CENTRAL AND EASTERN EUROPE AFTER TRANSITION

Studies in Modern Law and Policy

Series Editor: Ralf Rogowski,
Professor of Law, University of Warwick

Also in the series

Democracy, Law and Governance
Jacques Lenoble and Marc Maesschalck
ISBN: 978-1-4094-0395-1

Judicial Accountabilities in New Europe
From Rule of Law to Quality of Justice
Daniela Piana
ISBN: 978-0-7546-7758-1

The European Social Model and Transitional Labour Markets
Law and Policy
Edited by Ralf Rogowski
ISBN: 978-0-7546-4958-8

The Changing Law of the Employment Relationship
Comparative Analyses in the European Context
Nicola Countouris
ISBN: 978-0-7546-4800-0

Property in Work
The Employment Relationship in the Anglo-American Firm
Wanjiru Njoya
ISBN: 978-0-7546-4587-0

Contract and Control in the Entertainment Industry
Dancing on the Edge of Heaven
Steve Greenfield and Guy Osborn
ISBN: 978-1-85521-561-0

Labour Law in the Post-Industrial Era
Lord Wedderburn, Max G. Rood, Gérard Lyon-Caen,
Paul F. van der Heijden and Wolfgang Däubler
ISBN: 978-1-85521-644-0

Central and Eastern Europe After Transition
Towards a New Socio-legal Semantics

Edited by

ALBERTO FEBBRAJO
University of Macerata, Italy

WOJCIECH SADURSKI
University of Sydney, Australia

ASHGATE

Published by
Ashgate Publishing Limited
Wey Court East
Union Road
Farnham
Surrey, GU9 7PT
England

Ashgate Publishing Company
Suite 420
101 Cherry Street
Burlington
VT 05401-4405
USA

www.ashgate.com

British Library Cataloguing in Publication Data
Central and Eastern Europe after transition : towards a new socio-legal semantics. -- (Studies in modern law and policy)
1. Sociological jurisprudence--Europe, Eastern.
2. Sociological jurisprudence--Europe, Central. 3. Culture and law.
I. Series II. Febbrajo, Alberto. III. Sadurski, Wojciech, 1950-
340.1'15'0947-dc22

Library of Congress Cataloging-in-Publication Data
Central and Eastern Europe after transition : towards a new socio-legal semantics / by Alberto Febbrajo and Wojciech Sadurski.
p. cm. -- (Studies in modern law and policy)
Includes bibliographical references and index.
ISBN 978-1-4094-0390-6 (hardback) -- ISBN 978-1-4094-0391-3 (ebook)
1. Constitutional law--Social aspects--Europe, Eastern. I. Febbrajo, Alberto. II. Sadurski, Wojciech, 1950-
KJC4445.C426 2010
342.47--dc22

2010007202

ISBN 9781409403906 (hbk)
ISBN 9781409403913 (ebk)

Mixed Sources
Product group from well-managed forests and other controlled sources
www.fsc.org Cert no. SGS-COC-2482
© 1996 Forest Stewardship Council
FSC

Printed and bound in Great Britain by
TJ International Ltd, Padstow, Cornwall

Contents

PART 2: THE LEGAL PROFESSIONS

List of Tables

List of Contributors

Paul Blokker is a post-doctoral fellow at the Department of Sociology, University of Trento, Italy. From 2007 to 2008, he was Marie Curie Post-Doctoral Fellow at the School of Social and Cultural Studies, University of Sussex. His current research focuses on constitutional crisis, constitutional anomy and participatory constitutionalism in new EU member states. Recent publications include *Multiple Democracies in Europe: Political Culture in New Member States* (2009).

Alberto Febbrajo is Professor of Sociology and Anthropology of Law at the University of Macerata, Italy. He has written widely on many aspects of the history of Sociology of Law and on socio-legal aspects of the social systems theory. Recent books include *Sociologia del diritto* (2009). His next co-edited book will be *Law and Intersystemic Communication*, Ashgate 2010.

Zdeněk Kühn is Associate Professor of Jurisprudence at Charles University Law School and Judge of the Supreme Administrative Court. His academic expertise includes the theory and practice of adjudication and fundamental rights. In addition to many articles published in the USA, the Netherlands, the United Kingdom, Russia, China etc. he has published three books in Czech. His English book on the transformation of the post-communist judiciaries is forthcoming from Brill.

David Nelken is Distinguished Professor of Legal Institutions and Social Change at the University of Macerata, Italy. He is also Distinguished Research Professor at Cardiff University, UK. Recent books include *Comparing Criminal Justice: Making Sense of Difference* (2010).

Vittorio Olgiati is Professor of Law, University of Macerata, Italy. Formerly Scientific Adviser, he is Fellow of the Onati International Institute for the Sociology of Law, Onati, Basque Country, Spain. Visiting scholar at the Centre for Socio-legal Studies, Wolfson College, Oxford. He is currently President of the Research Committee on Sociology of Law (RCSL) of the International Sociological Association (ISA). He has published numerous books and articles on the sociological theory of law, legal profession, legal education and EU governance.

Daniela Piana is Associate Professor of Political Science at the University of Bologna. She has extensively published on constitutionalism, judicial reforms and enlargement in international journals. She is coordinator of an international network on judicial and legal training in Europe. Her most recent book, *Judicial Accountabilities in new Europe*, has been published by Ashgate in 2010.

Paulina Polak, PhD, works at the Institute of Sociology at the Jagiellonian University, Kraków, Poland. She has widely researched corruption, legal cultures and healthcare administration. Her next book will feature a systemic analysis of corruption in the Polish pharmaceutical industry.

Jiří Přibáň is Professor of Law at Cardiff Law School, Cardiff University. He is author and editor of many books in English and Czech, in particular *Legal Symbolism* (2007), *Dissidents of Law* (2002), *Liquid Society and its Law* (2007), *Systems of Justice in Transition* (co-edited with P. Roberts and J. Young, 2003), *Law's New Boundaries: The Consequences of Legal Autopoiesis* (co-edited with D. Nelken, 2001) and *The Rule of Law in Central Europe* (co-edited with J. Young, 1999).

Wojciech Sadurski is Challis Professor of Jurisprudence at the University of Sydney and, currently, Visiting Professor in Comparative Law at the University of Trento, Italy. He is also Professor at the University of Warsaw. He taught previously at various universities in Poland, Western Europe, the United States and Australia, and from 1999 to 2009 was Professor of Legal Theory and Philosophy of Law at the European University Institute in Florence, where he also served as Head of the Department of Law. He has published numerous books and articles in the philosophy of law, legal and political theory and comparative constitutional law. His most recent books are *Rights Before Courts: A Study of Constitutional Courts in Postcommunist States of Central and Eastern Europe* (2005 and 2008) and *Equality and Legitimacy* (2008).

Gisela Shaw is Visiting Professor of German and European Studies at the University of the West of England, Bristol, UK. Since 1989 the main focus of her research and publications has been the impact of the processes of transition on the European legal professions in general and on the notariat in particular.

Grażyna Skąpska is Professor of Sociology and Director of the Interdisciplinary Centre for Socio-Legal Analyses at the Jagiellonian University, Kraków, Poland. She has held teaching positions at the University of New South Wales and the University of Sydney, both in Australia, at Cornell University, USA, and at the University of Trier, Germany. She is a fellow of the Alexander von Humboldt Foundation and the Max Planck Institut, in Germany, the Collegium Budapest, the Wissenschaftskolleg zu Berlin and the American Bar Foundation. Her last book on constitutionalism after communism is currently in print.

Daniel Smilov teaches comparative constitutional law and politics at the University of Sofia and is Programme Director at the Centre for Liberal Strategies, Sofia, and

Recurrent Visiting Professor of Comparative Constitutional Law at the Central European University, Budapest. He holds doctorates from the University of Oxford and the Central European University, Budapest. He held previous research positions at the Centre for Policy Studies, CEU, and the European University Institute, Florence (Jean Monnet Fellow). In 1995 he was a visiting scholar at the Boalt Hall School of Law, University of California, Berkeley. He is co-author (with Martin Tisne) of *From the Ground Up: Assessing the Record of Anticorruption Assistance in Southeast Europe* (2004), co-editor (with Denis Galligan) of *Administrative Law in Central and Eastern Europe* (1999) and co-editor (with Jurij Toplak) of *Political Finance and Corruption in Eastern Europe* (2007).

Introduction

Twenty years on, it is clear that the transition from communism to democracy in Central and Eastern Europe (CEE) was the most important event in European history since the 1950s. The upheaval of the transition came from a series of micro- and macro-decisions, made not only by politicians and legal professionals but also by ordinary men and women. So a social and legal revolution took place, which, in a relatively short period, managed to clear the main obstacles blocking the elimination, after over 40 years, of an artificial division in the heart of Europe.

From a cultural point of view this transition required a critical re-examination of the communist period, a disposition to accept imported foreign legal models and institutions, and a re-emergence of the local legacies of the pre-communist past. The result was profound change for national identities subjected during the communist era to humiliation and oppression, which (re)discovered the opportunity of establishing the rule of law and democracy in CEE countries.

The complexity of the transitional process is widely recognized in scholarly literature, as the selected international bibliography at the end of this volume, at least partially, shows. The large number of books and articles on the subject underlines not only the unquestionable achievements in many countries both before and after the EU accession, and the several problems that the transitional process had to face, but also the differentiated strategies adopted in the social and cultural situations of these countries.

Communist regimes, in spite of violent pressures from the dominant Soviet power, had to tolerate a certain level of differentiation among CEE countries. It is thus not surprising that, in the following period, relatively high levels of normative and operative variation, both strategically and historically inspired, were displayed by CEE states, notwithstanding the great number of EU integrating mechanisms and vast set of 'guidelines' imposed on prospective members by EU authorities after 1993. This EU-related 'conditionality', while not coercive (in the sense that no CEE country was 'compelled' to join the EU), in fact exerted a strong pressure to conform to what was considered to be the EU model of organizing a country's political and legal affairs. Furthermore, the whole process of conditionality reflected, occasionally, a good degree of hypocrisy and 'double standards' on the part of the EU (for instance, CEE applicants were tested, among other things, on their knowledge of minority rights, while no authoritative instruments relating to this matter had been endorsed or implemented by the 'old' member states at the time).

Now that the accession phase is formally concluded and the conditionality requirements are often substantially absorbed, what seems particularly fruitful is to consider the reasons behind its differentiated realization in CEE countries and the problems connected with its conclusion. The basic formula of transition, considered as a segment within a general process of social change defined by a given point of departure and by one anticipated outcome, justifies an analysis of what was done in both institutional and cultural terms. It also seems necessary to identify the conditions of a 'post-transitional' phase, where a series of characteristics of the former phase, such as the asymmetric relationships between new and old members, could seem part of the problem rather than the solution.

This implies the perception of a double-tracked process of differentiation. At a first level, the integration produces different results within the same country; at a second and more general level, within the wide category of post-communist EU members the single countries are testing and combining different ways and strategies of governance.

This volume assumes that both trends combine to create new, autonomous differences at state and supranational levels and that, in their aim to overcome asymmetric relationships, they are two sides of the same coin. Accordingly, the volume focuses attention on these aspects, which will be among the most urgent issues of EU countries in the future. Each chapter adopts a comparative perspective, considering the experiences of a plurality of countries. Moreover, the contributors to the volume are representative, in a balanced way, of old and new EU members, thus providing a broader set of cultural points of reference. Within the research group involved in the preparation of this volume, the confrontation of insiders' and external perspectives presents an opportunity for the enrichment and refinement of individual positions and stimulates a constant exchange of views. In this way, the work tries to overcome the 'asymmetric' pattern that, as the following pages demonstrate, is one of the main characteristics of the EU as a whole.

Analysing the different solutions to transitional problems, a question emerges concerning the supranational context in which the so-called 'post-communist' EU members are now formally included: can the post-transitional phase also be defined in a positive, as well as in a negative way? Are post-communist countries comparable to the post-glossators, about whom, for a long time, there did not seem to be anything remarkable to say? A thing 'y', about which nothing more is known than that it comes after 'x', can be named by reference to 'x'; but all this introduces is a very particular kind of formalism.

The apparent emptiness of the 'post-x' description, in the case of post-communism, is to some extent deceptive. Therefore what seems particularly urgent, at the theoretical level, is the development of a new semantics that is adequate for describing the present situation in positive, more scientifically plausible and socially adequate ways without making use of the already large constellation of 'post-' terms: post-communism, post-statualism, post-normativism, post-post. This is the *fil rouge*, the common thread, of this entire volume, which tries to define the basic aspects of a post-transitional phase that is characterized by the increasing internal differentiations of the post-communist area. The post-communist area, as such, is destined to disappear, being articulated already in a series of qualifications which are emerging, at least implicitly, in order to substitute the merely negative jargon used for defining the trends of post-statalism and post-normativism.

The fact that all the countries discussed in this volume share a common immediate past is a platform of some solidity from which it is possible to understand their present condition. After all, 'communism' (or, to use the odd phrases of the ideologists of old, 'state socialism', or 'really existing socialism') was a strong unifying factor, and a factor that gave a very definite slant to the shape of society, the state and the law. In consequence, all these countries – notwithstanding their differences – inherited many similar problems at the point of their departure from the authoritarian regime. This can be seen particularly (but not only) in their constitutional trajectory. They all had to dismantle the USSR-imposed or -borrowed sham constitutionalism characterized by disregard for things like the separation of powers, the independence of judiciary, and guarantees of civil and political rights. This 'path dependence' rendered 'transitional constitutionalism' in the post-communist context a very distinctive and substantively specific phenomenon. In other words, the term 'post-communism' is more than just a sign of perplexity in characterization: it is also a relatively specific description. Or, at least, the balance sheet of the transitional period prior to the entrance into the EU of many CEE countries assumes.

The semantics to be adopted in this context are challenged by a double process of innovation. One part takes place at a constitutional level – that is, at the level of the fundamental texts on which the new legal order is based, as well as of the institutional guardians of their interpretation, the constitutional courts. The other part happens at the level of the effective role played by professional actors, including the judiciary and other legal professionals. Both points of reference are among the most visible parts of a wide cultural interaction, which is able constantly to correct itself in each EU country through a combination of normative and cognitive, legal and political, moral and economic attitudes.

This volume is therefore divided into two parts so as to group together those chapters which are relevant to the two main foci of attention: the constitutional framework, where political culture is strictly connected with legal culture; and the legal professions, where the formal legal cultures are challenged in particular by the expectations and different external legal cultures of the citizen seen as law-consumer.

In the opening chapter Jiří Přibáň reconsiders the importance of a series of 'asymmetric interdependences', which characterize the whole transitional process from the point of view of the CEE states as the procedures of 'importing law' and understanding the democratic deficit in interstate relationships. These factors are based on the nature of the EU, which, as a supranational organization without a European demos, 'draws heavily on the administrative state's legitimacy, based on efficiency and outcomes rather than on values and democratic procedures'. Nevertheless, for Euro-enthusiasts these settings demonstrate 'just a minor structural deficiency fully compensated for by the common benefits of EU membership'. EU membership was considered 'the best protection for emerging constitutional democracies [...] against illiberal and authoritarian politics', and the legislative harmonization demanded by the EU's bureaucratic class was used by the judicial branch 'as a form of self-empowerment against the legislative and executive branches of their nation states'.

These and other social balances produced the present 'European constitutionalism without constitution', which, 'unlike a state-like sovereignty achieved by means of a legislated constitutional settlement, [...] can evolve only because of its internal constitutional differentiation' and therefore requires a new EU legal semantics. A theoretical view is needed that does not limit itself to contrasting 'the diminishing role of member state governments' with 'the ascending supremacy of European forms of governance'. As a matter of fact it offers 'a distorted picture of the complexities of the differentiated self-constitutionalization of European society, which actually proceeds by internalizing state sovereignty as one of its systemic operations'.

In the following chapter, Alberto Febbrajo analyses the concepts of 'legal culture' and 'transition', which are often applied to achieve a better understanding of the events that took place in CEE countries after the collapse of communism. Adopting the comprehensive approach of social systems theory, which avoids a deterministic vision and instead absorbs some typical elements of the 'classic' contributions of Ehrlich and Weber, social and legal evolution are considered through an autopoietic scheme characterized by a critical analysis of the state-based normativism and the circularity of the main moments of selection, stabilization and variation. On this basis it is possible to construct a two-step, ideal-typical model of transition. The first transitional step tends to be 'oriented towards stabilizing the structures necessary for transforming already acquired achievements into points of no return'. This step is characterized by 'a greater degree of clarity at the level of the goals than at the level of the tools', and by a new constitution, which can be considered an 'evolutionary invention' and the precondition for producing an autopoietic, self-referential law.

The second transitional step requires 'the revision and adaptation of the newly created norms' and the development of a higher level of self-reflection, which 'allows a normative order to assume a cognitive orientation in order to correct its inefficient norms'. This step is characterized by 'a certain range of "redundancies", from among which legal professionals could select, when necessary, further adjustments'. The semantics of the transitional phase must take into consideration this new CEE constitutional framework 'as part of a larger process of differentiation, stimulated by the increasing complexity of a series of instruments of structural couplings'.

Paul Blokker draws on an extensive theoretical classification of different forms of constitutionalisms, which during a transition represent a complex field of partially overlapping possibilities. Avoiding 'looking at constitutional democracy from a legalist or monist perspective', Blokker argues that 'constitutions cannot be read solely in a negative, limiting way, as much of the legal, political-theoretical and political-scientific literature does'. Instead it is possible to identify 'two meta-languages of constitutions […], an instrumental language and a symbolic one', both connected with the Weberian ideal-types of rationality. In particular, a constitution articulates an instrumental language, in that it 'formulates the functional differentiation of society, the limitation of political power', and it expresses a symbolic language in that it 'invokes the substantive groundings of the political community'.

Focusing on some CEE cases, Blokker points out four different ideal-types of constitutionalism that could relate to distinct dimensions of constitutions: the '*liberal*' *constitutionalism*, according to which the constitution is essentially regarded 'in a regulatory and limiting sense'; the '*communitarian*' *constitutionalism*, in which there is evident attention to 'the symbolic dimension in general' and the dimension of identity in particular; the '*republican*' *constitutionalism*, which 'prioritizes political participation and self-government', and the '*substantive or positive*' *constitutionalism*, which is related to 'an ethic of distributive justice and to a positive, interventionist view of the constitution'.

The next two chapters are concerned with the activity of the Constitutional Court, seen as a central element in the political and constitutional landscape of CEE post-communist states. In Chapter 4, Wojciech Sadurski tackles the role of constitutional courts, focusing his attention on their so-called 'activism'. The impact of constitutional courts upon constitutional culture was often interpreted on the one side as 'salutary', because they 'repaired many of the legislative acts', and on the other as 'educational' as they contributed to a general awareness about the respect for constitutional values.

But constitutional courts can also have a negative impact when they encourage the feeling that 'all other branches of government are free to disregard constitutional strictures and should take into account only policy considerations'. This is because, in this way, they are contributing to the 'perception that other institutions – including "regular" courts – do not really have a responsibility for constitutional maintenance'. Thus, the assessment of the role of constitutional courts must be nuanced, depending on a series of variables such as the modes of appointment and the tenure of judges, the types of review, the degree to which the society as a whole considers constitutional strictures as significant, the importance of the law invalidated and the nature of the reasoning leading to its invalidation, the level of precision of the constitutional text, and the political landscape in which the courts operate. This means that 'a great deal depends upon the relationship between the Constitutional Court and the other branches of government, and that '[a] robust Constitutional Court may clash with some of our intuitions about democratic, parliament-centred law-making but [may also] accord with our views about the primacy of constitutional factors in legitimate law-making'.

In Chapter 5, Daniel Smilov examines the contribution of constitutional courts to 'the development of a specific culture of constitutionalism'. For a general framing of the problem, Smilov resorts to the metaphor of the judge Ulysses, considered as an ideal-typical figure who 'takes the fact of pluralism seriously' and finds himself in perpetual opposition to the 'thoroughly coherent', Dworkinian judge Hercules. Unlike Hercules, who is more concerned with implementing comprehensive doctrines, Ulysses follows a methodology based on the general Principle of Economy, according to which '[t]he justification for the method of resolution of adjudicative disputes among competing comprehensive doctrines should be grounded in as few elements [...] as possible'.

Applying this frame of reference, post-communist Europe becomes a test case for the 'non-coherentist minimalism' of Ulysses, especially in situations, as in Bulgaria during the 1990s, when society was deeply divided ideologically and the minimalist jurisprudence of the Constitutional Court was quite appropriately introducing progressive policies in many areas, without becoming 'the focus and forum of ideological conflicts'. Techniques for avoiding global coherence should be based on a series of presuppositions, in that conflicts between basic constitutional principles may sometimes be resolved by means other than a precise interpretation of the principles, and that decisions involving rules at a lower level of generality should not always be taken into account. On this basis Ulysses, in a manner that is particularly important in a transitional phase, 'is bound to consider different types of question, to which Herculean jurisprudence is insensitive'.

The last chapter of Part 1 is authored by Grażyna Skąpska. She takes as her target the problem of lustration, seen not as a simple way of dealing with the recent past, through the applications of legal sanctions against those who collaborated with the communist regime, but as a crossroads where legal, moral, political and social evaluations overlap. In this way an open conflict between internal and external legal cultures emerges and it is difficult to bargain a ceasefire, especially concerning issues such as lustration, where a compromise could appear unacceptable to many.

From a positivist point of view, the solutions are clearly based on the obligation 'of the law-governed state [...] to punish crimes and redress wrongs'. But, in the same vein, the principles of 'non-retroactivity' and of 'the individualization of guilt' are of equal moment, because the presumed collaborators were acting in an anonymous 'system', in which they were often involved 'not in clear-cut roles, that is, not only as direct perpetrators'. The result is a sort of ambiguity on the subject of lustration, because 'evidence of crimes was not only illegally destroyed by interested parties [...] but was also illegally copied, stolen, or even hidden in order to be used as an instrument of blackmail'. Lustration therefore presents different solutions (which are not simply positivist) in different situations giving 'the post-communist reconstruction a moral impulse and enabl[ing] the formation of a positive constitutional consensus around some positive values, directed at human rights protection'.

A closer examination of the limits of the positivist approach is offered by the second part of the volume, which is especially concerned with the legal professionals, that is, with the roles that operate within the legal order and in relation to its traditionally differentiated functions (prevention, defence and decision, through legal arguments, of social conflict). In the chapter which opens Part 2, Zdeněk Kühn observes that, in post-communist countries, one of the 'problems [...] reflected very frequently in popular complaints is the quality of the judiciary'. This attitude comes partly from the high expectations that, in a transitional phase, are suggested by the ideals of the rule of law; partly from a series of structural factors such as the growth of litigation, the length of procedures, the unsatisfactory methods of judiciary recruitment; and partly from factors concerning the internal legal culture of judges, as an excess of formalism, and privileges that are unjustified by the mere protection of judicial independence. Of course, the situation for the lawyers is completely different. While they were 'pariah' figures in the early communist system, their role has been enhanced through post-communism.

From a methodological point of view the cultural legacies of the past, which in different historical situations were 'both antiformalist/activist and formalist/statist', selectively influence the courts that, in the transitional phase, are no longer considering themselves 'unwilling and mechanical enforcers of rules made through the political process in parliament'. New aspects of societal evolution must be taken into consideration, which, in turn, requires 'the collapse of the original, strictly conceived model of the separation of powers' and a 'progressively increasing judicialization of politics and society'. New complex theories concerning law and its application must be developed because, 'all too often, the post-communist conception of law has remained imprisoned in parochial, outmoded positivist approaches'.

In Chapter 8, Daniela Piana demonstrates that, in CEE countries, judicial institutions have undergone two types of transformation: the first aimed 'at de-politicizing judicial organizations by introducing reliable mechanisms for the fair and transparent appointment of judicial staff'; the second at developing 'new forms of expertise, including managerial know-how' in the courts. The type of judge who emerges from these transformations is thus a judge with a Janus identity. On the one hand, 'he should be respectful of the legality principle and look to the law for the answers to his doubts'; and, on the other, he should also consider 'a different realm – the realm of management'. Therefore the 'borders of these renewed judicial systems', which are inevitably porous, place the judges in a context in which they 'are supposed to be autonomous (but not too autonomous)'.

From this perspective, a fair trial is not only based on procedure, but must be 'run and managed efficiently and transparently'. This implies 'two dimensions of accountability' and a fragmented cultural process, where organizational practices must enter into judicial education as essential for making 'judicial actors independent from possible influences coming from political and corporate power'. Such a model should go hand-in-hand with an internal cohesive bureaucracy that does not exclude external guarantees of independence and 'the way such a mechanism of accountability is enacted', which, according to the different situations, may vary 'from one domestic system to another'.

In Chapter 9, devoted to the 'legal culture' of Polish prosecutors, David Nelken applies this crucial concept to the reality of CEE countries with the support of Polish researcher Paulina Polak, who interviewed several Polish prosecutors of varying age, sex and standing. The collaboration of these two scholars, one from old EU member states and the other from CEE countries, embodies the general ambitions of the research project, which intended to develop an open encounter and confrontation of the different cultural attitudes in both areas, resulting from a combination of insider–outsider viewpoints.

Well apprised of the difficulties of applying the concept of legal culture, Nelken limits himself to very general statements. Legal culture is seen as 'one way of describing relatively stable patterns of legally oriented social behaviour and attitudes'. In this context, important 'identifying elements' for comparative purposes are at an institutional level – the number and role of lawyers and the ways in which judges are appointed and controlled; at a practical level – various forms of behaviour such as litigation and prison rates; and at a cultural level – more nebulous aspects of ideas, values, aspirations and mentalities, particularly of Polish prosecutors.

The research, part of a wider project on changes in legal culture in CEE states, is based on a series of semi-structured interviews. Interestingly, most of the subjects interviewed insisted that 'it would be very difficult or risky for them to put up resistance if politicians, via the minister of justice' wished to affect the outcome of corruption cases. Besides, confirming the hypothesis that different legal cultures coexist in the same country, the interviewed persons espoused different internal ideologies concerning the concept of independence, not necessarily assuming a positivist approach (as an extreme case, for one prosecutor independence meant the ability to '"take decisions consistent with his beliefs and conscience", rather than having to do with being subject to the law and the law alone').

In the following chapter, Gisela Shaw sets out to discuss empirical comparative research on the notaries who, as an independent legal profession, were traditionally charged in Europe 'with varying statutory functions within each country's non-contentious jurisdictions'. In CEE countries, after four decades of communism, 'notaries' found themselves 'deprofessionalized' and 'at the bottom of the pile of legal professionals'. Nevertheless, because of their relatively restricted number, in comparison to other legal professions, they were able to pass through a 'speedy transformation' of their 'role and status'. According to the different situations this renewal supported the 'bonds with continental European traditions and countries' as well as the integration into the EU, facilitating 'governments' control over economic developments, especially in the context of privatization'.

This development is highly differentiated in CEE countries. In the former German Democratic Republic, the traces of the communist legacy are rapidly fading with statal consensus and, especially amongst the notaries appointed after 1990, a new professional culture is emerging; in Poland, where a strong notariat had stabilized its position in the wake of the transition, notaries have had to cope with serious attacks from their own government and 'in the process have lost some of their professional autonomy and economic advantage'.

In the final chapter Vittorio Olgiati takes as his target the 'exhaustion' of the traditional 'cultural/technical mandate' of legal professionals as 'nation-state builders'. Not only in CEE member states but also in European societies both the transition to the EU constitutionalization process and the rise of an

EU governance are connected with a further deconstruction of the European legal professions. This has enhanced a new technical and cultural identity, inspired by a new EU-styled 'constitutional patriotism'. European higher legal culture cannot be conceived anymore as a science devoted to national public issues, but is 'committed to and accountable for the kinds of performances, plans, activities and so on that European society (individuals and organizations) is entitled to carry on within the constitutional framework of EU governance'. Therefore, science and governance are now strictly connected and this facilitates, not only in legal terms, 'a sort of "social contract" between European science and European society', and foregrounds 'the post-national question of European intellectuals'.

Besides, the principle of subsidiarity, allowing a legitimate degree of flexibility to the legislation of each member state, plays, structurally and functionally, an essential role that 'implies a highly refined' legal instrumentarium, but that also follows the typical pre-modern device that qualified 'the Gothic law of *the Ancien Régime*'. This grants EU institutions the power to regulate both social differentiation and legal complexity.

All the chapters presented here generally touch upon the different situations of CEE countries as considered from a comparative perspective. The two parts of the volume try to describe the basic features of a submerged cultural revolution, which, through the interaction of national constitutions as well as of legal professionals, contributes to the legal and social development of a new equilibrium. This equilibrium is characterized by less asymmetrical relationships within the EU and by increasing internal differentiation.

The co-existence of so many national ways of adjusting and innovating the legal orders of single members can suggest the image of an orchestra, in which, prior to rehearsal, each member is tuning his or her own instrument despite both the conductor and the common full score being missing. This happens because of the different accents and languages with which the national constitutions continue to be read by EU members, including CEE countries.

In this context constitutional courts and legal professionals could efficiently fulfil a social engineering role, orienting the crucial moment of the interpretation of law to a cultural exchange connected not only to imported law and to supranational influences, but also to law-consumers and local influences. The political elements, brought into the picture by the activism of constitutional courts, and the economic elements, included into the daily activity of legal professionals, can thus be presented as parts of the same, still open process of interpretation. A new semantics is gradually emerging, inspired by the fading out of the centrality of state sovereignty as well as of purely positivist restrictions, and by the intense horizontal interrelations between homologous professional actors. Correspondingly, the EU space seems now to be culturally predisposed towards continuing the search for an essential sense of identity, through a complex web of interactions based on the gradual stratification of a common 'material' constitution, and on a transnational *Juristenrecht*.

PART 1
The Constitutional Framework

Chapter 1
Constituting the Heterarchy of European Constitutionalism in the EU's New Member States[1]

Jiří Přibáň

Introduction

This chapter focuses on institutional and jurisprudential reflections on sovereignty and constitutionalism in the context of European integration of post-communist nation states and their political and legal systems. The EU's constitutional domain is subsequently used as an example of profound changes in contemporary European societies and their constitutional systems and cultures.

After importing laws and constitutional doctrines during post-communist legal and political transformations, constitutional courts of new member states needed to adopt constitutional concepts and arguments related to EU membership and specific structural preconditions of European legal and political institutions. While the 1989–2004 period was concerned with defining the principles and jurisprudence of the sovereign constitutional state and the democratic rule of law, the post-2004 period has been characterized by attempts to assimilate the notion of divided sovereignty and thus to grasp complexities of EU law and national constitutional systems and cultures. The concept of divided sovereignty was therefore adopted by the constitutional courts of new member states, and internalized as a form of emerging EU constitutional jurisprudence and a common legal culture for European society in the post-national constellation.

'Asymmetric' Europeanization of Post-communist States

Between 1989 and 1993, post-communist states made establishing EU membership a foreign policy priority, an objective which was not perceived as clashing with the

1 This chapter synthesises two streams of its author's recent research, parts of which already have been published. See 'Multiple sovereignty: On Europe's self-constitutionalization and legal self-reference', *Ratio Juris*, 23/1 (2010), 41–64; and 'From "Which rule of law?" to "The rule of which law?": Post-communist experiences of European legal integration', *The Hague Journal on the Rule of Law*, 1/2 (2009), 337–58.

coeval process of rebuilding national sovereignty, constitutional statehood and the rule of law. EU membership was considered to be a matter of national interest, despite there existing a profoundly asymmetrical relationship between the ever more economically and politically integrated EU and emerging post-communist democracies.

This 'asymmetric interdependence' defined the whole period between the 1989 revolutions and the 2004 EU enlargement.[2] Critics comment frequently on the EU's vague promises to accept post-communist countries 'in five years', which it has been making ever since the fall of the Berlin Wall. Nevertheless, post-communist political and constitutional transformations of the early 1990s and the profound coeval transformation of the European Community into the EU after the ratification of the Maastricht Treaty in 1992 eventually led to the outline of a specific integration policy for post-communist countries. Thus, in 1993, the newly established EU adopted a set of EU membership conditions for candidate states. These conditions became known as the 'Copenhagen criteria' and formed the basis of the conditionality process for EU accession.

As Milada Vachudova pointed out, the leverage of the EU over candidate states was originally passive and limited to the most general attractions of EU membership; however, it was transformed into active influence after the introduction of the Copenhagen criteria by the EU in 1993.[3] The Copenhagen criteria were adopted by the European Council in June 1993 and divided the EU accession conditions into three different categories – political, economic and legal. While economic conditions specified the need to establish a functioning market economy compatible with market pressures, competition and regulations within the EU, political conditions made it necessary to guarantee the institutional stability of emerging democracies and their constitutional systems, including the rule of law principles and human rights catalogues.[4] Political conditions even included respect for and protection of minorities, for which there were no grounds within the framework of European law.[5]

The asymmetrical relationship between the EU and post-communist accession states was justifiable by the EU's role as a political stabilizer at the time of social transformation.[6] There were also accompanying ethnic and national tensions in the

---

2 M. Vachudova, *Europe Undivided: Democracy, Leverage, and Integration after Communism* (Oxford: Oxford University Press, 2005), 109.

3 Ibid., ch. 3 and 5.

4 M. Novak, 'Human rights "conditionality" in relation to entry to, and full participation in, the EU', in P. Alston, M.R. Bustello and J. Heenan (eds), *The EU and Human Rights* (Oxford: Oxford University Press, 1999), 687–98.

5 B. De Witte and G.N. Toggenburg, 'Human rights and membership of the European Union', in S. Peers and A. Ward, *The European Union Charter of Fundamental Rights: Politics, Law and Policy* (Oxford: Hart Publishing, 2004), 59–82, at 67–68.

6 For a more general discussion, see W. Sadurski, A. Czarnota and M. Krygier (eds), *Spreading Democracy and the Rule of Law? The impact of EU enlargement on the rule of law, democracy and constitutionalism in post-communist legal orders* (Dordrecth: Springer, 2006).

region of Central and Eastern Europe.[7] Until the Copenhagen Council, the issues of democracy and the rule of law were automatically associated with member state governments and no formal criteria for applicant countries were defined by the EU. As Wojciech Sadurski commented:

> [T]hese matters – democracy, the rule of law and human rights – have largely been taken for granted within the Community itself, and never before 1993 were they included in a formal set of criteria for *former* applicant countries, whose democratic and human rights credentials always seemed impeccable to the members at the time. But after 1993 the contrast between the rules for existing members and the admission criteria for prospective newcomers became sharp.[8]

During the accession process, political and economic targets coincided with the legal requirement that all candidate states had to harmonize their national legal systems with the body of European *acquis*. Substantive political and economic achievements were thus accompanied by the instrumental need to adopt the EU *acquis* to adhere to the political, economic and monetary goals of the EU. The harmonization of European and national laws, along with the incorporation of European legal regulations, became a major political objective.

The system of Europe agreements which obliged candidate states to harmonize their laws with EU law formed the legal basis for the European integration of post-communist countries.[9] Strengthening the instrumental control of the accession process, the Commission introduced its *Agenda 2000* in 1997, which focused on the need to assimilate the enormous body of the EU *acquis*, including the treaties, secondary legislation and case law of the European Court of Justice.[10] In 1998, the Commission formed accession partnerships with individual countries which incorporated the legal systems harmonization deadlines and priorities. These partnerships further led to the formation of national programmes for adopting the Community *acquis*, in which candidate states were required to specify their harmonization policies including the adoption of legal acts, institutional reforms and financial resources. These policies were then assessed annually in the Commission's progress reports.[11]

---

7 J. Přibáň, 'European Union constitution-making, political identity and Central European reflections', *European Law Journal*, 11/2 (2005), 135–53.

8 W. Sadurski, 'Charter and enlargement', *European Law Journal*, 8/3 (2002), 340–62, at 343.

9 F. Schimmelfennig, 'The Community trap: Liberal norms, rhetorical action and the Eastern enlargement of the European Union', *International Organization*, 55/1 (2001), 47–80.

10 M.J. Baun, *A Wider Europe: The Process and Politics of European Union Enlargement* (Boulder, CO: Rowman & Littlefield, 2000).

11 See, for instance, M. Maresceau (ed.), *Enlarging the European Union: Relations Between the EU and Central and Eastern Europe* (London: Longman, 1997); M. Cremona (ed.), *The Enlargement of the European Union* (Oxford: Oxford University Press, 2003).

While the 1993–1997 period generated little more than general remarks regarding democracy and the rule of law reforms, the progress reports turned political conditionality into a detailed monitoring technique after 1997. The first reports were published in the autumn of 1998.[12] They consisted of a number of subsections evaluating different branches of government, detailing the justice system and its efficiency, judicial professions, corruption and anti-corruption measures, protection of civil and political rights, social rights, minority rights and policies and so on. The reports assessed progress in legislation and administrative measures in specific policies in individual countries, described accomplishments, and prescribed further measures to keep the whole process from coming to an end. National governments were asked to set out short- and medium-term priorities for the adoption of the *acquis* and were provided with financial assistance to achieve these goals.[13]

Was the EU a 'Patron' of the Democratic Constitutionalization of Post-communist States?

The Copenhagen criteria and subsequent progress reports and other policies introduced by the EU, like any other external policies, largely depended on internal conditions and factors facilitating their adoption by candidate states.[14] They had to be reformulated at national level as political interests, party ideologies, and governmental and constitutional programmes changed. Though incorporated EU laws heavily influenced constitutional and political developments in post-communist countries,[15] the effect of such laws became entirely dependent on national and cultural legal and political institutions.[16] The EU was able only to monitor this process of legal harmonization.[17]

From the perspective of democratic constitutionalism, the Copenhagen criteria and the Commission's progress reports (designed with conditionality in mind) had very mixed results. EU membership was considered such a political priority in all candidate states that the laws were approximated without appropriate democratic deliberation and then justified as historical necessity. The candidate states did

12 A. Williams, 'Enlargement of the Union and human rights conditionality: A policy of distinction?', *European Law Review*, 25 (2000), 601–17.

13 M. Vachudova, supra n. 1, 125–32.

14 J. Kelley, 'International actors on the domestic scene: Membership, conditionality and socialization by international institutions', *International Organization*, 58/3 (2004), 425–57.

15 G. Pridham and T. Vanhaven (eds), Democratization in Eastern Europe: Domestic and International Perspectives (London: Routledge, 1994).

16 E. Stein, 'International law in internal law: Toward internationalization of Central-Eastern European constitutions?' *American Journal of International Law*, 88 (1994), 427–50.

17 J. Elster, U. Preuss and C. Offe, *Institutional Design in Post-communist Societies: Rebuilding the Ship at Sea* (Cambridge: Cambridge University Press, 1998).

not participate in the creation of EU *acquis* and their contribution to the Europe agreements and conditionality documents was very limited.[18] Nevertheless, the candidate states did enjoy racing in what was nicknamed the EU accession 'regatta', competing with each other in terms of their number of completed chapters of EU negotiations.[19] In this context, one can legitimately ask whether metaphors of races at sea should be replaced by an old-style East European metaphor of 'Potemkin villages' scattered along riverbanks of Central and East Europe.

Despite fundamental criticisms, however, the whole process of European integration had an enormously positive and stabilizing effect on post-communist candidate states throughout the 1990s and early 2000s. While drawing on the difference between 'insiders' and 'outsiders', and using the rule of law, constitutionalism, democracy and human rights criteria as political pressure devices, the conditionality of the Copenhagen criteria successfully pushed 'outsider' post-communist countries to enact specific policies and comply with standards of democratic constitutionalism and the rule of law.

After the fall of communism, the process of Europeanization was always closely associated with the processes of democratization and constitutionalization. Some academics even wrote about the 'accession's democracy dividend' when examining the force, impact and limitations of the EU's external pressure on the accession countries.[20] EU membership was considered the best protection for emerging constitutional democracies in Central and Eastern Europe against illiberal and authoritarian politics, corruption, arbitrary use of power by civil servants, lack of public accountability, and many other sorts of political failure. In other words, EU institutions were expected to promote and police exactly the same goals which defined post-communist constitutional and political transformations. Weak national political and legal institutions, which were suffering from insufficient resources and experience, and were prone to political cronyism and corruption, were expected to be externally supported and stabilized during the transitional period by the EU.

The EU was a major point of reference and represented a 'normal state of things' towards which post-communist countries in transformation were heading and which, therefore, could and actually did have a strong synergistic effect in

18 F. Schimmelfennig and U. Sedelmaier, 'Governance by conditionality: EU rule transfer to the candidate countries of Central and Eastern Europe', *Journal of European Public Policy*, 11/4 (2004), 661–79.

19 The 'regatta principle' was introduced at the EU Helsinki Summit in December 1999. According to the principle, each candidate state could complete the accession talks at any time without being held back by other candidate states and their negotiations.

20 W. Sadurski, 'Accession's democracy dividend: The impact of the EU enlargement upon democracy in the new member states of Central and Eastern Europe', *European Law Journal*, 10/4 (2004), 371–401.

European politics.[21] The candidate states' 'patronized status' did not change until the EU's engagement in the constitutional treaty-making process. Opened by the Convention in 2002, it was continued by a draft of the constitutional treaty being approved in 2004, though it eventually failed owing to the 'no' results of ratification referenda in France and the Netherlands in 2005. During the Convention's work on the constitutional treaty, the candidate states were invited to contribute to its drafting but they were not able to block any consensus that could be established amongst member states at the time. In other words, the post-communist states' status changed from passive recipients of EU laws to active participants in EU constitution-making.

Furthermore, the stabilizing effect is still detectable five years after the 2004 EU enlargement, even in such Eurosceptic countries as the Czech Republic. The EU finds itself in the paradoxical situation of being the sort of highly suspicious political organization typical of impersonal administrative power and already imposing too many of its regulations on post-communist countries, whilst containing even worse political inclinations of national political and bureaucratic elites.[22] Traditional Central and Eastern European distrust of the state as an alien and incomprehensible institution has been associated with the EU bodies, yet the same bodies are locally believed to have powers to make national politics more accountable and bring it under the public's control. The dividend pays off in spite of local distrust of the company's management because all other alternatives would amount to political losses rather than profits.

Democratizing Effects and Democratic Deficits of EU Accession

The EU can demand its member states and candidate states to be democratically governed and rule of law-based. However, the EU as a supranational organization itself is short of democratic governance. The EU draws heavily on the administrative state's legitimacy, based on efficiency and outcomes rather than on values and democratic procedures.[23] It resembles earlier political developments within the nation state in the late nineteenth century, when bureaucracy became the most important legitimizing part of political will and the rationality of bureaucratic order informed the notion of legitimacy by legality. Regulatory 'necessities' and efficiency measures encourage the EU to copy the design of the administrative

---

21 See, for instance, A. Evans, 'Voluntary harmonization in integration between the European Community and Eastern Europe', *European Law Review*, 22 (1997), 201–20.

22 J. Rupnik, 'From democracy fatigue to populist backlash', *Journal of Democracy*, 18/4 (2007), 17–25.

23 D. Beetham and C. Lord, 'Legitimacy and the European Union', in A. Weale and M. Nentwich (eds), *Political Theory and the European Union: Legitimacy, Constitutional Choice and Citizenship* (London: Routledge, 1998), 15–33, at 17.

state and invoke 'the common benefit' rather than seek legitimation through 'representative democracy'.

In this situation of 'things administering themselves',[24] political goals of democracy, human rights and the rule of law can be formulated by the EU as external conditions but not as EU internal principles, which need to be adopted at post-communist nation-state level. These goals can be referred to as 'member state intrinsic principles' and as such can be legitimately expected of candidate states. However, this 'horizontal argument' is impossible to supplement by the 'vertical argument' of an EU democratic rule of law permeating the candidate state political and legal institutions.

The EU, therefore, is best described as having the rule of law without legitimacy by democratic procedures, yet legitimized by democratic constitutionalism at member state level.[25] In European legal and political studies, this structural setting is widely discussed as the EU's 'democratic deficit'. For some, the lack of democracy at EU level merely proves how wrong all Euroenthusiasts have been in pursuing their visions of European statehood. For others, the deficit has been just a minor structural deficiency fully compensated for by the common benefits of EU membership and democratic legitimacy guarantees as facilitated by the political institutions of member states. Nevertheless, both sides of this argument admit that European integration has been running as a profoundly legalistic and depoliticized project short of substantial democratic deliberation.[26]

From the perspective of constitutional separation of powers, the executive branch of national government benefited while the legislature was reduced to a body mechanically implementing EU *acquis* during the accession process. Parliamentary debates were initially limited to a few plenary sessions in most candidate states and this atmosphere of political ignorance lasted until the final stages of legal harmonization.[27]

Accession conditions were hardly disputed by national parliaments and were swiftly accepted in the hope of speeding the process of EU integration. Special

24 C. Schmitt, *Legality and Legitimacy* (Durham: Duke University Press, 2004), 5–6.

25 See, for instance, the Treaty of Lisbon, especially its Article 10 which reads: '1. The functioning of the Union shall be founded on representative democracy. 2. Citizens are directly represented at Union level in the European Parliament. Member States are represented in the European Council by their Heads of State or Government and in the Council by their governments, themselves democratically accountable either to their national Parliaments, or to their citizens. 3. Every citizen shall have the right to participate in the democratic life of the Union. Decisions shall be taken as openly and as closely as possible to the citizen. 4. Political parties at European level contribute to forming European political awareness and to expressing the will of citizens of the Union.'

26 J. Přibáň, *Legal Symbolism: On Law, Time and European Identity* (Aldershot: Ashgate, 2007), 116–19.

27 Z. Mansfeldová and M. Klíma (eds), *The Role of the Central European Parliaments in the Process of European Integration*: Proceedings of International Conference, Prague, 12–14 September 1997 (Prague: Academy of Sciences, 1998).

committees administering European integration commonly discussed acts of legislation before they were submitted to ordinary legislative procedures, and EU legal regulations were adopted through fast-tracking parliamentary procedures to meet deadlines set up during accession talks. For instance, the Czech government set up a special department which scrutinized all legislative proposals in terms of their compatibility with EU law and recommended to the government whether or not to proceed with legislative acts.

Meanwhile, the power of national bureaucracy was being enhanced by reports and political changes demanded by the EU's bureaucratic class.[28] Knowledge, finances and human resources gave the executive branch privilege over the legislature and, to a lesser extent, the judiciary.[29] Further, key national ministers, together with EU officials responsible for enlargement, formed a special group of administrators to manage the accession process. Instrumentality of accession procedures prevailed over, and occasionally even imperilled, substantive goals of democracy, human rights and the rule of law.

In regards to the justice system, legislative harmonization obviously needed to be accompanied by judicial harmonization which would guarantee the consistent interpretation of EU laws and legal acts approximating national and EU laws by the judicial branch.[30] With few exceptions, such as the Polish Constitutional Tribunal and cases concerning the different retirement age of male and female employees, the judiciary supported harmonization and a generally pro-EU interpretation of laws.[31] Judges even used EU laws as a form of self-empowerment against the legislative and executive branches of their nation states. Again, the power of expert legal knowledge served to conform to the general political trend of European integration.

Central European Constitutional Reflections on the *Kompetenz der Kompetenz* and 'no *demos*' Dilemma

How much EU 'law in books' influenced candidate states' 'law in action' will always be the subject of political disputes and academic interest. Nevertheless, the very existence of EU political conditions constituted a specific limitation of post-communist political power and successfully contained some excesses of political populism. Though inappropriately deliberated at nation-state level, legal rules of EU *acquis* still served as instruments of political reform enhancing

28 P. Mair, 'Popular democracy and EU enlargement', *East European Politics & Societies*, 17/1 (2003), 58–63.

29 H. Grabbe, 'How does Europeanization affect CEE governance? Conditionality, diffusion and diversity', *Journal of European Public Policy*, 8/6 (2001), 1013–31, at 1016.

30 A. Albi, *EU Enlargement and the Constitutions of Central and Eastern Europe* (Cambridge: Cambridge University Press, 2005), 52.

31 Ibid., at 52–54.

democracy and political accountability in candidate countries. In other words, the conditionality process weakened democratic deliberation but strengthened democratic institutional designs in those countries. The harmonization of EU and national legal systems happened as a rapid fast-tracked process of importation of laws but it also permanently affected legal and political institutions. It thus contributed to the much slower and ongoing process of transformating the legal and political cultures of candidate states, involving changes in the argumentative styles of the judiciary, administrative governance and so on.

During the 1990s, post-communist countries reinvented their national sovereignty, drafted new constitutional documents, and subsequently used their newly built constitutional sovereignty in EU membership negotiations. With the exception of Hungary and Poland, post-communist states joining the EU in 2004 had all been 'new states' – Estonia, Latvia and Lithuania reconstituted their statehood against the background of the collapsing Soviet Union, Slovenia left behind former republics of Yugoslavia in violent turmoil, and the Czech Republic and Slovakia peacefully abandoned common Czechoslovak federal statehood. For these states, EU membership was yet another form of their new existence and a proof of their identity in the world of international politics and law.

In contrast to the post-1989 process of rebuilding the constitutional sovereignty and national independence of post-communist countries, the EU requires its member states to delegate substantial sovereign powers to its institutions, including monetary policy, foreign affairs, border controls, judicial power, policing and so on. In all post-communist countries, these sovereign powers have been in the process of being reconstituted since 1989, yet they were coevally limited during the accession process.

This process of self-limitation of constitutional sovereignty was intended to cement rather than weaken the liberal democratic rule of law at post-communist nation-state level. Nevertheless, it also revealed structural shortcomings of the EU as a supranational organization reaching far beyond a common international law framework, yet falling short of any form of federal or confederative democratically legitimate statehood. It is not surprising, therefore, that the issue of constitutional sovereignty and its limits has returned as the most prominent constitutional problem in the wake of the EU accession of former post-communist states. The public, its political representatives and various constitutional bodies have gradually begun to emphasize the need to protect national statehood, associating it closely with the protection of constitutional democracy and human rights.[32]

Reflecting on the prominent position of constitutional courts during post-communist transformations and the legalist character of EU integration, it is clear how these judicial bodies became a centre for constitutional debates. Constitutional ambivalence about the accession process was addressed differently by different constitutional courts in different post-communist countries. As

32 A. Moravcsik and M. Vachudova, 'National interests, state power and EU enlargement', *East European Politics & Societies*, 17/1 (2003), 42–57.

early as 1998, the Hungarian Constitutional Court raised the question of the legitimacy of the harmonization process in its 'Europe Agreement Case', in which it reasserted constitutional sovereignty of the Republic of Hungary against the direct applicability of EU law and stated that a transfer of sovereignty to a foreign legal system needed to be explicitly authorized under the Hungarian constitutional rule.[33] In the judgment, it also emphasized that the constitutional amendment must follow the prescribed constitutional procedure rather than be stealthily enforced by means of parliamentary ratification of an international treaty.

Similarly, the Slovenian Constitutional Court argued that 'the Constitution places the public interest, for the State not to commit itself under international law to fulfil obligations which are not in conformity with its Constitution, at the level of a constitutional value'.[34] Should the court find some provisions of an international treaty unconstitutional, the ratification would be subject to the state's reservations being added to the treaty, its renegotiation or to a prior constitutional amendment.

It is interesting to see how constitutional courts' commitment to the rule of law and constitutional sovereignty during the accession process opened up a debate which logically followed the 1993 German Constitutional Court's 'Maastricht Case' decision, addressing the same problems from the perspective of a court of a member state.[35] In this landmark decision, German judges discussed the wide technical implications of the political fact that there is no European *demos* and that the EU, therefore, falls short of the substantive democratic legitimation necessary for any project of supranational statehood based on the supremacy of its legal system.[36] In what has become known as the *Kompetenz der Kompetenz* dilemma, the court reiterated its ultimate power to review and protect constitutional rights of German citizens, even against the EU.

Constitutional courts of Central and Eastern European candidate states originally interpreted the relationship between EU and national legal systems as a matter of intergovernmental negotiations drawing on national mechanisms of democratic legitimization. However, since the accession of post-communist countries to the EU in 2004, jurisprudence and theory of EU law in those countries has been witnessing much more diverse doctrinal responses to the process of EU integration, mainly reflecting on the importance and central role of the concepts of constitutional sovereignty. In this constitutional state, the German 'Maastricht

33 A. Tatham, 'Constitutinal Judiciary in Central Europe and the Europe Agreement: Decision 30/1998 (VI.25) AB of the Hungarian Constitutional Court', *International and Comparative Law Quarterly*, 48 (1999), 913–20.

34 Decision No. RM-1/97, 5 June 1997, Uradni list RS, No. 40/97, on Europe Agreement. Quoted from Albi, supra n. 29, at 116.

35 Ibid., at 135.

36 For a different view favouring the supremacy of European law, see K.J. Alter, *Establishing the Supremacy of European Law: The Making of an International Rule of Law in Europe* (Oxford: Oxford University Press, 2001).

Case', arguing that any EU limitation of the constitutional sovereignty of member states can always be reviewed and reconsidered by the constitutional courts of those states,[37] became a major point of inspiration for constitutional courts of new member states.

However, the constitutional courts of new member states do not always walk in the German Constitutional Court's footsteps. For instance, the Constitutional Review Chamber of the Estonian Supreme Court concluded that the system of EU laws enjoyed supremacy over the Estonian Constitution because:

> [...] within the spheres, which are within the exclusive competence of the European Union or where there is a shared competence with the European Union, the European Union law shall apply in the case of a conflict between Estonian legislation, including the Constitution, with the European Union law.[38]

On the other hand, the 'Lisbon Treaty' judgment of the Czech Constitutional Court reiterated the German constitutional principle of *Kompetenz der Kompetenz* and, although declaring its commitment to the 'pro-European' interpretation of EU treaties, stated that:

> [I]n the case of a clear conflict between the national Constitution and European law, which is impossible to mitigate by any reasonable interpretation, the constitutional order of the Czech Republic, especially its substantive core, takes precedence.[39]

Similar examples of reformulating the principle of constitutional sovereignty in post-accession new member states may be found, for instance, in the Polish Constitutional Tribunal's 'Euro-Warrant Case',[40] and in the early post-accession judgments of the Czech Constitutional Court, especially the 'Sugar Quota Regulation II' judgment of 8 March 2006, which stated:

---

37 For further discussion, see J. Přibáň, 'Is there the spirit of the European law? Critical remarks on EU constitution-making, enlargement and political culture', in V. Gessner and D. Nelken (eds), *European Ways of Law* (Oxford: Hart Publishing, 2007), 231–52, at 246.

38 Constitutional Judgement of the Supreme Court of Estonia on the interpretation of the Constitution, No. 3-4-1-3-06. Available online at <http://www.nc.ee/?id=663> [accessed 21 March 2010].

39 See section 85 of the judgment No. 19/08 Pl. US of 26 November 2008 regarding the constitutionality of the Treaty of Lisbon.

40 M. Fichera, 'The European Arrest Warrant and the sovereign states: A marriage of convenience?', *European Law Journal*, 15/1 (2009), 70–97.

> Naturally [...] the Czech Republic is bound by the principles of European law. As such rules take the form of national law, they must simultaneously be in conformity with the Czech constitutional order.
>
> The Constitutional Court is thus convinced that, although the applicable legal rules are rules of national law, to which apply the criteria flowing from the constitutional order of the Czech Republic, nonetheless, it cannot, without more, disregard the fact that they relate to an issue, the origins of which spring from Community law, a legal system produced by an international organization to which the Czech Republic has, by virtue of its accession pursuant to Art. 10a of the Constitution of the Czech Republic, transferred some portions of its state sovereignty. In consequence thereof, this system has, in those portions, become directly binding for the Czech Republic, also within the legal order of the Czech Republic.
>
> Although the Constitutional Court's referential framework has remained, even after 1 May 2004, the norms of the Czech Republic's constitutional order, the Constitutional Court cannot entirely overlook the impact of Community law on the formation, application, and interpretation of national law, all the more so in a field of law where the creation, operation, and aim of its provisions is immediately bound up with Community law. In other words, in this field the Constitutional Court interprets constitutional law taking into account the principles arising from Community law.[41]

This early formulation of the doctrine of self-limiting sovereignty in the 'Sugar Quota Regulation II' judgment was subsequently reiterated by the same court in the 'European Arrest Warrant' judgment, according to which:

> [...] the Constitutional Court refused to recognize the ECJ doctrine insofar as it claims absolute primacy of EC law. It stated that the delegation of a part of the powers of national organs upon organs of the EU may persist only so long as these powers are exercised by organs of the EU in a manner that is compatible with the preservation of the foundations of state sovereignty of the Czech Republic, and in a manner which does not threaten the very essence of the substantive law-based state. Understandably that, unless such an exceptional and highly unlikely eventuality comes to pass, the Constitutional Court, guided by the above-mentioned ECJ doctrine, will not review individual norms of Community law for their consistency with the Czech constitutional order.[42]

---

41 The 'Sugar Quota Regulation II' Judgment of the Constitutional Court of the Czech Republic, No. 50/2004 Pl.

42 Section 53 of the 'European Arrest Warrant' Judgment of the Constitutional Court of the Czech Republic, No. 64/2004 Pl.

The growing variety and complexity of constitutional jurisprudence in Central and Eastern Europe proves that former candidate states have joined other member states in attempting to find reasonable responses to legal and constitutional dilemmas relating to the current EU rule of law of democratic constitutionalism at nation-state level. Furthermore, these recent constitutional issues confirm that post-communist states have joined EU member states in embracing their complex constitutional structures and semantics, both embedded in and transcending the nation state. They actively participate in the construction of a specific European supranational polity, which may lack the characteristics of a modern democratic nation but which can still effectively enhance the rule of law based on human rights shared equally by all EU citizens.

In other words, the constitution-making and democratization problems faced by CEE countries in the 1990s have become an intrinsic part of European governance, which may primarily be driven by instrumentality and complex techniques of supranational administration but which, nevertheless, cannot eliminate issues of substantive democratic values and their recognition by a supranational community of EU citizens. Following the 2004 and 2007 enlargements of the EU, the problem of post-communist constitutional and political transformation has become part of the much wider and more complex problem of constitutionalization and democratization of the EU, stretching far beyond matters of technicality and 'things administering themselves'. The remaining sections of this chapter will therefore attempt to summarize recent Central and Eastern European constitutional transformative and integrative experiences, and to put them into the more general context of EU constitutionalism, constitutional and political cultures.

The Heterarchy of European Constitutionalism and the Concept of Divided Sovereignty

The European constitutional debate illuminates the main challenges of constitutional pluralism because EU law is impossible to conceptualize in the conventional jurisprudential terms of legal monism and dualism. Nation states are no longer the ultimate centres of constitutional authority and the European integration process has always been developing beyond the traditional limits of international law, constructing its own constitutional domain. However, recent constitutional aspirations and the imagination of the EU are coeval with the continuing constitutional regulations, aspirations and imaginations of both its old and its new member states. While EU member states are significantly limited as sovereign entities, holding superior power in their territory only by the self-referential principle of European law's supremacy in European matters, the same states also continue to exercise sovereignty both inside and outside the EU institutions.

Hierarchical explanatory models, such as the above discussed *Kompetenz der Kompetenz* dilemma and the 'no *demos*' thesis, which was outlined by the

German Constitutional Court in its 'Maastricht Judgment' and was adopted, for instance, by the constitutional courts in the Czech Republic and Slovenia, are certainly important for the internal operations of national constitutional systems and their relation to the system of European law. However, these explanations of the foundations of constitutional law and its legitimacy are of little use in understanding the self-regulatory character of the European law system, which recently accommodated the national legal systems of new member states accessing the EU in 2004 and 2007.

Similarly, calls for building European statehood[43] and constitutionalizing the principle of the supremacy of the jurisdiction of the European Court of Justice [ECJ] over national constitutional courts[44] can hardly result in the establishment of a monistic European constitutional system because the principle of respect for national constitutional systems is guaranteed by the body of European law. Observing the ECJ's drive towards the constitutionalization of European law and increasingly diverse national responses to it in both old and new member states, it is possible to see horizontal and heterarchical rather than vertical and hierarchical dealings between the member states and the EU's legal and political systems.[45]

New and often paradoxical concepts and metaphors have been developed to cope with the divisions, fractures and complexities of the body of European law and its both national and supranational constitutional contexts. Unity means diversity, integration means differentiation and so on. Within the legal system, the principle of the supremacy of European law is inseparable from the principles of proportionality, subsidiarity and self-containment.[46] European constitutionalism involves both 'a state-building dynamic' questioning the existing supranational regulatory practices of the EU[47] and the principle of mutual 'constitutional tolerance'[48] between EU law and national constitutional and legal systems and cultures.

43 G.F. Mancini, *Democracy and Constitutionalism in the European Union* (Oxford: Hart Publishing, 2000), 51–66.

44 See E. Claes, *The National Courts' Mandate in the European Constitution* (Oxford: Hart Publishing, 2006), 723–24.

45 N. Walker, 'The idea of constitutional pluralism', *Modern Law Review*, 65 (2002), 317–59, at 337.

46 See, for instance, T. Trimidas, *The General Principles of EU Law* (Oxford: Oxford University Press, 2006); and A. Estella, *The EU Principle of Subsidiarity and its Critique* (Oxford: Oxford University Press, 2002).

47 N. Walker, 'Europe's constitutional engagement', *Ratio Juris*, 18/3 (2005), 387–99, at 394.

48 J.H.H. Weiler, 'In defence of the status quo: Europe's constitutional *Sonderweg*', in J.H.H. Weiler and M. Wind (eds), *European Constitutionalism Beyond the State* (Cambridge: Cambridge University Press, 2003), 7–23, at 15ff.

The specific EU sovereignty paradox may be formulated as 'sovereignty manifesting itself by its limitations'.[49] In this unique legal and political condition, the paradoxical concept of divided sovereignty has become an important point of reference in debates concerning European constitutionalism and further political and legal integration. It replaces the Kelsenian monistic theory of legal validity and norm formation with an epistemology built on the notion of social difference, cleavages, fractures and the multiplicity of social communication.

European constitutionalism is therefore best addressed as a form of social constructivism.[50] Nation states, their constitutional cultures and their state-centred notions of sovereignty have been fundamentally transformed during the process of European economic, political and juridical integration. The interdependence of national economies, labour markets, security policies, political cultures, social welfare and migrations has led to a European politics beyond state sovereignty. The 'sovereignty argument' based on the assumption that a constitutional and legal order can function only if legitimized by a unitary political community, or *demos*, is brought into question by the fact that the body of European law has been shaped in the manner of constitutionalism in practice for decades,[51] without any recourse to the principle of democratic sovereignty. Unlike the sovereign nation state, the EU is shaped by the 'plurinational' coexistence of many nations and nationalities, both with and without statehood, which builds a series of interlinked normative orders and enjoys the practice of cultural, political and constitutional pluralism.[52]

Constitutionalizing Europe by Epistemological Communities and their Cultures?

European 'constitutionalism without a constitution'[53] has been emerging as a legal-technical project of the epistemological community of lawyers, which made effective use of the internal paradoxes and external aspirations of European

49 See, for instance, M.H.M. de Bonth, 'Sovereignty revisited', in A. Schrauwen (ed.), *Flexibility in Constitutions: Forms of Closer Cooperation in Federal and Non-federal Settings; post Nice edition* (Groningen: Europa Law Publishing, 2002), 97–105, at 101.

50 This constructivism is far away from the notion of social engineering and often draws on evolutionary social models. See, for instance, T. Christiansen, K.E. Joergensen and A. Wiener (eds), *The Social Construction of Europe* (London: Sage, 2001); and J. Shaw and A. Wiener (eds), 'Evolving norms of constitutionalism: Special issue of *European Law Journal*', *European Law Journal*, 9/1 (2003).

51 J. Přibáň, 'European Union constitution-making, political identity and Central European reflections', *European Law Journal*, 11/2 (2005), 135–53, at 146.

52 M. Keating, *Plurinational Democracy: Stateless Nations in a Post-Sovereignty Era* (Oxford: Oxford University Press, 2001), 140–41. For the constitutional theory argument of the plurinational state, see also S. Tierney, *Constitutional Law and National Pluralism* (Oxford: Oxford University Press, 2004).

53 Ibid., at 113.

integration. This 'constitutionalism in practice' mainly signifies the absence of either a real constitution or a process of constitution-making by other means.[54] The history of European constitutionalism is the social history of a legal utopia pursued from the earliest stages of European integration by a very specific group of lawyers, most notably judges and advocate-generals of the ECJ, legal experts in the European Commission and the Council of Ministers, legal advisers to national governments, and EU law theorists.

The impossibility of achieving a European constitution in the 1950s led to the gradual constitutionalization of European law by the European Court of Justice.[55] The political act of constitution-making and building a federal Europe was replaced by the transformation of constitutionalization politics into legal-technical matters. Since the landmark decision *Costa v. ENEL* and the Court's view that the Treaty of Rome has 'the nature of a real constitution',[56] EU jurisprudence has built upon the legal fiction of considering the treaty 'as if it were a constitution'.[57] The fiction includes the assumptions that the member states 'have limited their sovereign rights, albeit within limited fields',[58] and that this limitation is permanent.[59]

The failed politics of constitution-making of the 1950s was replaced by the constitutionalization of politics accommodated by the ECJ in the mid 1960s. However, the Court's enforcement of the principles of supremacy and the direct effect of European law should be perceived '[not] only as the translation of a political mobilization into the language of law, but also as the legal expression of the social autonomization of a specialized body of lawyers',[60] which requires a shift of 'analytical focus from the type of polity toward social practices'.[61]

To a large extent, the heterarchy of European law has been evolving through the differentiated multiple channels of European 'lawyers' law' or *Juristenrecht*[62] *– law enacted, interpreted and communicated by European lawyers as social groups with distinct constitutional ideologies, political agendas and practices.*

---

54 A. Cohen, 'Constitutionalism without constitution: Transnational elites between political mobilization and legal expertise in the making of a constitution for Europe (1940s–1960s)', (2007) 32(1) *Law & Social Inquiry*, 32/1 (2007), 109–35, at 112.

55 For this very early stage of European constitutionalism, see R.T. Griffiths, *Europe's First Constitution: The European Political Community, 1952–1954* (London: Federal Trust, 2000).

56 *Costa v. ENEL* CJCE 1964, 1178.

57 E. Stein, 'Toward supremacy of treaty-constitution by judicial fiat: On the margin of the Costa case', *Michigan Law Review*, 63/3 (1965), 491–518, at 513. For the quote, see A. Cohen, supra n. 53, at 126–27.

58 Case 26/62 *Van Gend en Loos* [1963] ECR 1.

59 Case 6/64 *Costa v. ENEL* [1964] ECR 585.

60 A. Cohen, supra n. 53, at 128.

61 A. Wiener, 'Editorial: Evolving norms of constitutionalism', (2003) 9 (1) *European Law Journal*, 9/1 (2003), 1–13, at 3.

62 For this remark, see M. Aziz, *The Impact of European Rights on National Legal Cultures* (Oxford: Hart Publishing, 2004), 17.

The sociological concept of Juristenrecht, introduced to legal science by one of the founding fathers of the sociology of law, Eugen Ehrlich, grasps the complexity of European constitutionalism, especially its reliance on specific professional knowledge groups, their distinct cultures and techniques of decision-making, and their capacity to operate beyond the body of legislated laws.[63]

Applying the concepts of divided sovereignty and constitutional tolerance in the judicial domain, the culture of 'judicial dialogue' amongst the national constitutional courts and the ECJ has been incorporated by European jurisprudence.[64] It echoes and radicalizes the German Constitutional Court's 'Maastricht Case' judgment, which called for a 'cooperation relationship' between the ECJ and national courts.[65]

The cooperation between European and national judges turned out to be beneficial for both groups because it generally expanded the influence of courts in both European and member states' politics and made them core institutions in building the rule of law in post-national Europe.[66] The legal method necessarily empowers judges as a professional group in the political systems of both the EU and its member states. However, the very concept of dialogue also shows the often contradictory nature of the relationship between the ECJ and the national constitutional courts, as recently experienced and addressed by constitutional judges of new member states. According to Miriam Aziz:

> The jurisdictional tug of war which has prevailed between the ECJ and the constitutional courts of the member states serves to illustrate the lengths to which jurists will go to have the last word as regards the locus of the ultimate authority.[67]

Nevertheless, national and European judges have common political and professional interests, and their tug-of-war enhances the process of the juridification of European politics.

---

63 E. Ehrlich, *Fundamental Principles of the Sociology of Law* (New York: Arno Press, 1975; originally published in 1936).

64 See A.M. Slaughter, A. Stone Sweet and J.H.H. Weiler (eds), *The European Court and National Courts: Doctrine and Jurisprudence: Legal Change in its Social Context* (Oxford: Hart Publishing, 1998).

65 For the discussion of the 'cooperation relationship' concept, see C. Joerges, 'The Law in the Process of Constitutionalizing Europe', in E.O. Eriksen, J.E. Fossum and A.J. Menendez (eds), *Constitution-Making and Democratic Legitimacy, Arena Report 5/2002* (Oslo: Arena, 2002), 13–48.

66 K. Alter, *Establishing the Supremacy of European Law: The Making of an International Rule of Law in Europe* (Oxford: Oxford University Press, 2001), 209–32.

67 M. Aziz, supra n. 61, at 45.

There are several competitors for final decision-making power in the EU.[68] The conflict-driven jurisdictional dynamic actually derives from the impossibility of determining which has the competence and overriding authority to decide on the applicability of EU law. Such a dynamic persuasively documents the operative power of divided sovereignty. Top national and European judges and legal elites still struggle to identify the ultimate arbiter, without any clear legal guidance but with the clear knowledge that their very conflict creates and sets in motion the operations of the EU constitutional domain.

Internal Paradoxes of the Democratization of European Constitutionalism

The EU is believed to be a deliberative order accommodating a number of complementary, overlapping and even conflicting national identities, in which there is no uniform constitutional and political design demanding the constitution of either a federal or a confederative state. At the same time, the European constitutional domain constructed by European judges and lawyers since the 1960s could not have dismantled the internal semantics of the constitutionalism discourse, especially its democratic polity-making and consolidating function. This is why, despite the wealth of debates on supranational governance, post-sovereignty, constitutionalism and the European Union as a polycentric polity,[69] the discourse of popular democracy and national or European sovereignty remains an important reference point in political debates and conflicts within the context of both the EU and its member states. It marks important political, juridical, economic and collective identity problems emerging coevally with globalization, Europeanization and the impossibility of continuing to build EU legitimacy on governance-driven efficiency rather than on democratic accountability.[70] The dynamics of a European polity are not reducible to institutional innovations and the linking together of multiple arenas of supranational governance.

Democracy is a theory of sovereignty which does not need any transcendental source of legitimation and which draws on the forces of political negotiation, deliberation and representation. No wonder that the EU project of ever-closer political union and integration by constitution-making, which involves the further transfer of powers from its member states and more EU majority decision-making

68 M. Aziz, 'Sovereignty lost, sovereignty regained? The European integration project and the *Bundesverfassungsgericht*', *Columbia Journal of European Law*, 9 (2002), 109.

69 See, for instance, M. Wind, 'The European Union as a polycentric polity', in J.H.H. Weiler and M. Wind (eds), supra n. 47, at 101–103.

70 For the view that EU does not need *demos* but efficiency, see J. Steffek, 'Sources of legitimacy beyond the state: A view from international relations', in C. Joerges, I.J. Sand and G. Teubner (eds), *Transnational Governance and Constitutionalism* (Oxford: Hart Publishing, 2004), 81–101.

(thus weakening the veto power of member states), has turned its attention to the problem of the European constituent power – the *demos* – or, rather, its absence.

As theories of democratic sovereignty and representation claim: '[T]he function of the majority rule is to establish a separation of powers, not between the classical *triad* of legislative, executive, and judicial power but between the *constitutive* and the *constituted* power.'[71] The growing exercise of majority power by EU institutions raises the question of compliance of dissenting states and communities within the EU. Can such obedience be justified by reference to the political community of which the dissenting parties are members and to which they give their unconditional loyalty? Does this construction of European society rely entirely on instrumental reason and political will, or does it also have the strong communal bonds and solidarity of an 'imagined community'?

The question of popular sovereignty at the EU level is inseparable from the process of the further constitutionalization of the EU without a constitutional document. The absence of a European *demos* cannot easily be dismissed as marginal on the basis that the EU uses specific forms of governance which are indifferent to the problem of democratic legitimacy. While it is true that nation-state constitutionalism is just one of many contextualizations of constitutionalism in the EU today, it cannot simply be rejected as 'dated and artificial',[72] because the constitutional sovereignty of the member states remains a constitutive part of the EU constitutional domain.

Neil Walker asked: 'If polities within a multi-dimensional order can be sectorally or functionally delimited, how far can such limitation be permitted without undermining the very idea of a constitutional *polity*?'[73] This is a crucial question: how far can the process of social and legal differentiation go without undermining the very meaning of constitutional law? Why do we insist on referring to societal constitutionalism if the sole function of nominally constitutional operations is the constitution of operability and autonomy for the differentiated subsystems of society, such as science, technology or the media? Is the constitution of social systems the same as the constitutionalization of a polity? And is it imaginable without political identity?

The question of the identity of the EU polity subsequently raises the problems of political inclusion and exclusion, as well as the boundaries of the EU polity itself and its effect on the constitutional polities of member states.[74] Translating the

---

71 L.J. Wintgens, 'Sovereignty and representation', *Ratio Juris*, 14/3 (2001), 272–80, at 279. The concept of 'the constitutive power' has the same meaning like 'the constituent power' preferred in more recent publications in the field of constitutional theory and used in this text.

72 M.P. Maduro, 'Europe and constitution: What if this is as good as it gets?', in J.H.H. Weiler and M. Wind (eds), supra n. 47, 74–102, at 74.

73 N. Walker, supra n. 44, at 347.

74 H. Lindahl, 'European integration: Popular sovereignty and a politics of boundaries' (2000) 6(3) *European Law Journal*, 6/3 (2000), 239–56, at 253–6.

sociological constitution of society as the unity of social plurality and multitude into the EU context, one is immediately reminded of the failed Constitutional Treaty preamble, speaking of 'unity in diversity', which has since been reformulated in the Reform Treaty draft as one of the EU's objectives.

The EU constitutional domain is both productive and reproductive of some form of European political identity. Like any form of constitutionalization, it is both constitutive (of European law and politics) and expressive (of European polity), which means that it enhances both the system of representative government and the normatively specific collective self-reflection of political identity. It is circular in the sense that the very existence of constitutional integration calls for political identity as its precondition, but it also already circulates the shared political values, policies and interests of the European polity in the form of constitutional communication.

Sovereignty is a 'product of the legal imagination';[75] and Habermas is right when he says that the problem of legal legitimacy is a central problem in modern political societies, emphasizing the foundational role of European identity-building.[76] The European Union can never achieve legitimacy without the constitution of a political identity. The EU sovereignty debate, which has been growing exponentially since the Maastricht Treaty and the subsequent constitution-making efforts and enlargement processes questioning the truth of the EU's 'widening is deepening' argument, is in many ways a legitimacy debate.[77] Nevertheless, analysis of EU legal semantics shows that the paradoxical concept of divided sovereignty has been operating far beyond the framework of a legitimacy debate. Instead, it functions in the profoundly self-referential and very productive mode within the context of the polycentric and pluralistic EU legal system.

From the point of view of legality rather than legitimacy, the EU divided sovereignty debate has never been a matter of constructing one overarching sovereign authority and delimiting all other 'minor' sovereignties, but a problem of internal explanation of the EU legal system's functioning. The concept of divided sovereignty is therefore best understood as a 'symbolic generalization'; it relates a legal plurality to the semantic unity which is part of the EU law's self-referential communication, and translates social experiences into legal meanings.[78] In other words, the concept is not an ultimate mirror of collective identity legitimizing EU integration, but a semantic instrument for managing the structural differences and complexities of the EU and its member states' legal and constitutional pluralism.

---

75 B. de Witte, 'Sovereignty and European integration: The weight of legal tradition' *Maastricht Journal of European and Comparative Law*, 2 (1995), 145–73, at 145.

76 J. Habermas, *Divided West* (Cambridge: Polity, 2006), 137–42.

77 See, for instance, R. Rogowski and C. Turner, 'Europe: Law, politics, history, culture', in R. Rogowski and C. Turner (eds), *The Shape of the New Europe* (Cambridge: Cambridge University Press, 2006), 1–22, at 7, 17.

78 N. Luhmann, *Law as a Social System* (Oxford: Oxford University Press, 2005), 92–6.

Concluding Remarks

European constitutionalism 'is a self-referential concept – not a reflection of something that contains or embodies something else (like values) but the reflection of the very thing itself'.[79] Its semantics do not cover the contingency of the collective will under the veil of a fictional moral unity. Unlike a state-like sovereignty achieved by means of a legislated constitutional settlement, which continues to be susceptible to all kinds of 'foundationalist' social semantics, the EU self-constitutionalizing legal system evolves because of its body of expert knowledge, operative contingencies, polycentric and heterarchical structures.

Turning away from the normative constructivism of polity-building by constitutional means, it becomes possible to rethink the paradox of constitutional sovereignty. Rather than perceiving it as the permanent oscillation of democratic legitimation between constituent identity and constituted power, it becomes a question of how to represent the contingency of political will as the founding principle of the political system of complex globalized societies.

The EU *Juristenrecht* is an example of contingency transformed into the living constitution of European politics and law. It also reveals the contrast between the jurists' European 'constitutionalism without a constitution' and efforts to legislate a constitution-like treaty for the EU. The popular sovereignty discourse appears in EU constitutional debates as either a specific supportive or critical response to the constitutional integration achieved by European legal and political elites.

The failed process of European constitution-making and subsequent serious setbacks accompanying the ratification process of the Lisbon Treaty persuasively show that, unlike a state-like sovereignty achieved by means of a legislated constitutional settlement, the EU constitutional domain can evolve only because of its internal constitutional differentiation into expert contingencies and legislated documents, which will effectively accommodate the paradox of divided sovereignty rather than seek a final solution to EU/member state constitutional sovereignty. Theoretical views that simply contrast the diminishing role of member state governments with the ascending supremacy of European forms of governance give a distorted picture of the complexities of the differentiated self-constitutionalization of European society, which actually proceeds by internalizing state sovereignty as one of its systemic operations.

---

79 J.H.H. Weiler and M. Wind, 'Introduction: European constitutionalism beyond the state', in J.H.H. Weiler and M. Wind (eds), supra n. 47, at 3.

Chapter 2
Legal Cultures in Transition: A System-theory Approach

Alberto Febbrajo

Introduction

This chapter discusses the different meanings of the concepts of 'legal culture' and 'transition', which are often applied, either explicitly or implicitly, to facilitate better understanding of the events that took place in Central and Eastern European (CEE) countries after the collapse of communism. The main hypothesis here is that some 'classics' of socio-legal theory, together with the recent and more comprehensive approach of the social systems theory, could contribute importantly towards defining these concepts and examining the substantial changes that occurred in the region over the last two decades.

Indeed, the social institutions of CEE countries during this transitional phase were in a sort of *statu nascenti*. Consequently, their cultural borders were not defined by already established filters, but were characterized by an exceptional fluidity. This means that they were passing, from the point of view of the social systems theory, through a complex process of differentiation, in which it is possible both to distinguish various phases and to use the concept of legal culture in a correspondingly flexible way.

As a matter of fact, a transition cannot be seen merely as 'a phase stretching between a point of departure and a point of arrival', where both are known in advance. The intuitive and 'simplistic' theories which are presuppositions of this scheme miss the crucial point of a real transition. It has to be interpreted not so much as 'an empty space between two well known and easily characterized resting-points' but rather as 'a path with highly contested features, many of them unanticipated, to a destination the character of which is far less obvious than once seemed'.[1] Transition, considered as a sociological concept, is destined to reach its ultimate stage, not only according to historians, but also according to the political actors who recognize that searches for certain outcomes are exhausted, and to the sociologists who observe their behaviour. These interpretations, historical and sociological, could obviously converge when the cultural aspects of transition, as

1 W. Sadurski, 'Transitional constitutionalism: Simplistic and fancy theories', in A. Czarnota, M. Krygier and W. Sadurski, *Rethinking the Rule of Law after Communism* (Budapest and New York: Central European University Press, 2005), 9–10.

in the case mentioned above, are so important that they cannot be ignored from either perspective.

The fact that, in a period of transition at least, a vague idea of the final outcome is shared by the actors involved, assures the fundamental convergence of their efforts. Transition can thus be seen as a special case of the several transformations that are constantly occurring in every society. While social change might be represented as a continuous series of micro-performances, produced by different actors and oriented along their particular horizons, transition is mostly oriented towards more general goals, even if admitting different alternative paths to reach them. Diffuse uncertainty concerning the tools of transition means that the ways in which transitions are accomplished might be completely different in different situations, depending on the various environmental conditions.

For a sociological analysis of transitions, it is necessary to focus attention not only on generally accepted goals, but also on a series of instrumental decisions and activities undertaken by different actors in different sectors of society. Avoiding a somewhat deterministic vision, and adopting a culturally more pluralistic approach, study of transitions might begin from two presuppositions: first, that it is almost impossible for a single mind to lead the events through a homogeneous and previously defined path; and, second, that their final outcome could turn out to be, by degrees, different from the original project.

The gradual nature and relative uncertainty of a transitional process is a consequence of the central role played by the different legal cultures, which are, in a sense, the selective lenses through which law is considered by social actors in the different social contexts. These lenses seem far more decisive than formal factors, such as written legal propositions and official agreements, in the search for meaningful explanations of effective behaviour. Behind each of these normative sources there are individuals, officials and populations who must translate their guidelines into practice, given different values, attitudes and interpretations of social (not only statal) norms.

The meaning of the concept of legal culture is, on closer scrutiny, as varied as that of the fundamental concept of culture. Therefore it is 'difficult to build such a protean term into testable explanations (especially as legal culture is sometimes taken as what needs to be explained and at other times is asked to play the role of explanation)'.[2] The wide range of possible meanings suggests some caution in the use of the concept and, at the same time, allows a number of possible facets. It could provide fruitful heuristic points of reference especially 'in explaining the type of legal changes which follow large social transformations',[3] or it could involve both the 'popular legal consciousness' and the 'legal ideology' emerging from the '"mandarin" materials of legal

2 D. Nelken (ed.), *Comparing Legal Culture* (Aldershot: Dartmouth, 1997), 2.
3 D. Nelken (ed.), *Comparing Legal Culture* (Aldershot: Dartmouth, 1997), 3.

scholarship'.[4] It could even assume the task of 'embrac[ing] provisionally an entire contextual matrix in which state law operates'.[5] In order to analyse the concept of legal culture we have to distinguish firstly between internal and external legal cultures. The former is based on a sort of insider's view, typical for professionals endowed with a direct knowledge of the law and of legal methodology, while the latter is based on the perceptions of the layperson as potential and occasional players in the law game. Although extremely important, this distinction does not imply homogeneity within either internal or external legal cultures. Internal legal culture could show relevant differences not only on the basis of general orientations towards single norms or the legal order as a whole, but also on the basis of specific roles exercised by legal professionals such as attorneys and judges. External legal cultures could refer to the views of ordinary citizens profoundly differentiated according to social categories based, for instance, on their age or level of income.

Moreover, the distinction 'internal/external' can be further articulated and applied separately to the roles or personal characteristics of the actors, and to the objects or the criteria they adopt.[6] Thus it is possible to imagine, for example, an internal actor applying external criteria of treatment to internal matters, as in the case of the ideological judge, or an external actor applying internal criteria to internal matters, as in the case of 'informal justice', where non-professionals legally control and determine relevant conflicts.[7]

Starting from these possible distinctions, it becomes evident that the key concepts of 'transition' and 'legal culture' could enlighten each other. From a socio-legal viewpoint, successful legal transitions particularly require the strong support of various legal cultures; that is, of the 'internal' legal cultures of the 'law-operators' with their different roles, as well as of the 'external' legal culture of the law consumers with their different needs. In order to incorporate these elements in a sociological theory of law, it is necessary to consider legal evolution not only compatible with, but essentially dependent on cultural factors.

4 L.M. Friedman, 'The concept of legal culture', in D. Nelken (ed.), *Comparing Legal Culture* (Aldershot: Dartmouth, 1997), 38.

5 R. Cotterrell, 'The concept of legal culture', in D. Nelken (ed.), *Comparing Legal Culture* (Aldershot: Dartmouth, 1997), 29.

6 A. Febbrajo, 'Cultura giuridica, Contenuti e funzioni di un concetto', in A. Febbrajo, A. la Spina and M. Raiteri (eds), *Cultura giuridica e politiche pubbliche in Italia* (Milano: Giuffrè, 2006), xi–lxii.

7 R.L. Abel (ed.), *The Politics of Informal Justice*, vol. 2, Comparative Studies (New York: Academic Press, 1982), 2.

A Theoretical Framework

Many theoretical models, influenced by particular political and social conditions, have addressed the issue of the relationship between centre and periphery, which is still one of the most important elements in the analysis of the present situation of the EU. It was considered mainly from a cultural point of view in some important socio-legal works at the beginning of the twentieth century. At that time the structure of the Austro-Hungarian empire was based on a real melting pot of different cultures and languages, integrated by ties much less rigid than formal appearances might suggest. In spite of that, or perhaps because of it, the empire was able to maintain a highly differentiated unity. Living in its periphery, and having as a source of inspiration a more pluralistic reality, Ehrlich developed a model of law in open polemic with the normative theory of Kelsen, who, living in Vienna, at that time the political and administrative centre of the Empire, had a completely different perception of the legal order – we could even say, a distinct juridico-cultural disposition.

On the basis of broad historical knowledge, especially of Roman law, Ehrlich displayed a deep appreciation of common law and insisted that the state has no exclusive law-making power. Even before the state created the formal legal order, which represents just a part of legal reality, social associations autonomously created the so-called 'living law'. This concept was defined by Ehrlich with reference not only to its effectiveness for individual actors, but also to its genesis, not from formal authorities but from normal social interactions, especially economic ones, in a certain cultural environment (this is probably the reason for the overwhelming importance of private law in his perspective).

The basic concept of living law draws attention to the connection between law and society in a double sense. In the first sense, living law is opposed to the inefficient and bloodless abstraction cultivated by legal scholars and jurists with no real contact with social life; in the second it is opposed to the arbitrary statal decisions of legislators, destined to remain 'paper law' owing to the ignorance of the legitimate norms autonomously produced by social associations, and to their cultural distance from this reality. This implies that living law can normally resist the centralized positive law, if the latter is incompatible therewith. Consequently, local legal cultures enjoy convenient conditions for their consolidation, such as the diffusion of regional languages and customs.

On one hand, the effectiveness of the state's use of force seems *over*estimated, because the natural forces of society are much stronger than the artificial ones at the disposal of the state. On the other hand, however, the role of law-operators, especially judges, is, at least in the continental vision of law, decidedly *under*estimated. The judges are not merely *la bouche de la loi*; rather, through their interpretation of positive norms in concrete cases, they perform the essential function of ensuring constant contact between living law and statal law, in order to correct the latter and give voice to the former, or vice versa. 'As soon as state law has actually become part and parcel of everyday life, and has exerted a moulding influence on it, jurists will no longer confine their attention to the words of the statute but will be concerned with the forms of life they have come into being under its influence.'[8]

Almost contemporaneously, but from a different perspective, Weber developed an approach inspired by a more centralized model of state and a more sophisticated methodology. Referring to a highly articulated typology of concepts, Weber was essentially preoccupied by using legal culture not only as a possible *explanandum*, that is, as an object of the research able to influence the minds of social actors, but also as a possible *explanans*, that is, as a hypothesis to be adopted by a neutral observer for his or her research.

Weber focused his attention on the large, and somehow mysterious, field which, for both sociologist and historian, is a sort of cultural black box – the field between social behaviour and positive law normally represented within the meta-cultural frame of the 'nation'. He was trying to isolate some typical features of Western social institutions on the basis of a comparative analysis of different contexts. Legal cultures, in particular, were studied not only through a combination of popular and professional cultures, but also by reference to their intense interactions with other types of culture (economic, political and even religious).

At least two Weberian typologies merit mention here: the first devoted to the different sources of legitimation of legal domination (merely emotional, value-rational, religious and guided by interest situations); and the second devoted to the different criteria of rationality, according to which it was possible to treat positive law in different situations (emotional, value-rational, traditional and purpose-rational). Both typologies offer an extremely rich conceptual arsenal for comparing established legal orders and for analysing their gradual, and inevitably approximate, realization as a consequence of the combination of different cultural factors. The concept of law is considered by Weber as a heuristic reference for both popular and professional legal cultures – a combination of abstract and concrete elements. It is thus defined as a *legitimate* order which 'is externally guaranteed by the *probability* that coercion (physical or psychological), to bring about *conformity* or avenge violation, will be applied by a *staff* of people holding themselves specially ready for that purpose'.[9]

On this basis, we can now observe that an adequate way for finding a useful theoretical scheme able to grasp the main characteristics of a transitional period must avoid, on the one hand, a purely normative approach, especially in its Kelsenian version, while rediscovering, on the other hand, a theoretical scheme which recognizes the sometimes hidden function of society to create new norms and to correct them when required.

8 E. Ehrlich, *Fundamental Principles of the Sociology of Law* (New York: Russell & Russell, 1962), 388.

9 M. Weber, *On Law in Economy and Society*, ed. by M. Rheinstein (Cambridge, MA: Harvard University Press, 1966), 5 [in this quotation the first two italics are added].

The social systems approach seems to be a promising theoretical attempt aimed at constructing a non-normative *and* sociological approach on the basis of the most important elements already articulated by the works of Kelsen, Ehrlich and Weber.[10] Starting from these presuppositions, the highest ambition of this approach is not only to identify the most important sociological institutions and their mutual interactions, but also to elaborate, from an evolutionary perspective, an autopoietic scheme, which in advanced societies is more adequate than a normative approach. For a social systems theory 'the legal system is no longer waiting in the wings for people to engage in a dispute in order that it can find a just solution that is in accordance with the law. Instead, law itself produces the situations, which trigger off conflicts, by regulatory manipulation of everyday life'. In other words 'law promotes itself'.[11] In general 'complexity as such improves a system's chance of adaptation', because 'evolution normalizes improbabilities, improbabilities being understood as the degree of deviation from an original situation'. This means that legal evolution 'operates in a circular fashion by responding partly with variation to external impulses, and partly by reusing its stabilisation as the motivation for innovation'. Social and legal evolution could thus be represented according to the scheme showed in Figure 2.1.[12]

The 'circularity' of this scheme is the most evident characteristic of social systems theory,[13] and should be specified to avoid misunderstanding. It implies not a simple reiteration of homologous models of action, but a self-constructing process constantly open to new outcomes; not a simple internalization of the perspective, but a double orientation towards internal as well as external factors; not a lack of interaction with the environment, but a regulated communication according to which actors within social systems know selectively what to learn or not to learn.

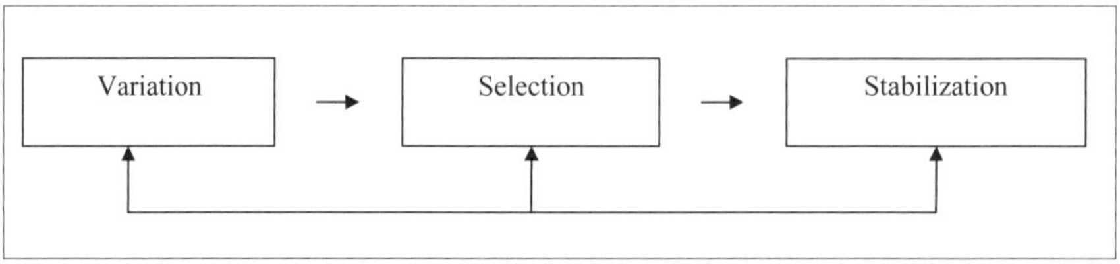

Figure 2.1 An autopoetic model of evolution

10 Cf. for recent contributions to these authors, R. Cotterrell, 'Images of Europe in sociolegal traditions, in R. Cotterrell, *Living Law* (Farnham: Ashgate, 2008), 145–63; A. Febbrajo, *Sociologia del diritto. Concetti e problemi* (Il Mulino, 2009).

11 N. Luhmann, *Law as a Social System* (Oxford: Oxford University Press, 2004), 267.

12 N. Luhmann, Law as a Social System (Oxford: Oxford University Press, 2004), 259. By permission of Oxford University Press.

13 A. Febbrajo, 'From hierarchical to circular models: Some introductory remarks', in *European Yearbook in the Sociology of Law* (Milan: Giuffrè, 1988), 3–21.

The events of the last 20 years in CEE countries could be considered a textbook case for the above-mentioned contributions. In autopoietic terms, they created the preconditions, as frequently happens in transitional phases, for overcoming the 'boundaries' of law through law.[14] Today these countries represent a sort of 'experiment' in relation to the question: how is a new legal order produced in a relatively short period and under external pressures. This somewhat forced process is based not only on internal and external legal sources but also on the decisive and continuous interventions of different non-legal factors, and on a constitution-making process, defined by political and bureaucratic institutions within a state-like entity rather than being endowed directly with the coercive means of the state.

Because the CEE countries involved could make reference to the legal system of other member states or to the legal order of the supranational EU structures, the 'internal/external' counterposition in relation to the borders of the legal system and to the 'centre of gravity' of legal development, may assume different dimensions, and can no longer be compressed into the alternative 'legal' or 'societal'.

A legal transition could be considered, at least implicitly, to be based on a combination of formal and substantive elements, not only on and the structural dimension of institutions with sufficient authority but also on a set of criteria for selecting individual decisions. It is here possible to use the image of hardware installation (structural dimension of the institutions) in order to produce 'stabilization', which has to be accompanied by the application of adequate software (instrumental dimension of the decisions) in order to produce 'variation'. Furthermore, the innovative solutions have to be selected through a particular combination of criteria of equality and differentiation, because only what is perceived as partially expected can be accepted, and only what is at least partially different can produce innovation.

A remarkable example of a transition, in the sense described above, is the result of architectural skills exhibited by many of the most well-known European city squares, which, typically, were constructed without a strict plan. Now they appear beautiful and almost perfectly harmonic, but they were built de facto over the years through a series of adjustments which substantially changed the original plan and interpreted it in a very flexible way. These different elements were able to integrate and enrich the original idea of a city square, by making reference to a widespread sense of beauty articulated at different cultural levels: the level of individuals connected by mutually compatible roles; the level of the roles

14 Cf. J. Přibáň and D. Nelken, *Law's New Boundaries: The Consequences of Legal Autopoiesis* (Aldershot: Ashgate, 2001). The concept of autopoiesis is without any doubt one of the most successful in the lexicon of new systems theory. For a sophisticated and convincing application, see G. Teubner, Law as an Autopoietic System (London: Blackwell, 1993). On the same subject, see also G. Teubner and A. Febbrajo (eds), 'State, law, and economy as autopoietic systems: Regulation and autonomy in a new perspective', in *European Yearbook in the Sociology of Law* (Milan: Giuffrè, 1991–1992).

connected by equivalent or convergent functions and the level of the functions connected by an integrated social system, that is, the city.

It is possible to distinguish, at historical level, several transitions during the construction of a square. Corrections will intervene on the basis of communication coming from complementary roles (for instance, from different masons and craftsmen) or individual actors (for instance, from celebrated architects and sculptors), but also from generous patrons related to functionally different sub-systems involved in the same project (for example, the owner of a Florentine bank or the members of a politically powerful family, who might be interested in having a representative seat at the borders of the square). Last, but not least among the cultural actors, mention must be made of the numerous citizens crossing the square and daily using its space to meet other people or to go about their business. In spite of the plurality of the actors involved and the difference of their cultural backgrounds, during the transition of some city precinct into a monumental square the harmony of the multiple individual decisions required was granted by an overarching aesthetic culture. It was based on the implicit adhesion to a generally accepted structural model which, with its internal proportions and symmetries, imposed a sort of general limitation to the imagination of architects and to the socially relevant interests.

In the analogy of the city square, it is easy to find important elements of the last period of reconstruction of Europe, both in terms of its potential and its limits. Following this argument a couple of questions have to be raised. How is it possible, in case of the reconstruction of a corner of an enlarged European square, to restructure certain buildings, clearly influenced by different styles, with the general consensus of their inhabitants? And how is it possible to grant a minimum level of adaptation of the architectural structures to the specific interests of legal, political, economic and religious institutions, and to the emergent needs of the ordinary citizens without compromising their fundamental unity? Before discussing these questions, it is necessary to analyse the typical characteristics of our dual model of transition, which, with its basic differentiations, offers a good ground for the application of a social systems theory approach.

Two Kinds of Transition

The typical features that would allow an external observer to distinguish (with a certain approximation) two different steps of transition could be heuristically characterized as shown in Table 2.1 below:

Table 2.1 The phases of transition

	First transition	Second transition
main reference point	goals	tools
typical strategy	systemic differentiation	cultural differentiation
prevalent attitude	defensive	pragmatic
final product	surface law	embedded law

As already suggested, in the initial phase of transition it is possible to observe a greater degree of clarity at the level of the goals than at the level of the tools. The pursued goals are normally shared by the actors while the tools are not yet established or tested. Therefore the first phase of transition in CEE countries typically shows an orientation towards abstract values applicable, through formal procedures, to a wide range of heterogeneous social sectors. According to the Copenhagen criteria for the accession into the EU, transition was an extremely pervasive programme inspired by formal rationality under the supervision of the rule of law. The pursued goals, whether directly or indirectly, concerned the most important social systems (the democratization of the political system, the liberalization of the economic system and the individualization of the moral system) in order to stress the limits of politics, and to signal the substantive and formal detachment from a previously predominant totalitarian, *dirigiste* and collectivist model.

In a first transitional phase, the prevalent attitude is defensive in relation to a not yet excluded risk of relapses into the past. Value orientations are influenced by the fundamental interest of escaping from a global empire; in so doing they basically converge towards a break from the past and an integration according to the EU *acquis*. Otherwise, post-communist institutions appeared to secure the domestic and international consensus they needed through a somewhat problematic combination of two elements. One, predominantly positive, was related to an activity and was produced by an active adherence to new democratic values. The other, predominantly negative, concerned a limitation, and was generated by a widespread fear of exclusion from the EU for failing radically to disassociate themselves from the former communist regime.

According to this 'defensive' attitude, accession to the EU is connected, as 'echoed in the public discourse and in the literature', with the very general idea that it 'will render democratisation irreversible'.[15] Given the opacity of the tools in this phase, the approach to the fundamental value of freedom is first interpreted not so much in a positive way, but rather as freedom from the risk of falling into the traps

15 W. Sadurski, A. Czarnota and M. Krygier (eds), *Spreading Democracy and the Rule of Law? The Impact of EU Enlargement on the Rule of Law, Democracy and Constitutionalism in Post-Communist Legal Orders* (Dordrecht: Springer, 2006), 27.

of communism again.[16] Moreover, legal norms are not sufficiently stabilized on the basis of pre-existing traditions. The huge number of EU guidelines has apparently reduced to a minimum the possibility of restoring pre-communist historical legacies, which were sometimes under the strong influence of both the *code Napoleon* and Roman law. We can thus speak of a 'surface law',[17] which refers to a *positive law* not yet embedded in a legal tradition but susceptible to perpetual reform and unilateral orientation towards the solutions proposed by EU bodies.

Unlike the previous, culturally more undifferentiated phase, the second period of transition corresponds to an increasing differentiation of internal cultures. The passive reception of EU guidelines is no longer as central as their selective adaptation to the emerging needs of specific sectors of society. This second phase puts the law in a wider, cultural context and reinterprets the general goals of the first phase, taking into account the living rules that develop on a social rather than on a statal basis. The progressive assimilation to the already established legal orders, represented by the older EU members, can now be balanced by reference to the legal milestones of the pre-communist period. This facilitates the emergence, towards both the incumbent supranational integration and its possible interpretations, of different cultural attitudes open to local re-examinations at the level of ordinary social actors as well as of legal professionals.

The complex interplay of external and internal, legal and non-legal cultural levels suggests a manifest adaptation of previously envisaged goals to a more realistic vision of the conceptual and institutional tools to be adopted in concrete situations. In this period, 'law has a special, extraordinarily constructive role', in that it does not merely provide settled guidelines for the present, but exercises its 'transformative potential' to engender the putatively different future which will come at the end of 'a bounded period, spanning two regimes'.[18] It is thus possible to interpret the value of freedom in a more positive and operative way; that is, as freedom projected into the future, oriented to a much wider range of possible actions.

We can here speak of an 'embedded law', seen as a sort of *living law*, which tries to adjust its content not merely to EU guidelines but, more importantly, to the complexity of society and to its various cultural tendencies. Referring to the possibility of developing such a deeply rooted law in a transitional phase, it is also necessary to notice different orientations respectively described as 'institutional optimism' and 'cultural pessimism'. These different perspectives take into

16 A. Sajó, 'Preferred generations: A paradox of restoration constitutions', *Cardozo Law Review* (1992/93), 847–63.

17 For this term cf. W. Twining, 'Surface law', in H. Petersen, A.L. Kjaer, H. Krunke and M.R. Madsen, *Paradoxes of European Legal Integration* (Aldershot: Ashgate, 2008), 157 ss. In this context, while expressions such as 'paper law' or 'law in the books' mostly relate to the effects of certain norms, 'surface law' takes their sources into consideration.

18 M. Krygier, 'Rethinking the rule of law after communism', in A. Czarnota, M. Krygier and W. Sadurski, *Rethinking the Rule of Law after Communism* (Budapest: Central European University Press, 2005), 267.

consideration the needs, on the one hand to change legal norms and institutions, and on the other to emphasize the difficulty of creating and supporting new law through law without adequate and sufficiently diffused cultural factors.

This dual model of transition, used for representing in very general terms the situation of CEE countries, underlines – from a socio-legal point of view – the paradoxes of an integration initially based on a legal culture artificially selected by formal institutions, and later destined to be increasingly influenced by autonomous and local legal cultures, which are able to produce unforeseeable differentiations.[19] Therefore the two-step process of transition may take into consideration the typical ways in which legal cultures transform living law into written law and written law into living law.

The legal transition is obviously not limited to 'paper law', or to the so-called 'law in the books', but includes the cultural orientations of the population that could influence the functioning of newly created institutions. This composite process is normally reconstructed, considering that legal professionals have to apply the norms mostly in conformity with a formal rationality (internal legal culture); social actors must react to legal decisions mostly according to a substantive rationality (external legal culture);[20] the public, though not directly involved, has to observe various forms of legal communication; and, last but not least, neutral sociologists in the Weberian tradition, attempting to give specific meanings to the legally relevant object of interpretation, have to resort to a heuristic combination of external and internal legal culture.[21] The specific historical situations of the countries involved, and the various ways in which the process of democratization is carried out, could moreover be perceived by different sectors of the same society in different ways. Referring to law it was therefore affirmed that 'social efficacy and official law requires, not merely that elites observe and seek to enforce it, but also that it enters into the normative structures which nourish, guide, inform, and co-ordinate the actions of ordinary people'.[22] Therefore, the reference to legal cultures appears as a filter for selecting and bringing into focus the lenses required for adapting formal law to different situations.

The circularity of this process could clarify the different aspects of transition, that is, the ways in which the present reception of norms and their future variations could be articulated at different levels: at the highest and most abstract level of the institutional reception of general values; at the more concrete level of their local adaptation; and at the pragmatic level of their implementation by individuals. The

19 H. Petersen, A.L. Kjaer, H. Krunke and M.R. Madsen, *Paradoxes of European Legal Integration* (Aldershot: Ashgate, 2008).

20 L.M. Friedman, *The Legal System: A Social Science Perspective* (New York: Russell Sage, 1975).

21 D. Nelken and J. Feest (eds), *Adapting Legal Cultures* (Oxford: Hart Publishing, 2001).

22 M. Krygier, 'Institutional optimism, cultural pessimism and the rule of law', in M. Krygier and A. Czarnota (eds), *The Rule of Law after Communism: Problems and Prospects in East-Central Europe* (Aldershot: Ashgate, 1999), 89.

fundamental relationship between vaguely defined goals (structural dimension) and possible tools (instrumental dimension) highlights the fact that the incoming new society, which is destined to realize the goals generally diffused in a period of transition, can only be innovated and adapted after having stabilized the first wave of normative production, not only through a new constitution, but also through practical activities of both legal operators and law consumers.

On the basis of this heuristic typology it is possible to discuss the problem of 'dealing with the past' – which seems preliminary in real transitions. It is necessary in order to give a specific identity to newborn legal systems, and to tackle the basic problems of stabilization (mostly oriented to the present) and variation (mostly oriented to the most urgent challenges of the future), which typically correspond to the main phases of transition we have outlined thus far. Table 2.2 below illustrates this further.

These three problems capture the basic aspects of a country involved in a profoundly regenerating transition (*who* I am, *what* I am, *how* I am) which requires a constant interplay between internal and external, legal and non-legal cultures.

Table 2.2 Preliminary and substantial problems of transition

Problem	Perspective	Focus	Effect
identity	past	selective memory	recognition
stabilization	present	constitution	legitimation
innovation	future	interpretation	adjustment

A Preliminary Problem: Legal Cultures and Collective Memories

From the point of view of social systems theory, institutions, states and even the world society could be represented as *self-describing* systems. Thus, if they are approaching a period of transition, the preliminary problem to be solved is constructing their own identity. They must present themselves as coherent points of reference: first, for the orientation of individuals living within their cultural borders; and second, for giving a sense to their action.

This is particularly evident in a period when the need to select the elements that could render a certain transition's point of departure plausible is necessarily connected with the control of memory. As a matter of fact, single events or entire episodes might damage the image of a certain society, or even threaten its survival. Every social system and every single institution needs to have a memory able to exclude things that are no longer acceptable. In other words, they have to 'remember to forget'.

It hardly needs emphasizing that a capacity for memory control is an essential instrument not only for retaining, in various ways, everything that may be useful for an adequate construction of a collective 'identity', but also for erasing that which needs to be forgotten in order to rewrite history. The tendency to follow widely shared patterns and highly selective criteria of relevance with pedagogic value requires a treatment of the past that can blank out certain events as if they never happened, or introduce a phase of collective critical reflection, giving rise, in both cases, to an 'official institutional memory'.

In a period of transition, such as the recent one in CEE countries, the time available for memory-building (or rebuilding) was sometimes dramatically short. Within a few years, both national public opinion and observers from the rest of the world had to be convinced of the fundamental discontinuity from the past and the seriousness of their radical processes of democratization, liberalization and individualization. The countries involved had to overturn, or otherwise overcome the many relics of the recent past still visible in their political, economic and moral spheres. It was thus necessary to find solutions, avoiding, on the one hand, the temptation to maintain the memory of negative experiences, whilst trying, on the other, to construct culturally acceptable and socially bearable criteria for an edifying use of remembrance.

The historically dominant experience was obviously the gigantic, Leviathan-like figure of the Communist party, able to interfere with almost every aspect of social life. But the communist era, which was the only past these countries needed to neutralize, did not eliminate other pasts: the more remote pre-communist traditions and the pre-democratic period immediately following the fall of communism – or, as in Poland, even occurring during its last years.[23] The more that cultural elements of the non-communist histories could be revitalized, the more reasons were given for strengthening, in a positive way, a collective sense of identity. Post-communist societies were thus exposed to a composite, simultaneously negative and positive, influence.

Among the strategies applied in this context, in almost all CEE countries before and immediately after their entrance into the EU, lustration was one of the most problematic. 'Lustration' or 'decommunization', that is, the purification of the new structures from the intrusion of those who had collaborated with the former regime, became a field of intervention of highly symbolic and substantial importance even if – or rather because – it was not compulsorily regulated by EU provisions.

In order to sever from the past without injuring the present, the identity problem could admit several solutions depending on different situations. In general, it was presented as being based on a crucial alternative symbolized by the difficult balance between Justitia and Nemesis. The blindness of both Goddesses could represent impartiality but also a symbol of the limited knowledge of human events. It therefore seems that 'in discussion of the extremely complicated problem of dealing with the past, the line is still, as it used to be, between those who have a limited concept of human justice – as represented by Nemesis – and those who look from the point of view of historical justice, Justice with a capital 'J', based on

23 Cf. P. Grilli, Da uno a molti: democratizzazione e rinascita dei partiti in Europa orientale (Bologna: Il Mulino, 1997).

principles considered universal in time and space, which have to be implemented regardless of social costs'.[24]

Translating these classical semantics into the language of social systems theory, the basic problem can be put in the following terms: what kind of memory is a social system able to sustain without reducing its capacity to react effectively to the environment? A social system must evaluate, in different situations, the social impact of a large amount of data concerning its past, and the internal stress that incompatible memories could provoke. In short, there is no doubt that, for a system, the past could be a burden. The problem does not have to be solved immediately in strictly technological or psychological terms, but it must be dealt with first in legal and political terms, that is, in terms of legality and of general consensus. It is also morally imperative to consider individual rights (dignity and privacy), and the human costs of reconstructing the real past of a huge number of people. Moreover, it is necessary to consider economic arguments, because the costs of a survey of documents and of the training of a large number of new cadres could be relatively high in comparison to the results expected, given the reduced role of 'ideologies in post-communist countries'.[25]

For all these reasons, dealing with the past requires a certain graduality, but the transformation time for EEC countries was remarkably short. Quick purification is not unique to post-communist countries. After World War II, countries like Italy, Germany, France and later Spain and Portugal, went through similar experiences, yet in fundamentally different situations. In those cases, clear evidence of discontinuity and a sort of lustration were already provided by the conclusion of a long war, accompanied, as in the case of France, by the official condemnation of the Vichy government, or, as in Italy, by a bloody civil war. As far as post-communist countries are concerned, it is necessary to recall that, in spite of previous fights for democracy and freedom valiantly attempted during the communist period, and of several examples of individual resistance to the regime, these countries were generally perceived by international public opinion as being members of a still-menacing empire, even after the 'Cold War' had subsided. Moreover, the need to clearly condemn the past was largely diffused among the population, given the high number of victims of past communist regime. The discussion of lustration was therefore of central importance, because it was necessary to 'measure' both the required intensity of the explicit repudiation of the past and the willingness to critically scrutinize the former political regime from legal, political, moral and even religious points of view.

In general, it is possible to distinguish between *Symbolic* and *Substantial* types of lustration, as Table 2.3 demonstrates.

24 Cf. A. Czarnota, 'Between Nemesis and Justitia: Dealing with the past as a constitutional process', in Czarnota, Krygier and Sadurski (eds), *Rethinking the Rule of Law after Communism* (Budapest: Central European University Press, 2005), 123.

25 Cf. J. Siklova, 'Lustration or the Czech way of screening', in M. Krygier and A. Czarnota, *The Rule of Law after Communism: Problems and Prospects in East-Central Europe* (Aldershot: Dartmouth, 1999), 248–60.

Table 2.3 Types of lustration

symbolic	moral	based on knowledge	diffuse
substantial	institutional	based on sanctions	limited

Where lustration was merely symbolic, evaluation of the quantitative level of possible cases of potential application, generally important from a socio-legal perspective, could almost be irrelevant, given the minor costs of moral sanctions based on the diffusion of the names of the collaborators with the former regime. By contrast, where lustration was substantial, prior evaluation of the quantitative level of potential applications could be decisive, because an excessive number of institutional sanctions could make such a programme almost unbearable for the social system as a whole. Obviously, for an efficient substantial lustration, even symbolic measures could have important effects, as with the option for victims to have access to the archives of the former police collaborators. Likewise, even substantial reactions, such as criminal trials against presumed collaborators, could produce overwhelmingly symbolic effects if they were limited to an extremely low number of cases.

It is also possible to distinguish among different types of policy, which ‘c[ould] focus upon perpetrators and on victims’. In both cases, as can be seen in Table 2.4 below, they could be made effective by means of legal or political sanctions.[26]

It is necessary to observe that memory of a social system by a selected number of people, especially if this memory concerns sensitive matters, could be a menace for democracy because of the potential blackmail power of the few who know the sins of the others. To reduce this risk, available information was possibly diluted over a longer period, involving different levels of selection. Therefore, the relevant facts, as in every communication process, were distilled by several filters (here, in particular, by personal, legal and political ones), each of them could contribute to the consolidation of an ‘official’ reality to be enriched and/or corrected from time to time by historical data. In this way a process opened up, which could periodically produce reassessments of the different criteria of selection, thus influencing official reality again.

26 C. Offe and U. Poppe, ‘Transitional justice after the breakdown of the German Democratic Republik’, in Czarnota, Krygier and Sadurski (eds), *Rethinking the Rule of Law after Communism* (Budapest: Central European University Press, 2005), 153.

Table 2.4 Policies of lustration

	Perpetrators	Victims
legal sanctions	criminal punishment	restitution/compensation
political sanctions	disqualification from public sector employment	'recognition'

Within this general strategy, the different ways in which lustration was implemented in EEC countries form a benchmark for various possible combinations of internal and external legal cultures. A few examples might be of service. One country in which lustration clearly appears to be at the crossroads between legal and non-legal cultures is Poland. Here the so called 'thick line' between past and present, between continuity and discontinuity, could find a strong support in the political role of religion. In Poland, lustration was presented, on the one hand, as the law of moral restoration, as a way to strengthen the role of positive law for guiding individual consciousness; on the other, as the beginning of a sort of moral abdication, as a way to reintroduce totalitarian methods, which were not only legally but also morally incompatible with the respect due to the individuals.

It was evident that lustration could systematically violate human rights, at least on procedural grounds (for example, verdicts could be pronounced without the presence of accused persons and without cogent evidence). Moreover, the lack of an exact definition of the term 'collaborator' was one of the main impediments to the implementation of lustration.[27] It was also for this reason that lustration acquired an ambiguous image.[28] The problem was not so much whether or not to apply lustration, but, rather, in what manner to exercise it and to what extent the measures to be taken ought to be proportional.[29]

The problem was discussed by the last members to enter into the EU. In Romania, a proposal for a lustration law, presented in 2006, about one year before Romania's entry into the EU, is yet to be translated into a bill. In Bulgaria, the lustration process was initially concentrated mainly on the educational system,

27 In Poland the Institute for National Remembrance (IPN) was created in order to analyse secret agents' lists. According to official evaluations, in the country 400–700 thousand people (out of a population of 38 million) had to be lustrated. Ad hoc courts of justice, with unlimited access to civil and military archives, were created in order to examine in single cases the level of complicity with the secret police. But the real meaning of the concept of 'collaborator' with the secret services SB (Sluzba Biespeczenstwa) remained unclear, and the attention in the public opinion was concentrated on some spectacular cases.

28 The ambiguities of the lustration process are analysed from a historical and comparative perspective by Grażyna Skąpska in Chapter 6, later in this volume.

29 Cf. A. Kaniowski, 'Lustration and decommunisation: Ethical and theoretical debates', in M. Krygier and A. Czarnota, *The Rule of Law after Communism: Problems and Prospects in East-Central Europe* (Aldershot:, Dartmouth,1999), 212–47.

where new elections in the administrative bodies of universities were provided to substitute individuals who were working inside the Party and in the National Security Service, and those who taught communist history in the educational organization of the Party.[30] But, after a first wave of lustration, the Constitutional Court declared the de-communisation law and, in particular, the exclusion of former secret service agents from chairing committees in parliament and from travelling abroad in official delegations to be unconstitutional and contrary to the European Convention of Human Rights.[31]

In general, we can thus affirm that the issue of lustration offers a good example of the decisive role played by a complex combination of legal and non-legal cultures. A process of lustration involves a combination of religious and political factors, moral guilt and legal accountability. It can have a cathartic effect on internal public opinion and can function as a sort of regeneration in relation to the international community.Concrete experiences depended to a large extent on the internal need to reconstruct collective memories, on the external need to reshape an internationally recognized identity and on the functional need to build a new elite.

The case of lustration sheds some light on those factors that could intervene in the process of implementing those strategies considered necessary from a legal and/or moral point of view to assure a smooth exit from the past. Nevertheless, it was the construction of new constitutions the basic element which (not only in a symbolic way) signalled official entry into the transitional period, putting some formal limitations on the lustration process and contributing to its definition.

The First Step: Transition through Legitimation

During transitions, considered the result of an unlikely combination of internal and external legal cultures, a central function of stabilization is certainly performed by constitutions. They could be seen as a sort of 'meta-structure', stabilizing the different structures of the social body and imposing certain limits on their possibilities for change. In particular, we can speak of constitution from a dogmatic point of view, as the normative source of the legal order, which has to select the lawful behaviour from the unlawful, and, from an empirical point of view, as the

30 Lustration required people to make declarations about past jobs, including describing activities carried out within the Communist Party by persons who held ruling positions inside scientific or academic institutions. According to the Sofia Social Research Institute, 50 thousand people lost their jobs, including 9,000 specialists from various companies, 1,400 officers of the National Security Service, 90 per cent of public employees, and one-third of Bulgarian diplomats, all because of files produced by the Secret Services (DS).

31 The Bulgarian Parliament simply approved a law regulating the disclosure of the content of Secret Service (DS) files, but without lustration requirements. The Romanian Constitutional Court recently declared unconstitutional a proposed reglementation of 'lustratzia' (decision n. 820, 7 June 2010).

generally accepted cultural source of these limitations. Consequently, a constitution can be regarded as the self-representation of the legal system, a combination of values and institutions, and of flexible software and more rigid hardware necessary for its functioning. Moreover, constitutions have the function of describing, at a very general level, acceptable points of equilibrium between individual interests and collective needs, different areas of influence and agencies of control. They constitute social games, which could admit different strategies and moves – and therefore different results for the future. Constitutions could thus be presented as protective 'harbours' where the needs and ideals of several future generations can find a favourable and safe place not exposed to social conflicts.

The prevalent semantics during the communist era, as in any totalitarian regime, did not clearly distinguish among the languages of law, politics, economy and religion. The state was the very centre of society and, as such, was an object of a sort of (induced) religious worship. In several post-communist countries, the necessity of changing too much too quickly,[32] and of finding a way out of the widespread interconnections of the former regime, require sstrategies of intersystemic communication, based on the mutual ability of social systems partially to recognize and ignore each other. It is thus possible, in the analysis of the first transitional phase, to find convergences among the typical codes applied by different social structures: legal, political, economic and religious ones. These convergences are obviously a homage to the intersystemic vision of Weber, but are also a recognition of the wide spectrum of legal and non-legal cultures that play a relevant role in a transitional phase.

This does not exclude the specificity of the binary codes of the different social systems, but rather requires at least their formal harmonization and stabilization within the constitutional text. In other words, constitutions are based not only on the formal acknowledgements of the binary codes typically applied by the different cultural systems, but also on the rule of law according to which the guidelines are defined for their fundamental combination at the level of parliament, free market, and of a background of religious or moral values on which to base a diffuse civic ethic. Needless to say, while law, politics and economy were officially included in the corpus of *acquis* elaborated by EU officials since 1993, and their transition could thus be guided by 'imported' rules, the reference to religion, and to its traditional influence on moral standards, underlines the importance of local and 'independent' variables. Table 2.5 illustrates this point.

32 Czarnota, Krygier and Sadurski, 'Introduction', in A. Czarnota, M. Krygier and W. Sadurski (eds), *Rethinking the Rule of Law after Communism* (Budapest and New York: Central European University Press, 2005), 2. Cf. also R. Dahrendorf, *Reflections on the Revolution in Europe* (London: Chatto and Windus, 1990).

Table 2.5 Intersystemic connections of the first transition

	Binary code	Cultural and institutional instruments of selection
law	legal/arbitrary	rule of law
politics	government/opposition	parliament
economy	individual/collective	free market
religion	good/evil	civil ethics

As we have seen, a transition tends first to be oriented towards stabilizing the structures necessary for transforming already acquired achievements into points of no return. The most visible symbol of this rite of passage is a constitution: according to social systems theory, a constitution can be considered as an 'evolutionary invention', an 'autological text', a part of an autopoietic, self-referential law that is able to legitimate itself.[33] Autopoiesis, in particular does not mean that legal systems cannot learn, but it does imply a way of learning characterized by the ability of law to reflect on law. Constitution represents this ability at the highest possible level. As a matter of fact, the more autonomy is obtained by a certain system, the more capacity it has to simplify its environment, and the more flexibility can be attributed to constitutions for selecting the relevant intersystemic relationships and translating them into a legal code.

The semantics used for the description of social structures by constitutions seem to be contradictory, as they suggest at the same time symbolic closure and pragmatic openness to society as a whole.[34] But they also reflect alternatives that allow a highly differentiated combination of autonomy and interaction. Fundamentally, constitution could be considered as a bridge between law and politics. It has the intersystemic function of contemporaneously defining the legal borders of politics and the political borders of law, and of providing a political legitimation of law and a legal legitimation of politics. Briefly, it represents the most legal part of the political system and the most political part of the legal system.

But in the constitution, seen as an essential factor for the stabilization and self-legitimation of a new legal order, other intersystemic connections are admitted. While its symbolic parts could have closer relationship with religion, its pragmatic parts could have closer relationship with economy. It is also important not to forget that, in the case of CEE countries, the standard rules borrowed from the EU or the European Convention on Human Rights are just a portion (and not the most important one) of the legal orders of these countries. Consequently, constitutions do not have total control over the legal order; they merely define the possible range of its innovations.

33 N. Luhmann, *Law as a Social System* (Oxford: Oxford University Press, 2004), 405 ss.

34 N. Luhmann, *Gesellshaftsstruktur und Semantik. Studien zur Wissenssoziologie der modernen Gesellschaft*, vol. 1 (Frankfurt a.M.: Suhrkamp, 1980).

The several issues connected with the presence of a new constitution in the first phase of a transition may be considered on the basis of a typology of temporal, social and spatial dimensions, inspired by social systems theory.

In a *temporal* dimension, it is necessary to mention the general paradox of every constitution, which, as the most durable normative act in a legal order, inevitably has to pay for its endurance in terms of threats to its effective legitimation.[35] Since social conditions constantly change, the longer a constitution survives, the less future generations will recognize themselves in its content. The challenge of time, crucial for life of every constitution, can be faced at different levels. Because of the relatively short period that in some cases marked the constitution-making process in CEE countries, in the first phase of transition constitutions could be 'light', in the sense that they had limited occasion to revitalize important traditions of the past, in particular the unforgotten cultural elements coming from the pre-communist period. But they could also be 'liquid', in the sense that they were destined to be constantly reshaped by other relevant cultural factors.

Moreover, constitutions have to be considered not only as products but also as producers of internal and external legal cultures.[36] In addition to the written constitutions, we have to consider, at a mere informal level, a plurality of emerging factors of stabilization which can also gradually change the internal, more formally oriented, legal culture. As a matter of fact, the 'unwritten' constitutional norms which are disseminated in the various legal traditions and legal cultures, constantly influence the public and the legal professionals.[37] In this complex cluster of factors of legitimation it should also be remembered the sometimes decisive acceleration of the process of constitutionalisation provoked by individual personalities, which could give different accents to important constitutional roles.

In a *social* dimension it is necessary to stress that every modern constitution must combine a double orientation: defence of what belongs to the realm of the personal and private dispositions of individuals; and protection of what belongs to the realm of public and political communities. It has therefore been observed that, especially in a first phase, 'value preferences in constitutions may be formulated as negative barriers to regulation, or [...] as positive duties to promote human and civic rights'. For both reasons, constitutions may be perceived as potential shields against communism and as 'political compromises between those political forces acting at the moment the drafting of the constitution occurs'. They cannot contain clear-cut distinctions, because they 'represent an arrangement which is expected to provide

35 L. Alexander, *Constitutionalism: Philosophical Foundations* (Cambridge: Cambridge University Press, 1998).

36 P. Haeberle, *Verfassungslehre als Kulturwissenschaft* (Berlin: Duncker & Humblot, 1982).

37 C. Mortati, *La costituzione in senso materiale* (Milano: Giuffrè, 1940).

fair opportunities in the future for all those involved in the process and, to a lesser extent, to unknown or not yet existing forces'.[38]

Examples of this ambiguity can be found in the realm not only of politics but also of economy and religion. Schematically, in the process of legitimation, each system could be associated with different combinations of typical orientation, as shown in Table 2.6 below.

Table 2.6 Orientations of legitimation

Politics	Economy	Religion
general interest	general values	general values
personal values	personal interest	personal values

These different orientations inevitably accentuate the *contingency* of law and show how important it is for analysing the increasing complexity of the relations between legal and non-legal cultures. They also show how unlikely it is to expect that all the social systems will keep pace with one another. Especially in the first period of transition, when different sectors of society have to be deeply transformed, constitutions could enlarge the base of their mediations. They could become a sort of 'multilateral compromise', in so far as they are influenced by legal cultures with a relatively low degree of normativity and with a relatively high degree of openness to economic, political, religious and even psychological aspects in order to improve their basis of legitimation.

Social systems theory has underlined the importance of composite mechanisms employed to save, and possibly to augment from several points of view, a normally scarce element of cohesion as legitimation. The traditional strategies of legitimation through legality are sometimes supported by norms with a mere symbolic function, or by legal decisions endowed with self-legitimating procedures in which the loser is denied the right to protest.[39] Similarly diffuse is the strategy that consists of a sort of 'double negation', that is, of a priori de-legitimation of possibile de-legitimations concerning the entire constitution or parts of it. In this context constitutions could be accepted, and socially defended, because of their stabilizing effects on society as a whole. The frequent lack of knowledge of the entire constitutional text among ordinary actors, and the diffusion of *pars pro toto* ways of legitimation, tends sometimes to transform constitutions into a sort of taboo, which in certain historical situations cannot be discussed even at the level of internal legal culture.

38 A. Sajó, 'Preferred generations: A paradox of restoration constitutions', *Cardozo Law Review* (1992/93), 847–63, 848 ss.

39 N. Luhmann, *Legitimation durch Verfahren* (Frankfurt a.M.: Suhrkamp, 1983).

In a *spatial* dimension, it is necessary to underline that the importance of the different levels of reduced sovereignty (which can no longer be connected to a measurable territorial basis) is growing, both with the gradual fading out of the role of the state and with the emergence of a more regionally and/or transnationally oriented European politics.[40] Paradoxically enough, the supranational governance that comes with EU membership leaves to individual members more room for differentiated governance at state and local levels. This requires not only an increasing coordination through an adequate 'regulation of regulations', but also a different relationship between the centre and the periphery, in comparison with both the communist and the pre-communist era.

The articulation of the different levels of governance is strictly connected with various levels of legal culture. Such levels are not confined within the limits of a traditional 'legal' order in the normative sense of the word; they also involve a plurality of non-statal and culturally relevant legal orders within the territory of one state. Today most of the new EU members, who occupy the geographical place once reserved for the pre-communist 'monocentric heterogeneity' of the Austro-Hungarian period, have tried in several ways to oppose the 'monocentric pervasive control' of the communist era. Probably as a consequence of their different traditions, the 'major laboratory of constitutional works', established during the long and differentiated phase of transition in CEE countries, created a noteworthy tendency against that 'single model' strategy which 'has come to dominate the constitutional landscape'.

In many cases, this variety of historically-produced constitutional models depends on domestic pre-communist traditions, which never culturally disappeared, and which the new EU member states tried to revitalize during the transition. There are, in this area, different solutions for different situations and it is possible to find many difficulties in attempting to classify the new constitutions according to generally accepted criteria. The constitutional drafters of the region 'have therefore produced "mixed" constitutions which are an amalgam of many well-known models'.[41]

The Second Step: Transition through Adjustment

After a transitional phase formally embodied by a heterarchical, not locally guided phase of constitutionalisation, the second step requires the revision and adaptation of the newly created norms. Referring to this situation, it was observed that 'if the problems of transition are unprecedented problems, so the

40 G. Teubner (ed.), *Global Law without a State* (Aldershot: Dartmouth, 1997).

41 R.R. Ludwikowski, '"Mixed" constitutions: Product of an East-Central European constitutional melting pot', *Boston University International Law Journal*, 16 (1998), 1–70; J. Batt, '"Fuzzy statehood" versus hard borders: The impact of EU enlargenent on Romania and Yogoslavia', working paper (Sussex European Institute, 2002).

means developed for dealing with them will need to be novel means'.[42] Even the constitutions, created for setting in motion a mostly goal-oriented period of transition, are destined to adjust, in a second phase, their instrumental parts, characterized by a more mature treatment of the necessary tools. It is thus not surprising that the second phase of transition becomes more ambiguous in relation to the selection of tools, and hence more open to various concrete outcomes. For a socio-legal scholar, this period of transition can be imagined as a journey towards high mountains. First seen on the horizon they will orient the traveller like a polar star, but from a shorter distance, they will reveal an increasing number of alternatives and probably, after a lapse of time, other mountains will be discovered beyond.

The revision and adaptation to social reality of the norms adopted by CEE countries are worked out principally by different internal legal cultures. As in a trial and error process, jurists, judges and legal scholars attempt, where necessary, to correct legal norms, even constitutional norms, taking into consideration their possible negative effects. This is true not only in common law countries, but also in continental Europe, where the great importance of producing adjustments in the legal order, through the so called *Juristenrecht*, is increasingly recognized. Like a beach constantly submerged and levelled by the sea, legal orders, including constitutions, are continuously corrected and rendered homogeneous with the newly emerging interests, by recurrent waves of legal decisions.

This phase of transition in CEE countries must, in a pragmatic process, tackle the new external and internal requirements of the 'post-communist' era. But what does it really mean to be in a post-communist era? It was observed that, whereas in a first phase the expression semantically accentuates the suffix *communist*, suggesting that 'the communist past, or its legacies, retain[s] present effects', in a second phase the emphasis seems to be on the prefix *post*, suggesting that 'we can regard the communist past as some sort of dream or nightmare, which dissipates on waking'.[43] This means that the search for constitutional stabilization, under the pressures of an increasing process of differentiation among social systems formerly integrated by a totalitarian regime, must be supported by corresponding legal cultures. In this phase for CEE countries, the main sources of variety are the vague definition of 'programmes and projects' concerning the EU as a whole and the differentiated local effects of the first wave of regulations following the indications of the EU. This is a process destined to continue, within an interstatal framework, at the level of law operators. In this context, differentiation and integration could both be reinforced.

42 A. Czarnota, M. Krygier and W. Sadurski, 'Introduction', in A. Czarnota, M. Krygier and W. Sadurski (eds), *Rethinking the Rule of Law after Communism* (Budapest: Central European University Press, 2005), 2.

43 M. Krygier and A. Czarnota, 'After postcommunism: The next phase', *Annual Review of Law and Social Science* (2006), 299–336, at 300.

From the point of view of social systems theory, the development of a higher level of self-reflection is closely connected with the mechanism of autopoiesis, which emerged in advanced legal orders as an instrument for triggering legal evolution. The active presence of a second level of observation, which this approach implies, allows a normative order to assume a cognitive orientation in order to correct its inefficient norms. All this presupposes that legal systems explicitly produce a certain amount of 'redundancies',[44] from among which legal professionals could select, introducing, when necessary, further adjustments. This does not necessarily imply a loss of importance of the normative characteristics of the legal system; simply a mutual acknowledgment of legal and non-legal systems. Only if economic logic is recognized by legal logic, and vice versa, will a channel of selective communication among these social systems become more than a pure utopia or a sort of normative invasion. In particular, the legal system seems capable of producing an increasing economization of itself, through the ability of legal decision-makers to translate into their own code the criteria of rationality adopted by economic actors.

In order to ensure an adequate basis for describing intersystemic communication, a new legal semantics must take into consideration the typical media and cultural points of reference of the socially most relevant sectors (politics, economy, religion). They could selectively 'irritate', through the mediation of their operators, legal professionals, who could then react, relying 'on their own network of operations'. In other words, the 'operative closure' of every system does not mean isolation, but a self-referential way of defining 'what belongs to the system and what belongs to the environment'.[45] Obviously, this refers to the influence of social systems on the legal system, and vice versa. The media connected to law, politics, economy and religion (legality, power, utility and faith) could thus respectively underline their cultural orientations (justice, consensus, profit, conscience) and contribute in this way to a gradual co-evolution of the different parts of the whole social system. Table 2.7 provides an illustration of this.

From this perspective, the cognitive and innovative potential of the legal system, based not so much on a hierarchical relation to society but on a more flexible and interactive concept of law, is particularly visible when more attention is given to the functioning of the other social systems. Starting from the presupposition that even the most distant sectors of society could converge, especially when the normative points of reference are so abstract, as in the case of constitution,[46] the legal system could play explicitly the role of the final factor of coordination for the different social systems, of a sort of 'meta-communicator' able to understand the different languages and typical codes of communication of the other social systems.

---

44 N. Luhmann, *Law as a Social System* (Oxford: Oxford University Press, 2004), 320 ss.

45 N. Luhmann, *Law as a Social System* (Oxford: Oxford University Press, 2004), 79–80.

46 N. Luhmann, *Grundrechte als Institution* (Berlin: Duncker & Humblot, 1965).

Table 2.7 Intersystemic connections of the second transition

	Law	Politics	Economy	Religion
operators	jurists	politicians	economists	priests
media	legality	power	utility	faith
cultural orientation	justice	consensus	profit	conscience

This semantic shift, based on the crucial concepts of autopoiesis and self-reflection of the legal system, could find in a second transition various examples in relation to temporal, social and spatial dimensions.

In a *temporal* dimension, it has to be underlined that the tools considered necessary to fill the gaps and the shortcomings of the new legal rules produced during the previous period, are based on legal argumentations that do not always specify and evaluate their future effects. Law-makers and legal professionals are often engaged in the production of new norms and legal decisions without having the possibility of collecting sufficient knowledge of the regulated matters. It is thus not surprising, in this context, that the tendency towards a fast production of new codifications is sometimes treated with suspicion.[47]

This kind of reaction corresponds to a widespread revaluation of the jurisprudence in comparison to an already inflated legislation, under the presupposition that 'law is something to be discovered more than to be enacted'. In spite of the apparent efficiency of a fast-food-like legislation, the slow food of a jurisprudential activity, normally connected with a deeply rooted cultural background, appears the more reliable response. From this perspective, as underlined by some theorists of its limits, legislation seems no longer 'to be a quick, rational and far-reaching remedy against every kind of evil inconvenience'. On the contrary, 'judicial decisions, the settlement of disputes by private arbiters, conventions, customs, and similar kinds of spontaneous adjustments [seem] a remedy for a legislation which may be too quick to be efficacious, too unpredictably far-reaching to be wholly beneficial'.[48]

Furthermore, there is no guarantee that all the elements of the composite field of cultural interactions will develop in a coherent way. Economic issues, for instance, were from the beginning at the very centre of the EU legitimation process, producing a constant amelioration of the living standards according to the principles of a free market economy. But it is especially in the economic field that the sovereignty of EU member states has been limited to some significant degree and subject to temporal

47 In Romania, for instance, it was suggested to slow down the drafting work for a series of new codifications. This request of a further reflection concerns all the country's main codification (*Codul civil, Codul penal, Codul de procedura civila, Codul de procedura penala*).

48 B. Leoni, *Freedom and the Law* (Princeton, NJ: Van Nostrand, 1961), 5.

constraints. Under the free market banner, programmatic and supranational long-term limitations are imposed (for instance, concerning certain levels of national debt). These restrictions, even if intended to be market-friendly preconditions, could be perceived in some occasions as compulsory renouncements of statal sovereignty, similar to those imposed by the typical 'five-year plans' of the communist era.

In a *social* dimension, the development of an adequate supply of legal norms in order to anticipate a corresponding demand, coming from external legal cultures, could produce many problems. It is important here to consider that the relation between the rules' precision and the adequacy of their interpretations is ambivalent. It is possible that the interpretation is perceived more as a menace than as an opportunity, and that it reduces the range of adaptability of the norms. Particularly when the norms are destined to be applied in different cultural situations, or even outside a single national context, several normative strategies can be adopted. The strategy of leaving to the interpreter a certain margin for flexibility – in our terminology of redundancies – could be used in different ways, depending on the requirements of the situation. For example, many years ago, on the label of the *Cinzano* bottle destined for the international market, two different recommendations were written. One said, in German: 'to be served at a temperature between *x* and *y*', precisely indicating the ideal range of temperature; the other, in Italian, said more simply: 'to be served neither cold nor warm'. It was clear that the unknown communicator was not really thinking that all German clients had a thermometer at hand, but that in Germany the average cultural 'expectations' for precision were much higher than in Italy. Nowadays, EU bureaucracies, when they have to solve analogous problems, take a less differentiated approach. The level of precision is often so detailed that it can exceed common cultural expectations. This is probably an attempt to render foreseeable the different outcomes, excluding innovative interpretations. The presupposition is that, in strict normative terms, a certain variety of interpretations is more likely to be a source of disorder than an enrichment of the legal order.

The ideals of the completeness and certainty of regulations are visible in EU norms in many other ways. In some cases EU officials prefer to resort to the 'list strategy', claiming that nothing important is excluded from the normative text and that the imagination of the law-maker can comprehend in advance all relevant events. In other cases, when the uncertainty is inevitable, they prefer to resort to the so-called 'precautionary principle', which tries to reduce the risks *ad abundantiam*, for the sake of citizens as well as of the officials responsible for the decision.

The idea that norms must be a precise mirror of future behaviour, and of their possible distinctions, has, as a consequence, a normative overflow which, paradoxically enough, renders more frequent the necessity of further interpretations. Indeed, an attempt to find an intermediate (less normative and more cognitive) point of reference for legal interpretation, originally proposed by Ehrlich, is now, in its essentials, maintained by Habermas. It is based on a sort of respectful orientation, not towards reality as such, but towards a living law, or, in an analogous way, towards the different 'life worlds'. The intention seems to be to reduce the polluting effects of positive law, and to prepare the interpreter to listen, not so much to the central voice of power, but to the voices coming from the different parts of society, which are interacting on the basis of a 'communicative rationality'.[49] Besides, the more or less extensive interpretation of new social rights, in many cases, could depend not only on complex legal argumentation, but also on the level of their moral acceptance and on the level of financial means available.

According to social systems theory, the principle of consistency has to be interpreted in a more flexible way. Variety means that even something which appears logically inconsistent could be admitted into the legal order, and eventually accepted or rejected on the basis of the different requirements of the situations.[50]

As a matter of fact, the key role of constitutional courts, as a factor of constant adjustment between the mostly-political power of law-makers and the mostly-legal power of judges, could be evaluated differently. Constitutional courts are sometimes regarded as crucial, but also risky, elements where both systems overlap. Especially in the second phase of transition, they could assume a dual task: to define both what is politically opportune within a legally selected number of possibilities, and what is legally correct within a politically selected number of possibilities. For the same reason, the political function of constitutional courts, owing to the fact that there are more than one possibility for their decisions, could be treated as an enrichment of their criteria, not as a treason towards formal logic. In Hungary, where the activity of the constitutional courts has reached its peak and has enjoyed widespread prestige, the Constitutional Court has been regarded as a crucial factor of legal evolution; whereas in Romania it is to some extent perceived, owing to its not only legal but also political role, as a potential threat to the very concept of parliamentary democracy. In the Estonian Republic, the constitution does not establish a Constitutional Court.

In a spatial dimension, given the increasing differentiation of the territorial validity of legal orders, it becomes ever more important to develop methodological approaches for adapting the norms to the different needs emerging from society at the local, state and supranational levels. For legal operators, the new programmes of legal education, aimed at the jurist of the future, cannot ignore the problems, especially in a period of generalized crisis, of statal centralism and hierarchical distribution of power. This is the reason why legal education in the new EU member states appears to be aimed, sometimes, more towards a 'global' than towards a 'European' jurist. Legal studies, following the usual interpretation of the so-called 'Bologna process', are actually characterized by the attempt to introduce a two-level curriculum, preparing, besides a full jurist, a sort of low-level legal operator with limited competences, but in some countries, as in Poland, the five-

---

49 J. Habermas, *Between Facts and Norms: Contributions to a Discourse Theory of Law and Democracy* (Cambridge, MA: MIT Press, 1999).

50 N. Luhmann, *Law as a Social System* (Oxford: Oxford University Press, 2004), 256 ss.

year curriculum for full jurists includes humanistic disciplines and the study of several foreign languages.[51]

In a period of transition especially, the traditional local-universal opposition, as once suggested by the contrast between legal positivism and natural law, appears more and more crucial and tends to be reconsidered. On the one hand, the radical positivism, according to which the lawyer 'does not constitute the law as a cultural object assuming a passive, solely cognitive attitude towards it',[52] could be perceived as dangerous, given the increasing relevance of local and supranational law-making processes. On the other hand, even in a system of legal education based on a formalistic model, some universal elements of natural law are not excluded, and a natural law approach could be presented as a reliable defence against the possible deviations of law-makers and for an extensive interpretation of constitutional values.

This combination of positivism and natural law could generate a sort of 'natural legalism'. The basic norm orientation of the interpreter becomes more comprehensive than in a positivistic approach, and includes the norms produced directly by society at local and suprastatal levels. Moreover, the various legal cultures, according to the 'internal' and 'external' distinctions and to their possible combinations, could outline legal instruments which suggest a highly differentiated approach. As we have seen, in the European cultural space the legal system is becoming, in general, more cognitive and less normative; more gradual, inconsistent and heterarchical, instead of efficient, consistent and hierarchical. But this does not exclude that the process of internal differentiation of the legal family of post-communist countries is destined to continue its pluralistic way, producing different legal models within the same society.

Concluding Remarks

Using a dual model of transition and a pluralistic model of legal culture, this chapter has sought to articulate legal transition, first in a mostly 'goal oriented' phase of stabilization, and second in a mostly 'tools oriented' phase of variation. Starting from this fundamental distinction, transition seems to be a sort of substantially controlled evolution. It is able to grant a more concrete quality to imagined goals, producing a sort of mild revolution or 'a peaceful movement which gradually

51 In many Polish universities (Warsaw, Szczecin, Krakow) some interviews with members of the academic staff underlined the importance of the 'Law Today' programme, which tries to integrate practical exercises, and provides a differentiated programme of 'study and work' curricula for future lawyers and judges.

52 M. Zirk-Sadowski, 'Transformation and integration of legal cultures and discourses – Poland', in Sadurski, Czarnota and Krygier (2006), 309 ss.

incorporates new elements and principles into the existing legal system', in order to transform it, with the aid of adequate tools, 'into an entirely different one'.[53]

During these transitional phases, legal cultures are inserted into a sort of 'policontextural' frame,[54] based on the circulation of different images of law not exclusively guided by a distinction between internal and external legal cultures. Law operators construct images of law that depend not only on their professional knowledge but also on their selective perception of other social systems; while the ordinary social actors elaborate images of law based not only on their direct experience in different realms of society but also on their indirect perception of written norms and, in particular, constitutional texts.

In the recent history of CEE countries, the two typical phases of transition, even if artificially compressed in a relatively short period, were able to produce some fundamental passages at the formal level of norms, as well as at the empirical level of social behaviour: a legal passage from totalitarian regimes to the rule of law, a political passage from communism to democracy; an economic passage from central planning to free markets; and an organizational passage from national to transnational governance.[55]

These passages, converging towards an integration produced by the reception and adaptation of common guidelines, appear nowadays to be, at least formally, accomplished. Obviously, the end of transition does not mean that all the problems are solved for CEE countries, but simply that the new problems are fundamentally similar to those of other EU countries. If transition is substantially exhausted it must be replaced with a new 'post-transitional' phase, characterized by a more egalitarian kind of co-existence among all EU members. The normal relations within EU organizations imply, at least in principle, a mixed distribution of active roles among new and older members. It will not only be possible but necessary to fully recognize the presence of new EU members and their ability to build up proposals, projects and programmes for the future development of the Union. The realization of a sort of 'unitas multiplex', of a unity in diversity, or of a centralized differentiation, requires a mutual interplay among all EU members, and in particular the overcoming of the simple, and in a post-transitional phase already obsolete, distinction between older members and post-communist members. If it is plain that 'not all wisdom moves from West to East',[56] we must also acknowledge that

---

53 Přibáň and Roberts, 'The Central European systems of justice in transition: Introductory remarks', in Přibáň, Roberts and Young (eds), *Systems of Justice in Transition* (Aldershot: Ashgate, 2003), 1 ss.

54 Cf. G. Teubner, 'Des Koenigs viele Leiber: Die Selbstdekonstruktion der Hierarchie des Rechts', *Soziale Systeme*, 2 (1996), 229–55.

55 J.J. Linz and A. Stepan, *Problems of Democratic Transition and Consolidation: Southern Europe, South America and Post-Communist Europe* (Baltimore: John Hopkins University Press, 1996).

56 W. Sadurski, A. Czarnota and M. Krygier, *Spreading Democracy and the Rule of Law? The Impact of EU Enlargement on the Rule of Law, Democracy and Constitutionalism*

wisdom, based fundamentally on specific recent experiences of different regimes as well as on pre-communist democratic traditions, plainly moves from East to West. In a post-transitional phase, older members of the EU will have no reason to retain the label of 'post-communist' countries; and even the less pejorative term 'Central and Eastern European countries' has now to be treated as a simple geographic expression.[57]

Yet further questions arise. After the so-called 'second transition', devoted to the differentiation of internal identities within post-communist countries, how is it possible to imagine the institutionalization of a 'normal', no longer asymmetrical relationship between the 'old' and the 'new' members of the EU? Are the EU member states prepared for this? And is there any possibility of preparing a concrete project for Europe that will be defined *with* the new members on a common cultural basis rather than being imposed on them?

The simple announcement of a post-transitional phase, without a subsequent structural and cultural change, could seem either inevitably rhetorical or, like many other promises connected with the EU, just a myth.[58] Indeed, a post-transitional phase requires, in the framework of social system theory, a higher level of complexity and a more diffuse interaction among different subsystems. This wider field of interaction could be described through an enlarged version of the fundamental concept of 'structural coupling'.[59] The concept is intended to convey, through selective interconnections, that a social system must deal structurally with a relevant set of features in its environment. As intruments of structural couplings, that is, as bridges from law towards politics as well as towards other social systems, it is possible to consider not only constitutions, in their normative and empirical meaning, but also the connected concepts of public opinion and democracy. In the concepts of public opinion, constitution and democracy, it is now possible to find adequate versions of the traditional pillars of a state-centred constitutionalism: a territorially defined *demos*, an organized community and a political decision-making capacity.[60]

These concepts are not black and white, but shades of grey, open to uncertain and mixed combinations. From this perspective, the transitional phase could be considered as part of a larger process of differentiation, stimulated by the increasing complexity of a series of instruments of structural couplings. The

---

in Post-Communist Legal Orders (Dordrecht: Springer, 2006), 5.

57 J. Přibáň and J. Young (eds), *The Rule of Law in Central Europe: The Reconstruction of Legality, Constitutionalism and Civil Society in the Post-Communist Countries* (Aldershot: Ashgate, 1999).

58 V. Tismaneanu, *Fantasies of Salvation: Democraqcy, Nationalism and Myth in Post-Communist Europe* (Princeton, NJ: Princeton University Press, 1998).

59 N. Luhmann, *Law as a Social System* (Oxford: Oxford Univerity Press, 2004), 440 ss.

60 Cf. J.H.H. Weiler, *The Constitution of Europe* (Cambridge: Cambridge University Press, 1999).

above-mentioned problems of identity, stabilization and variation, which, during the period of transition, were concentrated within the statal limits of the EU's prospective members, must now be submitted to a process of externalization involving the EU as a whole. According to this process it is necessary to define *who* must manage *which* social changes, and *how*.

The problem of identity in a post-transitional phase becomes more comprehensive: it could lead not only to a convergent reconstruction of the past, but also to a common perception of Europe and a shared concept of European citizenship. According to a systems theory approach, only a strong sense of cohesion, produced by the system's greater complexity, could tolerate a higher level of differentiation. In particular, differences in the distribution of roles on the European stage are partially connected with the difficulty of concealing, at a formal *and* at a substantive level, the negative evaluation implicitly imposed on new post-communist members of the EU. The current '"thin" sense of European identity could eventually support the establishment of the "thick" European people'. The development of a European identity, as well as of the EU, is an 'open-ended' process, which 'must respect the continent's pluralistic nature': it can thus 'emerge only as a symbolic space of heterogeneity, permanent contestation of existing practices, [and] compromise-oriented negotiations'.[61]

Balanced communicative criteria of relevance among EU members and a comprehensive European public opinion are still lacking, hindering the development of a truly symmetrical relationship. So far it is clear that CEE countries are not yet equal in the eyes of the media, and have no balanced capacity for drawing the attention of other countries. A 'cultural' sense of unity presupposes uniformity in recognizing what is important and what is not. It makes sense that events concerning the private life of a *chef d'état* of an older member state should attract significant attention. But it is less comprehensible that, in a post-transitional phase, the institutional problems of new member states could be completely ignored by the European public.

In relation to the most urgent issues at stake in Europe, the lines of cohesion cut across old and new EU members alike. The distinctions between believers and sceptics, rich and poor, secular and religious are clearly no longer embodied by the difference between older and post-communist members. In the context of a more mature attitude towards the challenges of integration, the presence of better living standards in Central and Eastern Europe is perceived, for instance, in a far more positive way in Poland and the Czech Republic, while in Hungary and Bulgaria people are much more sensitive to a series of issues, such as increasing insecurity, limitations in the protection of human rights and economic competitiveness.[62]

61 J. Přibáň, 'Happy returns to Europe? The Union's identity, constitution-making, and its impact on the Central European accession states', in W. Sadurski, A. Czarnota and M. Krygier (eds), *Spreading Democracy and the Rule of Law?* (Dordrecht: Springer, 2006), 193 ss.

62 Cf. Eurobarometer 2009, Views on European Union Enlargement, 2004–2007.

From this perspective, the emergence of a unitarian idea of Europe could be a suitable basis from which to accept potential divergences among member states. In terms of a social systems theory, the question of future territorial and cultural borders might appear to be crucial for the post-transitional destiny of the EU. So far, enlargement has been the necessary substitute for a sufficiently defined European project or European ideas, but since the transitional phase appears to be almost accomplished, attention increasingly needs to be paid to consolidation instead of enlargerment.

The problem of stabilization in a post-transitional phase can be solved through a post-constitutionalization process, in which constitutions will maintain their centrality, at least at the local level, but will reduce their capacity for self-legitimation. A constitution, seen as an important instrument of structural coupling, 'provides political solutions for the problem of the self-reference of the legal system, and legal solutions for the problem of the self-reference of the political system'. It 'fulfils the function of coupling – regardless of whether it is understood as a people-in-a-form, as an institution, as an organization or just as "government"'.[63]

In an open process of structural couplings, constitutions not only signal particular connections with the political system, but, as we have seen, they also do not exclude connections with the economy, religion and other social systems. The recent history of the concept of 'constitution' reveals the difficulty of maintaining the classical idea that politics could be constituted only within a state-centred legal order. Constitutions are closely connected with the presence of a sovereign state. Consequently, at supranational level they require a sort of meta-constitution, while at a formal level they require a sort of unwritten law. Therefore, in a post-transitional period especially, it is necessary to bet on a new kind of 'constitutional pluralism'[64] and on the principle of 'subsidiarity', possibly inspired by a differentiated typology of self-government, according to the complex structure of commonwealth so frequently here mentioned.[65] To preserve the dignity of the connection state-constitution an imitation of the traditional theory of the state is emerging, based on *constitution-like*, *parliament-like*, *sanction-like* and *population-like* entities, which appear to obfuscate, or to render acceptable, the present lack of an adequate semantics.

In this context, it is easy to understand the growing importance of the economic aspects of social life and the decreasing importance of the state. The economic system, particularly the free market which is basically connected with constitutional values, appears, as does the traditional state, to be a pervasive

63 N. Luhmann, *Law as a Social System* (Oxford: Oxford University Press, 2004), 410.

64 N. Walker, 'The idea of constitutional pluralism', *The Modern Law Review*, 65/3 (2002), 317–59, at 339.

65 N. MacCormick, 'Democracy, subsidiarity, and citizenship in the European Commonwealth', *Law and Philosophy*, 16 (1997), 331–56.

instrument of structural coupling. Thanks to its 'recursive closure' the economic system does not destroy for the future choices eliminated in the present, and it allows selective interaction that can take political, legal and even religious attitudes into consideration. Consequently, also in EU space, the state-constitution nexus is manifestly weakening. It is therefore widely recognized that the state is no longer a hierarchical organization but a more flexible and communicative series of networks. This allows the emergence of a plurality of 'constitutions' based on communities of individuals or on social institutions that are no longer connected with the territory but mostly interest oriented.[66]

Finally, in a post-transitional period the problem of variation requires a process of trial and error, which increasingly involves, as in an open game, the process of democracy. The fundamental systemic features of democracy consist in the possibility of submitting every political and legal regulation to future revision on the basis of selected communications emanating from other social sectors. This quality, which must be strengthened to face the present challenges of social change, makes it possible to replace past decisions by reusing or adapting alternatives already displaced. Democracy needs the support of political parties, which in turn must be able to interpret the real attitudes of their electorate in European matters. On several occasions, and in particular in the case of the failed ratification of the so-called 'European Constitution', the results were totally different from the positions officially declared by the majority of political parties represented in national parliaments. Therefore, political parties suffered a dangerous lack of feedback, even in relation to relevant European issues.[67] What can be seen here is a clear lack of political discussion on important issues. This is a problem that does not only concern political parties. Even the segments of the population that could, looking into the future, develop, better than others, European orientations, that is, the so-called 'bridge generation', does not seem to have demonstrated recognizable European loyalties or preferences.[68]

It is important to remember that the process of European democratization does not show a linear evolution; rather, it is a cyclical process of historical highs and lows, light and darkness. Moments characterized by particularly high levels of enthusiasm and participation could signal tensions and problematic balances within powerful institutions. For old members of the EU, the process of democratization

66 C. Joerges, I.J. Sand and G. Teubner (eds), *Transnational Governance and Constitutionalism* (Oxford: Hart Publishing, 2004).

67 A. Febbrajo, 'Europa come 'idea' e 'progetto' o come 'retorica' e 'processo'? Verso un nuovo modello di transizione', in C. Mongardini (ed.), *L'europa come idea e come progetto* (Roma: Bulzoni, 2009), 91–114.

68 I. Bialecki, B. Fatyga, K. Kosela, J. Kurczewski and P. Zielinski, *The Bridge Generation: Complexities, Issues and Perspectives of Youth in Poland* (Milano: Bruno Mondadori, 2005). According to the results of this research a sort of 'European indifference' of the 'bridge generation' seems to be testified by a strong dependence on extra-European artifacts and ways of life.

that took place following World War II was the result of external pressures multiplied by the negative outcome of the war and/or by internal plurisystemic developments. Especially among new members, emerges a more positive attitude, content-oriented instead of routine-oriented, towards democratic institutions. The quality of democracy, measured according to ideal-typical paradigms, differs according to the situations of various countries,[69] but to use democracy flexibly seems to be an adequate prerequisite for EU countries with complex challenges yet to face.

In summary, some cultural needs are strictly connected with a further evolution within the EU: the level of mutual knowledge of the different members must be increased; the extent of a real, symmetrical discussion on European issues has to be enlarged; and the role of members who might qualify as 'more equal than others' must be somewhat restrained or, at least, legitimized. The difficulties of the present EU situation, that is, the uncertainty of its cultural borders, the fragmented sovereignty of its member states, and the still-unequal influence on future decisions, could, in a sense, justify the absence of a recognizable idea for the future of Europe.

In this context, the classic image of the square (illustrated above), where the relevant aspects of the life of the city (political, economic, legal, religious) could find a harmonious coexistence, must be partially revised. What this revision leads to is the post-modern image of a cityscape, with each skyscraper belonging to a single state. They have an internal channel of communication, going both from top to bottom (normative-oriented) and from bottom to top (consensus-oriented). They are also interconnected by a series of external passages and are linked to a central building still under construction, which ensures, at interstatal level, not only a free circulation of persons and goods but also a heterarchical circulation of norms. Everyday life is organized in such a way as to subjugate the different communities and inhabitants of the single buildings to acceptable rules (formal state constitutions), according to the guidelines of the administration of the whole complex (substantive meta-constitution). In order to avoid the cityscape – with its plurality of *demoi* and constitutional and democratic structures – becoming a sort of non-lieux, it needs a diffuse perception of its essential cultural identity. But this presupposes an open process of change, based de facto and not only de jure, on the contribution of all the inhabitants and on their mutual recognition as parts of the whole, regardless of individual citizenship.

References

Abel R.L. (ed.), *The Politics of Informal Justice*, vol. 2, Comparative Studies (New York: Academic Press, 1982), 2.

69 L. Morlino, *Democrazie e democratizzazioni* (Bologna: Il Mulino, 2003); J. Zielonka and A. Pravda (eds), *Democratic Consolidation in Eastern Europe*, vol. 2, *International and Transnational Factors* (Oxford: Oxford University Press, 2001).

Alexander L., *Constitutionalism: Philosophical Foundations* (Cambridge: Cambridge University Press, 1998).

Batt J., '"Fuzzy statehood" versus hard borders: The impact of EU enlargement on Romania and Yugoslavia'. Working Paper (Sussex European Institute, 2002).

Bialecki, I., B. Fatyga, K. Kosela, J. Kurczewski and P. Zielinski (eds), *The Bridge Generation: Complexities, Issues and Perspectives of Youth in Poland* (Milano: Bruno Mondadori, 2005).

Blokker, P. (ed.), '1989 and social theory', *European Journal of Social Theory* (Special Issue), 12/3 (2009).

Cotterell, R., *Living Law* (Farnham: Ashgate, 2008).

———'The concept of legal culture', in D. Nelken (ed.), *Comparing Legal Culture* (Aldershot: Dartmouth, 1997), 29.

Czarnota, A., M. Krygier and W. Sadurski (eds), *Rethinking the Rule of Law after Communism* (Budapest and New York: Central European University Press, 2005).

Ehrlich, E., *Fundamental Principles of the Sociology of Law*, ed. by R. Pound (New York: Russell & Russell, 1962).

Febbrajo, A., *Sociologia del diritto. Concetti e problemi* (Bologna: Il Mulino, 2009).

———'Europa come 'idea' e 'progetto' o come 'retorica' e 'processo'? Verso un nuovo modello di transizione, in C. Mongardini (ed.), L'europa come idea e come progetto (Roma: Bulzoni, 2009).

———'Cultura giuridica, Contenuti e funzioni di un concetto', in A. Febbrajo, A. La Spina and M. Raiteri (eds), *Cultura giuridica e politiche pubbliche in Italia* (Milano: Giuffrè, 2006), xi–lxii.

———'From hierachical to circular models in the sociology of law: Some introductory remarks', in *European Yearbook in the Sociology of Law* (Milano: Giuffrè, 1988), 3–21.

Fogelklou, A. and F. Sterzel (eds), *Consolidating Legal Reform in Central and Eastern Europe: An Anthology* (Uppsala: Iustus Foerlag, 2003).

Forrester, S., M.J. Zaborowska and E. Gapova (eds), *Over the Wall/After the Fall: Post-Communist Cultures through an East-West Gaze* (Bloomington, IN: Indiana University Press, 2004).

Friedman, L.M., 'The concept of legal culture', in D. Nelken (ed.), *Comparing Legal Culture* (Aldershot: Dartmouth, 1997), 38.

———*The Legal System: A Social Science Perspective* (New York: Russell Sage Foundation, 1975).

Gessner, V. and D. Nelken, *European Ways of Law* (Oxford: Hart Publishing, 1997).

Haeberle, P., *Verfassungslehre als Kulturwissenschaft* (Berlin: Duncker & Humblot, 1982).

Krygier, M. and A. Czarnota (eds), 'After postcommunism: The next phase', *Annual Review of Law and Social Science* (2006), 299–336.

———*The Rule of Law after Communism: Problems and Prospects in East-Central Europe* (Aldershot: Ashgate, 1999).

Joerges, C., I.J. Sand and G. Teubner (eds), *Transnational Governance and Constitutionalism* (Oxford: Hart Publishing, 2004).
Leoni, B., *Freedom and the Law* (Princeton, NJ: Van Nostrand Co., 1961).
Linz, J.J. and A. Stepan (eds), *Problems of Democratic Transition and Consolidation: Southern Europe, South America and Post-Communist Europe* (Baltimore: John Hopkins University Press, 1996).
Ludwikowski, R.R., '"Mixed" constitutions – product of an East-Central European constitutional melting pot', in *Boston University International Law Journal*, 16 (1998), 1–70.
Luhmann, N., *Law as a Social System* (Oxford: Oxford University Press, 2004).
———*Legitimation durch Verfahren* (Frankfurt a.M.: Suhrkamp, 1983).
———*Grundrechte als Institution* (Berlin: Duncker & Humblot, 1965).
MacCormick, N., 'Democracy, subsidiarity and citizenship in the "European Commonwealth"', *Law and Philosophy*, 16 (1997), 331–56.
Makariev, P., A.M. Blasko and A. Davidov (eds), *Creating Democratic Societies: Values and Norms* (Washington, DC: The Council for Research in Values and Philosophy, 1999).
Morlino, L., *Democrazie e democratizzazioni* (Bologna: Il Mulino, 2003).
Nelken, D. (ed.), *Comparing Legal Culture* (Aldershot: Dartmouth, 1997).
Nelken, D. and J. Feest (eds), *Adapting Legal Cultures* (Oxford: Hart Publishing, 2001).
Offe, C. and U. Poppe, 'Transitional justice after the breakdown of the German Democratic Republic', in A. Czarnota, M. Krygier and W. Sadurski (eds), *Rethinking the Rule of Law after Communism* (Budapest and New York: Central European University Press, 2005).
Petersen, H., A.L. Kjaer, H. Krunke and M.R. Madsen (eds), *Paradoxes of European Legal Integration* (Aldershot: Ashgate, 2008).
Plasser, F. and A. Pribersky (eds), *Political Culture in East Central Europe* (Aldershot: Ashgate, 1996).
Pollack, D., J. Jacobs, O. Mueller and G. Pickel (eds), *Political Culture in Post-Communist Europe: Attitudes in New Democracies* (Aldershot: Ashgate, 2003).
Přibáň, J., 'Happy returns to Europe? The Union's identity, constitution-making, and its impact on the Central European accession states', in W. Sadurski, A. Czarnota and M. Krygier (eds), *Spreading Democracy and the Rule of Law?* (Dordrecht: Springer, 2006), 193 ss.
Přibáň, J. and D. Nelken (eds), Law's New Boundaries; The Consequences of Legal Autopoiesis (Aldershot: Ashgate, 2001).
Přibáň, J., P. Roberts and J. Young (eds), *Systems of Justice in Transition: Central European Experiences since 1989* (Aldershot: Ashgate, 2003).
Přibáň, J. and J. Young (eds), The Rule of Law in Central Europe: The Reconstruction of Legality, Constitutionalism and Civil Society in the Post-Communist Countries (Aldershot: Ashgate, 1999).

Sadurski, W. (ed.), *Constitutional Justice East and West: Constitutional Courts in Post-Communist Europe in a Comparative Perspective* (The Hague: *Kluwer Law International*, 2002).

Sadurski, W., A. Czarnota and M. Krygier (eds), *Spreading Democracy and the Rule of Law? The Impact of EU Enlargement on the Rule of Law, Democracy and Constitutionalism in Post-Communist Legal Orders* (Dordrecht: Springer, 2006).

Sajó, A., 'Preferred generations: A paradox of restoration constitutions', *Cardozo Law Review* (1992/93), 847–63.

Skąpska, G., 'Restitutive justice, rule of law, and constitutional dilemmas', in A. Czarnota, M. Krygier and W. Sadurski (eds), *Rethinking the Rule of Law after Communism* (Budapest and New York: Central European University Press, 2005).

Teubner, G. (ed.), *Global Law without a State* (Aldershot: Dartmouth, 1997).

———'Des Koenigs viele Leiber: Die Selbstdekonstruktion der Hierarchie des Rechts', *Soziale Systeme*, 2 (1996), 229–55.

———*Law as an Autopoietic System* (London: Blackwell, 1993).

Tismaneanu, V., *Fantasies of Salvation: Democracy, Nationalism and Myth in Post-Communist Europe* (Princeton, NJ: Princeton University Press, 1998).

Walker, N., 'The idea of constitutional pluralism', *The Modern Law Review*, 65/3 (2002), 317–59.

Weber, M., *Max Weber on Law in Economy and Society*, ed. by M. Rheinstein (Cambridge, MA: Harvard University Press, 1966).

Weiler, J.H.H., *The Constitution of Europe* (Cambridge: Cambridge University Press, 1999).

Zielonka, J. and A. Pravda (eds), *Democratic Consolidation in Eastern Europe*, vol. 2, *International and Transnational Factors* (Oxford: Oxford University Press, 2001).

Zirk-Sadowski, M., 'Transformation and integration of legal cultures and discourses: Poland', in W. Sadurski, A. Czarnota and M. Krygier (eds), *Spreading Democracy and the Rule of Law?* (Dordrecht: Springer, 2006).

Chapter 3
Democratic Ethics, Constitutional Dimensions and 'Constitutionalisms'

Paul Blokker

Introduction

Constitutions should not be regarded as foundational documents circumscribing closed legal orders. In Richard Bellamy's words, 'the constitution cannot be viewed as an objective fount of moral and political wisdom' (2007: 166). Constitutions are 'instituted' and, as such, tend to reflect prevalent political cultures of constitution-making actors. This means that, in reality, constitutional documents seem to show a plurality of politico-ethical values (cf. Rosenfeld, 2006), even if they do not always invoke these explicitly. Once instituted, constitutions cannot be regarded as sources of meta-political norms that merely need implementation. Constitutional norms and values, and law in general, are open to continuous (re)interpretation and contestation, and so can have validity only if they reflect cultural repertoires present in society (cf. Přibáň, 2002).

This chapter develops a number of analytical tools and ideal-typical models to investigate the relationship between constitutions and their politico-cultural environment. One can distinguish a number of ways in which constitutions can be open to politico-ethical repertoires: they can reflect them, as well as being the object of, an influence on or a reinforcement of them. One way of approaching the legal politico-cultural entanglement analytically is to distinguish between a range of constitutional dimensions. The predominant, negative understanding of constitutionalism prioritizes an instrumental or political dimension – that is, the constitution understood as a 'political map', as a way of both limiting power and delimiting spheres of autonomy – as well as a formal-participatory dimension in which participation is limited to the retrieval of existing rights. However, the constitution can also be said to reflect another, cultural and symbolic dimension, which more specifically includes a normative dimension in terms of the expression of ultimate, politico-ethical values, an identity-shaping dimension, a positive, aspirational dimension of substantive ends, and a politico-participatory dimension.

Another way of approaching the relationship between the constitution and its environment is to distinguish between different politico-ethical visions of the constitution. It can be argued that different perceptions of the constitution or 'constitutionalisms' are informed by different democratic ethics. There are at least four relevant ethics: the ethics of rights, identity, participation and distributive justice (Blokker, 2008; 2009). Liberal, communitarian, republican and substantive constitutionalism respectively prioritize these ethics, but this does not mean that they ignore other ethics. Rather, while prioritizing one ethic over another, they tend to hierarchize and interpret these ethics differently.

A distinction between different understandings of the role and status of the constitution in a plurality of 'constitutionalisms' not only serves heuristic purposes, enabling the comparative study of constitutions, but can also function as a way of indicating the perceptions of constitutions among societal and political actors (thus relating to the 'constitutional reality' as well as to the constitutional text). From this view, the various 'constitutionalisms' can be seen as distinct interpretations of a political community and as a means of understanding ways of integrating such communities (cf. Rosenfeld, 1998a; 2006). 'Constitutionalisms' can be related to distinct political cultures, which are themselves organized around the aforementioned democratic ethics, that is, 'key concepts' or 'symbols' that orient such cultures, and tend to prioritize distinct constitutional dimensions over others.[1]

This chapter begins by exploring the two meta-languages or dimensions of constitutions – the instrumental and symbolic languages – and related specific constitutional dimensions. It then discusses how such meta-languages in general, and distinct constitutional dimensions in particular, are reflected, hierarchized and interpreted in distinct perceptions of the constitution. Existing constitutional documents in the Central and Eastern European context, especially the Hungarian, Polish and Romanian cases, are used to illustrate certain points.[2]

Constitutional Dimensions

Constitutions can be understood as 'meta-texts' that, from a primary, analytical point of view, articulate two meta-languages. First, a constitution expresses an instrumental language or rationality: it formulates the functional differentiation of society and the limitation of political power; and it defines in this the relations between state and citizens, as well as among state institutions, government and opposition (Přibáň, 2007: 20; Scholl, 2006: 36). This instrumental rationality can be understood in Weberian terms as permitting the purposive rationalization of politics and the political community (Přibáň, 2007: 3). It also informs the predominant understandings of liberal constitutionalism (see below), in which constitutions are portrayed as documents that ground legality and a depoliticized

1 This chapter substantively expands and elaborates the discussion elsewhere of constitutional dimensions and a plurality of 'constitutionalisms' in the context of multiple political cultures in new EU member states (see Blokker, 2009, Chapter 5).

2 There will be occasional reference to a wider comparative constitutional context, beyond the Central and Eastern European context.

set of rights, making a strong distinction between public and private, as well as between politics and the rule of law. One important reading of the instrumental view of constitutions takes the form of 'legal constitutionalism', which regards constitutions as closed legal universes that arrange the contours of politics and of a neutral state, but which themselves should not be open to change by democratic politics (Bellamy, 2007).

Second, a constitution articulates a symbolic language that invokes the substantive groundings of the political community in terms of the normative principles on which it is based, its collective identity and traditions, and the aspirational and participatory ideals of that community. The symbolic dimension, in contrast to the negative political dimensions, is not concerned with the universal values of constitutionalism and their interpretation within a closed system of law, but with the embedding of such universal values in a local, historical and cultural context (in a similar sense to Hegel's 'national spirit', or Montesquieu's 'spirit of the laws'). In other words, from one perspective, constitutions express the 'fundamental ethos' of distinct societies. They attempt to codify a 'characteristic way of life, the national character of a people, their ethos or fundamental nature as a people, a product of their particular history and social conditions' (Pitkin, 1987: 167).

The symbolic rationality of constitutions can be related to the Weberian notion of value-rationality and substantive law, which 'reflects extra-juridical elements and accommodates moral, economic or traditional and religious criteria in the domain of positive law' (Přibáň, 2007: 20). The symbolic dimension of a constitution invokes ultimate values, extra-societal markers such as natural rights, societal traditions and identity, which need to be protected and promoted by the constitution. It can be argued that there is a collective dimension to the symbolic language of a constitution, in that constitutional symbolism 'expresses the moral authority of a political collectivity over individuals' (Přibáň, 2007: 21). The constitution articulates through its symbolic dimension a (constructed) collective unity and a form of collective self-understanding. This particularist constitutional dimension is often portrayed in an extra-temporal or essentialist way but, in reality, will always be open to contestation and change, as new interpretations of collective identities emerge, or older ones are reproposed. In this way, constitutions can be understood as symbols of unity (Scholl, 2006: 38). The symbolic dimension is also about giving political meaning to and embedding abstract legal terms into a socio-cultural language. Through the language, traditions and history of a particular society, a constitution gives meaning to that society's legality, that is, the political forms and specific views of its system of justice. Symbolism is equally important for the expression of the normative principles and aspirational values, or 'idées directrices', of a political community. In this sense, the symbolic dimension can be seen as an attempt to integrate modern pluralistic societies.

It is clear that modern constitutions will display both instrumental and symbolic dimensions to various extents. This must be the case, because instrumental rationality will always need to be paralleled by some kind of socio-cultural embedding and registry of ultimate values; and a purely symbolic constitution would lack the regulatory, ordering language needed to functionally integrate a political community.

Instrumental Rationality

The instrumental rationality of constitutions can be said to express a predominantly negative view of constitutions, in which constitutions limit government, stipulate rights (which provide for negative freedoms) and endorse stability and order (cf. Barber, 2006). The following subsections show how instrumental rationality relates to two main constitutional dimensions: the political dimension and the formal-participatory dimension.

Political Dimension

The political dimension of constitutions is at the heart of what is currently understood by 'constitutionalism'. As András Sajó argued:

> Constitutions – since the basic laws of the Greek city states (polis) until today – concern the relationship of the state's fundamental organs and its institutions. If during the process of creating this basic arrangement the principles of constitutionalism are kept in mind, these relations establish a system of limits that allow the freedom of the citizenry to prevail. Constitutions are about power; a constitution impregnated with the ideas of constitutionalism is about limited power (1999: 2).

The political dimension – political in the sense of providing the rules of the political game – expresses instrumental rationality fully in that the constitution contributes to the rationalization of the political order, by confining political decision-making to a distinct sphere of professional politics and by invoking a specific type of political participation, thereby making politics orderly and predictable, as well as a matter of calculability. This can be better understood as the regulating side of the constitution. In other words, the political dimension, in what could also be called the 'functional meaning', outlines the institutional order or sphere of politics on which democracy is to be based, 'framing the regular powers of a society and of its political system' (Castiglione, 1996: 420). The political dimension can be related to a 'pragmatic' or 'constitutional' image of democracy, in which the constitution plays the role of a regulating principle.

This regulating idea is often related – although not necessarily so – to the function of the constitution as a limiting, negative one. Regulation is then perceived predominantly in a negative way, in that it sets out – by means of a 'set of principles, manners, and institutional arrangements' – to limit government or majority rule in order to prevent the state from subjugating individuals (Sajó, 1999: xiv; cf.

Barber, 2006). Thus, separating powers and stipulating the inviolability of a set of rights to be enjoyed by individuals in the constitution become the fundamental constitutional principles preventing political power from being abused and turned against society, particularly minorities.

Apart from the regulating aspect, that of institutionalizing politics, the state and citizenship, there is a more foundational side to the political dimension of constitutions. In this latter sense, as a constitutive or foundational act, the constitution actually creates or establishes a political community. Although the constitutive dimension is then a *conditio sine qua non* for the instrumental rationality of the constitution, its nature is better understood as symbolic (see below). In its guise as a foundational act, there is a mythical aspect of the constitution involving concealment or suspension of the political (cf. Lefort, 1988: 11), in that the political violence that is the basis of any political order is made subordinate, functional or even invisible to the creation of a formal and legitimate constitutional order.

Formal-participatory Dimension

The political dimension invokes a mostly negative, regulating and foundational perception of constitutions. But constitutions are not reducible to foundational acts or descriptions of the political and legal system, nor to elaborations of separations of power or limitations on social interaction. Constitutions clearly also provide for an enabling, democratic dimension through civil rights (freedom of expression, consciousness, association) and political rights (active and passive voting rights) that enables citizens and political actors to act politically, even if it is within the limits set by the very same constitution. One of the essential functions of a constitution is channelling the political will of citizens – in other words, expressing popular sovereignty.

It can be argued that there are two approaches to enablement and popular participation. The first is based on a traditional constitutional model in which participation is confined to the activation of constitutional rights, and is much less about change, amendment, or, in other words, 'constitutional politics'. The second approach, labelled 'new constitutionalism' by the late Vivien Hart (2003), does not confine participation to the enactment of existing rights, but explicitly endorses participation in constitutional politics (see discussion of the politico-participatory dimension below).

Thus, while the participatory or 'enabling' dimension of constitutions can, in principle, be said to touch upon an idea of popular sovereignty, when taken in a purely formal-legal sense (the first mentioned above) it can still be understood within a largely instrumental rather than substantive language. Participation in a formal-legal sense is related to the constitution's role in 'codifying the rules of the democratic game' (Bellamy and Castiglione, 1997: 595), its provision of a framework for the actualization of subjective rights by individual citizens, and conflict resolution on the basis of constitutional norms. It is, however, less concerned with ideas of public participation, inclusion and civic voice and virtue as intrinsic aspects of constitutional democracy, and with what one could call 'democratic imagination' and (radical) democratic change.

Symbolic Rationality

A good part of legal and political scientific studies of constitutional orders focuses on instrumental rationality, the dimensions of political order and, to a lesser extent, participation. Relatively little attention is given to the politico-cultural or symbolic dimension of constitutions, in particular the way in which constitutions are related to politico-ethical discourses and (latent) perceptions that constitute views on politics and the political community held in a particular society (political imaginary). The symbolic rationality of constitutions – hingeing on value-rationality – can analytically be understood as including a number of dimensions that are indispensable to the constitution of a modern political community, that is, the normative, identitarian, aspirational, and participatory dimensions. The symbolic dimension indicates that the legal system can be never completely closed off from the societal and cultural spheres and is always permeated by the latter.

Normative Dimension

Constitutions are generally considered to be a 'basic law' (cf. the German *Grundgesetz*). As such the fundamental 'meta-text' or norm constitutes the legal order, which derives its ultimate references and values from the constitution. Sajó described the constitution '[a]s the starting point and the closing argument of a legal system' (1999: 39). It can, however, be argued that any formal constitutional document needs to refer to things outside its own legal domain, in other words, a kind of embedding in extra-legal, fundamental values. The axiological dimension of a constitution entails an attempt to ground a particular political community in a set of ultimate values in order to provide the necessary substantive meaning, which a purely formal constitution would not be able to provide. Without some kind of extra-legal, substantive dimension, a constitution would remain 'both overformal and relativistic' (Castiglione, 1996: 419).

Dario Castiglione argued that the normative, 'absolute' dimension can be grounded in a set of fundamental, ethico-normative principles, in the existentialist origin of the constitution (emphasizing its original nature), or in a reflection of organic, societal fundamental principles (1996: 420). But the normative dimension of a constitution does not necessarily entail the expression of a unity based on a singular, relatively coherent set of values. As the example of the Polish Constitution of 1997 shows, a constitution can be based on 'axiological pluralism' in which no singular ontological view on values and their identification exists (Winczorek, 1999). The Polish Constitution, particularly in its preamble, displays a dualistic vision that invokes both natural, religion-based values and universalist, civic ones (cf. Zubrzycki, 2006; see also Blokker, 2009; Brier, 2006; Hałas, 2005).

The dimension beyond and additional to a purely formal one articulates ultimate values by means of reference to symbols. In this, as argued by Joseph Weiler, the constitution's symbolic function can be *implicit*, that is, a constitution's ethos might result indirectly from the political dimension and the stipulation, and hierarchization, of specific rights. Alternatively, this dimension can be *explicit*, as is often the case when the distinct values and traditions of a specific political community are included in the constitution's preamble (2003: 55–6). In the latter sense, the emphasis is not so much on a normative, legitimatory dimension, but rather on the identification of a collective identity.

Identitarian Dimension

The symbolic side, then, not only entails the formulation of a set of ultimate values, but, in a related way, refers to an identitarian dimension, which is the expression of the collective identity of a particular political community. Hans Vorländer contended that the constitution fundamentally expresses an idea of unity or identity, in that it pretends to constitute a political community (Vorländer, 2006; cf. Rosenfeld, 1993). As argued above, modern pluralistic and secularized societies cannot integrate purely on the basis of reference to extra-social markers such as religion or tradition, but need to look to imminent, intra-social values. In this, the constitution provides a typically modern answer to the integration of heterogeneous or pluralistic societies (Vorländer, 2006: 230; cf. Lefort, 1988). As Ulrich Preuss explained: 'The power of the modern state […] requires a secular justification. And while, in the perspective of political theology, the people and its sovereign power have replaced an almighty God, it is the constitution which supplants the Holy Scripture' (1995: 99).

Whereas the normative dimension refers to generalizable or universally formulated fundamental principles, the identitarian dimension delimits the constitution as the fundamental declaration of a particular polity. The normative and identitarian dimensions are equally relevant for any constitutional order in that they both entail a way of giving fundamental meaning to the legal system within a specific historico-cultural context. Whereas the codification of ultimate values is an expression of the prevailing values and beliefs that are relevant for a particular political culture (or, often more accurately, a plurality of political cultures existing in a specific polity), and in this forms a legitimating mode, the identitarian dimension attempts to portray the collective as a singular entity or as 'people-as-one', in an endeavour to integrate a diversity of individuals and groups on the basis of a common identity.

Tensions can then emerge between a universally formulated set of values (which might promote diversity over identity or commonality) and the explicit formulation of a (majority) identity (which might favour homogeneity and assimilation). But the normative dimension can also be said to rely on the identitarian dimension, in as far as the legitimating of norms needs reference to a specific socio-political context. This can take the form, for instance, of a circumscribed sovereign nation or a particular constitutional self (Rosenfeld, 1993: 499). In other words, there needs to be some identity between a set of fundamental values and a particular political community, in which certain commonalities are emphasized while particular differences are minimized (Rosenfeld, 1993: 500). In this regard, it is important to underline the necessity of the identitarian dimension as providing some kind of more durable basis for the constitution of a political community, which might also appeal to future generations (Rosenfeld, 1993: 511).

The codification of a collective identity is then an attempt to make visible or to express symbolically the singularity of a collective or political community. A clear example of an outspoken identitarian dimension can be found in the Romanian Constitution of 1991, which, even if it only explicitly invocates the notion of 'nation' twice (see Regia Autonomă, 1998; Lungu, 2001; Preda, 2002), contains numerous references to a national community. The national community is regarded as the inheritor of the state and its sovereignty forms the foundation of the post-communist, democratic state (as expressed in article 1).

Expressing identity in ethno-cultural terms is obviously not the only option for a collective identity. The well-known analytical distinction is between ethnic and civic understandings (cf. Přibáň, 2007; see also Preuss, 1993), even if, in reality, some reference to an ethno-cultural understanding of a political community is unavoidable (Rosenfeld, 1993). The latter becomes, for instance, clear from the Hungarian Constitution (which, according to Scheppele, reflects a 'strongly liberal universalist, human-rights-centered version of constitutionalism' (Scheppele, 2004)), in which there is an almost total absence of what could be called an 'ethic of identity'. In this sense, the spirit of the constitution is mostly prospective and based on a notion of civic or state nation (cf. Přibáň, 2007; Majtényi, 2005). The ethno-cultural, identitarian dimension, however, comes through when the constitution invokes a (singular) reference to the cultural nation made up exclusively of ethnic Hungarians, in the article related to the status of Hungarians living outside of the Hungarian state (article 6(3)). In comparison, while the Romanian Constitution of 1991 predominantly articulates the identity of the majority, the Polish Constitution has a more dualistic approach that invokes both the idea of an ethno-national community as well as a civic one.

Aspirational Dimension

The identitarian dimension can take the form of a specific reading and interpretation of the past intended to create an image of unity and to endorse social cohesion and consensus in the present. A further, diachronic dimension to constitutions, also clearly visible in many of the constitutions of the new democracies in Central and Eastern Europe, is the future-oriented invocation of an ideal future society. This can be referred to as an aspirational or teleological dimension, in that the constitution is understood as a normative, programmatic statement of aims to be achieved by the political community, informing a process of societal change and the promotion of welfare generally.

The aspirational, positive dimension is often viewed with ambivalence (see, in particular, Sajó, 1999; Preuss, 1995), as it may include a policy-oriented, teleological quality that consists of the stipulation of a 'more or less detailed catalogue of state goals' (Preuss, 1995: 99), especially in terms of social policy-making (taking the form of, for instance, social rights and policy goals). Ulrich Preuss has indeed argued against the aspirational dimensions of many of the post-communist societies, which invoke images of democratic rule as well as substantive values, such as solidarity and welfare (Preuss, 1995). In this latter, policy-related sense, the critique is often, first, that there is a risk of constitutions stipulating teleological goals that may jeopardize the limiting, negative political dimension (Preuss, 1995: 101; cf. Barber, 2003); and, second, that the invocation of social rights undermines the overall credibility of the rights dimension of a constitution, because social rights cannot be guaranteed and are not defensible in judicial courts (Sajó, 1999). But, at the same time, it needs to be acknowledged that the teleology of constitutions signals an attempt to contribute to the enhanced social solidarity of a political community and, by doing so, to add to a cohesive, integrative dimension.

Politico-participatory Dimension

The participatory dimension is generally formulated in terms of enabling rights (civil and political rights, but also social and cultural rights). As indicated above, a basic distinction can be made between rights-based understandings of formal participation and more substantive understandings of effective participation, in which participation is valued as an aim in itself (cf. Rosenfeld, 2006). The politico-participatory dimension is about creating spaces or moments of equal participation, taking an active view of the democratic process and understanding participation as active self-rule, an end in itself. In this sense it is akin to the value-rationality of the symbolic dimension. The politico-participatory dimension can then be seen in contrast to the traditional view of constitutionalism, in which the constitution is understood as an 'act of completion', consisting of a 'final settlement or social contract in which basic political definitions, principles, and processes are agreed, as is a commitment to abide by them' (Hart, 2003: 2). Indeed, '[t]raditional constitution making as a conclusion of conflict and codification of a settlement that intends permanence and stability can seem to threaten rather than reassure' (Hart, 2003: 3). Instead, the politico-participatory dimension is about the constitution as a process, a form of 'conversational constitutionalism', in which the idea of a constitution as a 'final act of closure' is rejected in favour of endorsing a 'freely accessible debate' as a 'permanently open process' and as a 'conversation, conducted by all concerned, open to new entrants and issues, seeking a workable formula that will be sustainable rather than assuredly stable' (Hart, 2003: 3). Participation is seen not as a way of claiming one's legitimate rights in the face of a stable, enforceable final text, but as involving a 'moral claim to participation' (2003: 4) that adds a foundational democratic dimension to the constitution as such.

To sum up, the politico-participatory dimension gives a self-reflexive, self-doubting substance to the constitution, in a way that changes the traditional idea of the constitution as a final text and foundational act. This dimension is evidently not available in all constitutions, especially not the most well-known traditional constitutions (including – as noted by Hart (2003) – the American Constitution). It can, however, be argued that such a participatory, dynamic dimension is evermore important in new constitutions, corresponding to a pluralistic, political and anti-foundational understanding of the constitution (cf. Bellamy, 2007; cf. Arato, 2000).

Constitutional Dimensions and 'Constitutionalisms'

The dimensions of constitutions so far discussed are variously present and interpreted in different perceptions of constitutions or 'constitutionalisms'. In this, various tensions can be pointed out: between the negative and positive interpretations of the constitution's role; between the instrumental and symbolic rationalities; between legal and political views of constitutions (see Bellamy, 2007); and between rule-of-law and identitarian 'constitutionalisms'. The next part of this chapter describes four different 'constitutionalisms' – liberal, communitarian, republican and substantive – and the way in which these 'constitutionalisms' invoke and fill in the various dimensions. The four types should be understood as ideal-types, useful as heuristic devices for comparatively studying predominant languages of constitutionalism in existing constitutions as well as in 'constitutional reality'. The four types clearly relate to distinct democratic discourses, themselves prioritizing distinct democratic ethics (for example, rights in liberalism, participation in republicanism), but obviously cannot be taken as an exhaustive list of possible interpretations of the role of constitutions in modern democracies.

Liberal Constitutionalism

A liberal conception of constitutionalism primarily views the constitution in terms of the aforementioned political and formal-participatory dimensions. It is primarily a negative constitutionalism, in that it regards the constitution essentially in a regulatory and limiting sense, that is, as the institutionalization and limitation of political power, as well as a framework of citizens' rights and liberties (cf. Castiglione, 1996; Ionescu, 1988; Ungureanu, 2007: 7). The idea is to ensure the limitation of state power and prevent its being concentrated in the hands of a 'few men', rather than ground it in the law. The relation between constitution and democracy is, in this sense, complementary rather than contradictory, in that the constitution secures the preconditions for democracy. Expressing a liberal view of constitutions, Stephen Holmes suggested that 'limited government and self-government are likely to become mutually supportive rather than mutually subversive' (1995: 136; cf. Bellamy, 2007). Constitutionalism is thus equated with liberalism (Ionescu, 1988).

In Central and Eastern European constitutions, the liberal, legal-constitutionalist view has evidently played a prominent role since the 1980s. Perhaps the most conspicuous example is the Hungarian Constitution, which, even if formally still grounded in the old, communist constitution, is widely held to express a liberal, legal-constitutionalist outlook. The negative, limiting dimension is importantly underpinned by a well-entrenched mechanism of judicial review by the Constitutional Court. The latter has an exceptionally wide mandate (Körösényi, 1999: 164), and, particularly in the 1990s, has interpreted its role in terms of the active safeguarding of constitutional principles and the Hungarian *Rechtsstaat*. Another peculiar example of a liberal, negative constitutional outlook is the explicit, but rather tardy, attempt to strengthen the liberal, limiting dimension by means of the amendment of the Romanian 1991 Constitution in 2003 – in the form of an explicit reference to both the separation of powers and the supremacy of constitutional law in articles 1 (4) and (5) (cf. Carp and Stanomir, 2008: 4–5).

A further primary emphasis in any liberal conception – next to the political-institutional aspect – is on the incorporation of a catalogue of inviolable individual rights and liberties in order to protect the individual citizen from unlimited and arbitrary interference of the state in individuals' lives. This is often, even if not always, concomitant with the idea of fundamental human rights, basic civil and political rights, and the clear delineation of a private sphere. In terms of a hierarchy of rights, this means that civil rights are normally deemed primary in liberal constitutionalism, while political rights and limited, constitutionally constrained government are derivative in the sense that, primarily, they serve to guarantee civil rights (Rosenfeld, 2006: 32). Seen this way, politics has an 'essentially negative role' in guaranteeing a private sphere (Rosenfeld, 2006: 33; cf. Barber, 2006). This also means that adherents of liberal constitutionalism watch social (and cultural) rights with suspicion, because they deem them an unwarranted legitimation for inappropriate state interference in private lives. It can therefore be argued that the aspirational dimension, in terms of programmatic constitutional aims, is commonly distrusted by those with classical liberal views.

From the point of view of the normative dimension of a liberal constitution, the 'overriding values' are individual liberty and equality, which can be best guaranteed through formal rights (Rosenfeld, 2006: 28). In a legalist reading, the idea is that these values are to be protected by 'exceptional legal entrenchment' and the liberal constitution is to be regarded as a 'higher law' (Holmes, 1995: 134). In this regard, it can be argued that an important drive in liberal constitutionalism is to diminish the sphere of politics and protect a set of fundamental, natural values from the encroachment of politics (cf. Bellamy, 2007).[3] As mentioned, this

3 This is evident, for instance, in the Hungarian and Romanian Constitutions (articles 8(2) and 148(2) respectively).

protection is further strenghtened through the mechanism of judicial review, which has indeed been prevalent in the constitutional changes in Central and Eastern Europe, particularly in the Hungarian case (most explicitly so during the Sólyom presidency).

The liberal view of constitutionalism would not normally endorse any kind of explicit symbolic dimension in terms of the articulation of a collective identity. This is related to the pluralist idea of state neutrality, in which cultural and religious matters are left to the individual, while the state takes the role of an impartial arbiter. State neutrality regarding religion is, for instance, expressed in article 60 (3) of the Hungarian Constitution. Also the Polish Constitution (despite other, identitarian tendencies) invokes such a notion in article 25: the state 'shall be impartial in matters of personal conviction, whether religious or philosophical, or in relation to outlooks on life, and shall ensure their freedom of expression with public life'.[4] In a strict reading of state-church separation, the state's role in a liberal conception of constitutionalism is then ultimately a procedural, and therefore mostly non-substantive, one, in that its role is to protect and enforce individual rights. Any symbolic, identitarian dimension is deemed to be in tension with the liberal constitutional spirit (Ungureanu, 2007: 7, 9–10).

The formal-participatory dimension is expressed in individual participatory rights (voting rights) and through the division of powers that creates the possibility of control of political power by various institutions, and therefore the possibility of control of the executive by the legislature (Bellamy and Castiglione, 1997: 598). Thus, liberal constitutionalism does not only contain a limiting and negative dimension, even if the positive, participatory dimension is mostly about citizens' capacity to restrain state influence on the private sphere and to redeem their own interests (see Michelman, 1989: 451). In other words, the participatory dimension in liberal constitutionalism is more about the activation and reproduction of the constitutional order, and much less about substantive civic participation and constitutional change.

Communitarian Constitutionalism

In a communitarian view of constitutions, there is evident attention to the symbolic dimension in general and the identitarian dimension in particular. This does not mean that the instrumental rationality of constitutions and a language of rights are necessarily secondary (contrary to Forst, who speaks of a 'relative neglect of constitutional safeguards', 2001: 358), but rather that such rationality is interpreted with regard to a particular collective entity or community. As Philip Selznick argued, '[c]ontextual thinking is not the enemy of ideas and principles; it is what makes them effective' (2002: 75). In most types of communitarianism, the

4 Sadurski notes that in the Polish case the notion of 'impartiality' is a compromise between secular and religious forces, appearing to indicate a less strict separation between state and church (2003: 14). Indeed, article 25(3) invokes 'the principle of cooperation for the individual and the common good'.

political dimension of constitutions is appreciated in that it fully acknowledges the limitation of state power versus civil society, as well as rights and their limitative import, even if the emphasis is on the specific, contextual interpretation of rights and their expression of a distinct community. Communitarian constitutionalism can then be understood as largely complementary to liberalism, even if it criticizes liberal constitutionalism as having too much of an impoverished view of both the individual and society. Communitarian constitutionalism is further complementary in that it reminds liberalism of the importance of the common good and an appreciation of the collective good shared by individuals (Selznick, 2006: 27).

In symbolic-identitarian terms, this means that the constitution is regarded as reflecting (or being in need of reflecting) the pre-political entity of the community and its innermost values and identity. In this regard, even if communitarian views see the constitution as embodying a language of both universal rights and particularist values, they will always see the former as embedded in the latter, rather than the latter overriding the former, as in a 'priority of rights' understanding of the polity (cf. Ungureanu, 2007: 4). Indeed, democracy is understood to be the 'rule of communal values' (Forst, 2001: 353). Communitarian constitutionalism is then explicit about the constitution's integrative function and its symbolic nature, that is, a constitution concerns the foundational expression of a community *qua* sharing a common identity and its perceptions of the common good. In Weiler's terms, a communitarian constitution will be explicit about its symbolic function (2003: 55–56; cf. Ungureanu, 2007: 5) and will understand symbolism as an essential part of the role of a constitution in democratic societies.

It is therefore not surprising that in the communitarian understanding of the constitution, a foundational part is played by the definition of citizenship, that is, who is part of the polity and on what grounds (cf. Walzer, 1983). Membership defines who enjoys the full set of rights stipulated in the constitution and who can participate fully in the political community. While a more universal understanding of citizenship is equally grounded in the nation-state concept, in the communitarian understanding of citizenship this often entails a more stringent, ethnic understanding of membership of the nation. In universalistic, civic understandings being physically part of a society would be the criterion (Preuss, 1995: 114–15; Rosenfeld, 1998b). An interesting but ambivalent example of how a communitarian view can play a role in definitions of citizenship is the Romanian case. In the 1991 Constitution, as argued by Barbu (1999: 143), a dual conception of citizenship seemed to emerge: a pre-political one based on ethnic identity and serving as the basis for popular sovereignty; and a civic-political one, in which all those residing on the territory enjoyed distinct rights and had distinct obligations. But by the time of the 2003 amendment, defenders of the latter dimension seemed to have gained in strength (externally supported by the requirements for EU accession), which has since led to an attenuation of the communitarian dimension.

As observed above, a communitarian outlook does not imply that individual rights are of minor importance or that a bill of rights is of no significance. With regard to national minorities, however, communitarian-based constitutions (at least in polities that understand themselves as homogeneous) will give priority to the majority (cf. Rosenfeld, 1998b: 217–18). Such a constitutional endorsement of a community understood in homogeneous cultural terms – despite a prevalence of a liberal-legal language – can be found in a number of constitutions in Central and Eastern Europe.[5] In some cases, including those of Hungary, Poland and Romania, this dimension also comprises a reference to diaspora communities, as part of a larger, communitarian understanding of citizenship.

With regard to its normative dimension, in the communitarian perception of the constitution the 'community is paramount and *communal solidarity* the overriding value' (Rosenfeld, 2006: 29). It is not so much the constitution itself that has foundational importance, but rather the pre-political values and history of the community, of which the constitution needs to be a faithful reflection. In a strict interpretation of the communitarian view, the constitution does not so much answer the question 'Who are we?' (cf. Sadurski, 2001), since the historical community already exists on a pre-political level, but makes the answer to this question visible in a codified, textual form. Regarding an ethic of identity and the communitarian quest for self-exploration and definition of the common good, communitarian constitutionalism 'grants a foundational importance to the communal identity and the historical values of the community' (Ungureanu, 2007: 3).

As should have become clear by now, in terms of participation, communitarian constitutionalism favours a politico-participatory dimension over a formal-participatory one (cf. Selznick, 2002). This is most evident in its perceptions of participation: first, as an expression of public autonomy and the responsibility of, or opportunity for, the individual to participate in the deliberation over and definition of the common good; and, second, with an emphasis on law as 'responsive law', that is, 'the idea that law should be responsive to changing circumstances and the needs of the community' (Selznick, 2006: 29). There is in this a focus on inclusion and deliberation over shared problems that calls for the participation of both majority and minorities (cf. Breslin, 2004: 151–52). But then again, the predilection for 'democratic consensualism' might involve rather strong pressures for conformity. This perception of law, and constitutionalism in particular, refutes the alleged neutrality and universality of the liberal arrangement, reflecting instead the idea that 'law is more just when it springs from the character and condition of the people, and when it is administered with due regard for the integrity of institutions and the vitality of civil society' (Selznick, 2006: 29).

Although the attention for identity and the ethical community is clearly predominant in communitarian constitutionalism, there is a recognition of the socio-material needs that may be critical for citizens to be able to participate in the political community and therefore to preserve the community as such (cf. Forst, 2001: 359; Selznick, 1998). This commitment to substantive values can take the

5 From a wider comparative angle, it should be noted that a similar communitarian outlook can be found, for instance, in the (unwritten) Israeli constitution, as well as in some forms in the German basic law (see Breslin, 2004, chapter 6).

form of references to social solidarity in constitutions. Breslin, for instance, detected such a communitarian dimension in, for instance, the 'mixed constitutionalism' of the German basic law. His argument was that such a communitarian dimension not only involves a certain cultural-historical understanding of an ethical community, but also social understandings of property and the promotion of the welfare and collective existence of citizens (Breslin, 2004: 197–201). He alluded equally to the mixed nature of Central and Eastern European constitutions, seeing in the latter a sensitivity to a socio-material dimension. However, it might be more accurate to relate this to a distinct socialist, rather than communitarian, heritage (see below).[6]

Republican Constitutionalism

Republican constitutionalism prioritizes political participation and self-government. In this regard, the political, limiting dimension is variously interpreted in different strands of republican constitutionalism. In what could be called 'substantive' understandings of republican constitutionalism (cf. Bellamy, 2007), a certain affinity between the republican aims of public autonomy and self-government and a liberal predilection for rights and the rule of law is presupposed, in the sense that the latter function as preconditions for the former (Bellamy, 2007: 155; cf. Tomkins, 2005: 42–46). In this legalist-republican understanding of the constitution, the emphasis is on preventing the emergence of arbitrary rule and adequate safeguards for democracy. Such a legal reading of republicanism translates into a constitutional design that promotes the equal participation of all in public life and political rule, but that also contains an emphasis on the prevention of unlimited and arbitrary state interference by means of the division of powers, checks and balances. In this, it becomes clear that republican and liberal visions of constitutionalism (at least in some readings of the first) cannot always be neatly separated and are sometimes complementary (cf. Bellamy and Castiglione, 1997: 596).

In other, more radical-democratic understandings of republican constitutionalism, the constitution is not so much considered the unalterable expression of pre-political, fundamental rights that are to function as ultimate safeguards, as it is the temporary outcome of a continuous constitutional 'conversation'. A distinct republican view of the role of the constitution is one that is conducive to reflection and deliberation about the nature of rights and the organization of the polity at large. In this, the role of 'constitutional politics' is explicitly allowed for. The constitution facilitates the ongoing quest for the identification of the set of rights and common good that best coincides with the political community. One way of formulating this is to perceive the constitution not as codifying the preconditions of democracy, but rather as a 'procedure for

6 An example is the social dimension to property in the Hungarian Constitution: 'Hungary has a market economy in which public and private property are to receive equal consideration and protection under the law' (art. 9).

resolving disagreements about the nature and implications of democratic values in a way that assiduously and impartially weighs the views and interests in dispute in a manner that accords them equal concern and respect' (Bellamy, 2007: 4).

It can then be argued that republican constitutionalism, even if it overlaps and adds to liberal constitutionalism in a number of ways, diverges from the latter in that it, firstly, entertains a different substantive understanding of the status and role of rights in the constitution and, secondly, values the role of constitutional politics, which is, thirdly, related to a strong emphasis on active citizenship, participation and deliberation as an intrinsic good to democracy. With regard to the first point, the republican vision of rights is not, as in the liberal perception, based on the idea of the constitution as a 'higher law' that enshrines already existing, pre-political rights (as in natural law). Instead, it rather understands rights as the outcome of a society-wide deliberation over and decision on the common good (Michelman, 1989: 445–46). In republicanism, rights are determined by the citizens of the democratic community and form political resolutions to the problem of living together. As Cass Sunstein explained, 'understandings that point to prepolitical or natural rights are entirely foreign to republicanism, [and] the existence of realms of private autonomy must be justified in public terms' (1987: 1551).

However, from a more critical and historical view, the republican project of an ongoing democratic quest of self-exploration can be said potentially to entail some pre-political presuppositions as to the nature of the political community, that is, in terms of a national community with a related identity. In terms of the identitarian dimension, it can be argued that the republican project of self-government cannot function without a fairly homogeneous and homogenized identity that is also reflected in its constitution. Less explicitly so than in communitarian constitutionalism, in republican constitutionalism the singularity of the members of the polity seems presupposed. The famous expression of this homogeneity in the American Constitution is 'we, the people', a formulation that has been repeated in different ways in other foundational documents. According to Roderick MacDonald:

> [S]ince the revolutionary period in Europe legal republicans have typically understood the State as the political reflection of a single 'people'. Initially, the reflected image was claimed to be that of a political community committed to a particular form of citizenship and secular authority through a founding constitutional document (2005: 4).

This can be reformulated as the idea that in classical republicanism there is a tendency to favour a level of homogeneity of the polity in cultural terms – akin to small communities – as the only environment in which civic virtues can flourish, which makes it somewhat similar to communitarian views (Rosenfeld, 1998b: 218–19). But the identitarian dimension does not only or necessarily take an exclusionary guise in republican constitutionalism. It should also be acknowledged that the republican view of constitutionalism entails an idea of 'constitutional patriotism', that is, the idea that – in contradistinction to pre-political views of nationalism – the constitution is the object as well as the outcome of a shared commitment to participation in public life, grounded in a kind of political and cultural 'republican patriotism' or public ethics (Viroli, 1999: 86, 90).

The normative dimension in republican constitutionalism is less extensive or present than in liberal legalism, in that the republican 'overriding value' consists of an absolute endorsement of deliberative self-government (Rosenfeld, 2006: 28–29). This means that in the republican view (at least in some of its readings), while the constitution needs to safeguard this overriding value, it can itself be the object of periodical modification in order to adapt the constitution to shifts or changes in the political will of the polity. Republicanism favours, in this, what Ackerman called 'constitutional politics' or what Michelman labelled 'republican' or 'jurisgenerative' politics.

It should be obvious by now that the participatory dimension of the republican constitution is paramount and involves a politico-substantive dimension, rather than a formal one. Regarding the role of active citizenship in republican constitutionalism and clearly related to the emphasis on the autonomous rule-setting by the citizens themselves in a republican polity, there is a strong emphasis on the participatory component of citizenship (Buttle, 2001). In other words, the enabling features of constitutions allow citizens to have influence on democratic rule-making and the adjustment or revision of the constitutional framework. Constitutions that are inspired by perceptions of democracy that value the public autonomy of citizens allow for civic participation in democratic rule-making (through participatory rights such as civil and political rights); value citizen input in legislation by means of direct democracy (as in referenda); emphasize in some cases the need for decentralization of the state administration in order to facilitate local and regional forms of democratic government (cf. Rosenfeld, 2006: 32, n. 37); and provide for, at least in some readings of republicanism, relatively easy amendment or modification of constitutions initiated by publicly emerging calls for change (that is, facilitating the influence of democratic politics on the constitution). The latter constitutional dimension might be taken as the most radical (cf. Tierney, 2009) and at the same time the most problematic in many constitutions.

In the three cases discussed most prominently here, civic constitutional politics is limited by stringent constitutional rules. While in the Hungarian and Polish cases, direct civic participation in constitutional politics is virtually excluded, the Romanian Constitution in the first instance facilitates civic initiative towards constitutional revision. At the same time, however, the amendment procedure as such has been made complex and substantially reduces possibilities for effective public participation. Indeed, according to Arato, the Romanian Constitution's 'revision rule is the most difficult in the region' (2000: 163; cf. Banciu, 2001: 404–5). But the republican dimension does play some role in Central and Eastern European constitutions. For instance, in terms of (local) self-government, references can be found in various places in the Polish Constitution of 1997. In the preamble the principle of subsidiarity is invoked, while in article 4(2) a reference is made to the 'direct exercise' of 'supreme power'. The Polish Constitution further refers to the decentralization of public power (article 15(1)) and local self-government (16(1,2)). In the Hungarian case, the 1997 amendment led to a certain constitutionalization of forms of direct democracy (Deszö and Bragyova, 2007: 70).

With regard to the aspirational dimension of constitutions, republican constitutionalism does not necessarily endorse programmatic statements or policy aims as part of the constitution. But in a derivative sense, it can be argued that on the basis of the republican ideal of independence (Richardson 2006), a republican constitution might involve an aspirational dimension in an attempt to guarantee citizens' capacity to act publicly. Sunstein argued that, '[f]or people to be able to act as citizens, and to be able to count themselves as such, they must have the kind of independence that such minimal protections [against starvation, homelessness and other extreme deprivation] ensure' (2001: 223). The constitutional call for state interference in order to attenuate a socio-economic distribution that is considered 'too unequal' might then be justified in the context of the larger attachment to the ideal of self-government.

Substantive or Positive Constitutionalism

A fourth model of constitutionalism, a substantive, 'aspirational' or 'teleological' approach (Preuss, 1995), is related to what could be identified as an ethic of distributive justice and to a positive, interventionist view of the constitution. This perception of constitutionalism could also be labelled 'positive' or 'welfarist constitutionalism' (Barber, 2003; 2006). In contradistinction to liberal constitutionalism, the political dimension is not deemed the primary dimension in positive constitutionalism, but is rather understood as instrumental to the predominant, positive purpose of the constitution, that is, the furtherance of the public interest. The limiting function of constitutions, in terms of the protection of citizens against arbitrary government as well as against third parties on the basis of fundamental rights, is deemed important; but it is secondary to the 'first and stronger concern' of the positive function of government in the name of the general welfare (Barber, 2006: 654, 657). In other words, limiting government is understood not only in a purely negative sense, that is, as preventing arbitrary interference into individual life paths, but also in positive terms, as a way of 'keeping government focused on its proper objects' (Barber, 2006: 657).

In a related way, rights in substantive constitutionalism are not understood solely in negative terms, but rather in a positive way, as contributing to a social function and, in more general terms, as providing or securing particular positive ends (such as the enjoyment of particular goods). A narrower socio-economic reading of positive constitutionalism shows it to contain a predilection for social rights. Such a predilection can take two forms: a derivative one and a fundamental one (cf. Barber, 2003: 6–7). In a derivative reading, social rights are deemed important in order to achieve some other goal (participation in the market or civic participation in politics). In this way, social rights are complementary to more traditional civic and political rights (as in the Marshallian reading), but have an importance of their own too, in that they ensure the effective enjoyment of traditional rights. Social rights thus constitute entitlements on the state that allow citizens to benefit fully from the guarantees and 'enablements' provided through civic and political rights. Rosenfeld expressed this relationship as follows:

> [I]f political rights are understood not only as rights of participation, but as rights of *effective* participation, then their realization may depend on the vindication of some social and economic rights. Indeed, only an educated electorate that is adequately housed and fed can fully and effectively exercise its right to participate in its polity's process of self-determination (2006: 12).

When, however, social rights are endorsed in a more fundamental sense, they are taken as furthering substantive ends that go beyond the mere guarantee of minimal social protection, the safeguarding of democratic citizenship, or antidotes for market failure. In other words, positive constitutionalism entails a 'pro-government aspect that emphasizes public purposes over private incentives and suggests broader constitutional responsibilities than agreggating private interests' (Barber, 2006: 666). The market, in this reading, is taken as a means for achieving general welfare (Barber, 2003: 9).

It can then be argued that constitutions emphasizing the positive goal of distributive justice will tend to have a 'programmed' nature; they might contain a rather elaborate catalogue of objectives for the state to follow as well as the guarantee of a set of social rights. In its ideal-typical form, substantive, welfarist constitutionalism promotes a democratic project of social aims, social justice and explicit social rights in the name of public welfare and social democracy as a distinct political form. Substantive ends outlined in a constitution need not, however, concern only social protection; they can, more in general, include ends like 'national security, freedom of conscience, domestic tranquility, and the people's economic wellbeing' (Barber, 2003: 1).

In normative terms, positive constitutions place ideas of social solidarity and equality on the highest level, and strongly emphasize the integrative function of constitutions. In other words, substantive constitutionalism is less about the democratic, participatory dimension that relates to popular sovereignty, and more about prioritizing an integrative function that 'contains the reasons why the citizens fulfil duties of solidarity towards each other' (Preuss, 1995: 100). Substantive constitutions endorse a view of social justice that flows from the idea that constitutions 'embody the goals, aspirations, values and basic beliefs which that society's members commonly hold and which bind them together' (Preuss, 1995: 99). The legal codification of the idea of solidarity reflects this idea and attempts to strengthen such solidarity and social cohesion. The state is entrusted with an extensive role of intervention in society in the name of redistribution, social justice and participation. From a more fundamental, welfarist point of view, public interest and general welfare are taken as the highest goals in themselves (Barber, 2006).

In terms of an identitarian dimension, the prioritization of the public interest and social solidarity is difficult to imagine without some idea of commonality of the members of the political community, that is, some notion of shared identity on which a form of social trust can be based. In this regard, it has often been argued that, in order to uphold a sufficient level of solidarity among the members of a polity, they need to identify each other as equals to some extent. A substantive, socialist view of constitutionalism tends to presuppose rather than generate an idea of commonality, and in this it can be said to show affinities with communitarian notions of the pre-political community. The symbolic dimension in substantive constitutionalism tends to be mostly of an implicit kind, in that it is the substantive dimension of social solidarity that is evident (in particular through social rights arrangements) rather than the invocation of a distinct political community and its defining characteristics.

It is of course well known that Central and Eastern European constitutions reflect an aspirational, positive dimension quite expansively. For instance, the Hungarian Constitution states in its preamble that the transition to a constitutional state is also about the 'conversion to a socially alert market economy', while it acknowledges the socio-democratic nature of Hungarian democracy. According to Gábor Juhász, while during communism social rights took the form of a kind of favour from the state, 'amendments to the Constitution in 1989 established a much stronger right to social security' (2007: 396). Also in the Polish case, a reference to 'social justice' in the prominent article 2 of the Constitution invokes a 'constitutional anchor' for possible redistributive policies. The article reads: 'The Republic of Poland shall be a democratic state ruled by law and implementing the principles of social justice.' The Polish Constitution further invokes an ethic of distributive justice in article 20, which contains the notion of a 'social market economy'. The Romanian Constitution refers to a social market economy in article 1(3): 'Romania is a democratic and social State.' Indeed, this definition of the Romanian state as a social state, as observed by Cristian Ionescu, is 'much more an aspiration than a reality' (2007: 280). Also Ioan Stanomir argues that the social state creates a 'horizon of expectations' (Carp and Stanomir, 2008: 196). Be that as it may, in the normative terms of the discussion of substantive constitutionalism, the formal aim is to implement policies that enhance social equality and solidarity.

In participatory terms, it can be argued that there is relatively little appreciation for politico-substantive forms of participation in positive constitutionalism. There is both an emphasis on government and administration and a constitutionalized endorsement of public interest, but citizens tend to be perceived as 'clients' of the welfare state (Murphy, 1990; Rosenfeld, 2006: 34, n. 41). In this, the focus is more on citizens' formal enjoyment of positive rights than on their civic input in defining such rights.

Concluding Remarks

In this chapter I have attempted to avoid a reductive understanding of constitutional democracy as can be found in a legalist or monist perspective. More specifically, its argument has been that constitutions cannot be read solely in a negative, limiting way, as much of the legal, politico-theoretical and politico-scientific literature does. Rather, two meta-languages of constitutions can be identified – an instrumental language and a symbolic one – that can be further deconstructed into a range of constitutional dimensions. This shows that the negative, limiting dimension, which is predominantly political, constitutes one, admittedly crucial, dimension among a variety of dimensions of constitutions. The variety of symbolic dimensions is often ignored in contemporary 'legal-constitutional' views. But by invoking this complex variety of constitutional dimensions, it also becomes clear that constitutional texts are bound to contain various tensions, which are often not easy to efface or avoid, and which will either remain latent or become the explicit object of controversies.

Such an argument becomes even more evident when one takes into account the plurality of 'constitutionalisms' that can be identified on a theoretical level, but that, equally, have found a certain sedimentation in the constitutional outlooks of relevant actors as well as in the constitutional texts themselves. In this chapter, this sedimentation was exemplified by references to the Hungarian, Polish and Romanian Constitutions as well as to a number of others. The examples show that various constitutionalist readings can be related to singular constitutional texts, even if, admittedly, much more comparative, socio-legal research needs to be done to further specify differences and commonalities, and the particular weight of these. But it seems fair to argue that a singular, legalist view of constitutionalism, present particularly in popular views of 'judiciary democracy', is hard to uphold. In a similar way, the idea that a constitution can be regarded as an 'act of completion' distinct from the political community as such, the meaning of which is relatively uncontestable and untouchable, is problematic.

What further emerges from the discussion of multiple 'constitutionalisms', along with the different emphases on and hierarchization of constitutional dimensions, is that constitutionalism itself is 'essentially contestable' and cannot, in this, be seen as a neutral discourse impenetrable by politico-ethical viewpoints or discourses. In effect, all identifiable ideal-typical sketches of constitutionalism contain clear-cut politico-ethical views of constitutional democracy.

Acknowledgement

The author acknowledges a post-doctoral fellowship provided by the Provincia Autonoma di Trento, held at the Department of Sociology, University of Trento, Italy.

References

Arato, A., *Civil Society, Constitution, and Legitimacy* (Lanham, MD: Rowman & Littlefield, 2000).

Banciu, A., *Istoria constituțională a României. Deziderate naționale și realități sociale* (Bucharest: Editura Lumina Lex, 2001).

Barber, S., *Welfare and the Constitution* (Princeton, NJ: Princeton University Press, 2003).

——— 'Constitutions in exile: Is the constitution a charter of negative liberties or a charter of positive benefits? Fallacies of negative constitutionalism', *Fordham Law Review*, 75 (2006), 651–67.

Barbu, D., *Republica absentă* (Bucharest: Editura Nemira, 1999).

Bellamy, R., *Political Constitutionalism: A Republican Defence of the Constitutionality of Democracy* (Cambridge: Cambridge University Press, 2007).

Bellamy, R. and D. Castiglione, 'Constitutionalism and democracy – Political theory and the American Constitution', *British Journal of Political Science*, 27 (1997), 595–618.

Blokker, P., 'Multiple democracies: Political culture and democratic variety in post-enlargement Europe', *Contemporary Politics*, 14/2 (2008).

——— *Multiple Democracies in Europe: Political Culture in New Member States* (London: Routledge, 2009).

Breslin, B., *The Communitarian Constitution* (Baltimore, MD and London: Johns Hopkins University Press, 2004).

Brier, R., 'A politics of meaning: Culture and constitution-drafting in Poland's Third Republic', unpublished PhD thesis (Frankfurt (Oder): European University Viadrina, 2006).

Brugger, W., 'Communitarianism as the social and legal theory behind the German Constitution', *International Journal of Constitutional Law*, 2/3 (2003), 431–60.

Buttle, N., 'Republican constitutionalism: A Roman ideal', *Journal of Political Philosophy*, 9/3 (2001), 331–49.

Carp, R. and I. Stanomir, *Limitele Constituției: Despre guvernare, politică și cetățenie în România* (Bucharest: Editura C.H. Beck, 2008).

Castiglione, Dario, 'The political theory of the constitution', *Political Studies*, XLIV (1996), 417–35.

Deszö, M. and A. Bragyova, 'National Referendums in Hungary', in A. Jakab, P. Takacs and A.F. Tatham (eds), *The Transformation of the Hungarian Legal Order 1985–2005: Transition to the Rule of Law and Accession to the European Union* (The Hague: Kluwer Law International, 2007), 68–82.

Forst, R., 'The rule of reasons: Three models of deliberative democracy', *Ratio Juris*, 14/4 (2001), 345–78.

Grimm, D., 'Integration by constitution', *International Journal of Constitutional Law*, 3/2–3 (2005), 193–208.

Hałas, E., 'Constructing the identity of a nation-state: Symbolic conflict over the preamble to the Constitution of the Third Republic of Poland', *Polish Sociological Review*, 1/149 (2005), 49–67.

Hart, V., 'Democratic Constitution Making', Special Report (United States Institute for Peace, 2003). Available online at <http://www.usip.org> [accessed 16 April 2010].

Holmes, S., *Passions and Constraint: On the Theory of Liberal Democracy* (Chicago, IL: University of Chicago Press, 1995).

Ionescu, C., *Instituţii Politice şi Drept Constituţional* (Bucharest: Editura Universitară, 2007).

Ionescu, G., 'The theory of liberal constitutionalism', in V. Bogdanor (ed.), *Constitutions in Democratic Politics* (Aldershot and Brookfield: Gower, 1988), 33–49.

Juhász, G. 'The development of social law in Hungary between 1985–1990 and 2005', in A. Jakab, P. Takacs, A.F. Tatham (eds), *The Transformation of the Hungarian Legal Order 1985–2005: Transition to the Rule of Law and Accession to the European Union* (Kluwer Law International, 2007), 395–406.

Körösényi, A., *Government and Politics in Hungary* (Budapest: Central European University Press, 1999).

Lefort, C., *Democracy and Political Theory* (Minneapolis, MN: University of Minnesota Press, 1988).

Lungu, I., 'Romanian constitutional nationalism', *Polish Sociological Review*, 4/140 (2002), 397–412.

MacDonald, R.A., 'Legal republicanism and legal pluralism: Two takes on identity and diversity', in M. Bussani and M. Graziadei (eds), *Human Diversity and the Law* (Brussels: Bruylant, 2005), 43–70.

Majtényi, B., 'Special minority rights and interpretations of the nation in the Hungarian Constitution', *Regio – Minorities, Politics, Society*, 1 (2005), 4–20.

Michelman, F., 'Law's republic', *The Yale Law Journal*, 97/8 (1988), 1493–1537.

———'Conceptions of democracy in American constitutional argument: Voting rights', *Florida Law Review*, 43 (1989), 443–90.

Murphy, P., 'Socialism and democracy', *Thesis Eleven*, 26 (1990), 54–77.

Offe, C., '"Homogeneity" and constitutional democracy: Coping with identity conflicts through group rights', *Journal of Political Philosophy*, 6/2 (1998), 113–41

Pitkin, H., 'The idea of a constitution', *Journal of Legal Education*, 37 (1987), 167–69.

Preda, C. (2002), 'La Nation dans la Constitution', in *Nation and National Ideology: Past, Present, and Prospects* (Bucharest: New Europe College, 2002), pp. 390–445.

Preuss, U., 'Constitutional powermaking for the new polity: Some deliberations on the relation between the constituent power and the constitutions', *Cardozo Law Review*, 14 (1993), 639–60.

———'Patterns of constitutional evolution and change in Eastern Europe', in J.J. Hesse and N. Johnson (eds), *Constitutional Policy and Change in Europe* (Oxford: Oxford University Press, 1995), 95–128.

Přibáň, J., *Dissidents of Law: On the 1989 Velvet Revolutions, Legitimations, Fictions of Legality, and Contemporary Versions of the Social Contract* (Aldershot and Burlington, VT: Ashgate/Dartmouth, 2002).

———*Legal Symbolism: On Law, Time and European Identity* (Aldershot and Burlington, VT: Ashgate, 2007).

Regia Autonomă, *Geneza Constituției României. Lucrările Adunării Constituante* (Bucharest: Regia Autonomă Monitorul Oficial, 1998).

Richardson, H.S., 'Republicanism and democratic injustice', *Politics, Philosophy, and Economics*, 5 (2006), 75–200.

Rosenfeld, M., 'Modern constitutionalism as interplay between identity and diversity', *Cardozo Law Review*, 14 (1993), 497–531.

———*Just Interpretations: Law between Ethics and Politics* (Berkeley, CA: University of California Press, 1998a).

———'Constitution-making, identity-building, and peaceful transition to democracy: Theoretical reflections inspired by the Spanish example', *Cardozo Law Review*, 19 (1998b), 1891–1920.

———'A pluralist theory of political rights in times of stress', in W. Sadurski (ed.), *Political Rights under Stress in 21st Century Europe* (Oxford: Oxford University Press, 2006), 12–54.

Sadurski, W., 'Conclusions: On the relevance of institutions and the centrality of constitutions in postcommunist transitions', in J. Zielonka (ed.), *Democratic Consolidation in Eastern Europe: volume 1: Institutional engineering* (Oxford: Oxford University Press, 2001), 393–415.

———'Constitutional courts in the process of articulating constitutional rights in the post-Communist states of Central and Eastern Europe: Part II: Personal, civil and political rights and liberties', EUI working papers, LAW 2003/1 (Florence: European University Institute, 2003).

Sajó, A., *Limiting Government: An Introduction to Constitutionalism* (Budapest: Central European University Press, 1999).

Scheppele, K.L., 'Counter-constitutions: Narrating the nation in post-Soviet Hungary', paper given at George Washington University (Washington, DC, 2 April 2004).

Scholl, B., *Europas symbolische Verfassung: nationale Verfassungstraditionen und die Konstitutionalisierung der EU* (Wiesbaden: VS Verlag für Sozialwissenschaften, 2006).

Selznick, P., *The Communitarian Persuasion* (Washington, DC: Woodrow Wilson Center Press, 2002).

———'The jurisprudence of communitarian liberalism', in P. van Seters (ed.), *Communitarianism in Law and Society* (Lanham, MD: Rowman & Littlefield, 2006), 19–32.

———'Foundations of Communitarian Liberalism', in A. Etzioni (ed.), *The Essential Communitarian Reader* (Oxford: Rowman & Littlefield, 1998), pp. 3–14.

Sunstein, C., 'Beyond the republican revival', *Yale Law Journal*, 97/8 (1987), 1539–1590.

———*Designing Democracy: What Constitutions Do* (Oxford and New York: Oxford University Press, 2001).

Tierney, S., 'Constitutional referendums: A theoretical enquiry', *Modern Law Review*, 72/3 (2009), 360–83.

Tomkins, A., *Our Republican Constitution* (Oxford: Hart, 2005).

Ungureanu, C., 'European constitution-making and the question of religion', EUI Working Paper SPS, 2007/01 (Florence: European University Institute, 2007).

Viroli, M., *Republicanism* (New York: Hill & Wang, 1999).

Vorländer, H., 'Die Verfassung als symbolische Ordnung. Perspektiven einer kulturwissenschaftlich-institutionalistischen Verfassungstheorie', in M. Becker and R. Zimmerling (eds), *Politik und Recht* (VS Verlag, 2006), 229–49.

Walzer, M., *Spheres of Justice: A Defense of Pluralism and Equality* (New York: Basic Books, 1983).

Weiler, J.H.H., *Un'Europa cristiana. Un saggio esplorativo* (Milano: BUR Saggi, 2003).

Winczorek, P., 'Axiological Foundations of the Polish Constitution', in M. Wyrzykowski, *Constitutional Essays* (Warsaw: Institute of Public Affairs, 1999), pp. 59–71.

Zubrzycki, G., *The Crosses of Auschwitz: Nationalism and Religion in Post-Communist Poland* (Chicago, IL: University of Chicago Press, 2006).

Chapter 4
Constitutional Courts and Constitutional Culture in Central and Eastern European Countries

Wojciech Sadurski

Introduction

The emergence of robust constitutional review through strongly independent, 'activist' courts exercising abstract review of statutes (and other legal acts), leading often to the invalidation of acts enacted by parliamentary majority (and, not infrequently, enjoying a majoritarian popular support), has been one of the striking features of the constitutional systems of Central and Eastern Europe (CEE). Of course, both the robustness of the review (measured by the frequency of invalidations and significance of the laws which were struck down) and the independence of the courts (measured by formal guarantees of tenure, institutional design of the modes of selection and details of tenure, such as (non)-renewability and informal criteria of de facto pressures exercised upon the courts by other branches of government), vary from country to country. This has been, by now, reasonably well described in the literature of the subject.[1]

The most important institutional variables, which define a dominant model among CEE states and which have a significant impact upon the democratic potential of these courts, are the following: (1) the modes of appointment and the tenure of judges; (2) *who* can initiate the review; (3) the type of review (*ex ante* or *ex post*, abstract or concrete); and (4) the finality of the review. In referring to these four categories in the most general terms, one may make a number of observations. First, there are three different models of judicial selection: exclusively by parliaments (for example, Poland and Hungary); collaborative appointment by two bodies, one of which nominates and another which selects from that list (for

1 For a book-length analysis of constitutional review in CEE, see Wojciech Sadurski, *Rights Before Courts: A Study of Constitutional Courts in Postcommunist States of Central and Eastern Europe* (Dordrecht: Springer, 2005). See also, in particular, Herman Schwartz, *The Struggle for Constitutional Justice in Post-Communist Europe* (Chicago, IL: University of Chicago Press, 2000); and Radoslav Prochazka, *Mission Accomplished: On Founding Constitutional Adjudication in Central Europe* (Budapest: Central European University Press, 2002).

example, the Czech Republic and Russia); and a shared system of appointment, with different bodies (for example, the president, the parliament and a judicial representative body) having its own 'share' of judges (one-third) to appoint (for example, Romania and Bulgaria). Second, the list of authorized initiators is quite diverse, varying from country to country, but typically including a group (defined by a number or percentage) of members of parliament, the president, the government, the ombudsman and so on. Third, the dominant type of review is abstract and *ex post*, though most of the CEE states also have a 'concrete' path of review (initiated by an 'ordinary' court encountering a constitutionally dubious legal rule in the process of hearing the case) and occasionally an *ex ante* review (for example, in Poland, initiated by the President, and also in Romania). Fourth, all the CEE states' decisions of constitutional review are now final, in the sense that there is no possibility of an appeal or override, though until recently there were the possibilities of parliamentary override in Poland and Romania.[2]

This chapter will reflect upon the impact of those constitutional courts upon constitutional culture in CEE, viewed from the perspective of their relationship with the other branches of government, in particular, the legislatures. It will adopt a simple, commonsensical understanding of constitutional culture as the degree to which a constitution *matters* in a given polity: the degree to which important collective decisions are in fact informed by constitutional constraints; and the degree to which the society as a whole considers constitutional strictures as significant and worth considering when evaluating proposed or actual collective decisions. This is, of course, a very simplified, perhaps simplistic understanding of 'constitutional culture' but, for the purposes of this chapter, it is as good a point of departure as any.

The initial hypothesis is that the 'activism' of constitutional courts (a term which will be clarified below) can have both adverse and positive impacts upon constitutional culture, understood in a way just articulated. On the one hand, strong constitutional courts may encourage and consolidate the feeling (erroneous, in my view), both among political actors and in a community at large, that all other branches of government are free to disregard constitutional strictures and should take into account only policy considerations because, if they contravene the constitutional norms, a strong constitutional court will intervene and correct the decision in a constitutional way. This is the adverse impact of the existence and activities of robust constitutional courts on constitutional culture. On the other hand, strong constitutional courts act as a powerful incentive for the executive and legislative branch to factor constitutional values into their decisions (because the prospect of a judicial override is politically costly), and also as an actual guarantee that an unconstitutional decision sooner or later (usually 'sooner', in a system of abstract review triggered by political actors, in particular by the parliamentary

2 For an up-to-date description of the dominant model in CEE, see Kasia Lach and Wojciech Sadurski, 'Constitutional courts of Central and Eastern Europe: Between adolescence and maturity', *Journal of Comparative Law*, 3/2 (2008), 212–33.

opposition or by a president hostile to the government of the day) will be removed from the books. This consolidates the view, among political actors and in the community, that the constitution indeed matters. This is the positive impact of constitutional courts' activism upon constitutional culture.

As these remarks indicate, a great deal depends upon the relationship between the constitutional court and the other branches of government: the parliaments and the executive. The horizontal relationship between these bodies is the space where the issue of courts' 'activism' occurs. Indeed, we cannot even begin to know whether to characterize a court's behaviour as activist unless we already have a prior conception about the proper role of these other political institutions. 'Activism' is an inherently relational notion, which depends upon a reflection on what the relationship is between courts and legislatures (and the executive branch), and also on what legitimate spaces are occupied by these different branches. Constitutional culture is therefore informed by the relationship between constitutional courts and the legislature, in particular in the process of law-making. A robust constitutional court may clash with some of our intuitions about democratic, parliament-centred law-making but, on the other hand, may accord with our views about the primacy of constitutional factors in legitimate law-making. This double-faced, Janus-like nature of constitutional courts needs to be explored against the theory and practice of inter-institutional relationships (between constitutional courts and the legislatures and executives) in CEE countries.

Before exploring these issues, however, it is necessary to clarify what 'activism' means when applied to constitutional courts. The concept itself is suspect to many legal scholars and practitioners,[3] but we do not need to get embroiled in that controversy. What *is* important is that the phenomenon the notion of 'activism' is supposed to denote is substantial and raises understandable concerns; namely, the substitution of the view of the parliamentary majority with that of the court's majority, concerning the proper articulation of the meaning of a constitutional norm, when these two views collide *and* when it is possible for the court, *within the set of argumentative resources available to it*, to uphold or strike down the law. This is a concern to which the notion of judicial activism responds and, however we dislike the very notion, the concern will not go away. So this understanding of 'activism' is not obliterated by the fact that, for example, courts do not normally control their own agenda and cannot refuse to deal with matters brought to their attention by politicians. 'Activism' is not a matter of illegitimate intrusion into a field into which the court has not been invited, so to speak.

As a working test, it can be suggested that an inquiry into the 'judicial activism' of constitutional courts involves two criteria: the importance of the laws being invalidated under the constitutional provisions pertaining to rights, and the nature of the reasoning leading to such invalidation. As far as the first

3 For a powerful plea against the use of judicial activism, see Aharon Barak, 'The Supreme Court, 2001 term – Foreword: A judge on the judging: The role of a Supreme Court in a democracy', *Harvard Law Review*, 116 (2002), 16–162, at 126–27.

criterion is concerned, though the 'importance' of laws is a largely subjective matter, common sense probably dictates that the significance of overturning a law on abortion, capital punishment or lustration is higher than that of overturning a law striking down a particular procedure for obtaining professional recognition as a practising lawyer. In terms of the nature of the reasoning – the second criterion – the above emphasis, '*within the set of argumentative resources available to it*', is deliberate. It is safe to assume that any court usually has some leeway of choice of an argumentative method which may support different conclusions. This is most evident when a court engages in a proportionality analysis – one of the favourite methods of constitutional courts, especially when the admissibility of legislative restrictions of constitutional rights is scrutinized. Proportionality analysis – and its twin tool, the balancing of constitutional values – is a method which ultimately may support either of two contrasting results in any given case, depending on the comparative weight assigned by a judge to competing constitutional values. As these weights are not – and cannot be – strictly prescribed by the constitutional text, the judges, within the set of argumentative resources available to them, may end up either upholding or striking down a challenged law. The tendency to do the latter rather than the former is an easy, commonsensical symptom of judicial activism.

Factors Affecting the 'Strength' of Judicial Review

To ascertain the relationship between the legislature and the constitutional court, it is possible to talk about the 'strength' of judicial review. This refers to the quantitative and qualitative dimensions of confrontations between the court and the law-makers, reflected in the number of successful referrals to the court (particularly by the parliamentary minority) and also in the relative importance of the laws invalidated for unconstitutionality. This is just another way of discussing 'judicial activism'. The strength has a quantitative dimension – a dimension of scope that refers to the range of issues within which the court's preferences collide with those of the parliament – and a qualitative dimension, that is, the salience of the issues that produce disagreement between the two institutions. There are many factors determining both the range and the significance of the clash between court and parliament; obviously, the institutional rules of access to the constitutional court and the range of actors entitled to initiate the review are among the more important ones.

The starting point of the analysis has to be the nature of the constitutional courts themselves. Irrespectively of whether one describes the constitutional courts as judicial bodies of a special type, or quasi-legislative institutions, the political dimension of the courts' activity is obvious. Firstly, there is an unavoidable connection with the political sphere, since the constitutional courts are often being asked to decide on matters that have great impact on the politics of the day. Secondly, and more controversially, the fact that politicians, either exclusively or predominantly, as is the case in the 'divided' or shared systems of judicial appointments,[4] elect judges might cast doubts on the political neutrality of the latter. It might also be used as a convenient argument against an unfavourable ruling by politicians who have lost their courtroom battles. In other words, there is an inevitable conundrum inscribed in the very concept and design of constitutional review. Consequently, the constitutional courts in the CEE region have had to face various challenges resulting form their dual, legal-political nature while carving out for themselves a place on the political scene. These processes have taken different forms in individual countries. They have been influenced by several factors, some of which could be described as country-specific, others as universal to the CEE region.

First, the very design of a constitutional court has a great impact upon the relationship between the court and other branches of the government. For instance, in Romania the availability of the *ex ante* control of the laws resulted in a specific perception of the role of the Constitutional Court by politicians. Parliamentary groups of senators or deputies most often initiated preventive control. Proposals for legislative acts were brought before the Court not so much in order to control their constitutionality as to secure the interests of political parties.[5] In effect, as a Romanian constitutional expert opined, the Court was cast in the role of arbiter of political disputes of the day and exposed to political pressures.[6] Also, the fact that the Court's decisions until 2003 did not enjoy a final binding force and could be overturned by a majority of two-thirds of both chambers of the Parliament created a particular situation. The rulings of the Court were regarded as yet another, perhaps more authoritative, opinion on the law debated by the Parliament, but not as ultimate legal decisions about contested issues. Yet, despite these institutional factors, the Romanian Constitutional Court managed to gain the respect and acceptance of its political actors.[7] The case of the Romanian Court will be discussed, in more detail, in a later part of this chapter.

4 The 'divided' system means that different bodies have their 'share' of judges on the constitutional court to appoint: typically, the president, the parliament and the representative judicial body (as, for example, in Bulgaria or Romania). The 'shared' system means that one body proposes the candidates and another body elects the judges from that list (as in Russia, where the job is shared by the Duma and the President, and in the Czech Republic, with the Senate and the President involved in the appointment process).

5 Renate Weber, 'The Romanian Constitutional Court: In search of its own identity', in Wojciech Sadurski (ed.), *Constitutional Justice, East and West: Democratic Legitimacy and Constitutional Courts in Post-Communist Europe in a Comparative Perspective* (The Hague: Kluwer Law International, 2002), 283–308, at 291.

6 Weber writes: 'MPs' perception that the Constitutional Court should serve their interest was better noted in those instances when the speakers of the Chambers or individual MPs asked for the Court's opinion on issues related to the interpretation of the Constitution without any connection to a particular law, in a procedure which was not within the competence of the Court', id., at 293.

7 Ibid.

Another factor that may determine the relationship between a constitutional court, on the one hand, and the parliament and government, on the other, is the character of the constitutional text. Depending on the level of precision of the provisions and their ideological coherence, that is, the extent to which they promote conflicting values that the court will have to balance while adjudicating, the position of individual courts *vis-à-vis* other branches of government will differ. For example, the Hungarian Constitution marked by its Round Table/transitional origin has given the Court considerable scope for manoeuvre. This is also true for other countries from the region.

Further, the relationship between the constitutional court and other branches of government may be determined by the attitude of the ruling party towards other independent sources of state authority. This was the case in Bulgaria. The Bulgarian Socialist Party (BSP), the successor of the Communist Party, in its attempts to minimize departures from the previous political regime, was particularly determined to subordinate the Constitutional Court.[8] The conflict escalated between 1995 and 1996. Interestingly, the BSP-dominated Government and Parliament did not launch an open attack. Instead, they resorted to more cunning practices, intimidating the Court by, for example, attempting to move its premises to a new location without obtaining the Court's approval.[9] The Court responded by declaring, pursuant to a petition submitted by the President of the Republic, the governmental decree unconstitutional.[10] The Court also withstood pressure while deciding politically controversial cases. In 1996, in the situation of absolute domination of the political scene by the Socialist Party, the Constitutional Court was asked to pronounce on the provision of the Constitution concerning the eligibility requirements for the office of the President of the Republic.[11] It interpreted the constitutional provisions narrowly, which in effect brought about the exclusion from the presidential race of the already nominated candidate of the Socialists. Foreign Minister Georgi Pirinski was unable to stand for the office for the reason that he did not obtain Bulgarian citizenship by birth, as the Constitution required.[12] Despite difficult beginnings and the initial struggle to establish its authority *vis-à-vis* other branches of government, the Bulgarian Constitutional Court eventually accustomed politicians to its presence and involvement in state affairs.[13]

---

8 Schwartz, *The Struggle for Constitutional Justice in Post-Communist Europe*, op. cit., at 164.

9 Venelin Ganev, 'The rise of constitutional adjudication in Bulgaria', in W. Sadurski (ed.) *Constitutional Justice*, op. cit., 247–64, at 252.

10 Ibid.

11 Decision 12/96, described in Ganev, id., at 255.

12 Ibid., at 256.

13 Ganev writes: 'Only days after NATO and Russia requested access to Bulgarian air space, the government asked the Court to specify the conditions under which such access may be granted'. Ibid., at 259.

Perhaps the most important factor having a bearing on the CEE constitutional courts' relationship with other branches of government has been the political landscape in which the courts operate. Generally speaking, the greater the tensions between political forces, the greater the possibility that, sooner or later, adversaries will turn to the constitutional court to contest policy choices of political opponents. The consequence of the court's involvement in politically coloured disputes, even if they have already been translated into the language of legislative acts, is the threat of compromising the court's neutrality (which is an important ingredient of its claim for legitimacy) and, consequently, its public credibility. In some extreme situations where a constitutional court's adjudication leads to decisions unfavourable to a ruling party, the danger is even greater – there might be attempts actually or formally to limit the court's independence.

Last, but not least, one needs to identify those factors determining the strength of judicial review that are anchored in the institutional design and operation of the legislature itself. In general, one can claim that the strength of judicial review is, to a high degree, a function of the structure of the legislative system (namely, the more 'veto points' there are in the law-making process, the weaker the clashes between the constitutional court and the legislature), and also of the nature of the party system as it operates in the parliament (namely, the greater the push for creating coalition governments rather than strong one-party majorities, the weaker the clashes between the constitutional court and the legislature).

Returning to the first factor, Alec Stone Sweet has convincingly shown that the strength of constitutional review is largely a function of how centralized government control is over the legislative process.[14] The more 'veto points' a system contains (such as a second chamber, the availability of presidential veto and so on), the less dramatic any confrontation between the constitutional court and the legislature is likely to be. This is because, where the constitutional court is only one among a number of effective filters, the parliamentary minority may be able to achieve its political aims without having to refer the law to the constitutional court. To put it crudely, the centralization of the system of law-making – where one political actor can effectively control the process from the early legislative initiative up to the final enactment of the law – makes the constitutional court a more likely arena for resolving disputes concerning legislative preferences, and less 'protected' against the effects of such a head-on clash.

The evidence from CEE countries in support of these hypotheses is very fragmentary, partly due to the fact that the force of variables related to the regime type is overshadowed by the force of variables related to the degree of consolidation of democracy in different CEE states, with the latter variable affecting the independent position of the constitutional court and thus the strength of judicial review. For example, the strength of the presidency only partly affects the existence of a 'veto point' that may deflect the clash of legislature and

---

14 Alec Stone Sweet, *Governing with Judges* (Oxford: Oxford University Press, 2000), 52–55.

constitutional court. Almost all consolidated democracies of CEE have opted for a parliamentary system with a relatively weak presidency. An exception is Poland, with its semi-presidential system, where the presidential veto power has indeed at times effectively released the Constitutional Tribunal from the need to consider (and, putatively, invalidate) controversial laws. However, not all of the powers of this relatively strong presidency are capable of weakening the legislature-constitutional court clash; indeed, the presidential power to initiate an *ex ante* review (incidentally, also present in Hungary) may exacerbate the disagreements, because the burden of invalidation then falls on the Constitutional Tribunal rather than on the President.

The other Central European consolidated democracies assign a weaker role to the president within the parliamentary system than Poland. In some cases, even though the president may be elected directly by citizens, implying a relatively high degree of political legitimacy, for example in Slovenia, he nonetheless does not possess any power of veto over legislation approved by parliament. In neither Hungary nor Lithuania does the president enjoy such a power of veto (even though Lithuania is often classified as an instance of semi-presidentialism, owing to the fact that the president has reasonably strong powers in the field of international relations, dissolution of assembly and legislative initiative). The presidential powers of veto in Estonia, Romania (another state often classified as semi-presidential) and Slovakia are more limited than in Poland, because in these countries his suspensive veto can be overridden by a simple parliamentary majority rather than by a qualified majority of three-fifths as is the case in Poland (in Bulgaria and the Czech Republic an absolute majority is required); hence the capacity of presidents to act as 'veto points' is more limited in these countries. All of this illustrates that, with the exception of Poland and, to a lesser degree, the Czech Republic and Bulgaria, the institution of president does not really constitute a significant 'veto point' affecting the strength of judicial review.

Apart from the president, another 'veto point' may reside in an upper chamber which may be effective in screening out the most problematic pieces of legislation, thus reducing the potential for conflict between the constitutional court and the parliament. In two of the Central European bi-cameral systems (Poland and the Czech Republic) the powers of the upper chambers are more limited than those of the lower chambers, as they possess only suspending vetoes *vis-à-vis* legislation (although, unlike the Senates in France or Spain whose veto can be overridden by simple majority of the lower chambers, the Senate's veto in Poland and the Czech Republic can be overridden only by an absolute majority thereof). In the third bi-cameral Central European system, in Romania, both chambers possess the same legislative powers. This, of course, renders the Senate much more significant and effective as a 'veto point' than the Polish or Czech Senates, especially owing to the fact that, in practice, the two chambers often compete with one another for the final word on particular pieces of legislation.[15] Nonetheless, even the merely suspending veto of the Polish or Czech Senates may, at times, deflect the force of the clash between the lower chamber and the Constitutional Court. An example is provided by the Czech Republic, in which the Senate occasionally sides with the Constitutional Court when the latter collides with the lower chamber. This may be partly owing to the fact that Czech senators are less bound by strict party discipline than the members of the lower chamber, and also because the relatively long term of senators' office (six years) brings their perspective closer to that of the judges of the Constitutional Court. (In this respect the Czech Senate is different from the Polish and Romanian Senates, where the term of office for senators is the same as for members of the lower chamber, that is, four years.) There have therefore been cases in which the Senate has formed an 'alliance' with the Constitutional Court against the lower chamber.

As an example, consider the Czech law of 1998, which reduced the salaries of public servants by annulling the traditional 'salary supplement' (the so-called '13th and 14th monthly pays') for all public employees, as part of the government's austerity measures. The Constitutional Court protested against the inclusion of judges' salaries in these restrictions, on the basis of judicial independence, and also on the basis of the special role played by judges in the protection of democratic values and the rule of law.[16] As a consequence, the Court rewrote the law by exempting judges from the universal pay reduction. The Court's decision was, as could be expected, unpopular with the general public and with politicians, including President Havel who went as far as to criticize the judgment publicly. The following year, the Assembly of Deputies (the lower chamber) enacted the austerity law, which basically replicated the previous year's measures, including the removal of pay supplements for judges. At this point, the Senate returned the law to the Assembly specifically on the basis that the parliament should respect the decision of the Constitutional Court. The Assembly chose, however, to ignore both the position of the Senate and the earlier decision of the Court (which had applied to an earlier, although relevantly similar, law) and enacted the 1999 law in its original form. This new statute came again before the Constitutional Court which, by this time, had changed its mind and found the law consistent with the Constitution. In this case of a parliament-constitutional court clash, it was the Court which eventually caved in, but not before discovering an ally in the upper chamber of the parliament, and realizing that its objections had been endorsed by the upper chamber and, presumably, considered seriously by the lower one.

---

15 Renate Weber, 'Constitutionalism as a vehicle for democratic consolidation in Romania', in Jan Zielonka (ed.), *Democratic Consolidation in Eastern Europe*, vol. I: *Institutional Engineering* (Oxford: Oxford University Press, 2001), 212–42, at 227.

16 Decision of the Czech Constitutional Court no. 13/99 of 15 September 1999; see Jiří Přibáň, 'Judicial power vs democratic representation: The culture of constitutionalism and human rights in the Czech legal system', in W. Sadurski (ed.), *Constitutional Justice*, op. cit., 373–94, at 387.

The Constitutional Court and the Parliamentary Minority

While, in general, the position of a constitutional court exercising robust judicial review puts it in a potentially (and, often, actually) antagonistic relationship *vis-à-vis* the legislature, this is, of course only partly true. The real potential institutional hostility lies between the court and the parliamentary *majority* after a recently enacted law has been judicially invalidated. At the same time, such invalidation creates a ground for an alliance between the court and the parliamentary minority, especially in cases where minority MPs have initiated the challenge to the law in question. Alliances of this type are a universal phenomenon whenever abstract review can be initiated by members of parliament, for the simple reason that '[o]ppositions judicialize legislative processes in order to win what they would otherwise lose in 'normal', unjudicialized processes (they would be outvoted)'.[17] This is a politically inexpensive and basically risk-free avenue for achieving political aims temporarily unattainable by the opposition through a legislative path. Stone Sweet has hypothesized (with regard to West European constitutional courts) that the likelihood of a clash between the court and the majority of legislature is higher soon after the alternation of power in the parliament (from the left to the right, or vice versa), because in such periods the court is likely to reflect the political views of the past but not the current majority.[18] This hypothesis, however, is obviously only of limited applicability in those systems in which the selection of judges is done only partly by the parliament (as is the case in Romania and, in a different way, in the Czech Republic), or where the majority has to build a consensus with at least a part of the opposition to agree upon a judicial nomination (as is the case in Hungary).

The relationship of the composition of the court to that of the legislature is a variable that may affect the attractiveness of judicial review to the parliamentary opposition. However, as a general rule, it seems obvious that the opposition must treat the court as its natural ally, particularly when the legislative system includes relatively few 'veto points' and internal 'checks and balances', and the political majority is reasonably disciplined and stable. This is the case, for instance, in Romania, and it is no wonder that the (then) President of the Romanian Constitutional Court could proclaim: '[T]he [Constitutional] Court is an effective defender of parliamentary oppositions. All of the draft laws that we considered were brought before us by minorities, by minority factions.'[19]

However, the assumption that a parliamentary minority has an obvious incentive to challenge laws in the constitutional court whenever it is outvoted in the parliament needs to be qualified. In some countries, the social perception of an opposition party frequently resorting to constitutional challenges of recently

17 Stone Sweet, op. cit., at 55.

18 Id., at 55.

19 Alina Mungiu-Pippidi, 'Interview with President of the Romanian Constitutional Court, Ion Muraru', *East Europ. Constit. Rev.*, 6/1 (Winter 1997), 78–83, at 81.

adopted laws may not be so positive: the party may acquire the image of being a 'trouble-maker' and undermine its chances of winning in subsequent elections. This, I believe, is the case in Russia.[20] While the *financial* costs of such a challenge are negligible, the *political* costs may be high, and the maxim 'there is no harm in trying' does not necessarily apply. Elsewhere, however, the public perceptions of such constitutional challenges may be different. In Poland, for example, party supporters usually expect that their party will challenge controversial laws in the Constitutional Tribunal whenever it has such an opportunity; such a challenge is not generally seen (even by opponents of the challenging party) as a violation of the democratic rules of the game or of political weakness. Rather, it is seen as a perfectly legitimate political tool; indeed the *failure* to bring the law in question before the Constitutional Tribunal may be seen as a sign of the opposition party's negligence, lack of skills or political will to win. The tentative conclusion of this comparison is that the incentives for opposition parties to enlist the constitutional court as a political ally against the majority and the government depend upon the public perception of these parties and on the public interpretation of the meaning of the constitutional referral as much as they do on the comparison of the (political) composition of the parliament with that of the constitutional court.

Case Studies of Three Countries: The Czech Republic, Poland and Romania

This section provides three illustrations of the earlier discussion of inter-institutional relations between the constitutional courts and the other branches of government: namely, the Czech Republic, Poland and Romania. The section does not claim that these three countries are necessarily fully representative of the patterns of inter-institutional relations in all CEE states; indeed, it seems that the level of tension and even conflict is higher there than elsewhere. As such, they may perhaps serve as examples of certain pathologies in institutional relations. But at the same time, they may be useful in identifying the impact of these inter-institutional tensions upon constitutional cultures – precisely because the conflicting nature of these relationships is a significant example for a study of how institutions influence constitutional culture.

The Czech Republic

The predicament of the Czech Constitutional Court resulted from a rivalry within the executive branch, as well as a peculiar understanding of the role of the Court exhibited by leading politicians. This is not to say that the first 10 years of the Court's activity were uncontroversial,[21] yet the situation became particularly complicated

20 See Sadurski, *Rights Before Courts*, op. cit., at 95.

21 For a good discussion see Přibáň, op. cit.

in 2003 when the Parliament elected Václav Klaus to the post of President.[22] Klaus, a former prime minister and leader of one of the major political parties, was notorious for his mistrust of lawyers and fierce criticism of the Constitutional Court for its alleged activism.[23] Since the term of office of nine judges expired in July 2003, and the President was the one to put forward new candidacies to the Senate, Klaus got an opportunity to shape the destiny of the so-disliked institution. Another dimension of the appointment process was the obvious hostility between the President and the Senate. The majority of the members of the upper house of the Parliament could hardly be regarded as enthusiasts of the new President. Consequently, Klaus's disrespect for the traditional selection procedures based on consultations with academic and judicial circles, coupled with Senate's reluctance towards most of the presidential nominees, led to a paralysis of the Constitutional Court. For over a year the Court could not pronounce on the constitutionality of law owing to the insufficient number of justices on the bench.[24] The nomination saga finally concluded in December 2005, after the elections to the Senate gave the majority to members of the President's party.[25]

Yet, the controversies surrounding the Constitutional Court did not end with selection of the judges. A more recent episode in the battle between the Court and the President was caused by Klaus's dismissal of the President of Supreme Court, Iva Brozova. The Constitutional Court's decision finding the dismissal unconstitutional triggered a fierce response from Klaus.[26] The President described it as 'an example of judicial corporativism [sic]' and a 'threat to democracy'.[27] He even went as far as saying that it could have a negative impact on the situation of the Czech judiciary.[28]

Poland

The troubles of the Polish Constitutional Tribunal started after the 2005 parliamentary and presidential elections.[29] The new government, led by the

22 On 7 March 2003.

23 Zdeněk Kühn and Jan Kysela (2006) 'Nomination of constitutional justices in post-communist countries: Trial, error, conflict in the Czech Republic', *European Constitutional Law Review*, 2 (2006), 183–208, at 195.

24 Between Summer 2003 and Autumn 2004. Id., at 198.

25 Id., at 205.

26 Decision Pl. ÚS 18/06.

27 'Klaus considers Constitutional Court ruling on Brozova erroneous'. Available online at <http://www.ceskenoviny.cz/news/index_view.php?id=209019> [accessed 30 March 2010].

28 Ibid.

29 Of course, some earlier rulings of the Tribunal, such as those concerning a tax amnesty or the National Healthcare Fund, created some controversies and were criticized by politicians, but the scale of the attack after 2005 has been unprecedented in the history of the Tribunal.

Law and Justice Party (PiS), perceived the Tribunal as an institutional barrier to reforming the Polish state – reforms aimed at ending the Third Republic controlled, as it was claimed by PiS proponents, by invidious 'networks', and creating a new and virtuous Fourth Republic based on law, justice and solidarity. Consequently, not only have the judgments of the Tribunal come under attack, but also the institution itself. The Tribunal was criticized for its allegedly arbitrary ways of rendering decisions, which Prime Minister Jarosław Kaczynski described as 'legal circus tricks'. Also attacked were the moral and professional standards of the Tribunal's members – described as 'disgusting, opportunistic cowards'.[30] The newly coined term 'impossibilism' was meant to describe the doctrine of the Tribunal, meaning that the necessary (in the eyes of the new majority) reforms were rendered 'impossible' under the Tribunal's interpretation of the Constitution (which, with the post-2005 division in the parliament, the new majority was incapable of amending).

After the 2005 political changeover, the Tribunal took several decisions which clearly went against the plans and preferences of the new President Lech Kaczyński and the government: it invalidated the amendment of a law on the broadcasting council, which enabled the new government to appoint its own protégé as the chairperson of the council;[31] it invalidated the provision on the law on public assemblies, according to which local authorities (including Lech Kaczynski, when he was still President of Warsaw) could refuse permission for gay parades to take place;[32] it struck down some crucial provisions of the so-called 'lustration' law on access to archives of the ex-secret police;[33] it struck down a pet project of the new Minister of Justice concerning the reduction of the bar association's control over access to the legal profession;[34] and so on.

All these decisions (and there were more) put the Tribunal on a collision course with the new President, the parliamentary majority and the government, but none was more controversial and caused more outrage from Law and Justice than the decision concerning constitutionality of the so-called 'lustration' law. The statute, as the pillar of Law and Justice's de-communization policy, was of great symbolic importance for the government. The opposition and various human rights groups were alerted not only by the controversial purpose of the act, but also by the employed legal means. Thus, the Tribunal found itself under enormous political pressure and strong public scrutiny as the proceedings were televised and widely commented on by the press. Eventually, after protracted and controversial hearings, the Tribunal invalidated a large number of the provisions on the basis of

---

30 Ibid.

31 Decision of 23 March 2006.

32 Decision of 19 January 2006.

33 Decision of 26 October 2005.

34 Decision of 19 April 2006.

their being unconstitutional, which for all practical purposes rendered the entire act void.[35]

The decision provoked outrage in the ranks of the Law and Justice Party, and led to its submitting to the parliament a draft proposing amendments (eventually aborted) to the statute on the Constitutional Tribunal. The ruling party sought to curtail the powers of the Tribunal by introducing a number of seemingly minor organizational and procedural changes. The party proposed that the President of the Republic of Poland would appoint the President and Vice-President of the Tribunal for a period of three years instead of the whole term of office, that is, nine years.[36] It advocated that the Tribunal should decide which judge would adjudicate a case, rather than the President of the Tribunal allocating cases according to alphabetical order. Also, the order of adjudication of cases would be determined by the order of their submission, which would prevent the possibility of the President of the Tribunal deciding about the sequence of decisions based on the relative importance of cases.[37] Finally, the so-called 'Full Chamber' was to be enlarged from 9 to 11 judges and all cases would be adjudicated by the Full Chamber.[38] According to many judges and legal scholars, such changes, if implemented, would prevent the effective operation of the institution and make it more dependent on the executive branch, in particular, on the President.[39]

None of these proposals was put in place, and the electoral defeat of the Law and Justice Party in 2007 put an end to a period of strong tension between the Constitutional Court and the parliamentary majority (and the government). But the continued Presidency of Lech Kaczyński was a way of actively maintaining the political claims of Law and Justice, and the ongoing tensions between the Tribunal and the President resemble the earlier open conflict between PiS (now a major opposition party) and the Tribunal.

Romania

When designing the Romanian Constitutional Court in the early 1990s, the Constituent Assembly partially followed the French model of the *Conseil Constitutionnel*. But, in the aftermath of the collapse of communism, many in the Constituent Assembly opposed the creation of a strong Court.[40] Thus, in its original design, the Court lacked a series of attributes that similar institutions in the other CEE countries enjoyed. Of these, three were potentially relevant limits

35 Decision K 2/07 of 11 May 2007.

36 Article 15, paragraph 1 of the submitted draft.

37 Article 37, paragraph 1.

38 Article 25.

39 Among others voicing such opinions was former President of the Tribunal Professor Marek Safjan; see Ewa Siedlecka, 'Osłabić Trybunał' ('To weaken the Tribunal'), *Gazeta Wyborcza*, 29 June 2007.

40 Mungiu-Pippidi, 'Interview', op. cit.

to the establishment of a strong activist Court. The first limit was represented by the constitutional provision allowing the parliament to overturn a Court's decision declaring the unconstitutionality of a law by a two-thirds majority.[41] Although in practice never successful, this limit was very telling about the attitude of the Constituent Assembly towards this new institution. Only with the constitutional revision of 2003 was this provision eliminated from the Constitution. A second limit was the possibility, expressly provided for in the law on the organization and functioning of the Court (Law 47/1992)[42] to file a recourse against a decision of the Court within 10 days, a provision which was eliminated in 1997. This provision was used frequently during the first half of the 1990s by the Public Prosecutor to oppose both the competence of the Court to adjudicate upon the constitutionality of laws prior to the 1991 Constitution and the solutions given by the Court. There have been cases where the Court accepted the recourse and modified its previous decision.[43] A third limit to the establishment of a strong review was the lack of competence of the Court to arbiter conflicts between public institutions. The 2003 revision of the Constitution remedied this limit by introducing a new provision, which granted to the Court the authority to solve judicial conflicts between public authorities.[44]

Given the initial limited attributions of the Court, it did not enjoy much visibility in the first years of its existence. However, despite its rather weak position within the institutional framework, the Court steadily affirmed itself. This trend can be noted from the increasing number of referrals it received over time. During the last legislature (2004–2008) the number of annual referrals for constitutional review sky-rocketed, reaching 2,458 in 2006, up from 1,039 in 2005, 728 in 2004 and 573 in 2003.

If we adopt a qualitative approach to the decisions of the Court, we note that it issued decisions declaring total or partial unconstitutionality of laws even during the early 1990s, against the same parliamentary majority which had appointed the constitutional judges in 1992. As an illustrative example, the Court struck down the provision of the law on the retribution and other rights of deputies and senators which exempted the retributions of MPs from being taxed.[45] It also struck down provisions in the Standing Orders of the parliament,[46] in the law on the status of deputies and senators,[47] on the judicial organization,[48] on the organization

41 Art.145 of the 1991 Constitution.

42 Art.25 of Law 47/1992.

43 Decision 56/1994, Decision 11/1994, Decision 38/1993.

44 Art.146 para.(e) of the revised Constitution.

45 Decision 19/1995.

46 Decision 87/1994, Decision 45/1994, Decision 46/1994.

47 Decision 122/1996.

48 Decision 88/1999; Decision 89/1999.

and functioning of the Court of Audit,[49] or on political parties.[50] The increasing affirmation of the Court culminated with the invalidation of some provisions in the law on the revision of the Constitution in 1996[51] and in 2003.[52]

One of the most controversial decisions of the Court dates back to July 2005 and regards the proposed reform of the justice system,[53] which was presented by the government as a legislative package for which it assumed responsibility in lieu of the parliament, according to Article 114 of the Constitution. The question of the reform of the justice system was a crucial issue in the process of EU accession, an issue to which the EU had attached a specific safeguard clause (the postponement clause),[54] which would have enabled the European Council to postpone Romania's accession in the community by one year if there had been clear evidence that Romania was not prepared for meeting the requirements of membership in a number of important areas.[55] Considering the importance of justice reform according to EU standards, a wide political consensus on the reform process, especially in the years immediately preceding accession, would have been very welcome. However, this was clearly not the case, as the two main political forces at that time (PSD in opposition and PNL-PD in government) had very different versions of how to proceed with the reform.[56] Against the proposed reform of the justice system three references for exceptions of unconstitutionality were made by PSD and PRM in the two chambers of the parliament and, separately, by the High Court of Cassation and Justice.[57] In its decision (375/2005), the Court declared some of the provisions referring to justice unconstitutional.

Given that the Court had struck down provisions in a legislative package for which the government had assumed responsibility, the reactions from the members of the government and from society in general have been very critical. They all questioned the willingness of the Court to allow the reform of the justice system to proceed, accusing it of trying to block the reform process and, indeed, Romania's accession to the EU. Emil Boc, leader of one of the governing parties (PD), commented that the decision of the Court 'is a blow to the reform of the judicial system in the direction of preventing the independence of justice and postpones the entry into force of the whole legislative package'. He added that

49 Decision 28/1999, Decision 29/1999.

50 Decision 35/1996.

51 Decision 85/1996.

52 Decision 148/2003

53 Law on the reform in property and justice, as well as some additional measures.

54 The postponement clause applied to Bulgaria and Romania.

55 To January 2008 instead of January 2007.

56 There are three different parties/coalitions: the PSD (Social Democratic Party, centre-left); the PRM (Greater Romania Party, nationalistic); and the PNL-PD (National Liberal Party-Democratic Party, coalition).

57 Letter no.51/666 of 22 June 2005 of the General Secretary of the Chamber of Deputies; reference no.116 of 24 June 2005 from the High Court of Cassation and Justice; Letter no.2.033 of 27 June 2005 the General Secretary of the Senate.

'this constitutes an invitation for the EU to use the safeguard clause provided for the justice system'.[58] Justice Minister Monica Macovei, who was the initiator of the reform and highly regarded in Brussels, made very critical comments where she questioned the neutrality of the Court:

> [N]othing in the proposed law is unconstitutional. As Minister of Justice, I expected judges to be above any personal interests or group interests and not to bend to external pressures. This is how the system works in a strong democratic country. But unfortunately, the Constitutional Court brings us one step backwards and shows us that we still have a long way before that.

She then accused some judges of the Court of having a conflict of interest:

> [T]hey are in a clear situation of incompatibility and unfortunately they did not follow the moral imperative of abstaining from vote [. ...] These are four cases of clear conflict of interests [...] although the conflict of interests is a rule applied in all advanced democracies, in Romania this rule is ignored by the Constitutional Court itself, which should not be above the law.[59]

But, most importantly of all, she openly accused the Court of having invalidated articles which contained modifications specifically recommended by the European Commission: 'I was told very clearly that it would be good if we organized some competitions before the finalization of the Country Report.'[60]

The culmination of political reactions to the Court's decision came when Prime Minister Tăriceanu announced his intention to step down and called for anticipated elections:

> The blocking of the justice reforms [by the Constitutional Court] compromises our chances to get a good report from the European Union. There is only one solution, to return to the people.[61]

Voices were also heard calling for the resignation of the constitutional judges who had started a political and constitutional crisis,[62] or for the modification of the law on the functioning of the Constitutional Court.[63] A few days later, after the

58 *Ziua*, 'The government is about to fall' [Guvernul stă să cadă], 7 July 2005.

59 *Revista 22*, No. 801 – Interview with Justice Minister Macovei.

60 *Ziua,* 'The government is about to fall' [Guvernul stă să cadă], 7 July 2005.

61 'Romanian cabinet to resign after ruling', Associated Press, 7 July 2005. Available online at http://www.globalgoodnews.com/government-news-a.html?art=112075511310434250 [accessed 9 April 2010].

62 Bogdan Olteanu, then (PNL) Delegate Minister for Parliamentary Affairs.

63 Emil Constantinescu, former President of Romania, asked for the modification of the law on the organization and functioning of the Constitutional Court and for the

intervention of President Băsescu in his quality of 'mediator between the Powers in the State',[64] PM Tăriceanu changed his mind about the resignation, mainly owing to the realization that the Constitution contemplated the organization of anticipated elections under strict circumstances which were not fulfilled in the specific case.[65]

After having nearly provoked the resignation of the government and having been accused of trying to block the reform of the justice system, and, as a consequence, after having been accused of blowing Romania's chances of joining the EU in January 2007, the Constitutional Court risked being annihilated as an institution. Indeed, as a reaction to Decision 375/2005, but also following another decision which did not please the governing parties – Decision 601/2005, which struck down the modifications to the Standing Orders of the parliament aimed at facilitating the replacement of the two Presidents of the Chambers, who were members of the main opposition party – voices called for the abolition of the Constitutional Court.[66] But this extreme solution found little support among the coalition government.

However, the controversies over the Court's decisions did not end there. During recent years, as a result of the cohabitation between a President and a PM who came from different parties (Băsescu was president of PD before winning the presidential race, and PM Tăriceanu was president of PNL), but also owing to the strong personalities of these two politicians, the Constitutional Court has been called several times to solve legal conflicts between public authorities. Whether on the right of the President to call a referendum, on the right of the President to ask for the beginning of investigations against ministers, on the review of the Standing Orders of the Chambers, or on the modification to the law on the referendum for the suspension of the President, the Court was called to arbitrate in politically sensitive instances and its decisions raised almost automatically the angry critiques of 'the losers'. There is probably no political party which has not criticized at least once a Court's decision issued during the current government.[67]

---

modification of the Constitution. PM Tăriceanu also suggested that he might reconsider his resignation if a general consensus among all political forces was reached on the continuation of the justice reform, the modification of the law on the functioning of the Constitutional court – the incompatibility issue – and the modification of the Constitution.

64 Art.80(2) of the Constitution.

65 Art.89 of the Constitution stipulates that the President may dissolve the Parliament 'if no vote of confidence has been obtained to form a government within 60 days after the first request was made, and only after rejection of at least two requests for investiture'.

66 Teodor Meleşcanu, vice-president of PNL, declared in February 2006 that the PNL members of the commission for the revision of the Constitution were considering to eliminate the Constitutional Court and to transfer its attributions to the Senate. See *Jurnalul National*, 'The Constitutional Court – PNL in attack, PD and UDMR on the defensive' [Curtea Constituţională – PNL la atac, PD şi UDMR în defensivă], 16 February 2006.

67 Even PSD representatives have criticized the Court. To give an example, the Court's decision on the law on ministerial responsibility was qualified by the president

To conclude this case study: the Romanian Constitutional Court has never really had a positive image in society or among political actors. In fact, for a long period it has been accused of siding with the PSD. However, the recent successes of presidential referrals to the Court have led some to accuse it of having switched sides in favour of Băsescu. But Băsescu himself, as a reaction to the Court's decision on the law on ministerial responsibility, accused the Court of being 'a real shield for parliamentarian law breakers ... or suspected law breakers'.[68] On top of everything, the European Commission criticized the Constitutional Court in its July 2008 Report for having issued a series of decisions that could 'seriously weaken the fight against corruption', also pointing out that the 'implementation of the changes [introduced by the Court] resulted in blockages and delays at the prosecution stage'.[69] While initially quite shy in its interactions with other political actors, owing both to the formal limits imposed by the constitutional and legislative limited prerogatives of the Court and to a de facto domination of PSD-connected constitutional judges in the composition of the Court, the Romanian Constitutional Court has increasingly used its prerogatives as a guardian of the Constitution and arbiter in legal conflicts between public authorities.

Conclusions

Constitutional courts became one of the key fixtures in the political and constitutional landscape of CEE post-communist states, and it is hard to imagine the political life of these countries without those quasi-judicial institutions. Certainly, any account of the politics of CEE states would be defective if it did not provide an in-depth description of constitutional courts.

But how have they affected the constitutional culture of these countries? The response must be nuanced. At one level – call it an outcome-sensitive level – their impact upon constitutional culture has been salutary. Constitutional courts in the region have repaired many of the legislative acts in the direction of a greater respect for constitutional principles and values, such as freedom of expression and

of social democrats, M. Geoană, as surprising and contradictory. T. Corlăţean, secretary-general of PSD, declared that 'in this absolutely depressing political show which has become permanent, the Constitutional Court is prisoner of the political battle between the President and PM and gives lamentable solutions both from a constitutional and juridical points of view, which do not honour this institution'. See *Mediafax*, 'Politicians comment the Court's decision regarding the appointment of Norica Nicolai' [Politicienii comentează decizia CC în privinţa numirii Noricăi Nicolai], 7 February 2008.

68 Declaration by the President at a radio station, quoted in *Gândul*, 'The President has changed opinion about the Constitutional Court' [Preşedintele şi-a schimbat părerea despre Curtea Constituţională], 7 May 2008.

69 European Commission, *Supporting Document accompanying the Report from the Commission to the European Parliament and the Council on progress in Romania under the Co-operation and Verification Mechanism*, Brussels, 23 July 2008.

religion, non-discrimination, freedom of association and protection of minority rights. The score-card, in this respect, is not unqualifiedly positive but, on balance, the specific outcomes of constitutional review of legislative actions have been positive from the point of view of constitutional values and principles.

At a second level – call it educational – the impact has been more mixed. On one hand, constitutionally, courts have certainly contributed to a general awareness – among both political elites and societies at large – about the significance of respect for constitutional values. In the region where a tradition of respecting constitutions as significant restraints upon the exercise of political power is quite weak, this has been no mean achievement. On the other hand, however, the monopoly on constitutional adjudication enjoyed by constitutional courts in the system of a 'concentrated' judicial review has contributed to a perception that other institutions – including 'regular' courts – do not really have a responsibility for constitutional maintenance because it is the exclusive domain of constitutional courts. The episodes of clashes between constitutional courts and supreme courts in a number of CEE states provide an illustration of this phenomenon of an assertion of monopoly of constitutional adjudication by constitutional courts – a phenomenon, ultimately, threatening the weakening of constitutional culture in the institutional systems of post-communist states[70]

This is not to say that a system of constitutional review, as such, is antithetical to spreading constitutional culture. It is rather a question of the choice of a particular model of judicial review – abstract or concrete, concentrated or dispersed, *ex ante* or *ex post* – and determining which of these models better lends itself to the promotion of an idea that constitutional values should be taken seriously by all institutions and, indeed, by all citizens of a constitutional-democratic state. Strangely enough, CEE has never witnessed a serious debate about this issue: the choice of a concentrated, abstract, *ex ante* model of constitutional review vested in 'elite' constitutional courts, guarding jealously their monopoly over the binding constitutional adjudication, was seen as a 'done deal' – not something that should be the subject of an open, robust and unrestricted constitutional debate. The absence of such a debate, in itself, was an unfortunate fact, and a symptom of an important defect in the constitutional culture of transitional democracies in Central and Eastern Europe.

70 See Sadurski, *Rights Before Courts*, op. cit., at 19–25.

Chapter 5
Constitutional Culture and the Theory of Adjudication: Ulysses as a Constitutional Justice

Daniel Smilov

Introduction

Constitutionalism and constitutional culture in Eastern Europe are an experiment. Never before in their history have societies in this region been strongly committed to ideas of limited government, separation of powers and the defence of individual rights. Of course, there are some exceptions – Czechoslovakia in the interwar period and possibly Austro-Hungary before that – but, in any event, these exceptions cannot conceal the lack of constitutional traditions in Eastern Europe. This lack of constitutional traditions became conspicuous with the fall of the Berlin Wall, when the newly established liberal democracies in Central Europe needed to catch up with their counterparts from the West.[1] After the initial enthusiasm in copying institutions – which resulted in the universal introduction of constitutional courts and constitutional review – different countries took different paths in the development of their own culture of constitutionalism. One option, illustrated by the Hungarian Constitutional Court, was the systematic 'importation' and 'transplantation' of developed constitutional doctrines and theories of interpretation from established democracies, mostly from Germany in the Hungarian case.[2]

Another option was to improvise, and this was the Bulgarian path, which is discussed in this chapter. Improvisation is not created *ex nihilo*, of course. It is based on certain familiar themes, presented in a novel light and adapted to the taste and capacity of the performer. Here, the analysis will focus on the Bulgarian Constitutional Court (BCC) and its contribution to the development of a specific culture of constitutionalism. It will be argued that the Bulgarian constitutional judges – inadvertently rather than intentionally – have helped to create a specific attitude towards constitutionalism and the rule of law: an attitude which puts

1 See Wojciech Sadurski, *Rights Before Courts: A Study of Constitutional Courts in Postcommunist States of Central and Eastern Europe* (Dordrecth: Springer, 2005).

2 See Catherine Dupre, *Importing the Law in Post-Communist Transition: The Hungarian Constitutional Court and the Right to Human Dignity* (Oxford: Hart Publishing, 2003).

less weight on the coherence and integrity of the law,[3] and more weight on the implications of judicial decisions in terms of political morality as it is broadly understood. Several preliminary notes are in order.

First, in contrast to the Hungarian Constitutional Court, the BCC did not embark on a massive effort of 'harmonization' of doctrines and theories of interpretation with the leading European courts. On the contrary, much of the jurisprudence of the Bulgarian judges remains context-dependent and even idiosyncratic. More importantly, in terms of doctrine- and theory-creation the Bulgarian judges remain decidedly minimalist and, in general, the court could be described as 'self-restricting'.[4] Yet this does not mean that the court has not been involved in important disputes. On the contrary, certain policy areas, such as the restitution of properties nationalized under the communist regime, regulation of public electronic media, judicial independence and self-government, and many others have been heavily affected by the jurisprudence of the BCC. Indeed, it could be argued that, especially during the 1990s, the court was in an active dialogue with the Bulgarian government and legislature in terms of policy-making.

Also, the doctrinal minimalism of the court does not mean that it has been completely atheoretical. As Cass Sunstein has argued, judges often involve mid-level theorizing in their search for under-theorized agreements in the process of conflict-resolution.[5] These mid-level theories could hardly survive strict scrutiny in terms of coherence with the principles and rules of modern constitutionalism. But often they prove quite helpful, and very often they are the best that judges could hope for in certain circumstances.

Secondly, according to Bulgarian legal doctrines, judges do not have discretion[6] – they cannot resort in their judicial decision-making to anything but the law, which is supposed to provide them with a single right answer in every dispute. Of course, in informal conversations some constitutional judges are inclined to speak frankly about the difficulties of interpretation, and the challenges of de facto judicial discretion. These judges are a minority on the Constitutional Court, however, and the dominant views are militantly doctrinaire in this regard.

Next, the stark rejection of judicial discretion is, of course, no coincidence, but has deep roots in Bulgarian legal history. There are three generally formative

3 For the concept of coherence in law, see Anton Peczenik, 'Coherence, truth and rightness in the law', in P. Nerhot (ed.), *Law, Interpretation and Reality* (Dordrecht: Kluwer Academic Publishers, 1990); and Joseph Raz, *Ethics in the Public Domain* (Oxford: Clarendon Press, 1994). For Ronald Dworkin's theory of 'law as integrity', see his *Law's Empire* (Cambridge, MA: Harvard University Press (Belknap Press), 1986).

4 Rumyana Kolarova, 'A self-restricting court', *East European Constitutional Review*, 2/2 (1993), 48–51.

5 Cass R. Sunstein, *Legal Reasoning and Political Conflict* (Oxford and New York: Oxford University Press, 1996).

6 Kino Lazarov, *Обвързана компетентност и оперативна самостоятелност* (Фенея: София, 2000).

periods from the point of view of legal culture in Bulgaria. First, there was the interwar period, when for the first time legal theory and jurisprudence made serious advances through the work of scholars like Venelin Ganev,[7] Vladimir Vladikin[8] and Stefan Balamezov.[9] Apart from being intellectuals, these were very influential public and political figures, who had a huge impact on a number of generations of Bulgarian lawyers. In fact, these three figures still remain the most respected legal theorists in the Bulgarian doctrine. It is important to note for our purposes that all of them were heavily influenced by the positivist ideas of Hans Kelsen, and his strict attempt to distinguish the law and legal science from any evaluative judgment. The resulting formalism in the understanding of the law was and still is the foundation of Bulgarian legal theory.

The communist period in Bulgaria (1944–1989) started with a stark rejection of legal formalism in the name of proletarian justice: the so-called 'People's Court' rendered numerous death sentences in dubious legal proceedings after the communist takeover in 1944. This tradition of 'substantive' justice was the dominant one until the beginning of the 1960s. Yet, in the late period of socialism, when the regime did not feel threatened by internal or external enemies as in the earlier years, formalism made a surprising comeback in Bulgaria. This time, it was as a means for the legal profession to assert a relative amount of autonomy and importance. Formalism was necessary for lawyers once again in order to stress the increasing significance of the legal domain being relatively autonomous from party politics. *Relatively* should be emphasized: the lawyers were by no means dissidents within the system but, rather, its firm supporters. Yet, this relative autonomy was necessary for them to defend their guild interests and to improve their social status as a group. Also, one should not exclude from consideration the genuine attempt by certain people to find niches in the law (some private law matters or Roman law, for instance) in which the influence of the communist party was not particularly visible on a daily basis.

Finally, after the fall of the communist regime formalism was further strengthened by certain constitutional and political considerations. The communist party, at the time of the Constituent Assembly (1990–1991), feared political persecution by the courts most of all. Therefore, it insisted on the inclusion of very strong judicial independence instruments in the 1991 basic law, which in fact made the removal of judges from the communist time completely impossible. Thus, the judiciary in Bulgaria remained largely non-reformed in terms of personnel.

---

7 See Venelin Ganev, *Трудове по обща теория на правото* (Проф: Марин Дринов', СИБИ, 1998).

8 See Lubomir Vladikin, *Курс по общо държавно право: част първа*, 3 доп. изд. (София: Университетска печатница, 1940) and *Общо учение за държавата* (София: 1940 част втора). See also his *Организация на демократичната държава* (София, 1937).

9 See Stefan Balamezov, *Конституционно право* (Част 1, 2, 3) (Софи-Р: София, 1993).

Formalism came in handy in this situation: it formed the basis of the argument that political identities and convictions do not play a role in judicial work.

This was the historical background against which the BCC developed its minimalist, under-theorized approach to jurisprudence. The analysis starts with the question of the legitimacy of judicial minimalism in the context of a society in transition. There are certain tensions between the search for under-theorized solutions to disputes and the ideals of equality before the law and the rule of law more generally. After the theoretical discussion, two specific case studies from the jurisprudence of the BCC are offered. These are meant to provide an empirical setting for a discussion of the advantages and disadvantages of Bulgarian-type judicial minimalism.

The Legitimacy of Minimalism in Theories of Adjudication

The metaphor of Ulysses has been rather extensively used in constitutional theory.[10] Any attempt to employ it yet again requires a very special justification. What the ensuing discussion presents in this regard is a certain novelty. Ulysses is not used here as an illustration of the advantages of pre-commitment.[11] Instead of focusing on the episode with the luring songs of the Sirens (which the ancient hero avoided by asking his crew to tie him to the mast of the ship), here the interest is in Ulysses' role in the Achaean camp during the Trojan War. The argument is that this role is analogous in important ways to the role courts play in contemporary society, and that constitutional judges could draw important lessons for their own work from Ulysses' experience.

Ulysses' ships provided the venue (the court, as it were) where the Achaeans held their legal/political meetings, but this is not a sufficient reason for making him a patron of modern judges. Rather, both the nimble-minded hero and present-day magistrates engage primarily in the resolution of disputes and problem-solving among diverse members of their communities. My specific interest in the Ulyssean policy of conflict resolution lies in the fact that he managed to embody some general sense of unity and common purpose, without ever imposing his own interpretation of this common purpose on the rest of his fellow warriors.

Ulysses never took the centre-stage in the *Iliad*. Yet, without his contribution both the beginning and the end of the whole epic story would have been different. In a similar way, courts and judges are not the major heroes in modern day social and political life. The people as an electorate, the legislatures and their parliamentary majorities, the political parties and the directly elected presidents are the Achilles, Hectors and Agamemnons of our times. These are the actors who

10 See, for instance, Jon Elster, *Ulysses Unbound* (Cambridge: Cambridge University Press, 2000).

11 For an overview of the pre-commitment argument, see Scott J. Shapiro, 'Ulysses Rebound', *Economics and Philosophy*, 18/1 (2002), 157–82.

advance complete programmes and visions for the development of their societies: in John Rawls' terminology, these are the actors best suited to advance different 'comprehensive doctrines' in their society.[12]

Coming closer to familiar debates in constitutional theory, Judge Ulysses can be seen as a more modest alternative to Ronald Dworkin's super-hero Judge Hercules. Hercules, as argued by Dworkin in *Law's Empire*, must represent in all his judgments the law as a system of norms exhibiting integrity of principle. Therefore, he needs super-human capabilities to examine the fit between all the norms and principles in the entire legal system in each and every judgment. In this sense, the judicial theory espoused by Hercules could be called *coherentist*, since it asks the judge to present the legal system as a coherent unity of different norms.

In contrast, Judge Ulysses does not try to elaborate and impose a fully coherent set of common principles on his fellow citizens. Rather, he aims to endorse ad hoc compromises and partial agreements among the heroes in his camp. His goal is to create opportunities for each of them to express and live by values which do not necessarily fit together into a best overall interpretation but which show each of them at his best. He is not unprincipled – it is rather that he does not allow himself to espouse a single, coherent set of norms in the resolution of disputes.

Ulysses' Commitments

Ulysses has two commitments that could be useful for contemporary judges. The first is positive: a special view of one's community and its members. The second is mostly negative: a commitment to prevent a single comprehensive doctrine or any alleged 'best interpretation' of the legal history of the community from being imposed on the rest of his fellow heroes. Both of these commitments make Ulyssean judges abandon the search for thorough legal coherence, although they do not endorse arbitrariness or a lack of justification in its place.

The positive commitment: Ulysses' defence of pluralism Ulysses takes the fact of pluralism seriously – he believes that 'different citizens do not share the same comprehensive doctrine'.[13] 'Comprehensive doctrine' is a technical term, borrowed from John Rawls, which stands for individuals' most extensive attempts to search for coherence among their beliefs: their attempt to make all their beliefs fit together in an ordered set of principles and considered judgements. A comprehensive doctrine is more extensive than judges' 'working conceptions' or even their full-blown judicial theories, as envisaged by Dworkin's *Law's Empire*. Yet, comprehensive doctrines, understood as wide coherence functions, are

12 J. Rawls, *A Theory of Justice* (Cambridge, MA: Harvard University Press, 1971).

13 Victoria Davion and Clark Wolf, 'Reintroduction: From Comprehensive Justice to Political Liberalism', in V. Davion and C. Wolf (eds), *The Idea of Political Liberalism: Essays on Rawls* (Lanham, MD: Rowman & Littlefield, 2000), p. 4.

important for every Herculean judicial theory: if it is to be thoroughly coherent, it must make use of and rely on some comprehensive doctrine(s), at least as far as it concerns issues of moral justification.[14]

The concept of 'comprehensive doctrine' is important for Ulysses as well. As mentioned above, he treats his fellow heroes as holders of different comprehensive doctrines – the essence of the fact of pluralism. He could be a value-pluralist. Or, more modestly, he could believe that in modern societies it is epistemically very difficult to establish the truth in cases of conflict among competing comprehensive doctrines. In both cases, Ulysses is committed to treating all endorsed comprehensive doctrines in his society as at least *potential* sources of value, from which the community as a whole could benefit.

Having this commitment in mind, the first goal which Ulysses pursues is to create conditions for the enrichment, or at least the preservation, of a plurality of sources of value in his society. Healthy competition among different comprehensive doctrines may be beneficial for societal development, as well as for the establishment of truth.[15]

Secondly, Ulysses is committed to treating the heroes in his camp *justly and fairly*. This means that he takes the fact of pluralism normatively, at least in an important sense: he considers that the diverse holders of comprehensive doctrines deserve respect and should be treated with justice. Ulysses is not only a sophisticated diplomat – he has a genuine normative agenda.

In circumstances of pluralism, it is by no means guaranteed that there is a universal conception of justice and fairness, independent of some comprehensive doctrine for the adjudication of cases of conflict. But, regardless of whether such a neutral and overlapping conception exists, for mortal heroes such as Ulysses, it is dangerous and an expression of hubris to act in its name. The danger consists in the fact that it is most likely that Ulysses would start endorsing a particular partial perspective, rather than a neutral and universal conception of justice. And

14 This is so because, firstly, the determination of the 'purpose' of law cannot be a priori and dogmatically imposed by the coherentist theorist on pain of violation of the 'Neurath boat' argument – that is, that every feature of law must be revisable in the process of constructive interpretation. Gradual changes in the body of law are always possible during the search for coherence – the law boat could be reconstructed at open sea, but only plank by plank. In order for the purpose of law to be revisable, however, the theorist must be prepared to consider questions about the role of law in modern societies, the character of modern legitimacy, the nature of individual rights and so on. Secondly, the requirement for 'moral justification' of the legal norms in 'constructive interpretation' requires from the judges, according to Dworkin's theory, the construction of something like a 'comprehensive doctrine' encompassing their moral beliefs and convictions. The ultimate result of legal interpretations depends on these comprehensive doctrines. Therefore, Dworkin depicts the judges as moral philosophers, ready to search for coherence among their deep moral convictions when trying to present the communal legal history in its best light.

15 Here Ulysses pays a tribute to Mill's view of the role of freedom of speech in modern societies.

if a judge imposes a conflict resolution procedure grounded in a *particular* rather than a *universal* comprehensive doctrine, he would fail both to take the fact of pluralism seriously and to respect the diverse holders of comprehensive doctrines in his society.

Therefore, the Ulyssean strategy must be minimalist and non-coherentist – the idealized judge must try to follow some minimal normative principles, principles not exclusively tied to a particular comprehensive doctrine. Thus, the major normative constraint of non-coherentist, Ulyssean jurisprudence must be as follows:

> Principle of Economy (EP): The justification for the method of resolution of adjudicative disputes among competing comprehensive doctrines should be grounded in as few elements of comprehensive doctrine as possible. In no case should the conflict resolution procedure be justified by a particular comprehensive doctrine taken as a coherent whole.

This principle should apply both to individual judgments and to adjudication over time – if it is impossible to justify an individual decision without reference to a particular comprehensive doctrine, the court should make sure that this doctrine does not prevail in its jurisprudence as a whole. In every dispute, no matter how it is resolved, there will be winners and losers. The EP tries to minimize the losses of the losers and the gains of the winners. In this sense, it is a modestly conservative principle leading to the reduction of the number of 'winner-takes-all' situations. The conservative character of the principle reflects well the institutional role of courts as secondary heroes – they should not revolutionize political life, but should bring calm and reason to the disputes of highly controversial problems. In short, the EP has a deflationary effect – it is meant to prevent particular controversies from being blown out of proportion.

The negative commitment: techniques of avoiding global coherence The rationale of EP is to prohibit the imposition of a particular comprehensive doctrine in the procedure for conflict resolution. It has been admitted that reference to *elements* of some comprehensive doctrine is unavoidable in justifying a resolution to a conflict. The question for the Ulyssean judge, however, is how to prevent such reference from leading to the endorsement of a comprehensive doctrine in its entirety.

Comprehensive doctrines, as already stated, are wide coherence processes or reflective equilibria between the totality of our considered judgments and general principles. In adjudication, comprehensive doctrines are equilibria between the totality of legal norms and their principles of justification. This being so, there could be two possible strategies of preventing the imposition of a *whole* comprehensive doctrine through reference to some of its (controversial) *elements* in a legal dispute:

- *Localization of implications by subject-matter* (L): Coherent comprehensive doctrines presuppose horizontal (from department to department) congruence between their elements. *Localization* is the strategy of considering only the most immediately relevant implications of a given element of a comprehensive doctrine for a particular dispute. The element should be stripped of its implied relations of justification with other elements of the comprehensive doctrine.
- *Discontinuity of generalization* (D): A coherent comprehensive doctrine presupposes vertical congruence between its elements as well – from the most concrete to the most abstract. The strategy of *discontinuity* requires that the introduction of an element at a lower level of generality from a comprehensive doctrine does not automatically introduce all elements of higher orders of generality, which justify it in a particular comprehensive doctrine. Discontinuity holds in the opposite direction as well – the introduction of a general principle does not necessarily entail all its concrete instances as specified by a particular comprehensive doctrine.

The Principle of Economy (EP), L and D permeate legal practice and the methods of adjudication used by judges. The very existence of *legal doctrines* within different branches of law, as well as within one and the same branch, are actually an implementation of the EP, L and D. Constitutional law itself is divided into different, relatively autonomous areas, such as freedom of speech, rights' protection, separation of powers and so on. The general rationale behind these doctrines is to limit the scope of judges' considerations to include only the most relevant legal as well as moral considerations, and thus *localize the implications* and *discontinue any generalizations* that these considerations entail.

EP, L and D are the major tenets of Ulyssean jurisprudence. In brief, Ulysses' secret amounts to rejection of global coherence, and abandoning the search for thorough vertical and horizontal integrity of the system of norms, according to which conflicts are to be resolved. Coherence for Ulysses is welcome if it happens to be the result of his judgement: he is not unduly bothered, however, if his judgements do not ultimately achieve the full substantive congruence required by Dworkin's 'law as integrity'. Of course, Ulysses is not so unsophisticated as to allow for logical inconsistency among his judgements, but this is mostly where his interest for 'integrity' dries up.

Application of the Principles of Minimalist Adjudication

What should a judge do, then, in order to emulate Ulysses? Below are some of the most basic rules, supported by examples of their application, which a judge, inspired by EP, L, and D, should follow:

a. It is not necessary to have *all* general constitutional principles clearly defined and made to fit with one another in order to resolve a dispute involving legal rules at a lower level of generality. For instance, a decision on the right of the members of an ethnic minority to use their native language in schools and public buildings could be based, not on a general theory about the existence (or lack thereof) of minority rights, but on the relationship between those rights and national sovereignty and so on. The court, in my view, may legitimately leave some of these questions open, and resolve the case on the basis of (for instance) the right to freedom of speech or academic autonomy. By leaving the more general questions open, the court will simply leave the future clear for both the supporters of minority rights and the believers in individual rights and civic citizenship. After all, both of these projects for the future of the community seem to be valuable and worthy of being kept on board – both of them are compatible with the option to use native languages in schools.

b. Conflicts at the highest levels of generality (between basic constitutional principles) may sometimes be resolved by means other than a precise interpretation of these principles. Ambiguity between two possible interpretations may be welcome in certain cases. For instance, for a certain period of time (at least), European constitutional courts are well advised to leave the issue of the conflict between national sovereignty and the powers of the EU sufficiently vague and ambivalent. Courts may propose certain policies, but they should not necessarily have a clear overall view of the 'right' balance between these two principles, because it may damage the whole process of European integration or the interests of their own country (the anxiety which the Maastricht case of the German Federal Constitutional Court caused is a case in point). This is not a call for complete deference to the legislature on matters of integration, but a call for the realization of the ambiguous status of the integration process at this moment, which should be reflected in the position of the courts.
c. Decisions involving rules at a lower level of generality should not always be taken into account when a decision about rules at a higher level of generality is being considered. For instance, if a court is to adjudicate a conflict about the constitutional priority of freedom of speech over the right of government to regulate the public media, past decisions granting power to the government to appoint directors of the national media or to determine their personnel policy and programmes and so on may not necessarily count against the right to freedom of speech. Vertical coherence should not even be a consideration, and in particular should not be an overriding consideration in this case.
d. Resolution of a certain conflict at a lower level of generality should not always count towards the elimination of ambiguity at more general levels of rules and principles. For instance, if a constitution is ambiguous on the status and rights of minorities, a decision prohibiting territorial autonomous minority governments should not be taken (necessarily) to count in favour or

against a certain particular interpretation of the general role of minorities and their constitutional status. (This is probably a version of the previous rule.)

e. Conflicts from different legal disciplines or different areas of one and the same discipline should not necessarily be resolved by appealing to the same general principles. The existence of some general principles in one area should not necessarily count in favour of their adoption in other areas. The fact that a minority has been given the right to regulate its cultural affairs should not count in favour of granting the right to this minority to regulate its financial affairs. The lack of a right to regulate police and security matters should not be counted against the right to regulate cultural affairs and so on.

Other more detailed rules may be elaborated on the basis of EP, L and D. For present purposes, it is important to stress the fact that these rules undermine Hercules' effort to achieve both vertical and horizontal coherence. If these principles are sound in certain cases, then Dworkin's 'law as integrity' will not be able to account for their existence.

Ulyssean Jurisprudence and Equality before the Law

There is a danger for the principles of Ulyssean jurisprudence elaborated in the previous section to be viewed as a gateway to arbitrariness in judicial work. A Dworkinian may argue that these principles will ultimately lead to arbitrary 'checker-board' decisions. Ulysses, the argument goes, will be forced to jump from comprehensive doctrine to comprehensive doctrine in order to avoid the dominance of a single perspective in his jurisprudence. By doing so, he would fail to respect well-established legal principles such as equality before the law – citizens would not be judged under one and the same set of norms.

This section will show how such criticism ultimately fails. As argued above, Ulysses abandons coherence not in the name of arbitrariness but in the name of justice. As long as he is deviating from global coherence in the name of creating an environment in which each of the heroes in his community can live by and respect his or her most cherished values, and can pursue his or her most valuable overall goals, Ulyssean jurisprudence will be justified.

In other words, our mythic judge respects his fellow citizens as *equals* in their most fundamental capacity – the capacity to construct their own comprehensive doctrines and to arrange their lives according to their own convictions. It is then a misunderstanding to argue that Ulysses is a champion of arbitrariness – his decisions are ultimately grounded in his commitment to defend justice and fairness.

Questions of Constitutional Policy

Both in the case of Ulyssean and Herculean jurisprudence, the question of judicial competence depends on whether the dispute involves legal questions relating to issues of justice and fairness. Since equality of treatment is an essential part of any doctrine of justice and fairness, the discussion of equality before the law cannot disregard this jurisdictional issue.

In terms of judicial jurisdiction, the Dworkinian scheme is simple: (1) matters of *principle* relating to justice and fairness are within the jurisdiction of the courts and are to be resolved by the imposition of a coherent set of general norms; and (2) matters of *policy* relating to ideas of the common good are to be dealt with by the legislature – for such matters coherence is not so essential.

The Ulyssean division of jurisdiction between the court and the legislature in relation to matters of justice is different. For Ulysses, a central problem of justice is the issue of equal respect for citizens as holders of diverse comprehensive doctrines. In order to ensure such respect Ulysses is bound to consider different types of question, to which Herculean jurisprudence is insensitive. Thus, the Ulyssean taxonomy of areas of jurisdiction is as follows:

a. *Matters of constitutional policy of justice*, which relate to the fundamental issue of non-dominance of a single comprehensive doctrine in a pluralistic society. These matters emerge because of the Ulyssean commitment to the fact of pluralism. Ulysses admits that such problems cannot be dealt with by the application of a coherent set of principles – in a sense, he admits that they are *constitutional policy* questions which need to be adjudicated on the merits of the political situation in his society, without searching for generally applicable norms. Thus, Ulysses separates coherence from justice, at this most fundamental level, and preserves jurisdiction over matters relating to justice, even if they cannot be treated in a globally coherent way, because of the conflict among competing comprehensive doctrines.
b. *Matters of principle*, or matters of local coherence. These are residual issues of justice and fairness which emerge after the major question of equal treatment of holders of comprehensive doctrines has been resolved. In these matters, Ulysses has to proceed by the construction of an area of local coherence. Having made sure that there is no dominance of a single comprehensive doctrine in the legal system as a whole, Ulysses may pursue 'local coherence' on particular issues, in particular areas, by the construction of local theories (doctrines). This is the most obvious aspect of judicial work: the creation of doctrines of free speech in the public media, equal economic opportunity in the banking sector, restitution of agricultural lands and so on.
c. *Matters of legislative policy*, which relate to the enforcement of different views about the common good. These are matters of *legislative policy*, which Ulysses leaves at the discretion of the legislature. If a particular

case raises *only* issues of legislative policy, without involving matters of (1) constitutional policy and (2) principles, Ulysses defers the case to the legislative branch.

The focus on coherence and integrity in Dworkin's theory leaves constitutional policy questions out of the jurisdiction of Hercules. Justice and coherence are intertwined in Herculean jurisprudence and, in this sense, the problem of the constitutional policy of justice cannot even be raised in a coherentist theoretical framework. This is a major weakness of Dworkin's theory of adjudication, which could lead to troubles and disregard of specific social groups in some plural societies, where conceptions of justice are hotly contested. Post-communist Europe provides a good test case for this claim.

Equality before the Law in the Jurisprudence of the Bulgarian Constitutional Court (BCC)

The Bulgarian Constitution, Article 6, states:

> (1) All people are born free and equal in dignity and rights.
>
> (2) All citizens are equal before the law. Prohibited are all restrictions on the rights or privileges, based on race, nationality, ethnicity, sex, origin, religion, education, convictions, political identification, personal and social status, or personal wealth.

The discussion thus far has suggested that there are crucial matters from the point of view of equality of treatment which cannot be dealt with by a single, coherent theory of justice and fairness embodied in the law. The EP, introduced earlier in the chapter, prevents the imposition of a single comprehensive doctrine in judges' jurisprudence. If equality emerges as a problem both at the level of constitutional policy and at the level of matters of principle (local coherence), it becomes necessary to distinguish between two types of equality questions. Firstly, there is the question of which constitutional *policy* would ensure equality among holders of different comprehensive doctrines. Secondly, there is the question of what particular *doctrines* of equality before the law exist in a given jurisdiction.

The difference between these two questions became apparent soon after the BCC was established. In the period 1990–1992 the issue of equal treatment gained considerable importance in Bulgaria, when the conflict between two interpretations of the principles of the new Constitution started to take shape. On one hand, the Constitution was understood by the former communists as an instrument of legalization of entitlements stemming from the previous regime. Property rights, positions, pension rights and so on, acquired during communist rule, were, according to this view, to be taken as fully legitimate. On the other hand, the political forces around the reform-oriented parties – the Union of

Democratic Forces (UDF) and its allies – were reluctant to grant legitimacy to many entitlements acquired under the old regime. Thus, most of the cases relating to equality before the law in the early jurisprudence of the BCC were in fact clashes between two different comprehensive doctrines, having largely different positions about the communist legacy in Bulgarian society.

Since, as it will be shown below, many such cases were brought before the BCC in 1992, at one point the judges were asked to interpret the general meaning of the equality clause – Article 6 of the Constitution. The request was on the edge of inadmissibility, because the petitioners had not specified a precise question for interpretation, but rather asked for a general clarification of the meaning of the provision. The judges ultimately considered that interpretation was necessary, and held the following:[16]

a. The equality of all citizens includes their equality before all normative acts.
b. The forbidden grounds for discrimination are enumerated exhaustively in Article 6(2).
c. Privileges are created for the protection of children, the elderly, the mentally or physically handicapped, for the elimination of existing inequality, and for the sake of the specific duties of certain officials, who are relieved from penal liability.[17]

Although seeming to repeat almost verbatim the constitutional provisions, this holding spelled out the constitutional policy of the judges in relation to the conflict between the two aforementioned comprehensive doctrines. The Court refused to endorse either of them expressly, as a *general strategy* of dealing with the communist past, thus, in practice, enforcing the Principle of Economy. Moreover, the Court did not develop a complete, coherent theory of equality before the law, but rather held that there were a number of concrete doctrines of non-discrimination in areas exhaustively stated in Article 6(2). Furthermore, equality, in the view of the Court, was to be sought in relation to (separate) *normative acts*, instead of regarding the legal system as a meaningful and structured whole. Thus, the judges preserved the right to develop concrete doctrines, or areas of *local coherence*, without the elaboration of a general overall theory of non-discrimination, ensuring horizontal coherence among these doctrines in the context of the entire legal system.

---

16 See the dissenting opinion of Judge Milcho Kostov on the inadmissibility of the petition. He argued that: (1) it is pointless to interpret a legal norm if the petitioner is not able to point out the deep principled differences in the content of the interpreted norm; (2) there is no evidence as to the circumstances on which the question for interpretation is based; and (3) the request for interpretation implies that the principle of equality is not properly applied in the Bulgarian legal system, but has no evidence in support of the claim.

17 Decision 14 of 10 November 1992.

In order to understand this concrete constitutional policy, a brief policy analysis of the situation in transitional Bulgaria in the period 1990–1992 is necessary. The ex-communist Bulgarian Socialist Party (BSP) was the dominant political force immediately after the changes started in 1989, and it was the biggest party in the Grand National Assembly, which adopted the Constitution in the summer of 1991. Immediately after that, however, the Union of Democratic Forces – a reform-oriented party – won the parliamentary elections and formed a government with the Turkish minority party, the Movement for Rights and Freedoms (MRF). There was significant ideological tension in Bulgarian society at that time – passions were high on both sides and the future was highly uncertain and unpredictable. Although there was no direct danger of civil war, the Court was facing a task similar to the Ulyssean task in the camp of the Achaeans: that of keeping the heroes together and creating some sense of common enterprise without imposing a single interpretation of the purpose of this enterprise on all of the heroes.

In order to achieve this task, the Bulgarian judges did not want to disappoint the parties to the political conflict in their most fundamental beliefs and convictions, that is, as holders of comprehensive doctrines. Yet, they wanted to preserve jurisdiction over *concrete* disputes between the supporters of these doctrines. Therefore, the judges enforced the EP and refused to pursue global coherence. As a consequence, equality before the law came to be interpreted as a set of specific doctrines of local coherence.

This political background makes the judgment of the BCC intelligible, and it also throws light on the string of cases dealt with by the Court in the period 1991–1992 in relation to Article 6. These cases involved an elaboration on the concrete doctrines of non-discrimination, or the areas of local coherence secured by the judges.

Thus, to start with, the Constitution explicitly prohibited discrimination on the basis of political identification, convictions and social status. However, many people thought that, even without the identification of crimes committed by them, certain rights of the former *nomenklatura* members could be restricted in the name of historical justice. Ideas of de-communization were popular among the emerging non-communist political elite and some quarters of society as well.

This clash of political convictions produced its first constitutional controversy on 27 July 1992 (Decision 8). The law on banks and credit activities had introduced restrictions on the appointment of former leaders of the communist party (and satellite organizations) to the governing bodies of banks. Here, the judges held that the restriction was unconstitutional, as a violation of Article 6(2). In the view of the judges, the equality clause was not subject to any restrictions in this area. They also argued that the restriction imposed by the legislation was in contradiction with the constitutional freedom of vocation (Article 48). Finally, the judges held that: 'The provision contradicts art. 2(2) and art. 6(1) of the International Covenant on

Economic and Cultural Rights and art. 2 and art. 25 of the International Covenant on Civil and Political Rights.'[18]

In a similar fashion, the 1992 law on pensions[19] had introduced restrictions on the eligibility of former members of the communist party elite (the *nomenklatura*) for pensions.[20] Time spent occupying a full-time position in the governing bodies of the Bulgarian Communist Party and its satellite organizations was not to be counted towards the work experience which was one of the factors for the determination of the total amount of the pension. The Court struck down the restriction as a violation of the equal protection clause and the right to social security (Article 51(1)) by arguing that: 'When society has reason to give a negative evaluation of a period in its history, a political regime or particular political organization, it has no right to do so through [...] the violation of basic rights [...].'[21]

The Court further held that it was not certain that the restriction would achieve social justice: moreover, the judges reasoned, there were less restrictive means by which the goal could be achieved. If the goal was to terminate the existence of illegitimate privileges, it should be pursued by constitutional means.

In these two cases, the judges defended the legitimacy of certain entitlements acquired under communism. No general theory of the relation between the communist past and the equal protection clause was discernable from the decisions – a fact revealing the application of the EP in the jurisprudence of the judges.

In the following case, however, the Court had to give a more complex interpretation of equality in a dispute concerning the law on nationalization of the property of the communist party and its satellite organizations.[22] The law was an effort to strip the BSP – the successor of the communist party – of its property. In 1991, although the communist party had changed its name, it was very much unreformed and, because of the enormous property it inherited, it enjoyed a clear advantage in political competition. Therefore, one of the first tasks of the newly elected reformist government of the Union of Democratic Forces was to introduce legislation on the nationalization of the property of the BSP. The Court approved the constitutionality of the law and rejected a number of challenges, the most important of which alleged violation of the equal protection clause.[23]

The Court argued that the major goal of the law was constitutional: to detach the communist party (its successors) from the state, as well as to remove the consequences of illegal enrichment on the basis of state funds. This, in the view of

18 Decision 8 of 27 July 1992.

19 *Official Gazette*, 52 (1992).

20 The organizations falling under the law were the BCP, the Fatherland Union, the Dimitrov Communist Youth Union, and the Union of the Active Fighters against Fascism and Capitalism.

21 Decision 11 of 29 July 1992.

22 *Official Gazette*, 105 (1991).

23 The other allegations of violation concerned the rule of law, separation of powers, political pluralism, the right to property and the right to association.

the judges, was dictated by Article 11(2), according to which no political party or ideology should be proclaimed as representative of the state.

As far as equality is concerned, the Court denied the claim that the law was a violation of Article 6(2). On the contrary, the judges held that it removed an unjustified advantage and privilege. The Court also rejected the claim that the party's right to property had been violated, holding that it was not the legitimate owner of the property. Finally, the Court ruled that: 'Because in the new political conditions, according to art. 11(2) of the Constitution there is no place for a monopoly of one party, the intertwining between party and state must be abolished, and this can be done only by means of legislation.'[24]

The decision was split: three of the judges dissented (mostly the judges appointed by political bodies which the ex-communists controlled). Neno Nenovski argued that the law violated the right to property. In his view, it was impossible to hold simultaneously that the property of these organizations was illegally acquired and illegitimate, *and* that they were merged with the state. This would mean that the state as a whole was illegitimate and illegal: if the opposite was true, at least some of the property of these organizations should be treated as rightfully acquired. Nenovski further held that both the principle of individual rights and the rule of law were violated by the nationalization law.

The other two judges added that the law violated both the separation of powers, because unlawful enrichment was to be dealt with by the ordinary civil courts, and the principle of the 'social state', because the law nationalized the property of the communist trade unions.[25]

The dissenting opinions make clear the absence of a coherent *general* theory in the holding of the majority of the Court, clearly elaborating the relationship between the communist past and the equality principle. The judges relied mostly on the principle of political pluralism, and the prohibition on the entrenchment of a single state ideology in Article 11(2). This provision is a direct entrenchment of the Principle of Equality in the Bulgarian constitutional system, which prevents the imposition of a single comprehensive doctrine as a state ideology. The reliance on separate provisions of the law, without full elaboration on how they relate to each other in this particular decision of the judges, was an application of the principles L and D discussed above – the limitation of implications by subject-matter and the discontinuity of generalizations. As to L, the Court did not specify exactly how this decision was to be made congruent with the previous decisions – for instance, was it relevant that the first two cases concerned individuals and their rights, while this case involved political parties and organizations? As to D, the judges did not advance a coherent theory on the extent to which the communist state was illegitimate and unable to give rise to legal entitlements under the 1991

24 Decision 9 of 27 July 1992.

25 See dissenting opinions of Judges Pencho Penchev and Luben Kornezov to Case 4, 1992.

Constitution. Was it that the whole political establishment was illegitimate or only certain parts of it? The case did not give a clear answer to these issues.

The application of L and D in the jurisprudence of the BCC became even more apparent when the judges re-examined their interpretation of the equality clause in a case concerning the constitutionality of restrictions on the right of particular groups of academics to be elected to governing positions in universities. In 1992 the National Assembly adopted a law introducing 'temporary additional requirements' for members of the governing bodies of major scientific organizations and the Supreme Commission of Attestation (a body conferring academic degrees).[26] According to the law, particular groups of academics – who had occupied high communist party positions under communism – were prohibited for a period of five years from running for high governing positions within academic institutions. The law was challenged as a form of discrimination on political grounds.

However, in contrast with the previous cases (the bank and pension laws), the Court here held that the law is constitutional because: 'The discrimination is not on the basis of [that] enumerated in art 6(2) criteria.'[27]

The Court held that 'professionalism' was the sole ground of discrimination in this case, not political beliefs and convictions. The judges in fact argued that people who engaged in activities foreign to the essence and goals of science, serving political and ideological purposes, had an inferior standing in terms of professional (academic) qualifications. As an additional argument the Court held that: 'The possibility to be a member of the governing bodies of the academic institutions is not a right – therefore, there were no violation of constitutional rights.'[28]

Both arguments tread on shaky ground. It is difficult to accept that 'professionalism' was the major consideration of the legislature in adopting the law; on the contrary, it is quite clear that it was a part of the 'de-communization' programme of the non-communist government, aimed at restoring historical justice. In a way, the Court decided to side-step its own ruling that the negation of a particular historical period should be done in a constitutional way.[29] In this light, its second argument about the lack of a constitutional violation due to the non-existence of a right to be elected to a governing position also seems quite controversial. After all, the Constitution explicitly declares freedom of vocation (Article 48(3)) and the right to labour (Article 48(1)) as basic rights. These provisions clearly cover the discussed case, and the judges needed to make a better argument in order to explain whether or not these rights had been violated. The mere statement that there was no right to occupy a governing position was

26 The law was published in the *Official Gazette*, 104 (1992).

27 Decision 1 of 11 February 1993.

28 Ibid.

29 See the discussion of the pension law above.

not sufficient justification. Not surprisingly, the decision provoked a number of dissenting opinions, which raised similar points.[30]

The real problem with this decision was not the lack of a coherent theory on the relationship between the communist past and the principle of equality. The problem was not the application of L and D either. Rather, it was the failure of the judges to ground their particular decision in a constitutional provision by means of a convincing argument. They could have resorted to the principle of non-dominance of a single ideology in public life (principle of pluralism – Article 11(2)), for instance, by arguing that the entrenchment of people from the former regime in the highest academic positions would lead to de facto endorsement of a certain ideology in an area crucial to the autonomy of the public sphere – academia. No matter whether this argument were ultimately convincing, it would at least be relevant for the justification of the decision. But instead, the judges resorted to arbitrary and artificial distinctions between this case and previous cases.

Having this in mind, it should be stressed that the principles of Ulyssean jurisprudence – EP, L and D – are not satisfied by arbitrary and artificial distinctions or by avoidance of relevant arguments. These are principles of *justification* after all, which need relevant and plausible arguments in their application.[31]

Testing the Cement of the Community: Regulation of Ethnic Political Parties and Ethnic Minority Rights

Bulgaria is a small country on the south-eastern periphery of Europe. Its history during the twentieth century was turbulent indeed: a long period of Russian-sponsored communist rule was preceded by a chaotic time of shaky democracy amid authoritarian spells of monarchic government. During the 1980s, the communist regime in Bulgaria induced a significant ethnic conflict when it forced Turks and gypsies living in Bulgaria to adopt Bulgarian names, before, in 1989, effectively expelling around 400,000 Turks from Bulgaria to Turkey.

30 See the dissenting opinions of Judges Nenovski, Zhabinska, Penchev, Kornezov and Arabadziev. Along with the violation of the right to labour and the equal protection clause, other unconstitutional elements found by the judges in the law were violation of academic autonomy, violation of international treaties and violation of precedent (the pension case). A strong argument put forward concerned the implicit introduction of the notion of 'collective guilt' through the law. Judges Nenovski and Kornezov argued for an individualized approach, taking into account the merits of every case.

31 The lack of a general theory about the communist legacy and its legitimate and illegitimate elements has not prevented the Court from condemning specific and clear abuses under the old regime. Thus, the application of EP, L and D per se has never led to a lack of position or arbitrariness in the jurisprudence of the Court. A case in point is the controversy surrounding the restoration of the property rights of ethnic Turks, forfeited during the anti-Turkish campaigns of the communist regime in the 1980s.

At the end of the twentieth century, with the collapse of the Berlin Wall, Bulgaria adopted a new Constitution (1991), established a Constitutional Court and set out to promote the principles of modern Liberal democracy: competitive elections, a market economy and protected human rights. The original names of the ethnic Turk citizens were restored, they were compensated for the expulsion and most of those who had been expelled returned to the country.

Against this general background of improved and friendly majority–minority relations, the 1991 Constitution included a provision banning the establishment of political parties on an ethnic and religious basis (Article 11(4)).[32] Thus, the Turks living in Bulgaria and some other minorities seemed to be prohibited from having their own parties running in democratic elections.

On this matter, in terms of *constitutional policy*, in 1992 the BCC adopted the strategy of non-exacerbation of the ethnic tension in society. For this purpose, it refused to endorse either nationalistic readings of the constitutional text, or readings stressing extensive and clearly defined minority rights. The application of the EP, L and D – the principles of Ulyssean jurisprudence – were quite instrumental in this regard. Ultimately, the judges left the issue of the overall reading of the Constitution to a large extent indeterminate, and thus did not disregard the most fundamental beliefs and aspirations of competing political forces. Yet they managed to eradicate the most troubling forms of oppressive majoritarianism.

As to the *matters of principle*, the BCC has developed a series of concrete doctrines of militant democracy, minority language rights and so on. Without necessarily fitting into a single coherent picture, they have managed to restrain the government and the political majority in this area of governance, which is very susceptible to oppressive majoritarianism.

Decision 4, 1992: The Constitutionality of the Movement for Rights and Freedoms

In the first case under review, 'The Constitutionality of the Movement of Rights and Freedoms' (MRF), a predominantly Turkish-by-membership party was challenged before the BCC immediately after the first elections were carried out under the new 1991 Constitution. The BCC dealt with the question of whether the MRF fell under the prohibition of establishment of political organizations on ethnic and religious grounds (Article 11(4) and Article 44(2)), and whether its activity was directed against the sovereignty and national security of the country, as well as the unity of the nation. The challenge was sponsored by parliamentary representatives of the Bulgarian Socialist Party (the former communists), who were trying to capitalize on the nationalistic feelings among large parts of the

32 This seems to be a feature of Balkan constitutionalism – a similar prohibition exists in the constitution of Turkey as well. The Greek and Macedonian constitutions also contain provisions against extremist and secessionist parties.

Bulgarian population; the socialists had been the major advocates for the inclusion of the ban in the 1991 Constitution.

In the central part of the argument, the judges admitted for consideration the challenges based on the general constitutional principle of Article 11(2) – the prohibition against establishing parties on an ethnic and religious basis. In their reading of this constitutional provision, the judges interpreted the various prohibitions contained in it as a single 'militant democracy clause' aiming to protect the constitutional democratic order.[33] They argued that the ban was directed generally against parties which threaten the constitutional order: from their wording, it was not clear what *separate* role the 'ethnic, racial and religious' element of the ban played, if it had any such role at all:

> The placing together in Art. 11(4) of the prohibition of establishing political parties on ethnic, racial, and religious grounds and the 'prohibition' of establishing political parties which aim to come to power through violent means, gives grounds for the conclusion that the former prohibition also has a protective function and aims to defend the state and state power from any extreme consequences, which might result from the development of a process of ethnic, racial, or\and [sic] religious confrontation [...] Being erected on the idea of the unity of the Bulgarian nation, the Constitution [...] simultaneously recognizes the existence of religious, linguistic, and ethnic differences [...] [T]he [Constitution] does not aim to establish a prohibition directed against a certain category or categories of persons distinguished by their ethnic, racial, or religious characteristics, but to disallow the establishment and functioning of political parties in a rigid frame defined by ethnic, racial, or religious characteristics, as well as parties inaccessible to persons lacking these characteristics.[34]

The judges further stressed the *open* and *voluntary* character of the MRF, demonstrated by its internal regulations, the membership of its governing bodies and parliamentary caucus, as well as by the presence (although by no means significant) of representatives of different ethnic groups among its rank-and-file members (the membership of the party was predominantly ethnic Turkish). The Court also examined the electoral platform of the Movement and ruled that, although it had set for itself the goal of amending the Constitution, and although it

33 The 'militant democracy clause' in German constitutional law is a doctrine that allows for the limiting of constitutional rights if their exercise threatens the free democratic order. (For instance, Article 21(2) of the basic law, declaring the unconstitutionality of political parties 'seeking to impair or abolish the free democratic order or endanger the existence of the Federal Republic of Germany [...]'.) See Kommers, *The Constitutional Jurisprudence of the Federal Republic of Germany,* 2nd edn (Durham, NC: Duke University Press, 1997), 217–18.

34 Neno Nenovski (ed.), Конституционен съд, Юриспруденция, 1991–1996 [Jurisprudence 1991–1996] (Sofia: Colpi, 1997), 52.

had used the term 'minority' (not mentioned by the Constitution), the organization had not violated the basic principles of the Constitution. The BCC ultimately held that the party *did not threaten the constitutional order* and dismissed all challenges against it.

The political soundness of the decision of the BCC is beyond question: the judges prevented the escalation of ethnic tension in Bulgaria at a time when the new constitutional order was far from established. The judges also diluted an express constitutional ban, which was embarrassing and damaging for the international reputation of the country. Not only was the result of the decision politically sound, but the constitutional reasoning involved was also correct, though not based on coherence considerations.

First, the judges avoided defining and elaborating on general concepts such as 'minority rights' and their relationship with the principles of the 'unity of the nation', 'national sovereignty' and 'democracy'. In so doing they employed the EP and D principles of constitutional adjudication. Their decision *discontinued generalizations* (D) by refusing to elaborate on all the abstract and general constitutional concepts implicated in the case, such as 'minority' and 'national sovereignty'. Furthermore, the judges did not answer fully the question of what it is to have a party established on an 'ethnic basis'. In short, from a Herculean point of view, their decision was a big disappointment, and a missed chance to create clarity in such an important area of Bulgarian constitutional law.

By contrast, Ulysses would have reasons to be content with the decision. Had the judges entered into all of these issues, they would not only have had to deal with the obvious and overwhelming nationalistic bias of the drafters of the Constitution, but would also have had to engage in ever deeper philosophical disputes between (colour-blind) civic republicanism stressing individual rights and group-rights-oriented forms of liberal nationalism. All of these philosophical debates are most interesting and have huge implications for the coherence of Bulgarian constitutionalism; yet their ultimate resolution (either way) could have been dangerous in the particularly unstable situation in Bulgaria a few years after the fall of communism.[35]

The case was ultimately resolved on the basis of a simple test of unconstitutionality: whether the MRF threatened the existing constitutional order. On this issue, the judges created a doctrine of *local coherence*, grounded in a limited number of principles. They held that, as long as the party programme and activities were not directed at the subversion of the constitutional order or at its violent change, and as long as the party was not exclusive and closed to members of other ethnic groups, it was not a danger to the constitutional order. Global interpretations and implications of the decision for global interpretations were avoided.

---

35 For the utility of strategies 'economizing' in terms of justification, see Janos Kis, *Constitutional Democracy* (Budapest: Central European University Press, 2003), 165–66.

Decision 1, 2000: The Constitutionality of OMO Ilinden-PIRIN

Followers of Ulysses, including the BCC, can make mistakes. Ulyssean jurisprudence may lead to decisions made on the basis of wrong policy considerations, since it leaves a degree of discretion to judges in the adoption and application of their constitutional policies.

Eight years after the MRF decision, the BCC judges faced a challenge against the constitutionality of a tiny Macedonian party. The challenge took place after the 1999 local elections, in which the party concerned – OMO Ilinden-PIRIN – collected only around 2,000 votes and managed to win only one mayoral place in a small village. Understanding the issue of the Macedonian national identity requires a long and complex discussion; yet, it is probably not too controversial to say that the modern Macedonian nation appeared only in the twentieth century on the basis of the Slavic population living between Bulgaria, Serbia, Greece and Albania. As the local elections in 1999 showed, a small part of the population in southern Bulgaria was willing to identify as Macedonian both politically and nationally.

The challengers in this case argued that the establishment and operation of OMO Ilinden-PIRIN violated Article 11(4) and Article 44(2) of the Constitution, as well as the constitutional principles of the preamble declaring the duty to protect the Bulgarian statehood and national unity. It was alleged that the party had a 'separatist character' and that its goals ran against the unity of the Bulgarian nation. One argument invoked by the petitioners was that the party was the successor of an independent Macedonian association OMO Ilinden (formed in 1990), whose goal was the 'founding of a Macedonian state through the secession of the Pirin region from Bulgaria'.

First, the judges considered the issue whether the registration of the party violated Article 11(4) of the Constitution. They held that: 'There is no separate Macedonian ethnos in the Republic of Bulgaria. Because of that, the Court does not find evidence that the registration of this organization violates Article 11(4) of the Constitution and the prohibition to establish parties on ethnic ground[s].'[36]

It seems that, at this point, the Court had reached the right conclusion for the wrong reason. The logic of this argument advanced an interpretation of Article 11(4) which is far less justifiable than the interpretation of this provision from the 1992 MRF decision. According to the new reading, Article 11(4) prohibited *minority ethnic groups* from establishing political parties. However, since there was no Macedonian ethnic group in the country (in the view of the judges) the Court did not find a violation of Article 11(4) in the OMO case.

In contrast, the old interpretation did not enter into the issue of what an ethnic minority party was, or the issue of whether there was a particular minority in the country. Rather, it simply permitted the registration of parties, as long as they were inclusive and did not threaten the constitutional order.[37]

36 Decision 1, 2000.

37 In the following paragraph, however, the judges resorted to a further argument, echoing the rationale of the previous doctrine: 'On the other hand, it could be asserted

Despite the dubious merit of the reasoning up to this point, the first three parts of the decision seemed to be more or less consistent with, or at least not to directly contradict, the doctrine of constitutionality of parties elaborated in the MRF judgment. The error in the fourth part of the decision, though, was far from insignificant. There the judges developed another doctrine on the unconstitutionality of parties based not on Article 11 but on Article 44(2), which contained a prohibition on parties whose activity was 'directed against the *sovereignty, the territorial integrity of the country*, and the unity of the nation'. The BCC held that OMO violated this part of the provision concerning the integrity of the country. The evidence revealing the violation, in the view of the judges, included the following:

a. A gathering of OMO supporters in 1991 and the adoption of a declaration calling for, among other things, the granting of political autonomy to Pirin Macedonia, the withdrawal of the Bulgarian 'occupational' armed forces and the disbanding of Bulgarian political parties.
b. The publication of two maps indicating the inclusion of Bulgarian lands in the territory of the Republic of Macedonia in 1993 and 1995.
c. Seven interviews, memoranda and press-conference statements in 1998 and 1999 by the leaders of OMO, in which they, among other things, 'treat[ed] the Pirin region as part of Macedonia [...] and agree[d] that the region should be cut off from Bulgaria, although they claim[ed] that the time for this ha[d] not come yet [...]'.
d. Two campaign statements of the leaders of the party (during the 1999 local elections), in which they threatened to raise the issue of secession in case their requirements were not fulfilled by the government.
e. Finally, the Court accepted as evidence a 1999 letter written on behalf of the party from a member of its governing body to the Open Society Institute, Budapest. The letter contained claims for the political autonomy of the Pirin region and a statement that the rights of the Macedonians ranked higher than Bulgarian national sovereignty. (After the admission of the letter as evidence, OMO denounced it as an expression of its official policy.)

---

that a party is based on ethnic ground, when its founding documents do not allow for membership of representatives of other ethnic groups. As evident from Art. 8 of the founding document of OMO Ilinden-PIRIN, all Bulgarian citizens can be its members.' The argument reinforced the requirement of 'party openness' and 'inclusiveness' from the 1992 decision but this time, it seemed, the Court considered openness not as a decisive consideration but, at best, as a supporting one. The central point the judges made was that in Bulgaria there was no Macedonian minority and therefore there could be no party on an 'ethnic Macedonian ground'. From their reasoning it was unclear whether, had there been a Macedonian minority in Bulgaria, it would have been sufficient for OMO to be open to other minorities in order to be recognized as constitutional. If openness is sufficient, the lack of a Macedonian minority argument would be irrelevant anyway – the judges' first argument would be redundant.

Not only did the Court hold that this evidence was sufficient to demonstrate that the activity of OMO Ilinden violated Article 44(2) of the Constitution – the part aimed at protecting the *territorial integrity* of Bulgaria – but the judges further argued that every separate piece of evidence constituted a sufficient ground for the establishment of such a violation. The Court expressed the view that no '*effective* impact on the protected [... territorial integrity] is necessary' for a declaration of the unconstitutionality of a certain political activity under Article 44(2). In other words, declarations, interviews, letters and statements – all of them forms of *speech* – could be interpreted as unconstitutional activity sufficient for the prohibition of a political party.

> The restrictions on statements, containing calls inflaming hostility, is based on the enshrined Constitutional values of tolerance, mutual respect, as well as the prohibition to propound hatred on racial, national, ethnic or religious ground[s]. These restrictions do not deny protection to the variety of contradictory beliefs, reflecting the competition of ideas and opposing view points.[38]

> The [hatred restrictions ...] definitely target statements, which affect the interests of social groups, formed on the basis of different characteristics – racial, ethnic, religious, political, national, social, sexual, and so on. The exclusion of such statements from the range of protected speech is consistent with the universal value of tolerance proclaimed in the Preamble to the Constitution, with the requirement of religious tolerance (Art. 37,1), and with the prohibition on the creation of organizations, whose activity is directed toward the inflaming of racial, national, ethnic, or religious hatred (Art. 44(2)).[39]

The political effects of the decision were purely negative. It contributed to the cooling of the relationship between Macedonia and Bulgaria. It is likely that the BCC's decision will also prove to be an embarrassment for Bulgaria, because the country is likely to lose the case brought by OMO in the European Court of Human Rights (ECHR).

From a normative point of view, both Ulysses and Hercules would find the judgment wrong, though possibly for different reasons. Hercules would probably have to construct an argument, according to which the best overall interpretation of the history of the Bulgarian community allows for the political participation of national minorities. Here Hercules might provide a definition of 'minority' that includes the Bulgarian Macedonians. Another route of Herculean reasoning would be to deny the existence of a Macedonian minority, even the possibility of political representation of minorities under the 1991 Constitution, but to hold that the party was banned for speech acts or acts of expression, which are constitutionally protected. On some such basis, a Herculean judge could have dismissed the case

38 Decision 7, 1996, Neno Nenovski, op. cit., at 140.

39 Ibid., at 145.

against OMO. On both versions, the judges should have delved into a plethora of philosophical/historical questions about the existence and scope of minority rights, and about the best interpretation of Bulgarian constitutional history as a whole. The judges should have sought vertical and horizontal coherence, by showing how their decision fitted best with the principles of territorial integrity, freedom of expression, unity of the nation, the right to association and so on. Every point of interpretation left open or ambiguous would have counted as a weakness of the Herculean decision.

Ulysses would have taken a different route. He would have stuck with the 1992 MRF decision and the 'local doctrine' of the constitutionality of parties developed within it. Thus, he would have avoided elaborating on many complex issues about the place of minority rights in the best overall interpretation of Bulgarian constitutional history. Ulysses would have asked a simple question: was the party a threat to the constitutional order?

The answer to this question is patently clear: OMO Ilinden could not have been a threat to the constitutional order. Its programme did not preach a violent overthrow of the government, it was not closed to other members of the public, and it was not involved in any sort of criminal or subversive activities. Moreover, this was a party with the electoral support of just 2,000 people, which *physically* was not enough to present a danger to the Bulgarian state and constitutional order in 2000. Therefore, the paranoid fears of the BCC – based largely on evidence concerning acts of speech – had to be rejected.

Ulysses would likely be wise enough to leave aside other speculations about the impact of his decision on the possible overall interpretation of the history of the Bulgarian state and legal system, as long as he had eliminated the most oppressive nationalistic or extremist readings of the Constitution. His example neither promotes nor disadvantages any overall interpretation of this history; he would be willing to keep both Bulgarian and Macedonian broader historical viewpoints on board. He would not want to blow a trivial dispute about a practically insignificant marginal party out of proportion. Ulysses was not pedantically obsessed with the finding of global principles.

Conclusions

The judicial minimalism of the BCC has had a profound impact on the legal culture of the country. One of the most visible negative outcomes of this interpretative strategy was the opening up of certain disparities between the jurisprudence of the BCC and the ECHR.[40] Further, the BCC has acquired a somewhat Delphic

40 The main disparity between the Strasbourg jurisprudence and the BCC is visible on the issue of the dissolution of political parties, and specifically on the case of OMO Iliniden discussed above. See *United Macedonian Organization Ilinden-Pirin and Others v. Bulgaria* (Application no. 59489/00) 20 October 2005, Final 20/01/2006.

character – in terms of the unpredictability of its decisions – which does not encourage ordinary courts actively to address the BCC through the procedure of referral (concrete review). On the more positive side, the BCC has prevented certain constitutional disputes from being blown out of proportion – there have, in fact, been very few cases of the Court which have become key to the ideological identification of political parties (in the manner of *Roe v. Wade*[41] *or Buckley v. Valeo*[42] in a US context, for instance).

From the point of view of constitutional theory, one of the main questions which minimalism raises is whether it is capable of encouraging a culture of respect for the Constitution and general foundational norms of the Bulgarian community. Some scholars have argued that respect for constitutional norms in Bulgaria is generally very low. For example, in their thoughtful paper 'Invisible contexts, invisible barriers: The limits of the normative explanation of constitutional change',[43] Ralitsa Peeva and Ivan Krastev set out to cast doubt on the very possibility of a general normative theory of constitutionalism in Bulgaria. Their main argument was that the elaboration of such a general theory would require a 'common context of different constitutional choices'. Such a common context, they argued, does not exist, which places a decisive limit on 'normative constitutionalism' and disables it as an analytical and explanatory tool. If one is to understand the processes of constitution-making, as well as the workings of constitutionalism, detailed contextual and historical analysis of the strategic choices of different actors should be carried out. In this analysis even minute contextual factors could have enormous explanatory power and would (sometimes) override the abstract, principled explanations of 'normative constitutionalism'.

Peeva and Krastev supported their major claim by embarking on an analysis of five specific choices of Bulgarian constitutionalism: the timing of the constituent assembly; the inclusion in the constitution of a ban on ethnic parties; the inclusion of a vice-presidential institution; the number of MPs; and the age, citizenship and residency conditions for presidential candidates. In all of these choices, the authors argued, the constitution-drafters were not led by general normative principles of constitutionalism, but by strategic considerations in the process of competing and bargaining with their political opponents. All of these choices were the result of deals, compromises and sometimes the consideration of seemingly irrelevant facts (such as the seating capacity of the plenary hall of the building of the National Assembly). Therefore, the authors claimed, general normative theory cannot account for or explain these specific choices, a fact which illustrates its intrinsic limitations.

41 410 US 113 (1973).

42 424 US 1 (1976).

43 In Stefan Voigt and Hans-Jurgen Wegener (eds), *Constitutions, Markets and Law: Recent Experiences in Transition Economies, New Thinking in Political Economy* (Cheltenham: Edward Elgar, 2002).

Peeva's and Krastev's paper contributes to the ever popular cause of particularism and contextualism in social sciences. The mistrust in rules and principles and the fascination with 'unintended consequences' which permeate the paper do indeed sharpen some aspects of the authors' political and constitutional analysis. Unfortunately, they also breed a degree of misunderstanding about the nature of constitutionalism, which makes one doubt the ultimate benefits of this methodological trade-off.

Misunderstanding stems from neglect of the fact that constitutionalism presupposes not everything in a polity can be the object of strategic bargaining among political actors. What is more, if everything could be an object of strategic bargaining and trade-offs, as Peeva and Krastev seemed to presume, constitutionalism would simply cease to exist. The authors could well have been right to say that in Bulgaria there is no difference between constitutional and everyday politics, and that 'constitutional bargaining takes place at the level of normal politics rather than at the level of high principles'. Yet, if they were right, their account was an account of the death of constitutionalism in Bulgaria, rather than a sophisticated explanation of its workings.

The analysis of the interpretative strategies of the BCC presented above provides a more optimistic picture of Bulgarian normative constitutionalism. Indeed, the jurisprudence of the BCC is minimalist, particularist and non-coherentist. In a certain sense it is also context-dependent. But these facts do not necessarily mean that this jurisprudence is not justified at a very deep level by fundamental normative principles of constitutionalism, such as respect for pluralism, and individual liberty and self-determination. With the help of the fictional Judge Ulysses, it was argued that minimalist and non-coherentist jurisprudence could ground itself in principles such as EP, L and D, which are derivative of the respect of pluralism. These principles, it was argued, help the Ulyssean judge to treat everyone in his or her community equally in a fundamental sense.

During the 1990s Bulgarian society was deeply ideologically divided and the minimalist jurisprudence of the BCC was quite appropriate for the circumstances. Overall, without antagonizing some of the main parties, the BCC managed to introduce quite progressive policies in many areas (the restitution of land and media regulation, for instance). The BCC helped the ideological transformation of Bulgaria and the consolidation of democracy, without becoming the focus and forum of ideological conflicts. This is not a small achievement by any standard.

One wonders, however, whether judicial non-coherentist minimalism is still appropriate for Bulgaria 20 years after the transition. At present, the country is not ideologically divided. Indeed, party ideologies, programmes and manifestoes play an increasingly marginal role in Bulgarian politics. In such circumstances, the unpredictability of the BCC's jurisprudence has discouraged various players from addressing it. Also, the reduction in ideological tension and the number of disputes has automatically reduced the need for an impartial Ulyssean arbiter to resolve such conflicts. As a result, the caseload of the BCC decreased rather seriously: in 2007–2008, for instance, the court had fewer than 10 cases per year.

Overall, if this institution is to remain viable, it needs to be opened to the public through the introduction of a procedure of individual complaint. It is obvious that institutional actors are no longer interested in addressing the BCC with the same intensity as in the 1990s. Therefore, bringing in the citizenry could revive constitutional disputes. If something like that happens, judicial minimalism and non-coherentism may face different challenges from the ones discussed in this chapter.

Chapter 6
Settling Accounts with the Past, the Conceptualization of Difference and the Dilemmas of the Law-governed State

Grażyna Skąpska

Never Again!

Settling accounts with the past has not only moral but also cognitive importance for the new, post-totalitarian societies in Central and Eastern Europe (CEE). One has to reckon with past legacies and expose the truth about former regimes in order to be faithful to moral standards, denounce crimes and hypocrisy, and disclose local social experiences not only of deprivation and fear, cowardice and cynical opportunism, but also of heroism, in order to reshape the political and legal cultures of post-communist society. One has to initiate the reconstruction around new values and standards. Here, the concept of difference plays a particular role as an important cognitive device of these societies, constitutive for their self-reflection and new self-definition. At stake are important rights, which emerged as a result of dictatorial regime overthrow attempts collapsing in Latin America and Europe: the right to truth, and the right to remembrance. Quite clearly, both of them present important cognitive devices of post-totaliarian or post-dictatorial societies in the reconstruction of their political and civic identities. There is also an important right to justice and to the fulfilment of social expectation that crimes will be punished.

However, from the political point of view, the attitude towards the past still continues to lurk in the shadows of doubt. How should states deal with such persons as Gyula Horn, who was involved in the crushing of the Budapest uprising in 1956 and became Prime Minister of the Hungarian democratic government, or General Jaruzelski, who imposed martial law in Poland in 1981, crushed the Solidarność movement, and yet became President of the new state in 1989?

Moreover, one has to take into account a quite particular legacy of the Round Tables in Central and Eastern Europe as vehicles of 'lawful revolutions', with their stress on legality, understood as protection of certainty and predictability. In this respect, it should be stressed that the new CEE democracies like to inscribe themselves within Western civilization in which the notion of the rule of law – or, in their case, the law-governed state – has emerged and developed. However, they are confronted by legacies of long dictatorship and tasks that are both risky and novel, and, indeed, go beyond the law, or at least beyond the written law literally interpreted. Hence, they have to appeal to extra-legal resources, and to make use of extra-constitutional rules and values wherever these exist in order to deal with the past atrocities. This could be contrary to the mentioned certainty and predictability, and to the predominant positivistic interpretation of the rule of law principle.

One also has to acknowledge the fact that past reckoning brings much temptation to new governments. The desire is to get rid of their political opponents by finding evidence, however feeble, that they collaborated in the functioning of the former system.

Considering these mixed and conflicting goals and pressures, important for the developing legal and political cultures and even for the new identities of post-communist societies, this chapter will debate three fundamental issues surrounding the political and legal transformation in Central and Eastern Europe, and the establishment of the rule of law. It will argue that the attitude towards previous human rights violations is constitutive for the process of differentiation of these societies from that which they do not want to be, and in consequence, for the formation of their new identities. However, both processes – the differentiation and the new identities formation – are challenged by the history of so-called 'peaceful revolutions', and their characterization as 'lawful' or 'constitutional'. This, in turn, has an impact on the very conceptualization of the rule of law and legality. Indeed, the legacy of human rights violations and the particular history of peaceful revolutions in Central and Eastern Europe present an important challenge to the classical conceptualizations of the rule of law, or *Rechtsstaat*, as insufficient and even 'toothless' when confronted with modern, mass-scale crimes and severe human rights violations. Perhaps that is the lesson lawyers can learn from the experiences of Central and Eastern Europe after the collapse of communism in 1989.

This chapter will be based mostly on data from Poland, with references to other countries in the region.

New Democracies and the Concept of Difference: A Critical View

The difference and the process of differentiation present initial steps in the shaping of new socio-political identities after the breakdown of the former regimes. They help the society to form its new identity as a politically organized community and to solve crucial dilemmas inherited from the past.

The concept of difference as a means of identity creation has a long genealogy in philosophy and is a crucial theoretical concept in contemporary sociology. Founded in the relational logic of Immanuel Kant, it was fully elaborated in sociology by Pierre Bourdieu and Niklas Luhmann. In Bourdieu's view, the concept of difference is closely related to that of *habitus* as a set of perceptual (cognitive) schemes through which an individual sees and interprets reality (Bourdieu, 1990: 58; see also Bourdieu, 1996). Consequently, situated in a social space, an individual shapes his own identity in relation to other actors and other social spaces by means of difference. In the theory of Niklas Luhmann, the difference presents a first step – the first operation of a system in its environment –- by which it tries to reflect on itself and build a theory of itself by means of further processes of differentiation initiated by the first one perceived by the system (Luhmann, 1984: 43). The difference means an initial opposition to or contrast with something that the newly created political system is not. For instance, it implies the definition of an individual by reference to inalienable human dignity, as opposed to the concept of an individual as a member of a social class; it defines the social, political and economic orders by their differentiation from the past and from their environment; and it provides crucial ideas about the goals and aims worth attaining. Thus, the conceptualization of a difference presents also the foundation of a new legal order.

The difference has both diachronic and synchronic aspects: it relates to differentiation from the past and from the current environment, a differentiation with respect to time – primarily the past – and space. The first step in the process of historical differentiation answers the question of what the new system is not in order to formulate more questions about: what the new system actually is. With regard to societies trying to build a liberal democracy, it is that initial cognitive operation which differentiates the new liberal-democratic order from undemocratic ones: authoritarian, dictatorial and totalitarian. This enables the steering of internal operations but, above all, facilitates communicative consolidation and the formation of a constitutional and legal community in a new democracy.

Diachronic differentiation represents a key component in the process of the theoretical self-representation and self-conceptualization of new democracies. It leads to the formation of a new political identity for the society – to its new self-definition. In the case of CEE post-communist societies, differentiation from the undemocratic past is even more important than elsewhere because – as members of the European Union – they exist in an environment which they would rather adapt to than differentiate themselves from, at least not with respect to the most important components of European liberal democracies.

For the conceptualization of this initial difference from the past, the phenomenon of rupture is of crucial importance; the rupture, the radical breaking away from the past consists, among other things, of a declaration of some elements of the past as illegal and de-legitimized in contrast with the legal and legitimized present order (Sarjomand, 2003: 23). Thus understood, the 'rupture' often overlaps with a 'constitutional moment' – that particular moment in the life of a politically organized society in which heated debates about new principles of political organization and foundations of a new identity start. 'Ruptures' and 'breakdowns' characterize great modern revolutions. The symbolic representation of rupture was the introduction of the new calendar after the French Revolution, starting with a symbolic 'point zero' in the history of the modern French nation. As emphasized by Zenon Bankowski, the rupture or breakdown of a political system brings about a paradigm shift entailing further rearrangement of the conceptual schemes of the society. This involves: 'changes not only in empirical beliefs but in the language in which this world is described, in goals of inquiry, in epistemic values, and in the standards of rational thought and intelligible explanation' (Bankowski, 1991: xii). Rupture also leads to a rhetorical change, expressed in slogans, analogies and metaphors.

The conceptualization of such a fundamental difference in Central and Eastern Europe was challenged by the very lack of a clear rupture, especially in case of pioneers of the transformation – Hungary and Poland – and the great stress on the legality of them, so characteristic of the Round Tables as events which led to the system collapse. As observed by two prominent authors, 'at least in Poland and Hungary, the break with communism and the building of new regimes has become to an important extent a legal problem, one of the transcendence of party-state legal structures and practices'. Moreover, as both authors stressed, 'the East European transitions did not only aim at constitutionalism and the rule of law, but also the process of change itself which, in all countries with the exception of Romania and Soviet Union, took a constitutional form. This paradoxically involved taking the existing communist constitutions seriously for the first time (an odd proposal of the dissidents!) and using their own mechanisms to produce constitutions with an entirely new spirit' (Arato and Sajó,1991: 101).

Therefore 'Round Tables' were political as well as legal events. As such, they contributed importantly to the inclusion of the rule of law (or rather the law-governed state principle) in post-communist constitutions. It is argued that a high respect for the law constitutes a type of 'civil religion' that indeed 'steps into the shoes of religion in an earlier era' (Dezalay and Garth, 2002). As such, it also legitimizes profound political change in the eyes of the outside world. Concerns with the 'legality' of efforts aimed at dismantling the CEE system prevailed and legality itself proved – besides the notion of 'self-limiting revolutions' – a key component of the semantics promoted by members of the democratic oppositions, setting the events of 1989 apart from earlier revolutions.

The initial description of these events as 'lawful revolutions' came from Hungary – notably from a prominent intellectual and participant of the Hungarian Round Table, Janos Kis, as well as from Kalman Kulcsar, the then Minister of Justice in the still communist government. For the former author, the parties seated at the Hungarian Round Table were mostly interested in securing stability and continuity for the legal order in Hungary (Kis, 1995b). There, the pre-1989 order was not questioned, 'not even for one day' (Kis, 1995a). This position was later strongly supported by the actions of the Hungarian Constitutional Court, especially by its then President, Justice Laszlo Solyom, who often stressed legal stability and certainty as dominant features of the Hungarian change (2000: 20, 21, 39) and himself described it as a 'revolution under the law' (2003: 39).

This attitude was also highly evident in Poland, having been practised by the oppositionists of the Polish RT, even at the price of losing their credentials among the people (Skąpska, 1992). In the then Czechoslovakia, as it is argued, Charter 77 was not a political program, but a 'list of human rights and civil liberties violations by the communist regime' (Přibáň, 1999: 33). In the struggle between the authorities and dissidents in Czechoslovakia, the strategy of the latter was 'legalistic'. This was clearly noticeable even after November 1989. The events of 1989 were characterized by a striking 'persistence of constitutional and legal documents adopted by communist legislation' (Přibáň, 1999: 47). In Czechoslovakia, as in any other CEE country, the slogan of the legal positivists – 'Justice according to the law' – bore strong critical and reconstructive meaning when confronted with the communist appeals to classlessness and the rights of particular social classes, not to mention the revolutionary consciousness of the proletariat. Thus, 'the rule of law became one of the most important revolutionary demands. The revolutionary vocabulary [...] was accompanied by a legal positivistic vocabulary demanding the re-establishment of legality, due process of law and generally binding impartial procedures' (Přibáň, 1999: 45). Similarly, in Poland the legality of the change was summarized in a postulate that the revolution be conducted by legal means (for example, by initiating legal proceedings against the government or sending petitions to human rights organizations) instead of an armed revolt.

In the case of Round Table talks held in Central and Eastern Europe in 1989, legality not only proved a key element in structuring the negotiations and lending a guideline for further change; it was also a crucial component of the whole package of concepts related to liberal democracy as a post-communist transformation *telos* – including human rights, freedoms and liberties, protection of private property and freedom of negotiations.

However, notions of legality and of lawful revolutions respectively could have several meanings. First, they could refer to the legal positivistic meaning of legality – unquestioned formal legality limited by previously existing law and procedures, and characterized by the literal interpretation of legal prescriptions. Second, these lawyers' notions of legality could be supplemented by the protection of human rights, which broadens the legality conceptualization, providing the system change with new semantics which appeal strongly to citizens. It paves a clearly defined path for future development, as in the case of German constitutionalism where the contents of rights are indisputable and their protection cannot be modified via normal politics. Third, the notion of legality could refer not only to human rights but also to the daily life experiences of citizens, linking the liberal ideal with locally rooted interpretations of it. In the second and third case, the notions of legality would import not only a formal, but also an important axiological and sociological rationalization and legitimization to Round Table outcomes. All three notions of legality bring some order to the potential chaos of the overwhelming change.

In the first case of the lawyers' notion of legality, order is protected by current law – that is, in the case of Central and Eastern Europe, by the still communist legal order because of its axiological foundations in principles of legal certainty and predictability. To some extent this is also true with respect to human rights protection, if such rights have already been expressed in communist constitutions, or guaranteed by the then existing law. In the third case of socially bounded notions of legality that extend the narrow lawyers' meaning, this refers to a contextually and even existentially bound order, one which could find resonance in the consciousness of citizens and reflect their expectations of human rights protection and justice. It is rooted in local knowledge and local experiences of people exposed to the functioning of a totalitarian or dictatorial regime. This relationship, between the formalized and general legal language of law and the authentic experiences of people living under communism, represented an important challenge to the interpretation of the rule of law provision when confronted with the task of human rights violations punishment, and the conceptualization of the initial difference.

The anti-communist opposition – predominant in Hungary, but also present in Poland and, to some extent, in other CEE countries – praised binding law as a positive contrast to the legal hypocrisy of late totalitarianism. The members of democratic opposition contrasted it with zealous, revolutionary consciousness, characteristic of preceding revolutions (the French and Bolshevik, in particular).

Especially with regard to the Hungarian Round Table negotiations, the notion of formal legality – and of legal continuity – was supported by the values of legal certainty and predictability (Sajó in Elster, 1996: 78). This adherence to formal legality and the prevailing value of legal certainty became a salient feature of negotiations in other CEE countries, too (with the exception of Romania and the Caucescu trial).

Round Table negotiations were able to pave the way for further institutional development: the compromises struck as a result of the negotiations were subsequently legalized by new parliaments. Hence, the notion of legality took on yet another meaning. The Round Table negotiations were seen as *sui generis* sources of law based on the normative proposition that *pacta servanda sunt*. Thus, the tables were characterized as pre-constitutional or quasi-constitutional events (Elster, 1996: 5), and, as observed with regard to Poland, 'mechanisms created at the RT [Round Tables] have survived the transition and have taken on a life of their own' (Osiatyński in Elster, 1996: 21, 22). Note also that a great deal of legislation, as well as provisions for future constitutions, emerged as a direct result of the demands of communist party representatives at Round Tables.

Considering legality to be one of the most important features in the overthrow of totalitarianism in Central and Eastern Europe, and the changes in the political, constitutional and legal cultures of post-communist societies, conclusions are not easy to reach and appraisals are ambivalent. On the one hand, negotiations were subordinated to existing law and to the meaning of legality as a 'lawyer's formal legality'. Adherence to the law, in effect, was part and parcel of the negotiations. This kind of legality is easily welcomed, especially by societies who would like to return to their daily affairs as soon as possible after years of struggle with an oppressive system and who are tired of the overwhelming politicization of their lives. It is to be questioned whether this kind of legality carries enough transformative potential and bears enough charisma to turn post-communist citizens demonstrating on the streets into members of a future polity composed of active citizens, undertaking responsibility for the future functioning of the state. It is also worth stressing that legality justifies the lack of a clear rupture, with all the consequences of this fact: social, political, mental and moral.

It is still not clear whether the main actors of the Round Tables could have foreseen the social dangers of continuation and preservation, not only of legal institutions in the name of legal certainty and predictability, but also of the political and social relationships lurking behind them, such as vested interests. Former functionaries wanted to protect existing rights and privileges inherited from the former regime, or immunity for gross violations of human rights, or what could be acquired through the privatization of the national economy. Certainly, as I am trying to demonstrate elsewhere, this kind of lawyers' legality is not a good method to protect the important rights to truth and remembrance, not to mention the social expectations of justice.

The most interesting concept of legality not debated at the Round Tables came from the Czech intellectuals. In their powerful critique, the 'socialist legality' concept was seen not only as a rhetorical veil of terror, but as a means of ritualization and petrification of public life, as well as bureaucratization of language, too. Thanks to such authors as Vaclav Havel, as well as other Czech dissident elites, quite novel ethical and existential aspects of law and legality came to be debated: those which referred to the democratic history of pre-war Czechoslovakia, to some indisputable human values and to the moral demands of human existence. One of them was inherent in a slogan of 'living within the truth' as a means of combating the totalitarian system (Havel, 1985).

The Constitutive and Moral Potential of the Difficult Past: The Right to Truth, to Remembrance and to Justice

Let us reflect on the constitutive and cognitive potential of dealing with past human rights violations. A prominent lawyer, the Executive Director of the Inter-American Institute on Human Rights in Latin America, argued that facing and reckoning past human rights abuse constitutes an obligation for new governments. They need to investigate, prosecute and punish; they also need to disclose to the victims and to society all that can be reliably discovered about the circumstances of such crimes, including the identity of the perpetrators and instigators. Such an obligation is translated into a society's right to truth (Mendez, 2009: 39; Roth–Arioza, 1995).[1] This right emerged in an age of gross violations

1 The 1985/86 Annual Report of the Inter American Commission on Human Rights reads:

> 'Every society has the inalienable right to know the truth about past events, as well as the motives and circumstances in which aberrant crimes came to be committed, in order to prevent a repetition of such acts in the future. Moreover, family members of the victims are entitled to information as to what happened to their relatives. Such access to truth presupposes freedom of speech, which

of human rights, giving rise to high numbers of perpetrators, instigators, collaborators and victims, and was formulated to deal with an unprecedented technical capacity of hiding the truth. Thus, the right to truth comprises a civic right of a new type, a response by a civic society to the increasing possibilities of concealing atrocities, destroying evidence and silencing people – behaviour typical of modern dictatorships and totalitarian regimes. As such, it is a most important contribution to interpretation of the law-governed state principle after the collapse of a totalitarian or dictatorial regime.

The right to truth is based on a belief that the truth about the past, if disclosed and disseminated, brings both restitution of dignity to victims and retribution for past atrocities. The right to truth represents a specific form of the broader civic right to information enshrined in every democratic-liberal constitution. In Central and Eastern Europe, such an obligation stems from the conviction that 'living within the truth' is a crucial part of the moral capital with which these societies initiated their transformation towards democracy. If taken seriously, the right to truth serves as crucial guidance in the process of differentiation of the new political system from the previous one. Therefore, the truth about the past is constitutive for new democracies. It contributes to the restoration of victims' dignity and the protection of their rights. Hence, for instance, it helps to redirect post-communist constitutionalism, and post-communist law in general, towards the protection of civic rights. It also comprises an initial step in the process of public self-reflection and of differentiation from the past – the mentioned initial step in the construction of a new political identity after the collapse of a totalitarian regime.

Further, the right to truth is directly and imminently connected with another one: the right to remembrance and to present one's own experiences, in the process of collective memory shaping. The right to remembrance places democratic governments under an obligation to document the particular experiences of individuals and broaden the official version of national history by local experiences. Wrongs must be documented, evidence collected and the 'white spots' of a nation's history filled in order to render the collective memory more democratic and, above all, include the memories of victims. To meet this obligation and protect the right to remembrance, new 'institutes of national remembrance', or similar institutions, have been established in the post-communist societies of Central and Eastern Europe. If protected, these rights to truth and to remembrance contribute to the process which could be labelled 'public enlightenment'.

The principle of the law-governed state also imposes upon new governments an obligation to compensate for wrongs and, as such, represent a mentioned 'moral impulse' in the process of public morality reconstruction.

In Central and Eastern Europe these issues are of still greater significance since the societies whose moral bonds were destroyed during the last half of the twentieth

---

of course should be exercised responsively' (as cited in Roth-Arioza 1995: 28). According to authors who investigated the reckoning of the past in South America, the right to truth is prior to accountability (Roth-Arioza, 1995: 89).

century are experiencing a lack of moral justifications and discursive resources with which to face the challenges incurred by the regime change. Dealing with the past offers such potential for the revitalization of public morality. It makes people consider and discuss moral issues and think about the victims, as well as about the public good, as justification for the constitutional principle of the law-governed state.

Interestingly enough, it is the civil society whose struggles against policies of past concealment contribute to this process of public enlightenment and large-scale public learning. As already witnessed during global processes of reckoning with the past, the quantum of victimization has seldom been exposed by governmental or international bodies (Bassiouni, 1996: 11). Likewise, in Eastern Europe that task has primarily been undertaken, with all its understandable limitations, by non-governmental organizations (NGOs) such as Charter 77 in Czechoslovakia, or the Committee for the Defense of Workers of the late 1970s and early 1980s in Poland, or the Memorial organization in Russia thanks to which we learn about the atrocities committed by the USSR. There are also organizations of victims of the tyrannical regimes, of slaves condemned to work in Siberian or other labour camps, of owners deprived of their property, of mothers, of dedicated journalists, and of committed researchers struggling to expose the truth and not forget it.[2]

In order to protect the right to truth in CEE countries, it was civil society and journalists who, at the beginning of the 1990s, alerted public opinion to the destruction of files and archives of the security police and the Communist Party, undertaken by members of these institutions under the express orders of high-ranking officials (Paczkowski, 1999: 49). In the end, it was civil society, at least in Poland, which has consistently since 1993 (as seen in public opinion polls) demanded the opening of files and accessibility for all interested parties.[3] With respect to the nationalization or confiscation of the property of individuals, communities or organizations, the engagement of civil society (again in Poland) has proved crucial in the struggle for property restitution.[4]

---

2 As noted with respect to Poland, initially nobody seemed interested in opening the files and disseminating the information – neither members of the former regime, nor the new officials, members of the former underground opposition (Paczkowski, 1999: 51).

3 According to historians, the destruction of documents and files in Poland started in September/October 1989. Furthermore, in October 1989, General Jaruzelski ordered the destruction of Central Committee meeting records spanning 1982–1989. This destruction of files and documents took several months (Paczkowski, 1999: 52, 53). In Poland and elsewhere, public opinion was often warned about this process by local media, thanks to information from citizens. Aside from their obliteration, files were removed by persons working in specific institutions and used for 'private collections' as hidden political bombs.

4 The engagement of civil society in property rights restitution is well illustrated by the Polish case. In Poland, many organizations of former owners – such as organizations of Lemkos or landowners, of persons resettled in Poland from Lithuania, Byelorus or the Ukraine after World War II – played crucial roles in the struggle for restitution or fair

The new governments are further obliged to the ratified European Convention on Human Rights and Fundamental Freedoms of 1950, not to mention the Universal Declaration of Human Rights of 1948; these and other covenants comprise part of the post-communist constitutional and legal orders. Among other things, according to these agreements, full information about past human rights abuse must be disclosed.[5]

Dealing with past human rights abuse attests to the sincerity of the slogan at the beginning of the chapter, 'Never again!'. It generates hidden, cognitive and axiological resources that would assist post-communist societies in restoring their integrity. From the classic sociological, Durkheimian perspective, revealing the truth about crimes and, above all, punishing perpetrators and instigators potentially contributes to the reinstatement of basic social values (Osiel, 1997). Above all, the very notion of the law-governed state, as well as legal concepts of crime, punishment, human rights, human dignity, perpetrators and victims, restitution and compensation function as crucial components of constitutional semantics. Therefore, dealing with the past links the meanings of constitutional provisions to those ascribed to them by their addressees. It furthermore appeals to the set of resources already available in a given society: to the hidden, cultural and moral resources that would assist post-totalitarian societies in restoring their integrity and internal bonds. Being constitutive of a community bound by shared meanings of both constitutional and legal concepts, confronting the past also performs a creative and performative function. In the case of property rights restitution, for instance, dealing with the past means honouring the constitutional principle of private property protection. It means, too, the recognition of individual property rights as civil rights, and of collective property rights (for example, of associations, churches, municipalities, charities and minorities) as the foundation of their autonomy as well as of their cultural or ethnic identity. Hence, the protection and restitution of property rights evokes – again in the classic Durkheimian sense – the recognition of social pluralism in a liberal democratic society.

Summing up, settling accounts with past human rights violations represents a first step in the process of distinguishing the new order from the previous one and is constitutive for a community united by a common understanding of its fundamental concepts and principles. If subordinated to the law-governed state principle, it also brings about the legalization of approaches towards the past, that is, the subordination of reckoning with the past to specific concepts, principles and procedures on which the general principle of the law-governed state is built. This principle means the judicialization of a handling of the past, that is, subjecting it to professional decision-making in appropriate courts. As a consequence, dealing

---

compensation. They were active in presenting cases, contacting governments, lobbying, representing owners before courts, and preparing complaints to be presented before the European Tribunal of Human Rights.

5 All new CEE constitutions refer to international law as part of the internal legal order and, indeed, to its priority over the internal legal order.

with past human rights violations under the principle of the law-governed state imposes legal definitions and reasoning on real-life situations, and subordinates social and political actions to legal procedures. Thus, it fulfils the promise of legality, so important at the beginning of a historical change. Moreover, it testifies to the sincerity of the high moral standards with which CEE societies started their transformation: living within the truth, and recognizing and compensating human rights violations.

However, settling accounts with the past also concurrently introduces a serious challenge to the principle of the law-governed state. First and foremost, not all cases of human rights violation were punishable under the old law. Obviously, collaborating with the former regime – internationally recognized as legal – or with its secret police was not punishable at all. Therefore governments that undertook the task of seriously dealing with the past found themselves forced to reach beyond a literal understanding of the law-governed state principle. They needed to bring in some ingenious methods for defining crimes and their punishment in a process known as decommunization and/or lustration, that is, of cleansing the public sector of high-ranking officials of the previous regime and people tainted by collaboration with its policing organs. These methods came to be known as transitory justice (Teitel, 2000). However, because of the often complex and unclear nature of the cases, as well as of the evidence itself, when free access to files is limited such methods easily turn into weapons in political struggles: they are used to compromise political opponents. Furthermore, in the case of the nationalization of property, that is, violation of property rights, restitution of property necessitates economic sacrifice on the part of society and its government, which have to compensate the losses, reprivatize public property, and find legal solutions to often unsolvable problems.

In consequence, the very principle of the law-governed state is used and misused by proponents and opponents of the reckoning with the past and opening of files, because of its entirely contrasting interpretation: either as justification for not dealing with it, or for dealing with it in a quite limited way; or as justification for its thorough investigation and punishment of perpetrators and instigators (Barańska, 2007: 112).

All these dilemmas overlap with those already characterized: the lack of a clear rupture in the process of regime transformation and the predominant lawyers' (that is, positivistic concept of legality) characterization of the legal culture and legal education of Central and Eastern Europe.

As an outcome, dealing with past human rights violations contributes to the ambiguities of transformation. First and foremost, it presents an unavoidable challenge to post-communist constitutionalism: either it culminates in the questioning of the law-governed state principle, at least in its most obvious, direct meaning, or it leads to the reproduction of constitutional fiction and hypocrisy.

The remainder of this paper will briefly outline the most typical approaches to the difficult task of past reckoning in Central and Eastern Europe, and the arguments that justify each of them.

Knowledge as Power: The Paradoxes of Democracy and Model Approaches

It is no wonder that legacies of state crimes evoke burning questions for governments and societies. These questions are still important in the countries in which the transformation started. Dealing with the past and settling accounts with it means deciding how new officials will treat the guilt of their predecessors. Evaluation of a system leads to the evaluation of its functionaries and their collaborators. Sometimes this ends in 'naming' and 'shaming', that is, in the stigmatization of perpetrators, instigators and collaborators; sometimes it ends in the 'cleansing' of structures of government, the 'ousting' of compromised officials. If dealing with the past is oriented towards prosecution and punishment – in all forms of stigmatization, lustration and decommunization – one could call such an approach to the past 'perpetrator-oriented' (Skąpska, 2003: 199–218).[6]

Dealing with the past could also lead to compensating and honouring its victims above all, and then to rectifying the wrongs committed by the former regime as far as is possible. The right to truth could be particularly instrumental as a basis for a 'victim-oriented' approach to the past. This could lead not only to the 'cleansing' of social institutions, but also to the honouring of the victims' dignity. The participation of victims in the procedures of truth-revealing and their compensation for physical and psychological injuries, as well as the restitution of property rights, restores their trust in law and justice and in the new government. Thus, it has a great legitimizing potential, which is so crucial for new democracies. It is further instrumental for victims to be involved in the process of post-communist, democratic reconstruction. Hearing victims, making their experience a matter of legal debate and, whenever such debates are made public, making their experience a matter of public concern is of great potential in overcoming their isolation and exclusion, and helping them out of the silence that surrounded them before, at least in the public sphere. Moreover, it helps to overcome the deficits of the narrow law-governed state principle interpretation by including human rights protection in it.[7] Dealing with the past could also build a foundation for the reconstruction of social bonds on the basis of reconciliation, and for the 'healing' of social wounds after the truth about the past is made public.[8]

6 The perpetrator-oriented approach seems to be the most compatible with the conventional understanding of the law-governed state principle. It also reflects some cultural features of those societies in which it was initially conceptualized and introduced into legal systems (see Skąpska, 2003b: 69 ff.).

7 In the reality of post-communist societies, the human rights-oriented approach seems closest to the definition of the law-governed state as victim-oriented. The effects of such a conceptualization are morally to justify and honour individuals and groups who resisted and fought against Stalinism. It presents, too, a foundation for the rehabilitation of those who suffered under that regime and for the restitution of their rights (including property).

8 Emblematic of a healing version of past reckoning is the famous Truth and Reconciliation Commission in the Republic of South Africa, established under the Interim

The approach to the past, especially learning the truth about it, has an important socio-political dimension. It constitutes a test for democracy in accordance with the Foucaultian argument about knowledge as power. The knowledge at stake is of a highly sensitive nature: it consists not only of information about participation or collaboration in human rights abuse, but – perhaps predominantly – of information about cowardice, opportunism, individual weaknesses, shameful behaviour and also some sensitive personal characteristics. It is a knowledge one would never reveal publicly. Such knowledge provides considerable power to those who have access to it. This power could be in the hands of politicians who know the files, experts working in archives or institutions of national remembrance, lawyers taking part in respective proceedings and any other functionary of the former or present regime who had or has access to the files. Thus, the current Chairman of the Institute of National Remembrance in Poland, an institution where security police files are collected and analysed, in a TV interview described his position as similar to that of God because of the enormous amount of sensitive information to which he has access.

Additionally, dealing with the past is the subject of political decision-making. It takes place in the context of existing power relations in all their aspects: symbolic power in the domain of public debate, political power in the domain of law-making, the professional power of lawyers in the process of adjudication and the above-mentioned power of knowledge about data collected in files. Hence, if the 'file' is not made public, it easily attains the status of a crucial instrument in political power struggles, in the 'outing' of political opponents. If it is made public, it might reveal not a blatant crime but rather a shameful weakness, not to mention other sensitive information collected by the former political polity to be used as a means of blackmail against political opponents. Therefore the difficult discourse about the past reveals deeply vested interests in hiding or exposing some of the 'truths' about it (Łoś, 1995).

Nonetheless, if the truth about the past is learned and debated amidst narrow circles of politicians, experts and government functionaries, then it is known only to the elites and the meaning of democracy is reduced to purely formal proceedings. This means a paradoxical revival of former divisions between those with access to sensitive data about citizens and those who control knowledge about key social phenomena and processes, while the rest of the citizens can only express their opinions once every four or five years by voting.

The meaning of democracy should be broader and deeper, including public debate and the possibility of freely expressing views and opinions, engaging

Constitution of 1993 in that country, as well as a number of such commissions in Latin America. According to its analysts, the Truth and Reconciliation Commission in South Africa was essentially seen as a forum in which the victims and perpetrators of apartheid could tell their stories. A link was drawn between 'confessional' and 'tribunal': a 'legal tribunal' and 'public confessional' (Christodoulis, 1999: 4, 5).

all interested persons in communicative action on an equal footing, according to the model of the legitimizing potential of communicative rationality. This deeper meaning of democracy, as well as the communicative legitimization of a democratic constitution, is of great importance for post-communist societies which have undergone long period of imposed silence and censorship. In CEE countries in general, their history is of deep divisions between enlightened elites (participants in public debates) and uneducated masses, who are treated with contempt as being in need of enlightenment and protection against their own vices. With regard to the period of Stalinism this entailed a division between the former dissidents who heroically opposed the oppressive system and the rest of society, which was treated as if it would taint entirely through collaboration with it, or as not having enough moral or intellectual ability to make reasonable judgements about the past.

Here one can refer to Michel Foucault's concept of pastoral technology, which can be applied to whole social sectors, not just to individuals. In the latter case, 'pastors' take care of their flock, preventing the 'simple people' from transforming the public scene into one the pastors assume to be based on sheer revenge. Settling accounts with the past by hearing victims and opening files presents an opportunity to overcome such legacies, to hear all voices and debate all experiences, to make knowledge about the past accessible to all interested and, above all, to supplement law with the experiences and expectations of ordinary people, thus enhancing expert knowledge with local knowledge.[9] In other words, democracy could be measured by equal protection of the rights to truth and to remembrance, granted to any person who has a proven interest in learning the truth about past atrocities as a victim of human rights abuse, or as a suspected perpetrator or collaborator. Files could be made entirely public – a situation that presents an important topic for public debate in order to entrench post-communist constitutionalism in the broadest social experiences.

On the other hand, reckoning with past human rights violations may present a serious challenge to the society itself, its own self-conceptualization and its identity as a victim of terror. Files were mainly prepared to compromise people and could therefore consist of information on private affairs (such as personal sexual preferences), revealing truths about such pasts that could challenge self-image. Files also reveal the extent of collaboration with the regime. Past reckoning could in this way become a source of possible social trauma, causing shame if the opening of a file reveals participating in or collaborating with the oppressive

9 Expert knowledge in this case functions predominantly in the form of the knowledge of legal experts, who are elaborating data according to legal prescriptions, that is, defining actions, establishing facts, and recognizing the causal nexuses between them. Local knowledge, however, functions in the form of vague definitions based on experiences, emotions and evaluations, providing daily-life definitions of situations, but not systematized observations.

regime, taking part in atrocities, or profiting from human rights violations such as the confiscation of private property.

Revealing the past could be especially painful in those societies that generally, as in Poland, define themselves as societies of victims, considering victimhood and the heroic struggle against oppression as crucial to their identity. In order to avoid such painful reconsideration of the society's own identity and to reduce possible social trauma, in 1989 the first democratic Prime Minister of Poland, Tadeusz Mazowiecki, proposed the concept of a 'thick line' dividing the past from the present.

In Hungary, initial approaches towards past human rights violations were summarized in the slogan 'Living well is the best revenge' (Halmai and Scheppele, 1997: 83). Handling the past this way then became about concealing or silencing uncomfortable opinions, closing files and leaving them to experts, and granting amnesty and actual legal immunity for perpetrators, instigators and collaborators. We are dealing here with another paradox of the democratic society confronted with its difficult past – that is, the paradox of democracy as a source of concealment of past crimes. This could result in actual popular outrage directed toward those pressing for the truth, as illustrated by the behaviour of some Argentinians toward the Mothers of Plaza Mayo (Cichecka, 2006: 67). There appears to be a temptation to hide the truth in the archives and grant access to files only to professional historians.

The concept of the 'thick line' and the resulting concealment of past crimes proved to be insufficient when confronted by legacies of past human rights abuse. One has to deal with the perpetrators and instigators of the most atrocious crimes committed by the functionaries of the old regime up until the very last days of its existence (Łoś and Zybertowicz, 1999). Moreover, it became apparent that it is not possible to get rid of a nation's history – answering questions related to the past is unavoidable not only because of the democratic nature of the new regime, but also because of new information technologies. It became quite clear, too, that all efforts to conceal the truth would provoke great political problems and lead to public cynicism. As it is argued, democratization represents circumstances under which officially sponsored versions of history and the tabooing of the past run out of control, along with historical myths and delusions. Then 'atrocities vehemently come to the surface' (Reinprecht, 2001:102). Here one can refer to the German experiences of 1968, when the youth revolt also encompassed a revolt against concealment of the Nazi past. If concealed, the past can easily turn into a political instrument for crushing political opponents, a moral weapon used against those involved in concealing the past, regardless of their motivations. Additionally, in Central and Eastern Europe, as anywhere else, it soon became clear that some approaches to the past – notably those connected with the 'thick line' policy proclaimed by the government in order to consolidate society – could acquire quite an authoritarian undertone, even if promoted by respected former dissidents, as in the above-mentioned case in Poland. If the voices and daily-life experiences of persons who lived under an oppressive regime are not taken into account, then, applying Alfred Hirschman's classic proposition, 'loyalty' disappears, the legitimization of the new, democratic government is questioned, and the danger of an 'exit', of a refusal to cooperate with and participate in democratic procedures becomes quite serious (Hirschman, 1970). The 'exit' translates into disenchantment with the new order and lack of trust in the new authorities and institutions. The past cannot be hidden from the public in democratic societies, especially if the mass media and Internet are at its disposal. On the contrary, if not revealed and publicly debated, the past could become a subject of political provocation and blackmail.

It seems, then, that the broadest public debate about previous human rights violations – even if it is painful and puts national myths in doubt – is a necessary, indeed a primary step in the process of democratization not limited to purely formal arrangements. It contributes to the sincerity of the founding slogans, it has a 'healing' quality in a rather surgical sense and it contributes to the overcoming of previous exclusions from the public sphere. As stressed above, it helps to define the crucial, primary difference in the formation of a liberal democratic constitutionalism and to include the broadest social circles in this process.

These are burning issues related to the understanding of the law-governed state principle in the new CEE democracies. They require resolve, great effort and civil courage on the part of societies, governments and lawyers. They also provoke some questions concerning the 'output' – the truth that emerges from trials and/or opened files, the institutional arrangements with regard to compensating victims, the degree of property rights protection resulting from regulations and judgments on restitution, the usage made of knowledge about the past by politicians and citizens, and the restorative effects of dealing with the past. The 'input' – constructing institutions and procedures to deal with the difficult issues of the past under the auspices of the constitutional law-governed state principle – manifests the profound differences among societies that have to face the reality of their own past, as separate from the questions and dilemmas they have in common.[10]

Thus, the new governments should decide whether they opt primarily to stick to the constitution and existing law, not negotiating its contents, or whether they intend to make the constitution and law expedient to other goals: financial stability, the involvement of former regime functionaries into the process of social reform, legal certainty and narrowly interpreted legal foreseeability. There are also other possible socio-political approaches. With regard to past human rights violations other than of property rights, they could follow the policy of the German Chancellor Konrad Adenauer. This policy was based on a proposition 'not to traumatize the already traumatized society' when he opposed the public debate on the involvement of German society in the functioning of Nazism after World War

10 There are significant differences between CEE countries. However, this process is still dynamic and the chapter on past reckoning in Central and Eastern Europe is not yet closed, as is evident in the Polish case.

II (Schwan, 1997: 43). In contrast, CEE governments could choose to be faithful to the initial principle of 'living within the truth'.

Combining approaches to past human right violations, one can differentiate between four models of past reckoning. The first involves implementing the classic law-governed state principle, interpreted narrowly and literally. The second, which refers to the right to truth and the general rights of a system's victims, is supported by international law and human rights protection. The third is known as the 'transitory justice' approach, one valid for a period of transition towards liberal democracy and an unquestionable rule of law. It is argued that the 'transitory justice' approach, after the first period of innovative practices, is based rather on some moral standards not conforming to existing law, which will transform itself into a 'regular' model of the rule of law once accounts with the past are settled (Teitel, 2000: 5). The fourth approach is based on the policy of concealment, illustrated by the idea of drawing a 'thick line.'

The approaches adopted towards the crimes initially were dramatically changing in such countries as Poland and Hungary, which were pioneers of the change. There policies of concealment of past crimes and immunity for state officials were subjected to strong criticism – data compromising state officials were constantly leaked from hidden files, published in newspapers and/or on the Internet, which led to a considerable change in the initial policies. Remarkably, a great distrust of the government is typical in Poland and Hungary.[11] Thus, in Hungary and Poland, as well as in all other post-communist countries, after some dramatic turns and events – mostly consisting of a so-called 'wild lustration', that is, the above-mentioned unauthorized publication in the form of leaks of the names of alleged collaborators, often prominent members of government (even presidents and prime ministers) – lustration laws were finally adopted, installing legal control over wild lustration and ending the officially sponsored concealment. This belated reckoning of the past, including lustration and decommunization, is as yet incomplete, as seen in the Polish case.

In Poland – once a leader of political changes in Central and Eastern Europe – the so-called 'lustration law' was introduced as late as 1997, the main characteristic of which was its legalistic approach toward the past. The law declared that civil servants, deputies, senators and judges, as well as candidates for these positions, must disclose whether they consciously collaborated with the secret police or worked for them between 1944 and 1990. Such an approach was also based on sequestration of the archival records of the secret service in the newly founded Institute of National Remembrance. Each citizen has a right to apply to have access to his/her file, provided that he/she has been victimized – only persons recognized as victims are granted access to their own files. This law was strongly criticized in Poland, not only because of doubts with regard to the evidence –

11 As empirical data illustrate, lack of trust in the government is highest in Poland (among all members of the European Union). In this respect, Poland is closely followed by Hungary.

secret police files – but also because of the limited access to files and the exclusion of the general public from the process. After a series of scandals, when whole lists of collaborators' names were published in newspapers and on the Internet, a new lustration law was proclaimed in Poland in 2006. Immediately following its proclamation, the President of Poland declared it to be not actually binding, even though its being binding had been formally approved by Parliament. The 2006 lustration law was amended and passed by the Polish Sejm in January 2007, but was invalidated by a verdict of the Polish Constitutional Tribunal in May of that year. Thus, the lustration law will once more be subject to parliamentary proceedings and perhaps to constitutional review as well; its future is far from predictable now. In the meantime, the most important political actors (that is, the President and the strongest political forces in the Polish Parliament) are calling for a change to the 1997 Polish Constitution and the lustration law in order (among other things) to redefine the position and prerogatives of the Polish Constitutional Court. The Polish case clearly illustrates how a policy towards the past, if not successfully, even if painfully commenced immediately after the overthrow of the former regime, can be used as a weapon in the political struggle, poisoning the public sphere and public debate, and leading to the questioning of the whole constitutional order.

Another important feature of the Polish approach to past human rights abuse was some (unknown) degree of support for the establishment of extra-judicial bodies and procedures, such as truth commissions or truth and reconciliation commissions, or, as is currently the case with the files of collaborators within the Catholic Church, commissions of 'truth and care' or 'truth and reconciliation', dealing with cases in which strict adherence to the rule of law principle has been unsatisfactory. However, starting only a few years ago, these truth commissions did not become popular and, according to authorial knowledge, are not working any more.

Another institutional attitude towards the past was taken by the Constitutional Court in Hungary, quite in accordance with the description of that state's revolution as 'lawful' in the strictly positivistic sense. As the most important agent in the formation of a constitutional community in Hungary after the collapse of the communist regime, the Constitutional Court there has several times referred to such values as legal certainty and clear definitions of legal concepts as the foundations of constitutionalism. In light of that approach, retroactive justice and the possibility of punishing political perpetrators, instigators and functionaries therefore run counter to the principles of legal certainty and are outweighed by the lack of a clear-cut legal concept that would enable precise definitions of crimes and punishments. Similar to the Polish case, this approach did not prevent wild accusations and the publication of lists of agents' names. Finally, a law was passed in Hungary according to which a very limited number of officials are subject to lustration. In 2009, after a series of scandals in recent years when lists of collaborators' names were published in the mass media and on the Internet, projects were developed to change the law substantially and open the files to everybody.

From among CEE countries, only the Czech Republic has undergone thorough and comprehensive lustration and decommunization, mostly because of approval by then President Vaclav Havel. Considering the difficulties inherent in just retribution, Havel signed the 1993 'law on the illegitimacy of, and resistance to the communist regime'. The effects of that law were perpetrator-as-victim oriented. Its aim was morally to justify and honour individuals and groups who, acting on moral conviction, resisted and fought against the former regime. Further, it provided a basis upon which to rehabilitate or elevate, as well as to compensate, those who had suffered under that regime, becoming the first issue dealt with by the new government. This specific legislation was not strictly legal but rather proclamative; it appealed to conscience and ethics, stressed the moral justification and honouring of victims, and emphasized their moral convictions in fighting against the criminal regime.

The Czech lustration law of 1990 had been strongly criticized, above all because of the presumption of guilt (Siklova, 1996; Gillis, 1999). There was also the problem of using secret police files as the main source of evidence, as well as the difficulty of verifying their contents, especially in their vast numbers. With respect to the 'transitory justice' model, one can observe that the Czechs have now put this period behind them. Independent of the different approaches taken, all CEE countries continue to face some unresolved issues that they inherited from the past. These, in turn, contribute to difficulties in the interpretation of the constitutional law-governed state principle, and the formation of a new social consensus in the respective societies.

Conclusion: The Dilemmas of the Law-governed State Principle after the Collapse of Communism in Central and Eastern Europe

The principle of the law-governed state represents a founding norm in all post-communist constitutions. Prima facie, this principle imposes on new governments an obligation to punish crimes and redress wrongs, to give back what was illegally taken and confiscated or compensate fairly for losses. Equally important is the principle of non-retroactivity as a basic component of the law-governed state. However, this most important principle – in the case of post-dictatorial and post-totalitarian regimes – contributes to ambiguities in the transition period: firstly, because the crimes were committed by functionaries of a state acting against the society but within then-existing law; and secondly, because those functionaries were involved in gross human rights violations but not in clear-cut roles, that is, not only as direct perpetrators but also as instigators, as highly placed officials issuing orders or defining policy aimed at the destruction of 'system enemies', as collaborators denouncing such 'enemies', or as persons placed in some crucial positions responsible for the functioning of the Stalinist system. Here we have in mind those performing political functions or functions in politically sensitive sectors, such as the communist party apparatus, police and army, or education and mass media.

In the case of direct perpetrators and instigators, the legal solution entails concepts of crimes against humanity, war crimes and so-called 'communist crimes', which are not subject to statutes of limitation on prosecution. With regard to post-communist constitutionalism, applying this solution necessitates a resolve to accuse the officials of communist governments as perpetrators and instigators of crimes against humanity in order to justify retroactivity. Such an act is especially difficult if the former instigators have been partners at Round Tables.

There are other important considerations with respect to the application of the law-governed state principle in the reality of the post-communist society: these refer to the individualization of guilt as another crucial component of the law-governed state principle. This concretization and individualization of guilt, typical of proceedings within the domain of penal law, preclude its being ascribed to functionaries of an anonymously acting 'system'. Here, in the form of retributive justice, the crimes are considered the acts of real individuals, of the functionaries or collaborators of the regime who were actively representing it and with whom one can actively deal today. This is no small feat in societies used to 'system thinking', who were formerly made to consider public officials, judges, prosecutors, investigators and their collaborators as 'puppets of the system,' absolved of personal responsibility. 'Never again!' is here supplemented by the conviction that 'killers should end up on the gallows'. Perhaps that will prevent other people from entering into the service of evil forces. However, one should emphasize that – in the multifaceted and muddied reality of the communist system, in which not only did division of power not exist but there was also a complex structure of informal or semi-formal rules and orders issued by communist party officials who were often acting collectively (that is, the 'Politburo') was emblematic – the task of distilling and defining the contribution to human rights violations of a specific person, especially in the case of instigators, is not an easy one.

As has been stressed, these serious conceptual, political, social and economic dilemmas in settling accounts with the past by applying the law-governed state principle after the collapse of totalitarianism or a dictatorship occur, especially if the principle is interpreted in the tradition of the legal positivism of civil law countries typical of Central and Eastern Europe, that is, as a directive to observe only existing law and interpret it literally (Morawski, 1999: 41, 42). This positivistic tradition was directly reflected in the verdict of the Polish Constitutional Tribunal in 1995, when it declared that the law proclaimed by the communist authorities in Poland, in accordance with the then-binding procedures, did not lose its validity even if it was unfair or non-humanitarian (as cited in Morawski, 2000: 49). If such a directive is additionally legitimized by the values of the legal certainty and predictability of law, then a temptation occurs not to redress past wrongs, especially if they were committed by public officials according to or in the 'shadow' of the legal code in existence prior to 1989. Thus, it must be noticed that the law-governed state principle literally interpreted is badly suited to dealing with former human rights abuse and, indeed, can be used as protection for old regime functionaries. In this way, it would contribute to the preservation of the status quo and to structural reproduction. Such a purely formalistic and literal interpretation of the law-governed state principle was adopted by the pioneers of post-communist transformation: the governments and constitutional courts of Poland and Hungary under the ideology of legality so characteristic of the Round Tables.[12] Another important motive stems from the conviction that society should unite its efforts to build a better future and a liberal democracy, not to scratch its wounds. Yet another motive was the fear of some democratic dissidents turned new political elites that society would not rise to expectations but would turn the public sphere into one of sheer revenge.

The initial policies of past concealment have proved to be entirely ineffective and the narrow, literal interpretation of the law-governed state principle in some cases dysfunctional. In contrast to the envisioned restoration of social bonds and political cooperation aimed at democratization and liberalization under the auspices of legal certainty and foreseeability, these policies led to growing social divisions and widespread moral disenchantment with the new governments, to popular cynicism, to the illegal openings of files and the leaking of their contents as a means of political blackmail, and to growing accusations by political opponents of collaboration with the former regime or participation in human rights crimes.

Moreover, a literal interpretation did not fulfil the expectations of protecting the right to truth and to remembrance. In this way, an important potential of post-communist constitutionalism, as well as its moral impulse, was lost. Instead of being innovative, it became complacent. It also became evident that the literal interpretation of the law-governed state principle on the part of the government and judiciary is either greatly naive or arrogant or both and, above all, is removed from the reality of post-communist societies. In that reality, evidence of crimes was not only illegally destroyed by interested parties – an argument raised often by opponents of any form of transitory justice – but was also illegally copied, stolen, or even hidden in order to be used as an instrument of blackmail. In any case, as

12 In Hungary, as in any other post-communist country, the main issues of legislative measures concerning human rights violations committed by the former regime were property restitution, compensation, lustration and criminal prosecution of crimes. As was stressed, the main concepts framing the review of transitional legislation in Hungary in the jurisprudence of the Hungarian Constitutional Court were legal continuity and the rule of law (Art. 2 (1)). However, it should be emphasized that the Hungarian Constitution does not establish a requirement of legal continuity. It is a jurisprudential concept which was developed in response to the government's attempt to lift the statute of limitations for crimes that were not prosecuted for political reasons in the previous regime (retroactive justice criminal cases). Thus, upon the preliminary review petition of the President of the Republic, a unanimous Constitutional Court abolished the retroactive criminal justice bill in its entirety. The entire position of the Constitutional Court in Hungary was summarized as follows: 'The Hungarian Constitutional Court clearly said that it is not willing to subject transitional rules to 'transitional standards' of constitutionality' (Uitz, 2005: 246).

political gossip currently claims, copies of the files are archived in Moscow. Finally, in Hungary and Poland, all of this led to important changes in initial policies and the later adoption of some models of effective handling of past crimes and models of transitory justice.[13] As a matter of fact, in Poland, this process of altering the original policy is far from over; as noted earlier, the most recent law on lustration adopted in 2007 was ruled invalid by the Polish Constitutional Tribunal.[14] This, in turn, as also noted above, has led some politicians to propose a crucial change in the 1997 Polish Constitution itself, especially with respect to the position and competencies of the Constitutional Tribunal.

Additionally – it is argued – the evaluation of communist law from the perspective of the law-governed state principle, even if motivated by legal certainty and predictability, creates a legal fiction with a distinctive projection of a hyper-reality. This, in turn, consists of an evaluation of a law-governed state as if it were real, although characterized by the breaking of this very principle. This was once known as 'legal hypocrisy' (Zajadło, 2003: 18). The legacies of the past open a unique opportunity to go beyond the narrow, formalistic definition of the law-governed state and to overcome the burdens of a positivistic legal culture: they create the possibility of expanding its interpretation firstly to the standards of international law and international human rights protection; and secondly, to local experiences and local expectations of civil society.

The questions of how to reconstruct morally devastated societies after totalitarianism are not new. Most prominently, they were present when Germany was rebuilding her constitutional order after 1945 and had to promote the formation of a new, liberal and democratic constitutional community after the Shoah. They were also present in other countries – after the collapse of authoritarian regimes in Spain, Portugal and Greece, dictatorial regimes in Latin America and apartheid in South Africa. This list could be extended to include other countries and continents in the foreseeable future.

However, the German example is of special interest here, not only because the country has gone through the process of political and social reconstruction twice in her contemporary history – after World War II and after the dismantling of the Berlin Wall. In both the first as well as the second case, external forces had an important impact on the emerging liberal democratic constitutionalism in that country, on the meaning and interpretation of the law-governed state and, consequently, on a new theory of German society expressed in the

13 After several years, the policy that 'Living well is the best revenge' and the formal interpretation of the law-governed state principle was changed, and Hungary, as any other post-communist country, has witnessed scandals connected to revealing files on the collaboration of prominent politicians with the former regime: an ironic version of the 'living within the truth' proposition.

14 In Poland, the last version of the lustration law of 2007 was partially invalidated by the Constitutional Tribunal in 2007. The debate on lustration and the best means of revealing knowledge about the past still continues – it has been nearly 19 years long.

German basic law of 1949. After World War II the external forces were the Allied Forces; after the Berlin Wall's collapse it was the Federal Republic of Germany, with her model basic law and other institutional arrangements at hand and ready to be implemented, which contributed meaningfully to the emerging subsequent constitutionalism. With respect to the comprehensive restitution of property rights in Germany, it is also sometimes argued that it was imposed 'from above' by the winners, that is, the West Germans. One has to add that, notwithstanding this external impact and the ready institutional framework, the Germans, too, experienced great difficulties in the process of handling the past and reconstructing society (Offe, 1994; Schwan, 1997).

Nonetheless, it is equally important to recall other typical features of past reckoning in Germany, which are crucial for the current debate on post-communist constitutionalism. Firstly, after World War II, German constitutionalism experienced a great revival of natural law theory reflected in the first 20 articles of the German basic law and, above all, in the principle of human dignity protection as its opening norm. Moreover, in post-1945 Germany, the so-called 'Gustav Radbruch formula' was used to evaluate Nazi law and justify retroactivity. Briefly, according to this formula, the law loses its validity if it flagrantly violates basic moral norms. This led to the concept of legalized illegality (*gesetzliches Unrecht*) and the fundamental criticism of legal positivism understood as a literal interpretation of the law and a strict separation of the law and morality. This would make it possible not to punish even the worst perpetrators if their actions were compatible with then valid law. The so-called 'thesis of separation of law and morality', as a Polish author argued, 'accepts dogmatically the priority of legal norms over moral rules in every situation; giving, thus, the practically unrestricted possibility of legalizing all kinds of atrocities' (Morawski, 1999: 47). Thus, in Germany, as with the Eichmann trial in Jerusalem, higher moral standards were used in order to evaluate the law and, consequently, the actions of governmental officials taken under it. The German experiences represent important issues of legal philosophy. Not only is the reinterpretation of the retroactivity principle in view of responsibility for crimes against humanity and war crimes at stake, but also 'the essence of law and its philosophy' (Zajadło, 2003: 20).

Secondly, in post-war Germany as well as in similar cases elsewhere, international pacts and covenants were used to identify a discrepancy between the totalitarian legal system and international human rights protection. This, in turn, enabled the declaration of respective dictatorial and totalitarian law as invalid and, as a consequence, made it possible to prosecute human rights abuse. Towards this aim were used the Declaration of Human Rights of 1948, in particular, as well as the Pact on Human and Political Rights of 1966 and the European Convention on Human Rights of 1952.

Thirdly, not only after 1945 but above all after 1990, the key role in the entire process of past reckoning and reinterpretation of the law-governed state principle was played by 'ordinary people': judges of the lower courts, public prosecutors of lower rank, as well as lay persons – including the budding civil society that protested against the destruction of files and, in fact, became leaders in their collection and preservation, as in the most prominent case of Joachim Gauck in Germany, but there are also other prominent examples.[15]

However, it is very difficult to refer to natural law at the beginning of the twenty-first century when the very source of natural law and its interpretation is in doubt. In accordance with the concept of contextualized constitutionalism and with the argument on the need for a positive constitutional consensus as the social foundation of a post-communist constitutional community, a possible approach to the interpretation of the law-governed state principle would be recognition of the aforementioned 'local knowledge': the experiences of people whose rights were violated on a mass scale. Thus, in order to render this principle legitimate and compatible with expectations of social justice, it is important to open its interpretation up to the experiences and expectations of the victims of totalitarianism and dictatorship. Again, referring to Michel Foucault, one can argue for a genealogy in the process of dealing with the past, subordinated to the law-governed state principle, that is, for a combining of legal expertise, historical knowledge and local remembrance of atrocities (Foucault, 1996: 22).

As is already known, not all cases of human rights violations were actual 'crimes' as defined in a criminal code. Novel and temporary institutions are in this way just another answer to the limitations of a formalistic interpretation of the rule of law principle (Offe, 1994: 184 ff.; Teitel, 2000). The model of transitory justice has two variations. The 'surgical' model of dealing with past human rights violations, consists predominantly of quasi-penalization of perpetrators and collaborators: it starts with their disclosure, targeting and screening; and then cleanses the state apparatus, system of justice, education and media of persons compromised by collaboration with the previous system; before finally ousting the communist *nomenklatura*, the political police and its collaborators from the public sector (decommunization). Of course, this does not preclude compensation of victims and fair restitution of property rights, but its fundamental aim is to strip the democratic state structures of persons involved in the functioning of the previous regime. This has an important sociological and political effect. It enables the new government to get rid of persons – for example, teachers, university professors, or administrative officials – who would otherwise form a considerable political force and would want to preserve the sort of legal order that would guarantee them at least security and immunity and would generally help them to maintain networks and connections in key institutions: political, educational and governmental. However, one needs strong legal and political instruments to control the functioning of transitory justice and prevent its transformation into a tool of political struggle. Hence, as the earliest and most recent Polish examples

15 The involvement of 'ordinary people' in the process of past reckoning is typical not only of Central and Eastern Europe, of course. The most prominent cited in this book is the example of 'Mothers from the Mayo Plaza'.

clearly illustrate, this type of transitory justice quite easily runs out of control and turns itself into a weapon for getting rid of political opponents.[16]

It seems the questions of how to establish and interpret the law-governed state whilst simultaneously reckoning past atrocities and wrongs are more pertinent, and the dilemmas created by past legacies more difficult, in the case of CEE post-communist democracies than in many other countries. They present the consequences of Stalinism and also of the negotiated character of transformation, of the lack of a clear rupture, a clear division between the old anti-democratic and the new democratic government. They result from legal continuity and, in Central and Eastern Europe, from the 'lawful' character of great change. The CEE past had quite a distinct character. In contrast with human rights violations created by occupation, war or civil war and the consequent clear division between perpetrators and victims, or with human rights violations conducted by a government unequivocally condemned – as was for instance the Nazi government in Germany – in the case of Central and Eastern Europe the communist governments were internationally recognized as legitimate, leading, as is already known, to a broad 'grey zone' of activities not easy to evaluate and legacies extremely difficult to deal with. The ambiguities are connected with the fact that not only the direct perpetrators, but also, or even above all, the instigators and collaborators were responsible for the regime's functioning, for the entire legal and constitutional hypocrisy and for the social destruction. Moreover, one can argue that the classic law-governed state principle, when faced with mass-scale human rights violations committed by state officials and their collaborators, is often toothless and, at the same time, does not cover all crimes or all persons involved in their commitment. The latter were those prominent politicians and members of government who were not actually torturing or killing, who were even – as in the case of the Polish Minister of Internal Affairs or the general who introduced martial law in Poland in 1981 – actively involved in the reform, but who, before this, had given orders to kill and torture, or were architects of the functioning of the late Stalinist system. There exists a danger that, in all such cases, the promise of the law-governed state written into the constitution may become quite hypocritical.

16 Modern usage of the term 'lustration' was initiated by the Czechs and their comprehensive lustration law of 1990. Under its provisions, every citizen gained the right to apply to a special office for the result of his/her lustration, a document stating whether he/she is or is not registered as a collaborator of the former secret police. This document is required in order to serve in certain state posts, to run for office, or to be employed in certain government institutions. Those who hold positions requiring lustration must resign if they refuse to provide this document. People who disagree with the findings in their report can seek redress from the Appeals Commission. In some opinions, the anomaly of the Czech lustration process is that it affects those labelled 'candidates for collaboration', that is, those whose collaboration was questionable. The worst perpetrators never applied for their lustration, quietly resigned from government posts and moved to new, more lucrative positions as entrepreneurs (Siklova, 1996: 58).

Quite unexpectedly, the alienating justice idea and the formal concept of *Rechtsstaatlichkeit* find some empirical illustration there, where concerns with the stability and autonomy of law resulted in the very slow changes of the inherited communist law, and law's continuity was not put into question. With regard to such issues, empirical researchers provide a lot of evidence of clashes between the expectations of persons who were regime victims and the legalistic approaches represented by constitutional courts, what had been aptly formulated as: 'we expected justice, and received the rule of law'. The possible solution presents a more comprehensive interpretation of the law-governed state principle, which is closer to the social reality and based predominantly on empathy towards victims of the system, on their truths and their rights to remembrance. This could give the post-communist reconstruction a moral impulse and enable the formation of a positive constitutional consensus around some positive values, directed at human rights protection.

As a concluding remark, one emphasizes that the past has moral content relevant to the present, to the extent that the present was shaped by the past. To this, one can add that this morally important past could give the present an innovative impulse: to broaden the list of human rights and supplement them by novel rights to truth and to remembrance; and to reconceptualize the rule of law after the collapse of dictatorial and totalitarian regimes.

References

Amir Arjomand, S., 'Law, political reconstruction and constitutional politics', *International Sociology*, 1 (2003), 7–32.

Arato, A. and A. Sajó (eds), 'Introduction', *Law and Social Policy*, 13/2 (1991), 101–106.

Bankowski, Z., 'Introduction', in Z. Bankowski (ed.), *Revolutions in Law and Legal Thought* (Aberdeen: Aberdeen University Press, 1991), v–viii.

Barańska, M., 'Zasada państwa prawnego w dyskursie politycznym na temat lustracji' (The law-governed state principle in the public discourse on lustration), *Studia Socjologiczne*, 2 (2007), 83–116.

Bassiouni, M.Ch., 'Searching for peace and achieving justice: The need for accountability', *Law and Contemporary Problems*, LIX (1996), 11 ff.

Bourdieu, P., *Distinction: A Social Critique of the Judgment* (Cambridge, MA: Harvard University Press, 1996).

———*Language and Symbolic Power* (Cambridge: Polity Press, 1990).

Christodoulis, E., 'Truth and reconciliation as risks', paper presented at the Legal Institutions and Collective Memories Workshop, International Institute for the Sociology of Law, Onati, Spain (22–24 September 1999).

Cichecka, J., *Rozliczenie zprzeszłością a łamanie praw człowieka w Argentynie* (Reckoning with the Past and Human Rights Violations in Argentina) (Kraków: Kielce, 2006).

Dezalay, I. and G. Garth Bryant, *Global Prescriptions: The Production, Exportation and Importation of New Legal Orthodoxy* (Ann Arbor, MI: University of Michigan Press, 2002).

Elster, J.(ed.), *The Roundtable Talks and the Breakdown of Communism* (Chicago, IL and London: Chicago University Press, 1996).

Foucault, M., *The Order of Things: An Archaeology of Human Sciences* (New York: Vintage Books, 1996).

Gillis, M., 'Lustration and decommunization', in J. Přibáň and J. Young (eds), *The Rule of Law in Central Europe: The Reconstruction of Legality, Constitutionalism and Civil Society in the Post-Communist Countries* (Aldershot: Ashgate, 1999), 56–81.

Halmai, G. and K.L. Scheppele, 'Living well is the best revenge: The Hungarian approach to judging the past', in J. McAdams, *Transitional Justice and the Rule of Law* (Notre Dame, CA: University of Notre Dame Press, 1997), 155–84.

Havel, V., *The Power of the Powerless: Citizens Against the State in Central-Eastern Europe* (New York: M.E. Sharpe, 1985).

Hirschman, A., *Exit, Voice and Loyalty: Responses to Decline of Firms, Organizations and State* (Cambridge, MA: Harvard University Press, 1970).

Kis, J., 'Between reforms and revolution: Three hypotheses about the nature of the regime change', in B. Kidaly and A. Bozoki (eds), *Lawful Revolutions in Hungary 1989–1994* (Boulder, CO: Atlantic Research and Publications, 1995a).

———'From costs and benefits to fairness: A response to Richard Posner', *East European Constitutional Review,* 4/3 (1995b), 84–87.

Łoś M., 'Lustration and truth claims: Unfinished revolutions in Central Europe', *Law and Social Inquiry*, 4 (1995).

Łoś, M. and A. Zybertowicz, 'Is revolution a solution? State crime in communist and post-communist Poland', in M. Krygier and A. Czarnota (eds), *The Rule of Law after Communism: Problems and Prospects in East-Central Europe* (Aldershot: Ashgate, 1999).

Luhmann, N., *Soziale Systeme: Grundriss einer allgemeinen Systemtehorie* (Frankfurt am Mein: Suhrkamp, 1984).

Mendez, J., 'An emerging right to truth: Latin-American contributions', in S. Karstedt (ed.), *Legal Institutions and Collective Memories* (Oxford and Portland, OR: Hart Publishing, 2009), 39–62.

Morawski, L., 'Positivist or non-positivist rule of law? Polish experience of a general dilemma', in M. Krygier and A. Czarnota (eds), *The Rule of Law after Communism: Problems and Prospects in East-Central Europe* (Aldershot: Ashgate, 1999).

Offe, K., *Der Tunnel am Ende des Lichts* (Frankfurt am Mein: Camppus, 1994)

Osiatynski, W., 'The roundtable talks in Poland', in J. Elster (ed.), *The Roundtable Talks*, op. cit. (1996).

———'Constitutionalism and rights in the history of Poland', in L. Henkin and A.J. Rosenthal (eds), *Constitutionalism and Rights: The Influence of the United States Constitution Abroad* (New York: Columbia University Press, 1990)

Osiel, M., *Law and Collective Memory* (New Brunswick, NJ,: Transaction Publishers, 1999).

Paczkowski, A., 'Poland: The enemy nation', in S. Courtois, N. Werth, J.-L. Panne and A. Paczkowski, *The Black Book of Communism* (Cambridge, MA: Harvard University Press, 1999).

Paczolay, P., 'Traditional elements in the constitutions of Central and East European democracies', in M. Krygier and A. Czarnota (eds), *The Rule of Law after Communism: Problems and Prospects in East-Central Europe* (Aldershot: Ashgate, 1999).

Přibáň, J., *Dissidents of Law* (Aldershot: Ashgate, 1999).

Reinprecht, C., 'The role of collective memory in the process of democratization: The Austrian experience', in H. Pascher and G. Skąpska (eds), *A Work in Progress: Social and Political Change in Contemporary Poland and Austria* (Kraków: Universitas, 2001).

Roth–Ariaza, N., *Impunity and Human Rights in International Law and Practice* (Oxford and New York: Oxford University Press, 1995).

Sajó, A., 'Roundtable talks in Hungary', in J. Elster, op. cit. (1996).

Schwan, G., *Politik und Schuld* (Frankfurt am Main: Fischer, 1997).

Siklova, J., 'Lustration or the Czech way of screening', *East European Constitutional Review* (Winter 1992).

Skąpska, G., 'Rozliczenie łamania praw człowieka w przeszłości: Analiza kulturowa' (Reckoning with the past human right violations: Cultural analysis), *Ius et Lex* (2003), 69–94.

———'The rule of law from the East Central European perspective', *Law and Social Inquiry*, 15/4 (1990), 699–706.

Solyom, L., 'The role of constitutional courts in the transition to democracy, with special reference to Hungary', *International Sociology*, 18/1 (2003), 133–61.

Solyom, L. and G. Brunner, *Constitutional Judiciary in a New Democracy: The Hungarian Constitutional Court* (Ann Arbor, MI: University of Michigan Press, 2000).

Teitel, R., *Transitional Justice* (Oxford: Oxford University Press, 2000).

Uitz, R., 'Constitutional courts and the past in democratic transition', in A. Czarnota, M. Krygier and W. Sadurski (eds), *Rethinking the Rule of Law after Communism* (Budapest and New York: Central European University Press, 2005).

Zajadło, J., *Opowiedzialność za mur: Procesy strzelców przy murze berlińskim* (Responsibility for the Wall: Trials of the shooters by the Berlin Wall) (Gdańsk: Arche, 2003).

PART 2
The Legal Professions

Chapter 7
The Democratization and Modernization of Post-communist Judiciaries

Zdeněk Kühn

Introduction

One of the most widespread problems in post-communist countries, at least as far as is reflected very frequently in popular complaints, is the quality of the judiciary. Delays, absurd and surprising decisions and a high level of formalism are often mentioned. Some authors claim that post-communist law, scholarship and the judiciary are in deep crisis.[1] These problems with the judiciary are often mentioned by international organizations as well as politicians. Few post-communist leaders, however, are as outspoken as the former Czech Premier Zeman (1998–2002), who has written in his memoirs that he knows of no 'lazier and more incompetent band than the Czech judges, who take lots of money for doing nothing'.[2] This quote shows most specifics of post-communist judicial cultures: first, the superior and dismissive attitude of politicians towards judges, often combined with open or hidden disrespect for their judgments; and second, deep distrust of judges among the general public.

The reason for this must be located in the past. The collapse of communism found socialist legal and political systems unprepared for the challenge of a new societal system: either completely unprepared, as in Czechoslovakia, East Germany and most other countries of the Eastern bloc; or prepared very poorly after limited

---

1 Cf. similar views are expressed on the Czech Republic, Hungary and Poland, respectively, by Professor of Commercial Law in Prague and Judge of the Court of First Instance of the European Communities, Irena Pelikánová, 'Nad posláním české právní vědy' [On the Mission of Czech Legal Scholarship], *Právní rozhledy*, 8 (2000), 187; a Law Professor in Budapest, Csaba Varga, *Transition to Rule of Law: On the Democratic Transformation in Hungary*, (Budapest: Hungarian Academy of Science, Institute for Legal Studies, 1995); a Professor of Law in Lodž and a Judge of the Supreme Administrative Court of Poland, Marek Zirk-Sadowski, *Transformation and Integration of Legal Cultures and Discourses – Poland*, a lecture at the conference 'Implications of enlargement for the rule of law and constitutionalism in post-communist legal orders', European University Institute, Florence, 28–29 November 2003. Available online at <http://www.iue.it> [accessed 19 April 2010].

2 Miloš Zeman, *Jak jsem se mýlil v politice* [How I Have Erred in Politics], Praha (2005), 197.

reforms, as in Hungary and Poland. Although there was some discussion initially about the proper direction to take after the collapse of communism, there was no question that legal systems should be radically reformed as soon as possible. In their shape in the late 1980s, they were simply incompatible with the ideals of a democratic state, as well as with the needs of a radically changing society heading towards a market economy.

While especially in the early communist system lawyers were pariahs, in post-communism their role was enhanced. Building a rule-of-law state to a certain extent also entails building a lawyers' state. Law is now one of the most prestigious fields of study; the legal profession is increasingly honoured both financially and in terms of prestige. This, however, did not discourage policies of the early 1990s, when most post-communist reforms, supported by foreign advisers, de-emphasized the importance of legal reforms. For instance, the Czech government, composed of liberal economists, repeatedly stressed the need to 'run away from lawyers' and develop the liberal economy without corresponding legal regulations.[3] The failure of these neo-liberal projects in the mid 1990s was followed by a virtual tidal wave of new legislation, ushered in by governments determined to lead their countries into the European Union.

The paths of Central and Eastern European systems were diverse and, at the same time, similar. There was only one exception: East Germany. When Germany was unified, the East German legal system was simply absorbed by the West German, entirely replaced by West German rules. Moreover, judicial and prosecutorial posts were filled by West German personnel.[4] In 1994, only 9.2 per cent of the judges who held office in 1989 still remained in their posts, and those who left had been replaced almost exclusively by Westerners.[5] Even in 2009, of the 16 Justices of the Federal Constitutional Court, none was from the new Eastern *Laender*.[6] As Markovits put it, '[t]he rule of law in Germany's Eastern half

3 Václav Žák, 'Economists or lawyers? Institutional foundations of emerging democracy: The Czechoslovak example' in Lene Bøgh Sørensen and Leslie C. Eliason (eds), *Fascism, Liberalism, and Social Democracy in Central Europe: Past and Present* (Aarhus: Aarhus University Press, 2002), 189 ff., at 195–97. For a comparison of the situations in Poland (with a key reformer L. Balcerowicz), the Czech Republic (V. Klaus) and Russia (Y. Gaidar), see C. Clement and P. Murrell, 'Assessing the value of law in transition economies: An introduction', in P. Murrell (ed.), *Assessing the Value of Law in Transition Economies*, (Ann Arbor, MI: University of Michigan Press, 2001).

4 On this process generally, cf. Inga S. Markovits, *Imperfect Justice: An East-West German Diary* (Oxford: Clarendon Press, 1995).

5 Inga S. Markovits, 'Children of a lesser god: GDR lawyers in post-socialist Germany', *Michigan Law Review*, 94 (1996), 2270, at 2271.

6 According to the official biographies provided on <http://www.bverfg.de> [accessed 2 April 2010], Justice Ch. Hohmann-Dennhardt was born in 1950 in Leipzig, then the GDR. But according to her biography on the Internet, she attended Western schools. I assume that her family left what was then the German Democratic Republic in the 1950s and emigrated to West Germany.

– conceived by Westerners, built by Westerners, staffed with Westerners, and, by all signs, efficiently and smoothly run by Westerners – is likely to remain for some time a largely Western enterprise.'[7]

In contrast to East Germany, there was no West Czechoslovakia, West Poland or West Hungary that might have easily repudiated and replaced the legal ideology and re-staffed judicial posts virtually overnight. But unlike East Germany, the rule of law is building from within in Central and Eastern Europe. This process is still underway, not yet completed, and post-socialist legislatures and lawyers are still looking for a more precise model which they would like to develop and which would best fit their societies.

A first challenge to the ordinary judiciary came with the new demands that the post-communist era put on all judges, in fact, on all lawyers. Many ordinary judges as well as many academic lawyers tried to avoid this challenge by stressing the difference between constitutional courts and ordinary courts, the former being activist tribunals assigned the task of enforcing the constitution, the latter being only mechanical agents who are supposed to read laws in a formalistic way. In effect, they claimed that these new demands were placed solely on the constitutional courts. The second, and even more important, challenge is coming now, with the recent EU enlargement, when the ordinary judges have to begin the review of their national government's policies against the backdrop of the principles of EU law. Suddenly, all judges started to encounter new problems with a vast political impact and, in keeping with the doctrine expounded, they may not attempt to assign this task solely to the constitutional courts.

This chapter, in a rather sketchy way, will show the trends in new laws on the judiciary in the 1990s and 2000s and introduce the post-communist judges. First, it will show the rise of pending cases after the fall of communism, a rise which is limited by the abilities of post-communist judiciaries to handle caseloads efficiently. Second, what happened to the 'old' judges will be discussed, including the chronic lack of judges in the first post-communist decade and a gradual filling of the judicial posts by the early 2000s. The third section analyses the problem of judicial independence in Central Europe on paper and in reality. It also discusses the personality of judges in Central Europe. The paper concludes with a brief introduction to a post-communist judicial philosophy.

The Rise of Litigation

Since 1989, the rise in the rate of litigation, already visible towards the end of the communist era, has accelerated. The number of cases at Hungarian district courts increased by almost 50 per cent between 1991 and 1998; those before the regional

7 Markovits, supra n. 5, at 2305.

courts nearly doubled in the same period.[8] The number of new cases at Polish ordinary courts increased between 1990 and 2001 by 246 per cent.[9] Slovak district judges faced a doubling in the annual number of new civil actions filed.[10] In the Czech Republic, between 1989 and 2000 the number of new civil actions filed in civil district courts increased by approximately 30 per cent, the total number of civil cases (both original and appellate) dealt with by regional courts doubled, and the number of civil appeals to the same courts more than doubled. At the same time, the number of serious crimes adjudicated by the Czech regional courts as courts of first instance increased fivefold. In contrast, Czech district courts dealt with approximately the same amount of criminal prosecutions as they did in the late 1980s.[11] This difference might be accounted for by decriminalization of the socialist era's petty crimes, especially parasitism (which were decided by district courts), and at the same time the emergence of complex cases of economic criminality, which the regional courts must deal with as first instance courts. The increase of litigation was accompanied by inevitable delays in deciding cases. These delays are now a common problem throughout the post-communist region.[12]

However, there is a significant potential for the number of proceedings to rise in the future, if the quality of judges improves. It seems that the insufficient quality of the post-communist judiciary has kept this number lower than it would otherwise have been. If developments in the former East Germany (GDR) after 1990 are compared with those in other post-communist countries of Central Europe, a striking difference is revealed. After the Federal Republic of Germany incorporated five new federal (formerly East German) *Laender* in 1990, thus making available its efficient judiciary to persons living in the former GDR, they have resorted to the judicial system far more often than have their counterparts in other post-communist countries. In 1988 a total of 62,210 first-instance civil cases were filed in those *Laender*.[13] That number rose to a total of 76,800 in 1991, but then increased sharply to 317,600 in 1994.[14] The civil litigation rates in the former East German *Laender* thus increased more than fivefold during the later years of

8 Office of the National Council of Justice, The Functioning of the Hungarian Judicial System, Budapest, 8 February 2000 (on file with author).

9 Polish statistics for the years 2003, 2002 and 2001, provided in English by the Statistical Office. Available online at <http://www.stat.gov.pl/english/index.htm> [accessed 2 April 2010].

10 Slovak statistics for 1999 provided by the Ministry of Justice. Available online at <http://www.justice.gov.sk/> [accessed 2 April 2010].

11 For further details, see judicial statistics. Available online at <http://www.justice.cz> [accessed 2 April 2010].

12 Cf. for further references R. Procházka, *Mission Accomplished: On Founding Constitutional Adjudication in Central Europe* (Budapest and New York: Central European University Press, 2002), at 102.

13 See Statistisches Jahrbuch Der Deutschen Demokratischen Republik 1989, at 399, quoted in Markovits, supra n. 5, at 2307.

14 Id., at 2307.

communism in 1988 and 1994. As I have shown above, in other post-communist Central European countries the litigation rate increased by only approximately half that much.

The Replacement of Old Judges and Creating a New Judiciary

One of the crucial questions of the post-communist transformation concerned what was to be done with the old judges. In fact, the ability of most socialist judges to serve under the new conditions might plausibly have been questioned. Spontaneous turnover through self-selection began shortly after the fall of communism. For instance, out of 1,460 Czech judges sitting in 1990, more than one-third (484) left the judiciary within three years.[15] In Czechoslovakia, as well as in most other post-communist countries, this development might be explained by the fact that many former communist judges left their posts for much more lucrative work as private attorneys. While some of them undoubtedly left because they were too compromised by their collaboration with the former regime, many others were the best people the judiciary had in the early 1990s.

In 2001, about 60 per cent of Czech judges had spent fewer than 10 years on the bench.[16] Similarly, in Hungary at present 70 per cent of trial court judges have fewer than 10 years' experience in their judicial posts.[17] That is why it is possible to say, already in the first decade of the twenty-first century, that the number of judges who had served on the bench before 1989 is low. Hence it would be technically incorrect to characterize Central European judges as former communist judges; on the contrary, for the most part they started their judicial career only after the fall of communism. This fact closely relates to the number of ex-communists within the judiciary. In 2005, there were only 714 former communist party members among 2,876 Czech judges, that is, less than one-quarter. In contrast, 15 years earlier, communists formed almost 60 per cent of judicial personnel.[18] However, as a result of a rigid career system it can fairly be said that the higher one goes in the structure of the judiciary, the higher the percentage of ex-communists.[19]

15 See Eliška Wagnerová, 'The position of judges in the Czech Republic', in J. Přibáň, P. Roberts and J. Young (eds), *Systems of Justice in Transition: Central European Experiences since 1989* (Aldershot: Ashgate, 2003), 163, at 170.

16 Id., at 170 (1,431 out of 2,465).

17 Zoltan Fleck, 'Judicial independence and its environment in Hungary', in J. Přibáň, P. Roberts and J. Young (eds), *Systems of Justice in Transition: Central European Experiences since 1989* (Aldershot: Ashgate, 2003), 121 ff., at 127.

18 Information provided to the author by the Czech Ministry of Justice, April 23, 2005 (on file with author).

19 At least in the Czech Republic the actual precise data are difficult to obtain and are often considered sensitive. A former senator Mejstřík tried to obtain the data through questionnaires, though only a minority of judges were willing to disclose their past. Still, his method showed that a lot of former communist party members are present at the High

One should not conclude from this data, however, that communist legal thinking has no impact. Quite the contrary: it was a distinctive feature of communist legal culture, including its law schools. Therefore, it was not only inherently connected to the judiciary, but also had a spillover effect into the rest of the legal profession. Moreover, institutions have a memory which persists despite personal changes (cf. section on post-communist judges below).

The chronic lack of judges after 1989 was not eliminated until judicial salaries, which were very low shortly after the fall of communism, were substantially raised in the course of the 1990s. EU pressure played a considerable role in this improvement. For instance the average salary of the Czech district court judge, which in 1990 hovered around the national average, is now approximately three times higher than the national average.[20] Understandably, by the second half of the 1990s, judicial wages no longer presented a problem in the Czech Republic, and judicial vacancies have been filled. The situation in Slovakia is similar.[21] In Poland, the situation was more problematic,[22] as the judicial salaries in Poland in the late 1990s were lower than elsewhere in Central Europe.[23] However, there were significant improvements between 2000 and 2002, and the average salary of a district court judge reached the level of about 2.5 times the national average by 2002. Regional court judges earned 3.2 times the national average in 2002.[24]

Although private practice would offer Central European lawyers substantially greater financial rewards, state employment offers other advantages, such as job security. It is therefore possible to say that Central Europe has put the chronic shortage of judges of the early 1990s behind it. Comparing data on the number of judges in post-communist countries of Central Europe (Table 7.1) will show that they roughly correspond to Germany.[25]

Court of Prague. See press conference of 3 October 2008. Available online (though only in Czech) at <http://www.martinmejstrik.cz/> [accessed 2 April 2010].

20 Data from the Czech Ministry of Justice. Available online at <www.justice.cz> [accessed 2 April 2010].

21 See CEELI, Judicial Reform Index for Slovakia (June 2002), at 14. Available online at http://unpan1.un.org/intradoc/groups/public/documents/UNTC/UNPAN017569.pdf [accessed 2 April 2010].

22 See 'Judges want better funding to overcome crisis in judiciary', PAP [Polish Press Agency] News Wire, 21 January 1997. Available online through LexisNexis www.lexisnexis.com.au [accessed 19 April 2010].

23 See 'Overview of the Polish judiciary', with information until 1998. Available online at <http://www.prawo.org.pl/> [accessed 3 April 2010].

24 Information available online at <http://www.stat.gov.pl/english/index.htm> (Polish Official Statistics of 2003) [accessed 2 April 2010].

25 Common law countries have a significantly smaller number of judges. Cf. David S. Clark, 'The relative importance of judiciaries in distinct legal traditions', in James A.R. Nafziger and Symeon C. Symeonides (eds), *Law and Justice in a Multistate World* (New York: Transnational Publishers, 2002), 609–27.

Table 7.1[a] **Number of judges**

	Population	Judges	Judges/100 000 inhabitants	Number of employees per judge
Czech Rep. (2001)	10 273 000	2 660	26	3.1
Austria (1995)[b]	7 800 000	1 561	20	N/A
Germany (1995)[c]	82 440 000	22 100	27	4.7
Slovakia (2003)[d]	5 379 000	1 302	24	3.0
Poland (2001)[e]	38 242 000	8 768	23	N/A
Hungary (2002)[f]	10 291 000	2 604	25	N/A

Notes: [a] Unless otherwise indicated, these data are drawn from out of Souhrn návrhů pro českou justici v oblasti organizace soudnictví, civilního a trestního řízení [A Set of Proposals for the Czech Judiciary in the Area of the Organization of the Judiciary and of Civil and Criminal Procedure], Twinning Project CZ 01/IB/JH/01 Judicial Reform and Court Management Czech Republic – Germany – United Kingdom (not published, on file with author); [b] David S. Clark, 'The relative importance of judiciaries in distinct legal traditions', in James A.R. Nafziger and Symeon C. Symeonides (eds), *Law and Justice in a Multistate World* (New York: Transnational Publishers, 2002), 609–27, at 611–12; [c] Clark, at 611–12; [d] Figures available online at <http://www.justice.gov.sk/> [accessed 19 April 2010, author's own calculations]; [e] EU Regular Report on Poland's Progress Towards Accession (9 November 2002); [f] EU Regular Report on Poland's Progress Towards Accession (9 November 2002).

Another problem is the equipment of the law courts. After 1989 the equipment was generally poor. This has changed in the course of the 1990s, in part through the support of the EU PHARE programmes, as a large amount of personal computers and other equipment was delivered to court offices.[26] However, the salaries of administrative personnel (support staff) are problematic and very low in comparison with similar professions in both the private and public sectors. As a consequence, support staff assisting judges are on the whole underqualified. This seriously affects the efficiency of judicial work,[27] and might also explain the much higher efficiency

26 Cf., for example, for Slovakia CEELI, Judicial Reform Index for Slovakia (June 2002), at 27–28.

27 For a recent work on this issue focusing on the Czech Republic, see Jens Dreßel, Zpráva o výsledcích analýzy právních předpisů v oblasti struktury soudnictví, rozdělení pravomocí uvnitř tohoto systému a organizace soudů v České republice [The Report of the Findings of an Analysis of Legal Regulations in the Area of the Structure of the Judiciary, the Distribution of Powers within the System, and the Organization of Courts in the Czech Republic], Twinning Project CZ 01/IB/JH/01 Judicial Reform and Court Management Czech Republic – Germany – United Kingdom (not published, on file with author). For Poland, see 'Overview of the Polish judiciary'. Available online at <http://www.prawo.org.pl/> [accessed 3 April 2010].

of German judges in comparison with their post-communist counterparts. From Table 7.2, one can see that a judge in the German land of North Rhine Westphalia, aided by competent support personnel, is approximately two to three times more efficient than his Czech counterpart.

Table 7.2[a] Efficiency of the courts' work

	Average length of procedure (in months), 2001				Number of resolved cases per judge, 2001	
	Civil		Criminal		Civil	Criminal
	District Courts	Regional Courts	District Courts	Regional Courts	District Courts	District Courts
Czech Republic	17.9	9.9	8.7	20.6	362.4	223.2
N.R. Westphalia (Germany)	4.3	7.2	3.9	5.2	690.0	600.0[b]

Notes: [a] Unless indicated otherwise, these data are drawn from Souhrn návrhů pro českou justici v oblasti organizace soudnictví, civilního a trestního řízení [A Summary of Proposals for the Czech Judiciary in the Area of the Organization of the Judiciary and of Civil and Criminal Procedure], Twinning Project CZ 01/IB/JH/01 Judicial Reform and Court Management Czech Republic – Germany – United Kingdom (not published, on file with author); [b] Including administrative offences, according to German law.

One can also see that the German judiciary comprises approximately the same number of judges per capita and with only about 50 per cent more support staff per judge than in most post-communist countries (refer back to Table 7.1).

The division of labour between post-communist judges and their support staff is very problematic. Most often, adjectives like 'inefficient', 'wasteful', 'disorganized', and 'chaotic' are used in relation to managerial work at Central European courts.[28] Because of the frequently changing judicial personnel, judges

28 Cf. Zpráva o analýze oblasti trestního práva a trestního práva procesního (Česká republika) pana Dr. iur. Franka Schreibera, předsedy senátu pro trestní právo u krajského soudu, Komora pro trestní hospodářské právo, Spolková republika Německo (Zemský soud Hagen) [Report of an Analysis in the Field of Criminal Law and Criminal Procedural Law (Czech Republic) by Mr. Dr. iur. Frank Schreiber, the Chair of a Criminal Senate at a regional court, Chamber for Economic Criminal Law, Federal Republic of Germany (Land Court Hagen)], Twinning Project CZ 01/IB/JH/01 Judicial Reform and Court Management Czech Republic – Germany – United Kingdom (2003, not published, on file with author), at 25; CEELI, Judicial Reform Index for Slovakia, June 2002, at 25.

spend much more time then should be the case in performing administrative tasks to the detriment of the quality of their judicial work proper. Many of these complaints would be familiar to judges in the same region between 1918 and 1939.[29]

Hungarian judges, for instance, spend approximately 27 per cent of their time in court, around 15 per cent of their time writing opinions and the rest on administrative tasks, such as the organization of their work, dictation of judicial protocols and statistical issues. Czech judges spend more than half of their time on administrative matters that might otherwise be handled by qualified support staff.[30] In Poland, therefore, the position of court managers was recently created in order to handle more efficiently the courts' work.[31] It will be good to keep these data in mind when one analyses the deficiencies of the post-communist judiciary. In no sense is it the intention of this chapter to assert that the methodological influence exerted by the old conception of law entirely explains all the deficiencies of post-communist judicial decision-making. More practical issues, such as the lack of qualified support staff, might also play a considerable role in these deficiencies.

---

29 The Austro-Hungarian successor states inherited judiciaries damaged by World War I and its aftermath. The efficiency of judicial administration was undermined by the war, the communist rebellion and later anti-communist terror in 1919 Hungary, the 1920 war between Poland and Soviet Russia, the ethnic uprisings in the Czech and Slovak borderland, an economic crisis and common turmoil embracing interwar Europe. In the war's aftermath, judges' salaries drastically declined. On 1 January 1921, the official journal of the Czech judges wrote: 'The judiciary is in a crisis which is not remembered even by the oldest colleagues.' (*Soudcovské listy*, 2 (1921), 1). Czechoslovak judges complained that the judiciary's institutional position and material conditions had worsened in comparison with those that prevailed under the Austro-Hungarian monarchy. The number of non-judicial personnel (clerks, secretaries, etc.) fell substantially below a reasonable level.

30 Zpráva o analýze oblasti trestního práva a trestního práva procesního (Česká republika) pana Dr. iur. Franka Schreibera, předsedy senátu pro trestní právo u krajského soudu, Komora pro trestní hospodářské právo, Spolková republika Německo (Zemský soud Hagen) [Report of an Analysis in the Field of Criminal Law and Criminal Procedural Law (Czech Republic) by Frank Schreiber, the Chair of a Criminal Senate at a regional court, Chamber for Economic Criminal Law, Federal Republic of Germany (Land Court Hagen)], Twinning Project CZ 01/IB/JH/01 Judicial Reform and Court Management Czech Republic – Germany – United Kingdom (2003, not published, on file with author), at 25.

31 'Monitoring the EU accession process: Judicial capacity in the Czech Republic' (2002), 40. Available online at <http://www.soros.org/resources/articles_publications/publications/judcap_20030101> [accessed 3 April 2010].

Introducing the Post-communist Judges

Institutional Settings

The status of judges in Central Europe had already begun to deteriorate after World War I, to the extent that some scholars now say that the longest and most stable period of judicial independence in the region was the era between 1867 and 1914, a period when the democratic institutions of the Austro-Hungarian monarchy functioned and the judiciary was guaranteed its independence by the reigning imperial majesty.[32] After 1945, Central Europe found itself in the Soviet zone of influence, in which 'popular democracies' were invariably installed. The discussion on judicial independence, which was increasing in the interwar period, was interrupted at once by force. The problem of judicial independence was claimed to be solved because, in comparison with the situation in 'bourgeois states', a socialist society 'strengthens and develops the principle of judicial independence'.[33] A revived discussion started in the course of the 1990s after the communist regimes had been overthrown.

The independence of judges was proclaimed in the constitutions of all post-communist countries, but its implementation differs. In the course of the 1990s, Hungary developed a system which gave judges extensive autonomy. The recruitment of the judiciary is now entirely up to the judges themselves. Consequently, the Hungarian model is one of the most autonomous among European systems in the early twenty-first century.[34] Poland and Slovakia have implemented a model of shared powers, in which autonomous judicial organs share the recruitment of the judiciary with the executive authority.[35] In Poland, the National Council of the Judiciary is the constitutional body which represents the judiciary as the third branch of the government. The Council was already established in 1989, and its existence was constitutionally guaranteed in the 1997 Polish Constitution.[36] Among its main functions is to propose judicial candidates

32 Cf. Wagnerová, supra n. 15, at 163 ff. (claiming that 'the longest period in which the judges in the Czech lands had the chance to establish themselves as independent was from 1867 to 1918'). This seems the most valid opinion.

33 Josef Macur, 'Některé aspekty soudcovské nezávislosti' [Some Aspects of Judicial Independence], *Právník*, 127 (1988), 197.

34 On the creation and establishment of this model see Fleck, supra n. 17, 128 ff.; 'Judicial capacity in Hungary' (Open Society Institute, 2002). Available online at <http://www.soros.org/resources/articles_publications/publications/judcap_20030101> [accessed 3 April 2010].

35 For a discussion of the Slovak Judicial Council, see Alexander Bröstl, 'At the crossroads on the way to an independent Slovak judiciary', in J. Přibáň, P. Roberts and J. Young (eds), *Systems of Justice in Transition: Central European Experiences since 1989* (Aldershot: Ashgate, 2003), 141 ff., 148 ff.

36 Art. 186 of the Polish Constitution (proclaiming that the Council shall 'safeguard the independence of courts and judges'). For the literature in English, see Ewa Letowska,

to the President based on its cooperation with the court colleges and general assemblies of judges of relevant courts, which assess candidates' qualifications and submit opinions to the National Council of the Judiciary through the Minister of Justice.[37] In its first decade of existence, this body has generally been judged to be successful.[38]

In contrast, the Czech Republic (together with Latvia) has maintained the most extreme system of centralized management of the courts, performed by the Ministry of Justice. The Czech political elite rejected the very possibility of creating a national council of the judiciary, as well as any important autonomous elements in the judiciary. The proposals to establish such a judicial self-governing body were rejected, primarily with references to the historical tradition of judicial administration before the communist era. Ironically, the old-fashioned and problematic system is defended simply because of its age. In this view, the system has inherent value because it existed prior to the advent of the communist regime.[39]

Although the principle of judicial independence is guaranteed, the administration of the judiciary, including the selection of judicial candidates, is controlled by the Czech Ministry of Justice. The presiding judges of courts (chief judges) exercise their powers more as the representative of the Ministry of Justice than as the representative of the independent third branch of the government. This situation is frequently criticized because of problems with the separation of powers and the facility with which the Ministry of Justice can manipulate the judiciary.[40] For instance, in a recent series of restitution lawsuits by a Czech aristocrat against the Czech Republic, the Ministry of Justice ordered chief judges to inform the

'Courts and tribunals under the Constitution of Poland', *St. Louis-Warsaw Journal of Transnational Law* (1997), 69.

37 Art. 179 of the Polish Constitution. The Minister of Justice has the power to submit candidates to the Council directly, but this seldom happens. For details see 'Judicial capacity in Poland (Open Society Institute, 2002), 158. Available online at <http://www.soros.org/resources/articles_publications/publications/judcap_20030101> [accessed 3 April 2010].

38 Letowska, supra n. 36. In 2001 Poland passed two new important laws on the judiciary, Law on Ordinary Courts, 27 July 2001, Dziennik Ustaw [Official Journal] 2001, no. 98, item 1070; and Law on the National Council of the Judiciary, 27 July 2001, Dz.U. 2001, no. 100, item 1082.

39 In more detail see Michal Bobek 'The fortress of judicial independence and the mental transitions of the Central European judiciaries', *European Public Law*, 14 (2008), 99–123. Also available online at <http://papers.ssrn.com/sol3/papers.cfm?abstract_id=995220&download=yes> [accessed 3 April 2010].

40 'Rozhovory o pravu' [Discussions on the Law], *Soudce*, 5 (2002), at 2. (In this interview, the honorary President of the Czech Judicial Union Vyklický, criticizes the administration of the judiciary, which never functioned properly in the country, and argues that the system is used as a means to deflect blame from the state administration for the frequent delays in the judiciary.)

ministry about all lawsuits made by that person in their court, including the name of the judge who was supposed to decide the case.[41]

The Czech Constitutional Court recently criticized interferences by the executive power with the judicial branch. In 2006 the Czech President dismissed the Supreme Court Chief Justice from her post. The Chief Justice challenged the dismissal before the Constitutional Court, claiming the violation of the principle of judicial independence. The Constitutional Court struck down the law which enabled the executive power to dismiss a chief judge from her post and criticized the Czech regulation of the judiciary.[42] The Court reasoned, inter alia:

> [O]ne of the basic preconditions to the rule of law is a strong and independent judiciary. In a state which should be considered a law-based state, the judiciary must be regarded as one of three powers, which has the same weight as the executive and legislative powers, from which the judiciary must be independent to the greatest degree possible, whereas the judiciary is the only one of the three powers for which especial emphasis is placed on the constitutional protection of its independence. This principle has been broadly embodied in the majority of the world's constitutions; sometimes even in those states where the judiciary was (or is) not actually independent. The danger remains that this principle will remain a mere theoretical edifice, unless it is supplemented in special provisions of the Constitution, or at least in the legal enactments governing the judiciary, by further principles which can be deduced from the constitutions of the majority of West European states, just as from the most important international documents relating to the issue of the independence of the judiciary. […] It is an indispensable requirement for safeguarding the independence of the judiciary that the conditions influencing the selection, recruitment, appointment, career advancement or removal from office of judges allow for independence from the executive and legislative powers. […] In spite of the plurality of institutional models for court administration, one can discover common characteristics in [Europe]. [Judicial independence] is guaranteed either by transferring significant powers to the supreme council of the judiciary (Italy, France, Spain), or by distinguishing judicial administration from state administration within the context of the classic model (Germany, Austria).[43]

---

41 Cf. the website of the plaintiff, <www.knize-kinsky.cz>, including legal opinions for the plaintiff [in Czech, accessed 3 April 2010].

42 For the best description of the dismissal case and the administration of the Central European judiciaries generally see Bobek, supra n. 39.

43 The judgment of the Constitutional Court of 11 July 2006, Pl. US 18/06, quoted according to the English version found at <http://angl.concourt.cz/angl_verze/doc/p-18-06.php> [accessed 3 April 2010].

Based on this reasoning the Court rebuffed the argument of the President (supported by the Czech government) that the power to dismiss a chief judge is vested in the hands of the same body which appoints judges:

> If the President of the Republic is entrusted with the power to appoint the Chief Justice of the Supreme Court, without concurrent action by any other state body, an entirely unlimited power to remove the Chief Justice of the Supreme Court cannot be found in the Constitution's silence. In the situation where the authority to remove the Chief Justice of the Supreme Court is not explicitly mentioned in the Constitution, to adopt an interpretation whereby the President's authority to appoint implicates also the possibility to remove the Chief Justice from office, was in conflict with the constitutionally protected value of the independence of the judiciary and its separation from the executive power. In this system, where the judiciary is not absolutely separated from the executive, the President of the Republic is thus entrusted solely with the authority to install the Chief Justice of the Supreme Court into office, whereas in terms of influencing his performance in office or the termination of that office, no power of the President is envisaged. *A rule which provides that 'he who appoints, may recall' is entirely logical in cases where a direct relationship of superiority and subordination is involved. However, no such relationship exists between the President of the Republic and the Chief Justice of the Supreme Court* (who, according to Art. 92 of the Constitution, stands at the head of the highest judicial organ).[44]

It is doubtful whether this argument would be praised by mainstream Czech legal academia. In fact, the most frequently claimed opinion, prior to the Constitutional Court's judgment, was the one close to the argument of the dissenting Justice V. Kůrka.[45] He rejected the starting premise of the Court's majority, which stated that direct control of the executive power over courts' administration is not comparable to standard administrative relations within the executive branch:

---

44 Id. (emphases added)

45 For just one example, cf. the article of Charles University Constitutional Law Professor Václav Pavlíček, 'Několik předběžných poznámek k jmenovacím a odvolacím pravomocem prezidenta republiky' [Several preliminary notes to the President's powers to appoint and dismiss] *Lege artis: odborný časopis pro právníky* 1/2 (2006), 42–45. The article was reprinted in the brochure published in support of the President's action: Marek Loužek (ed.), *Soudcokracie v ČR: fikce nebo realita?* [Judgeocracy in the Czech Republic: fiction or reality?] CEP, Praha (2006), 71–79. The little brochure was written in order to condemn the Constitutional Court's judgment, which in the view of all authors means the rise of 'judgeocracy' (the term 'invented' by President Klaus personally, close to the classic 'government of judges' problem). Interestingly, some authors, lawyers close to the President, even call for the return of the communist principle according to which the term of all judges was limited, subject to repeated reappointments after a short period of time. It includes a foreword written by President Klaus personally.

> Thus, the court administration which (in contrast to state administration of courts) the Constitutional Court has been considering, is not, in content and regime, distinguished from state administration nor from administration as such; thus, *it is unjustifiable to assert that the principle of superiority and subordination, which is otherwise characteristic of administration, does not apply within its framework*. It is an untenable notion that where the Ministry performs the administration of courts through its chief judge, the court's chief judge is not in a relation of subordination towards the Ministry [...].[46]

However, with regard to the selection of judges of ordinary courts, neither the system with strong judicial councils nor the system with a strong executive branch role appears to work much differently. First, the judicial autonomy which increasingly pervades post-communist systems seems to support the inclination towards a professional career judiciary (see the section on judges below). For instance, the judges who exercise decisive functions within the Hungarian judicial system, the most autonomous judicial system in the region and one of the most autonomous in Europe, openly prefer young candidates without experience in other legal professions over candidates with practice off the bench.[47] The situation in the Czech Republic, the country strongly influenced by the Minister of Justice and with no judicial council whatsoever, surprisingly goes in the same direction, as the real power in selecting judges is exercised by chief judges of regional courts and the actual role of the ministry is usually purely formal.

Although open politicization of the professional career model combined with extensive judicial autonomy is unlikely, the negative side of this model is an increasing insulation of the judiciary, which is generally considered unaccountable and unresponsive to the needs of practical life.[48] Moreover, it seems to support the tendency of law courts 'to close ranks and resist substantive change', as an important Hungarian legal scholar put it.[49] Facing a uniform perspective on the

46 See the dissenting opinion by V. Kůrka, published in English supra n. 43 [emphases added].

47 Judicial Capacity in Hungary, supra n. 34.

48 Critical observers have remarked that, in fact, the six members of the National Judicial Council (out of a total of 15) who are representatives of non-judicial professions constitute the only link that Hungarian judges have to the rest of society. The Hungarian National Judicial Council consists of 15 members: nine judges elected by secret ballot of the Judges' Conference, the President of the Supreme Court (who is also the president of the National Judicial Council), the Minister of Justice, the Attorney General, the President of the Hungarian Chamber of Attorneys, and representatives of Parliament's Constitutional and Judiciary Committee and Budgetary and Financial Committee. Act on the Organisation and Administration of Courts, LXVI/1997, Art. 35. See Judicial Capacity in Hungary, supra n. 42, at 116.

49 See the interview with Zoltán Fleck, 'There is a curious alliance of interests', HVG hetilap, 28 June 2006. Available online at <http://hvg.hu/english/20060628zoltanfleckeng.aspx?s=24h> [accessed 3 April 2010]. Cf. also Zoltán Fleck, 'Architekti demokracie'

proper personality of an ideal judge, the judges tend to be very similar in background and ability. Therefore, the judicial system lacks an enriching variety of experiences and insights. Selection of judges is often based on personal networking that tends to cement existing hierarchies within the judicial system. What is even worse, a non-transparent selection often inclines to choosing relatives of sitting judges,[50] a phenomenon quite well known in France prior to 1789.

Judges

The judiciary in Central Europe remains a predominantly female profession. In Hungary, for example, 72 per cent of the judges at the district courts in 2000 were women.[51] In 1990, when the Polish communist regime fell, 61.6 per cent of Polish judges were women, and by 2000 this percentage had increased to 63.6 per cent (66.2 per cent at first-instance courts). One finds almost identical numbers in the Czech judiciary (63 per cent in 2001).[52] In Slovakia, women occupied almost 64 per cent of the posts at district courts.[53] In contrast, there were far fewer women at the higher courts: in Poland only 22 per cent of judges at the Supreme Court in 1997 were women[54] and only 24 per cent at the Czech Supreme Court in 2004.[55]

These figures indicate that the judicial profession remains rather less prestigious in the post-communist region. Generally, it might be said that the percentage of women on the bench is in inverse proportion to the general level of prestige enjoyed by the profession. In the countries where the judiciary enjoys high prestige, that is, common law countries or Germany, the number of female judges is traditionally

---

[Architects of Democracy], *Sociologický časopis* [Czech Sociological Review], 4 (2005), 601–15.

50 Cf. the country report on Hungary from Freedom House, with further references for Hungary. Available online at <http://www.freedomhouse.org/template.cfm?page=47&nit=453&year=2008> [accessed 3 April 2010]. Similarly Fleck, supra n. 17, at 129 (discussing the 'uncontrolled system tending towards oligarchization'). As far as is possible to know, the situation is rather similar in both the Czech and Slovak Republics.

51 Office of the National Council of Justice, The Functioning of the Hungarian Judicial System, Budapest, 8 February 2000 (on file with author).

52 Wagnerová, supra n. 15, at 170.

53 Author's own estimate based on figures contained in CEELI, Judicial Reform Index for Slovakia, June 2002, at 9.

54 Małgorzata Fuszara, 'Women lawyers in Poland under the impact of post-1989 transformation', in Ulrike Schultz and Gisela Shaw (eds), *Women in the World's Legal Professions* (Oxford: Hart Publishing, 2003), 375.

55 Author's own estimate based on figures contained in the website at http://www.nsoud.cz [accessed 3 April 2010]. In Slovakia, nearly 40 per cent of the Supreme Court posts are held by women (author's own estimate based on figures contained in CEELI, Judicial Reform Index for Slovakia, June 2002, at 9).

much lower.[56] In contrast, the countries where a judicial career is much less prestigious, typically the countries of Romanist legal circle (for example, France and Italy), have achieved, in general, a gender balance, or even gender imbalance in favour of women, like in the ex-socialist systems.[57]

Nowadays, Central European judges are formally appointed by their country's president but the overall process is openly based on the professional career model of the judiciary, where younger candidates are favoured and older candidates with professional experience outside of the judicial branch are disadvantaged or at least discouraged.[58] This effectively means that, at the level of trial courts, cases are adjudicated by the least experienced lawyers, usually recent graduates after a short period of preparation. Although it is an old continental tradition, even before communist rule ended the Hungarians began to question to what extent the system might continue to work in this way.[59] In the view pronounced in Hungary three years before the fall of the communist system, a truly independent and reliable judiciary would be created only if the judiciary itself were composed of experienced lawyers who had had substantial life and legal experience off the bench.[60]

The classical continental paradigm of drawing judges from recent law school graduates is now increasingly questioned throughout the region.[61] The situation is slowly changing, mostly by statutory enactments. The minimum age at which a person is qualified to become a judge in the Czech Republic is now 30 (but until 2003 it was 25 years). In Slovakia, since 2000, the minimum age to become a judge has been 30.[62] Many judges appointed in the Czech Republic until 2003 were not much older than 25. In 2003 the Czech Minister of Justice (since 2003 Chief Justice of the Constitutional Court) wrote that when he saw 'the kids at the Prague Castle who were taking the judicial oath', he became even more persuaded

56 Ulrike Schultz, 'Introduction: Women in the world's legal professions: Overview and synthesis', in Ulrike Schultz and Gisela Shaw (eds), *Women in the World's Legal Professions* (Oxford: Hart Publishing, 2003), xxv, xxxvii. (The respective numbers in 2000 were at around 10 per cent – for example, in the US females make up between 10 and 12 per cent of the judiciary; in Australia approximately 10 per cent, but 22.6 per cent in family courts; and in the UK 11.8 per cent).

57 In Germany 26.31 per cent in 1999. Id.

58 I can recollect from my personal experience, drawn from an interview conducted in 1997 at the Prague Municipal Court, that the interviewer, a judge of the court, quite openly told us, all recent graduates, that personally he did not like experienced candidates, as they would be inclined to bring strange things into the judiciary. Facing this experience, I decided to join the legal academia instead.

59 Cf. critically Cs. Kabódi, 'La juridiction est-elle une prestation?', *Acta Juridica Academiae Scientiarum Hungaricae* 28/1-2 (1986), 149–62.

60 Id. In Kabódi's opinion, a judge dealing with the issues of fact, that is, a judge at the lowest (trial) level, should be an experienced person, not a recent graduate.

61 Id., at 112.

62 Law No. 385/2000 Z.z., § 5 (1.a). Cf. in English, CEELI, Judicial Reform Index for Slovakia, June 2002, at 7.

that the Czech legal order must abandon this harmful practice and opt instead for judges with sufficient life experience and at least 10 or 20 years of previous legal experience.[63] In the Czech Republic a minimum age of 40 is being considered for the future.[64]

The most severe critique of the present situation has been written by Deputy Chief Justice of the Czech Constitutional Court, Eliška Wagnerová. In her view:

> Continental Europe has been abandoning exaggerated legal positivism in favour of sociologising lines of thought which necessarily change the institutional framework. A judge untouched by life is no longer sought after. As the law ceased to be a science about itself but is about life then an exponent of the law must know life.[65]

It seems safe to say that a judge educated in the continental professional career model is the least suitable person to overcome the dogmatism and formalism typical of the Central European judicial profession. A young lawyer is from the very beginning of her professional career moulded by this outmoded system, which understands itself as a bureaucratic machine and emphasizes formalism over substantive values, and simplified solutions over more complex ones. Young Central European judges, during the few years of their judicial candidacy immediately following largely dogmatic law education at the university, encounter nothing other than the mores of their older colleagues. The values of dogmatism and formalism, omnipresent throughout their first professional years, are likely to become firmly internalized because the young judges are never exposed to anything but formalist and textual law application.[66]

High Courts and Constitutional Courts

Judicial posts at the high courts in Central Europe are usually filled by career judges who have made the journey throughout the judicial ranks, beginning at the lowest judicial level and ending at the supreme court of the ordinary judiciary

---

63 Pavel Rychetský, Reformu justice pro občany, ne pro soudce! [The Reform of the Judiciary for Citizens, not for Judges!], the daily Právo, p. 6, 12 April 2003.

64 Koncepce stabilizace justice [The Conception of the Stabilization of the Judiciary], a document of the Czech Ministry of Justice (2004), at 10. Available in Czech at <http://www.epravo.cz> [accessed 3 April 2010].

65 Wagnerová, supra n. 15, at 178. It is a translation of the article, which was originally published in Czech.

66 Cf. this description of the Italian situation: 'Law graduates become judges by way of a public examination. Once admitted to the judiciary they enter a bureaucratic culture lacking in a tradition of excellence and hard work. Excessive importance is given to formalities.' Adrian A.S. Zuckerman, 'Justice in crisis: Comparative dimensions of civil procedure', in A.A.S. Zuckerman (ed.) *Civil Justice in Crisis: Comparative Perspectives of Civil Procedure* (Oxford: Oxford University Press, 1999), 3–52, at 24.

after 20 or more years on the bench. Most of these people have never had any career experience other than in the judiciary. This is a typical example of both the Czech and Slovak Supreme Courts, composed almost exclusively of professional career judges. The sole exception is the Czech Supreme Administrative Court, the body much more diverse than a typical post-communist high court, which includes academics, former attorneys-at-law, former high state officials and so on.

The Polish high courts, in contrast to a typical post-communist supreme court, have been transformed not only in terms of personnel, but also professionally. After the end of communism the Polish Supreme Court and Supreme Administrative Court were re-staffed with a considerable number of academics and other 'outsiders' to the judicial echelons. Thereby the post-communist Polish judicial system vastly utilized the Polish academia, not so compromised by the former communist regime as was its Czech-Slovak counterpart. In the summer of 2003, out of 29 judges of the civil section of the Supreme Court almost one-quarter (seven) hold professorial degrees.[67] One professor of the Warsaw University, himself a judge at the Supreme Court, noted that the composition of the court is shaped by the academics, most of them lacking previous judicial experience.[68]

One must bear these numbers in mind. They might explain why the Polish high courts often provide different results than their counterparts in other Central European legal systems. The Polish high courts were far more receptive to a new concept of law and a 'new constitutionalism' than the majority of other post-communist high courts.[69]

Unlike a typical post-communist high court, which is usually perceived as a symbol of legal continuity, the task of the post-communist constitutional courts was to annihilate old paradigms. As Ruti Teitel put it, [l]aw in periods of radical upheaval is commonly conceived as antistructural, as eluding principle and defying paradigm. The period of normative shift is commonly thought to be antiparadigmatic.'[70] This 'antiparadigmatic' purpose could not be achieved by self-restrained constitutional courts. And activist constitutional courts might only develop if peopled by judges of a very different sort than those sitting in the ordinary judiciary.

Who are the constitutional justices in the Central European region? First, unlike ordinary career judges, they are political appointees with a visible professional past behind them. For instance, the American model is followed in Russia, Slovenia

67 According to the data provided by the Polish Supreme Court on its Internet page at <http://www.sn.pl> [accessed 3 April 2010].

68 W. Sanetra, 'Sąd Najwyższy w systemie wymiaru sprawiedliwości' [The Supreme Court in the system of the judiciary], *Przegląd Sądowy*, 9/7-8 (1999), 3–15, at 15.

69 Cf. in more detail Z. Kühn, 'Making constitutionalism horizontal: Three different Central European strategies', in Andras Sajó and Renata Uitz (eds), *The Constitution in Private Relations: Expanding Constitutionalism* (Utrecht: Eleven International Publishing, 2005), 217–40.

70 Ruti G. Teitel, *Transitional Justice* (Oxford: Oxford University Press, 2000), at 215.

and the Czech Republic, where the constitutional justices are appointed by the President with the approval of the Senate. In Slovakia, the Parliament nominates two candidates for each vacant post and the President chooses from among these candidates. In Hungary and Poland, the Justices are elected by Parliament; in Poland by the lower chamber of the Parliament (the Hungarian Parliament is unicameral).[71]

The Federal Constitutional Court in Germany, a paradigm for the post-communist courts, has traditionally been dominated by academics. A similar situation exists more or less in the four Central European post-communist countries. In February 2003, of the 15 justices at the Polish Constitutional Tribunal 10 were law professors; in Hungary it was as many as nine of 11.[72] Between 1985 and 2001, 26 Polish justices served at the Tribunal, which included 24 law professors (five of whom were also experienced practitioners), five ordinary judges, three prosecutors and two practising attorneys.[73] The number of academics is considerably lower in the countries of former Czechoslovakia. Perhaps this reflects the difficulty in finding academics not compromised by the Czechoslovak communist regime.[74] Since 2000, when the Slovak court was newly composed, it has had five law professors out of 13 justices; in the Czech Republic in spring 2003, only one-third of the bench was comprised of law professors (five of 15), in 2009 only two law professors remained.[75]

In all four courts we can find outstanding figures able to give the Court's reasoning appropriate direction toward sophisticated Western-style adjudication. Such exceptional figures were necessary, if we consider the very nature of the activity of the new courts: to introduce new conceptions of constitutionalism in a society governed by very different ideals. Constitutionalism challenges the space in the legal system which, in Kahn-Freund's meaning, is more organic,[76] and the resistance to change in law would be very high 'when law is tightly coupled

71 Cf. European Commission for Democracy through Law, *The Composition of Constitutional Courts* (Strasbourg: Council of Europe Publishing, 1997).

72 Data located on the Internet sites of the corresponding courts.

73 Leszek Lech Garlicki, 'The experience of the Polish Constitutional Court', in Wojciech Sadurski (ed.) Constitutional Justice, East and West: Democratic Legitimacy and Constitutional Courts in Post-communist Europe in a Comparative Perspective (The Hague: Kluwer Law International, 2002), 265–82, at 269, notes 16 and 17 and the accompanying text.

74 In this sense, a former Slovak prime minister, Vladimír Mečiar, remarked that it is impossible to disguise the fact that 'there were not even 10 experts on constitutional law in Slovakia'. See Herman Schwartz, *The Struggle for Constitutional Justice in Post-Communist Europe* (Chicago, IL: University of Chicago Press, 2000), at 201.

75 Data located on the Internet sites of the corresponding courts. The former Czech data relate to the 'first' court, appointed by President Havel; the latter to the 'second' Court appointed by President Klaus.

76 O. Kahn-Freund, 'On use and misuse of comparative law', *Modern Law Review*, 37 (1974), 1.

in binding arrangements to other social processes'.[77] The leading figures of the constitutional courts were scholars who had a background in Western doctrine while not being compromised by relations with the former regime.[78] An important role was also played by charismatic lawyers who emigrated during the communist rule,[79] or who were persecuted by the communist regime. The relative lack of such exceptional figures on the Slovak Constitutional Court throughout the 1990s very likely constitutes one of the reasons for its rather rigid jurisprudence.[80]

Judicial Philosophy and its Transformation

It can be said that the application and methodology of communist and post-communist law is an understudied phenomenon, especially if compared with numerous volumes written on the law and its application in Nazi Germany. Even recent publications dealing with the 'darker legacies of law in Europe' persistently elaborate only national socialism and fascism, as if European legal culture had no other 'darker legacies'.[81] It can be said that, in communist totalitarian systems, a distinctive legal culture fully developed, so that it evolved to a much greater extent than did the legal culture in the Nazi era, which lasted for only 12 years. In contrast with the short-lived Nazi regime, Russian communism lasted for over 70 years, and communism in Central Europe for over 40 years. In this way, communist reasoning, communist legal culture and its aftermath offer us a very interesting backdrop against which to analyse the development of legal culture and its methodology in a long-lasting system that was intellectually almost completely separated from the outside world.

Even those authors presently dealing with the post-communist region primarily analyse the processes of transition from communism while mostly omitting persistent legacies of communist legal culture and communist legal

77 Günther Teubner, 'Legal irritants: Good faith in British law or how unifying law ends up in new divergences', *Modern Law Review*, 61 (1998), 19.

78 Examples of such figures, in Hungary, are L. Sólyom (the Court's President between 1990 and 1998) and Attila Harmathy (from 1998); in Poland Lech Garlicki, an internationally renowned constitutional comparatist, was a justice until 2001; in the Czech Republic Pavel Holländer, a legal theoretician and philosopher, who was reappointed for a second term in 2003; in Slovakia, Alexander Bröstl (from 2000) represents such a figure.

79 Such as Vladimír Klokočka of the Czech Constitutional Court (1993–2003) or Eliška Wagnerová of the same Court (from 2002).

80 See Procházka, supra n. 12, at 249. Cf. id., at 262 (observing the presence of the former communist apparatchiks at the Slovak Constitutional Court in the 1990s, claiming that 'one's ability to appreciate what no legal text can offer is something that will require years of humble learning').

81 Christian Joerges and Navraj Singh Ghaleigh (eds), *Darker Legacies of Law in Europe: The Shadow of National Socialism and Fascism over Europe and its Legal Traditions* (Oxford: Hart Publishing, 2003).

methodology.[82] Analyses of the judiciaries in the post-communist region focus mostly on the new and rapidly developing phenomenon of constitutional courts. There are very interesting treatises describing the emergence and first decade of the new constitutional judiciaries. More critical analysis of the post-communist constitutional judiciaries has appeared recently.[83] On the other hand, the phenomenon of post-communist ordinary courts has been largely neglected, as the novelty of constitutional courts has attracted all of legal scholars' attention.

While post-communist law has been substantially modified since 1989, all too often the methods of reasoning about that law remained unaffected. Considering the fact that, to a substantial extent, the same persons continued in both judicial offices and academic positions, this finding should come as no surprise.

It seems there were two periods in the development of communist legal style and legal culture: first the Stalinism of the 1950s; and then the declining socialism of the 1970s and 1980s.[84]

The Stalinist conception of law suffered from an inner contradiction, as it included both anti-formalist/activist and formalist/statist versions. If one were to characterize Stalinist legal philosophy fully, it is fair to say that it was Janus-faced. On the one hand, the era of Stalinism emphasized the activism of individuals who were willing to achieve extraordinary working results and fight a foreign enemy. Stalinist judges had to join this trend and they also had to show that they contributed to the rapid building of socialism. Facing the specific atmosphere of the time, judicial reasoning became surprisingly activist in *all* cases, not only in political cases of the suppression of the opposition. In that period judicial reasoning radically departed from its continental roots. On the other hand, however, the very basic principles of Stalinist legal philosophy were remarkably formalist, dogmatic and state-centred. Formalism of jurisprudence on the one hand and activist legal reasoning on the other hand came into tension, and, after the end of Stalinism, were finally resolved in favour of formalism.

What follows is the era of post-Stalinist dictatorships which, following Václav Havel, can be referred to as 'the post-totalitarian era',[85] the era of allegedly Marxist cliché to which, deep down, virtually nobody was committed. In this era Socialist fervour died out everywhere, including in courtrooms, and survived only in the numerous conferences of the Communist Party. Despite the fact that the

82 However, one should mention Inga Markovits, a scholar who consistently deals with the issue of the application of communist law in East Germany. See, for example, 'Justice in Lüritz', *American Journal of Comparative Law*, 50 (2002), 819; or *Imperfect Justice: An East-West German Diary* (Oxford: Clarendon Press, 1995).

83 Wojciech Sadurski, *Rights Before Courts: A Study of Constitutional Courts in Postcommunist States of Central and Eastern Europe* (Dordrecht: Springer, 2005).

84 In more detail see Zdeněk Kühn, 'Worlds apart: Western and Central European judicial culture at the onset of the European enlargement', *American Journal of Comparative Law*, 52 (2004), 531–67.

85 Václav Havel, *The Power of the Powerless* (New York: M.E. Sharpe, 1985), at 27.

communist rulers of that time were obsessed by rules, law in fact mattered very little, and many important issues were resolved outside the legal system proper. After all, socialist ideology held that law was destined to disappear during the course of the successful socialist development.

Stalinist judges were radical activists and anti-formalists who did not hesitate to rewrite the law in order to satisfy the ideals of the ruling ideology, the aims of societal transformation, or, most likely, the needs of the ruling party. After the decline of Stalinism, however, socialist legal scholarship produced, and the Socialist judiciary put into effect, a strange mix of old-fashioned pre-socialist positivism and Stalinist and post-Stalinist legal doctrine veiled in Marxist pseudoscientific orthodoxy. The strong formalism of the Stalinist conception of law was fully utilized only after Stalin's death. The argument here targets the era of the two last decades of the communist regimes, when this conception of law and a new ideology of judicial decision-making were already firmly in place.

The events of 1989 returned the democratic conception of the rule of law to the region. The problems of post-communist judicial argumentation seem to be a direct continuation of the last phase of Central European communism. After the end of communism, the old 'socialist legal family', which most comparative law treatises had posited, had seemingly been replaced by a legal black hole.[86] Although, as a result of the EU enlargement, the 'other Europe' became part of the European Union, it would be too simplistic to assume that all features of the old legal culture disappeared with the fall of the Berlin Wall, so that those countries' legal systems thereby automatically assimilated to the EU norm. The communist legal system had been simplified during the four decades of the self-proclaimed Central European socialism. This simplification has had a dramatic impact on post-communist legal problems. In order for the new laws and institutions to reflect the burgeoning life of the post-communist society, new complex theories of law and its application needed to be rapidly developed. Yet, all too often, the post-communist conception of law has remained imprisoned in parochial, outmoded positivist approaches.

In fact, the analysis of Imre Szabó written in the 1970s is fully applicable in the early 2000s. Legal scholarship used to be, and still is, based on the position of simplistic textual positivism, in that it takes 'an apologist's view in respect of the existing […] legal systems'. Academia and the old-fashioned parochial legal education are left 'with hardly any other role but to provide explanations justifying positive law, while the study of the conditions for continued evolution, including a criticism of existing law, [is] relegated to the background'.[87] This prominent

86 Cf. Rafał Mańko, 'The culture of private law in Central Europe after enlargement: A Polish perspective', *European Law Journal*, 11 (2005), 527, 547–48, discussing the fact that the most recent edition of Zweigert's and Kötz's treatise on comparative law simply discarded the socialist legal family 'without writing anything in their place' (id., at 548).

87 Imre Szabó, 'The socialist conception of law', in *International Encyclopedia of Comparative Law,* vol. II, *The Legal Systems of the World: Their Comparison and*

feature, accompanied by insufficient funding of higher education throughout the region, has to a remarkable degree assisted the old ideology of the judicial application of law in being surprisingly resistant to the challenges of the post-communist era.

The empowerment of the judiciary via the European enlargement might be considered a sort of treatment for many problems described in this work. Although European law will face a number of obstacles, a kind of 'spillover' effect will probably slowly occur, as national judges begin to make use of the new tools provided by EU law even in purely domestic cases. As in the old EU member states, 'the increasingly intensive penetration of a patulous Community law into the fabric of the domestic legal systems' will bring about 'a dramatic alteration in the constitutional status of the national judicial authorities'.[88]

Yet perhaps another sort of spillover effect will also occur. The ideology of excessive formalism is not likely to survive the challenge posed by the realities of an empowered judiciary; a new ideological conception of the judicial function will be even more urgently needed. National ordinary judges have acquired new competencies, above all the power given by Community law to set aside national legislation, thus creating a decentralized system of judicial review in the countries where it has traditionally been centralized. Their exercise of that power in particular will inevitably call for more sophisticated explanations of the significance of precedent (whether or not it is recognized as having binding force), as that is a precondition of any sensible application of Community law in the member states. Post-communist legal scholarship will have to develop new doctrines and a methodology that will be better able to account for judicial decision-making, and will provide post-communist lawyers with more practical ideologies for the judicial application of law.

Moreover, the ongoing European integration increases the importance of comparative legal research and comparative legal studies.[89] This is one reason why a significant increase in the role of comparative law can be expected in the eight post-communist nations that joined the EU in May 2004.

Unification, Chapter 1: 'The different conceptions of the law', (Mouton, The Hague: J.C.B. Mohr, Tübingen, 1975), at 52.

88 Ami Barav, 'Omnipotent courts', in Deirdre Curtin and Ton Heukels (eds), *Institutional Dynamics of European Integration: Essays in Honour of Henry G. Schermers*, vol. II (1994), 265, 301.

89 Cf., for example, A5-0384/2001 European Parliament Resolution of 15 November 2001 on the approximation of the civil and commercial law of the member states (COM(2001)398, C5-0471/2001,2001/2187(COS)), para. 14(f), urging the Commission to submit an action plan comprising, inter alia, 'measures to promote the dissemination of comparative analysis and common legal concepts and solutions in academic training and in the syllabuses of the legal profession, as well as promote dissemination of Community law to the same academic and legal circles'. The resolution is available online at <http://europa.eu> [accessed 19 April 2010].

With the ongoing empowerment of the post-communist ordinary judiciary, serious discussion about the proper level of judicial self-restraint and the limits of judicial function will inevitably start. Although the empowerment of the judiciary is wholeheartedly to be supported, this is far from advocating one-sided judicial activism or naively believing that all human wrongs and the ills of society will be redressed by all-powerful judges who act as social engineers.

Discussions concerning the proper limits of judicialization are entirely legitimate and very important. With the collapse of the original, strictly conceived model of the separation of powers, courts are no longer unwilling and mechanical enforcers of rules made through the political process in parliament. The progressively increasing judicialization of politics and society seems to be 'a partial aspect of societal evolution',[90] and future legal theory must focus on developing new schemes which would be able fully and properly to account for such judicial activity. If, in the long run, the judiciary comes to represent a serious obstacle to widely accepted societal reforms, it would undermine the process of judicialization in Central Europe and lead to a new era of judicial self-restraint, as occurred in France after 1789. However, for as long as the process of judicialization is generally considered 'one of the most powerful barriers that has ever been devised against the tyranny of political assemblies',[91] the rise of judiciaries in Central Europe is likely to go on.

90 Günther Teubner, 'Juridification: Concepts, aspects, limits, solutions', in Teubner (ed.), *Juridification of Social Spheres* (Berlin: Walter de Gruyter, 1987), 27.

91 Alexis de Tocqueville, *Democracy in America: Book I* (New York: Vintage Books, 1945), at 107 [original 1835].

Chapter 8
Bureaucratic and Managerial Cultures in Central Eastern European Courts

Daniela Piana

Between the idea
And the reality
Between the motion
And the act
Falls the shadow.

T.S. Eliot, 'The Hollow Men' (1925)

Introduction

The large majority of European judicial systems features a bureaucratic organization (Guarnieri and Pederzoli, 2002) and, by and large, sticks to a deductive conception of law (Raz, 1971).[1] This model of governance epitomizes the Weberian conception of bureaucracy, in which formal and impersonal rules define the scope and boundaries of roles performed under the control of hierarchical mechanisms of enforcement (Weber, [1914] 1968, Part III, Chapter 6).

In all bureaucratic judicial systems, adjudication legitimately performs its social function as long as formalized boundaries keep the judiciary isolated from undue influences possibly coming from external actors and institutions. In doing so, these formalized boundaries set a net distinction between an internal logic of action (based on the legality principle) and the several different logics that are eventually followed by other parts of the social system to which the magistracy belongs (Kallinikos, 2004 and 2006).[2] These characteristics are summed up by a prototypical feature of all civil law systems of justice administration, namely legal codification, whereby cases are adjudicated on the basis of a proceduralized series of actions described in legal codes (civil and penal procedural codes).[3]

1 As long as law was for the first time deemed to be a consistent and coherent system of rules, spanning from general to particular, the organization that was asked to apply these rules had to be hierarchically ordered (Damaska, 1986).

2 These parts may be functionally different – for example, hospitals, schools and so on – but may also include different normative orders, such as the market.

3 In the majority of European countries the application of a Weberian organizational model is, by and large, co-responsible for having put forth the seductive promise of fair justice with an impersonal face. Formally defined functions, together with a legal decisional

Viewed alone and separately from one another, none of these features suffices to create a modern, bureaucratic system of adjudication.

Over the last two decades, Central and Eastern European judicial institutions have undergone multiple processes of change (Kriger and Czarnota, 1999; Přibáň, 2001; Kühn, 2004) in which domestic forces and international donors intensively marked the pace and direction of judicial reforms (Dakolias, 1999; Morlino and Magen, 2008; Piana, 2009).

Under their influence judicial institutions have endured two types of transformation. The first one was aimed at de-politicizing judicial organizations by introducing reliable mechanisms for the fair and transparent appointment of judicial staff (Přibáň, Roberts and Young, 2003). As a matter of fact, judges and prosecutors appointed under communist rule were either kicked off the bench or re-socialized in a new legal culture. The second transformation took place a bit later on, when the bulk of legal reforms had already been realized and the political systems were somehow moving toward their consolidation. At this second stage, which overlapped with the pre-accession period, post-communist countries embarked on a process of modernization which, in principle, asked courts to develop new forms of expertise, including managerial know-how. The core business of this second wave of reforms was more about capacity-building than institutional design (Coman, 2007; Dallara, 2009). If, at first, post-communist judicial systems had been asked to become impartial and to ensure their isolation from politics, they were now being targeted by a number of policies aimed at developing managerial know-how in its new members. In a nutshell, courts were now also expected to pursue goals of efficiency and effectiveness.

The intertwining of these two transformations has been underexplored by scholars (with few exceptions, such as Frydman, 2007; Piana, 2009). Though deep and extensive empirical research should be conducted in order to properly address this issue, by devoting attention to the type of values and logics of action promoted by European institutions in post-communist judicial systems, one may open a vista and provide a few clues about the knots left hanging by scholars on the effects – whether intentional or not – that the pre-accession strategy had on these systems. In trying to cast better light on the criticalities they are associated with, the following pages will deal inevitably with four issues: (1) which consequences might arise in Central and Eastern European countries from the implementation of two different rationalities, one legal and the other managerial; (2) whether there was anything specific about countries that were exiting from non-democratic experiences or whether one could say that the same problems confronted by these countries arise in advanced democracies as well; (3) to what extent it is legitimate

rationality, were expected to result in impartial and impersonal adjudication. According to this view, bureaucratic organizations of judicial roles should be able to protect magistrates from undue influences and thereby guarantee impartial adjudication. Thus, as long as judges adjudicate on the basis of law and behave as bureaucratic actors, legitimacy of the adjudication is guaranteed.

to speak of a post-bureaucratic setting when one is speaking of post-communist judicial systems; and (4) whether a fully-fledged system of bureaucratic judicial governance ever existed in these countries.

Bureaucracy, Modernity and Judicial Governance in CEE Countries

In a bureaucratic judicial system, legal and bureaucratic logics of action – which prescribe that decisions should be based on legal norms and should also be respectful of the legal doctrine set down by senior judges and prosecutors usually sitting in the high court (Cassation or Supreme) – co-participate to put in motion a distinctive pattern of judicial governance in which the independence of a single judge is substantially subordinated to the independence of the magistracy as a system. The rationale for this goes in the same direction as the principle of autonomy of public administration from political institutions. As Max Weber correctly pointed out, judges who work in bureaucratic settings benefit from very peculiar types of guarantee, such as independence and professional status. Once recruited by means of a general, standardized procedure (which very much resembles the procedure adopted to recruit civil servants and bureaucrats) they are inserted into a machine in which they will spend all of their careers. Each judge is expected to behave in a way that is respectful of several different rules and standards. His behaviour should be lawful and it should respect: the organizational values that constitute and shape the identity of the judicial system in which they work; the professional deontology of the legal professions; a standard of effectiveness and efficiency in the use of the organizational resources; the rights of the citizens, the ultimate holders of democratic sovereignty. 'This complex picture figures out a situation where judges expect costs and negative rewards if their behaviour does not respect a set of several different standards. Some of them are weaker and informally enforced, while some of them are harder and legally binding' (Piana, 2009). One may safely say that the bureaucratic judge (a judge who is working within a bureaucratically organized judicial system) is held accountable by means of a vertical chain of mechanisms of rule enforcement, whose effectiveness depends on the internal cohesiveness of the judicial hierarchy.

What ensures the legitimacy of a decision on a case is the balanced combination of a procedurally correct process of decision-making in relation to the case (evidence taking, hearing of witnesses and so on) and the cohesiveness of the judicial decisions taken in previous years/decades and among different courts belonging to the same system. The consistency of the judicial hierarchy and the respect for legal procedures are all aimed at ensuring the impartiality and imperturbability of the bench *vis-à-vis* possible influences coming from the external environment, whether politics, or society, or the market, or other foreign legal systems.

As we all know, this portrait no longer corresponds to the real state of affairs in which adjudication takes place. Judges are now placed amidst a complex, multi-layered and multi-centred global system, which generates norms that should be accommodated mostly on a case-by-case basis rather than on the basis of deductive and intra-systemic reasoning. Ordinary judges are allowed to be attentive to the normative creation of foreign courts and, accordingly, to bypass or overrule the doctrine endorsed by senior judges who are responsible for their own career promotion. In issuing a sentence judges are no longer simply interested in domestic reputation, but can be particularly sensitive to the reaction of foreign colleagues he or she may have met during international meetings or seminars. It is not only the legal procedure which starts to be in touch with 'heteronomic' inputs (that is, inputs coming from different 'nomos', different normative orders), but also the judicial hierarchy, who are put under pressure by the increasingly important interaction of colleagues beyond the formalized borders of the bureaucracy in which the hierarchy is embodied.

Non-democratic judicial systems fit into this picture with some nuances and under specific conditions. It should be remembered, for example, that in authoritarian regimes judges are usually not subjected to any particular form of politicization, whereas the scope of their action is mostly and considerably reduced by limiting the number and the types of cases on which ordinary courts adjudicate. In this respect, the development of a hierarchical judicial organization is less important for authoritarian rulers, because they do not aim to influence society through adjudication. Sensitive cases and politically delicate issues are treated outside the ordinary courts in special judicial bodies (military courts are a fairly common example). Unlike authoritarian regimes, totalitarian regimes desperately need the support of the bench in applying the law in line with the dominant (and unique) ideology. Courts adjudicating under totalitarian rule are asked to become part of the system rather than being left to one side (Arendt, 1951). Accordingly, judicial behaviours are inclined to become over-proceduralized in order to mask, through the sacred value of procedure (impersonal by definition), the arbitrariness (from the point of view of citizens) of their decisions. Moreover, judicial hierarchy is vital in the effective transformation of courts within the regime. The more cohesive the hierarchy, the more value is injected into the system from the top of the hierarchy, namely at the level of high-ranking judges, whose decisions are more likely to be enforced along all levels of the judicial system, from supreme courts to ordinary courts. Strong socialization to ideology is distinctive of this type of system (Bihari, 1979 Lane, 1996). Whereas high-ranked judges are appointed by political bodies, ordinary and low-ranked judges are often influenced by senior colleagues and opportunities for career promotion (decided by senior judges).

Central and Eastern European countries are, in theory, representative of this second model. With the passing of time, socialist states rapidly experienced the collapse of authority and cohesiveness. Organizational units, in principle belonging to the state, were in reality under the influence of external interests and unable to stick to a common, organization-based set of values, due to the lack of a fully-fledged impersonal approach. Therefore, in post-communist societies, bureaucracies are in a very uneasy position. On the one hand, they are a vital instrument for the processes of institutional change and institutional rebuilding necessary to democratize the state. On the other hand, they are the focus of reforms aimed at de-politicizing and moving public sectors away from non-democratic legal and political cultures. Besides the problem of the fact that public institutions have been both the instrument and target of reforms during the post-communist period, post-communist bureaucracies have also faced the problem of capacity-building. In fact, in these societies the legacy of the non-democratic regime has mainly consisted of a largely politicized state, which has, in the last decade, undergone a process of de-legitimization. As a matter of fact, at the sunset of communism, states turned out to be captured by a political elite threaded throughout the dominant party and masked behind heavy proceduralization and comprehensive formal legalism. Beyond the façade of this compact structure, local elites were tied to public officials and civil servants, whose loyalty had been turned away from the central hierarchy towards local networks and clubs of influential people working between politics and bureaucracies. The coherence and cohesiveness of the state in the moment of the decline of the communist regime were both very low. This lack of hierarchical coherence, coupled with the legacy of a regime that had dismantled any capacity to undertake individual enterprises, was matched by the hyper-bureaucratization of the all-public sector. 'Socialist rule of law' was the label used to refer to a state that was organized according to the law, performed according to hierarchical rules – with a corresponding deductive system of legal sources – and was respectful of the legal correctness of its procedures. However, beyond this mask, and to differing degrees, all Central and Eastern European countries experienced, at the end of the communist regime, a weak state wrapped in procedural splendour (Ajani, 1996).

Judges did not remain exempt from this process. In communist judicial systems, the hierarchical organization of functions had been kept firmly immune from any change for decades. However, the communist ideology penetrated – more so, to some extent, in countries such as Czechoslovakia or Bulgaria, less so in others like Hungary and Poland – judicial function: the more the communist state developed, the more the high court became politicized, including prosecutors, whose limits, scopes, instruments and aims were completely handled by a restricted and exclusive political elite. Therefore, in the aftermath of the fall of communism, all CEE countries introducing the democratic rule of law featured a bureaucratic and proceduralized, but not apolitical, state. The *procuratura* has been thought as the paladin of political power. The unachieved or unaccomplished separation of normative institutional orders based on different values (basically morality, politics and law), which characterized the totalitarian experience, left a deep mark on the way that bureaucracy was participating in the governance of CEE countries. Even though it is risky to venture into an analysis of the relationship between totalitarianism and modernity, for the sake of argument, here it should be pointed out that legal rules of an impersonal nature and the division of politics from morality and law had only been partially achieved in post-communist social systems. This is despite the fact that they featured bureaucratic structures, based on legal rationality and proceduralized ways of dealing with collective actions.

A Place for Governance in Post-communist Judiciaries?

In a bureaucratically organized judicial system, legal, institutional and professional accountability has, for centuries, had a dominant and almost exhaustive role in keeping the behaviour of judges and prosecutors coherent and aligned with the institutional spirit of the organization in which they work. Concretely, this means that judicial behaviours have been assessed on the basis of their compliance with legal standards (the legality principle), with the doctrines set down by senior judges sitting in higher courts (values embodied into the judicial institution) and with deontological standards (the standards set down by legal professionalism).[4]

The interaction of these dimensions of accountability seems to have happened fairly easily. In particular, they are co-extensive and they target the same normative and institutional order: a hierarchy, whose professional standards are set down by its senior members and whose boundaries refract possible interferences coming from different normative orders, such as the market, morality or politics.

It was only after World War II that bureaucracies started to be touched by a wave of managerialism and efficiency-oriented reforms that emerged in the United States and crossed the ocean to reach first England and then, afterwards, continental Europe. In the countries in which the process of democratization unfolded during the eighteenth and nineteenth centuries, the complexity and fragmentation of the public sector came about in the middle of the twentieth century. Then the later democratized countries started to confront the types of problem derived from both the hollowing out of state power and the overloading of the public sectors. With different gradations and different paces, almost all old democracies confronted serious problems in the organization of the state and, in particular, in the decrease of efficiency in the public sector (Peters, 2000; du Gay, 2005). Put simply, managerial accountability looks at the behaviour of public officials from the perspective of a cost–benefit rationale. Accordingly, behaviour is assessed as positive if it is efficient and scores highly in the cost–benefit ratio.

The concept of judicial administration is to be framed within this context. Judicial administration has primarily been used by Americans to describe the assemblage of practices and routines used to manage courts (but not the judicial system as a whole) in order to ensure the proper and efficient use of human and material resources. Managerial accountability is of particular value in the case of judges who perform managerial roles, especially chief justices and chief prosecutors who have specific mechanisms for career promotion. These mechanisms set up a relationship between court management capabilities and performance and the probability of promotion in the hierarchical scale. The way such a mechanism of accountability is enacted varies from one domestic system to another. In Europe, the wave of managerialism that hit the public sector in the 1990s took some time to impact on judicial systems. As such, managerialism, which is closely related

4 This point is developed in Piana, 2009, ch. 2. On professionalism, see Abbott, 1988, and on legal professions, Halliday, Karpik and Feeley, 2007.

to the main stream of new public management, results from the contamination of the bureaucratic orders with the market, and the countries which are better off are those in which the market has, over the decades, maintained a dominant position over the state. The introduction of managerialism into the judicial field highlights some of the effects witnessed by other sectors, such as health care, education, security and so on. Yet judicial systems, by incorporating indicators of performance and efficiency into their bureaucratic order, have wound up with slightly porous boundaries between the actions of the inner system and the external environment in which the system operates. In other words, it has allowed new, non-bureaucratic values and extra-legal ways of governing human behaviours to penetrate the texture of the hierarchy, thus changing (even if only partially) the conception of the judicial role. This conception may eventually become more complex, multidimensional, manifold and finally open to personal choices. Judges who perform the role of manager exhibit some of the psychological and sociological characters of leaders: they take decisions as to the allocation of resources and they are encouraged by the daily circumstances of their work to think not only legally, but also in terms of their performance and efficiencies.

When communism fell and pro-democratic elites took power in CEE countries, there were a number of factors driving Western policy towards post-communist countries. Opportunities for economic exchange were the first concern of Western political actors, who pushed national governments towards defining strict conditions in order to allow private enterprise and public institutions to open up economic and political dialogues with those countries.[5] The legal environment emerged as a turning point in the process of reforms initiated in the post-communist setting. This was true even before the European process of pre-accession started, since the Council of Europe was in favour of pro-rule of law reforms in all post-communist countries (Piana, 2006). Judicial education has been shown to have dramatic leverage in transforming the legal environment of CEE countries, and it has been considered one of the key conditions in making judicial actors independent from possible influences coming from political and corporate power. In particular, in the early 1990s, the Council of Europe started to monitor, step-by-step, the implementation of constitutional principles within the new constitutional charters (Bartole, 1993).[6] The Venice Commission, by monitoring constitution-making, influenced the drafting of constitutions and the application of judicial

5 Western governments have used their seats in various organizations to push for the definition of conditions that enable membership for CEE countries: two such bodies are the Council of Europe, a truly intergovernmental institution, and the European Union, in particular in the meetings of the European Council. Enlargement to include CEE countries was in fact decided in two European Councils, in Edinburgh in 1989 and in Copenhagen in 1993. For a historical reconstruction, see Torreblanca, 2000..

6 The Czech Republic became a member on 30 June 1993; Hungary on 6 November 1990; Bulgaria on 7 May 1992; and Romania on 7 October 1993.

review (Schwartz, 2000).[7] For countries such as Poland, Hungary and the Czech Republic, whose constitutional legacy had been preserved within academia, the Venice Commission featured as the first successful example of an epistemic community working for the coordination of domestic constitutional policies (Wyrzykowski, 2000). The Council of Europe has progressively developed a set of recommendations dealing with the independence of judges, which also touch upon judicial education (Oberto, 2003). Furthermore, several non-governmental organizations (NGOs) and professional associations provided standards for re-assessing judicial training programmes (Piana, 2010). International organizations (IOs) and international NGOs had started to pave the way towards the reform of systems of judicial education, even before they started to be requested by the European Union at the dawn of the pre-accession process in 1997.[8] The creation of a competent and reliable judicial staff has been on the agenda of all democratic reforms by the European Commission. When the pre-accession process started, the European Commission nudged this process along and asked that judicial staff learn the *corpus juris* of the *acquis communautaire* and be adequately trained in order to work cooperatively within the European legal space (Piana, 2005). It is for this reason that socialization and social learning have turned out to be the main elements of pressure applied to the judiciary.[9]

With the pre-accession strategy, the European Commission decided to allocate 30 per cent of PHARE funds in institution-building projects (European Commission, 1998c).[10] In fact, since 1998, the training of judges and prosecutors has been strongly supported by the European Union through the 'twinning' exercise (Papadimitriou and Phinnemore, 2004). One part of these projects aimed to foster the managerial capacities of courts. The main point raised by the Regular Reports and the Council of Europe after 2000 was the lack of efficiency in the use of human and material resources and the increasing backlog in the courts. More than the rule of law, the theme of the last part of the pre-accession reforms was mostly the promotion of quality justice and reasonable timeframes for judicial

7 The Venice Commission was created in 1990 and was vested with the role of advising the Council of Europe on constitutional matters. In particular, the Commission is composed of professors and experts in constitutional law, who advise democratizing countries. See online at <http://www.venice.coe.int/site/main/presentation_F.asp?MenuL=F> [accessed 14 April 2010].

8 The pre-accession negotiation includes discussion and agreement of a National Plan for the Adoption of the Acquis Communautaire. This was initiated by the European Commission with the first group of countries in 1997, a second group then being admitted to the negotiations in 1999. For a critical view of the requirements of the Commission, see Nicolaides, 2003.

9 The European Council has decided to create a European Judicial Network, which should foster judicial cooperation among national judges.

10 In the beginning, the targeted countries were CEE countries. Thereafter, twinning was extended and widely adopted in the neighborhood policy and in the stabilization process in the Balkans and South-Eastern Europe.

proceedings. In a nutshell, the culture of the rule of law that was promoted in judicial reforms comprised both a legal and a managerial dimension.

In terms of legal accountability, many inputs referred to the necessity of keeping judges and prosecutors strictly accountable to the law. First of all, the creation of a constitutional court, even if not asked for or imposed by the EU, has been welcomed by the EU and the Council of Europe as a significant and positive step forward in the implementation of constitutionalism. However, it is important not to overestimate the weight of European pressure on constitutional design:

> [I]t is rather unlikely that the prospect of the accession to the EU has had a visible, measurable impact on constitution-making in the CEECs (other than through adding certain specific 'European clauses' to constitutional texts, to be mentioned below). New post-communist constitutions had been firmly in place, and accepted as settled and stable in all CEE states (except for Hungary) well before the prospect of joining the EU became a real one (Sadurski and Morlino, 2010).

With regard to the creation or non-creation of constitutional courts, this means that the choices made by CEE countries seem to have derived more from domestic forces and factors rather than from external pressures. Yet, the European Convention on Human Rights has played an important role in providing norms and principles for the drafters of constitutions. More than anything else, the European Commission exercised persistent pressure by asking CEE countries to address, as soon as possible, the need of ensuring their citizens the right to a fair trial. This means, in concrete terms, that all CEE countries have been asked to adopt new or considerably renewed civic and penal procedural codes respectful of fundamental rights. Furthermore, all Regular Reports mention the importance of providing judges and prosecutors with adequate and comprehensive programmes of judicial training. All judicial staff were expected to be trained – or retrained in cases where the judiciary had not fully replaced staff inherited from the previous regime – in domestic and EC law, the latter gaining increasing importance in view of the accession. The legality principle has been thought of as the pillar of legal and judicial reforms enacted by candidate countries. In other words, candidate countries were assessed by the EU on how effectively they had entrenched the legality principle in their legal codes and judicial institutions.

The bulk of pre-accession financial aid was devoted to creating arenas and institutional contexts in which judges were able to find legitimate legal knowledge. Judicial schools were in this respect the epitome of legalism, at least if we consider exclusively the training programmes. All new schools created at the end of the 1990s and at the end of the accession offered a variety of courses and seminars that, according to the Roman tradition, help judges to learn the substantial law – civil and penal, national and European. As the Regular Reports of the European Commission recommended, CEE countries should provide judges with a solid and reliable system of training, both initially and in-service, in order to clean out the generation of judicial actors socialized during the socialist regimes and to make sure that adjudication is based on the law. Training served both to re-socialize judges appointed under socialist rule and to strengthen the bureaucratic order of judicial systems. Training was supposed to work to create a fully-fledged *esprit de corps*. In this respect, the pre-accession process has fostered the bureaucratic dimension of the CEE countries' judicial systems (Albers, 2008). One indicator of this is the spectacular diffusion of judicial schools, specialized institutions whose main function is generally to assist the recruitment of competent judges and prosecutors and, in some cases, to maintain the competence of judicial staff during their service. A judicial school offers standardized and centralized programmes of initial training. The model followed by CEE countries has been based on the French and Spanish ones, both of which present a judicial school with a fairly developed and detailed offer of training sessions, courses and seminars. The adoption of this model witnesses the existence of two different forces, whose effects seem to converge in a common and stable result. Post-communist judicial systems were in strong need of a reliable, legitimizing institution responsible for guaranteeing the good behaviour of judges and prosecutors. Judicial schools were in this respect something of a watershed, marking a clear and net point of discontinuity with the past. Furthermore, the adoption of the French and Spanish models has been encouraged and helped significantly by the policy instruments adopted by the EU to finance judicial reforms in the candidate countries. In many twinning projects, financed under the PHARE programme in previous decades, the judicial schools of the old member states have developed detailed and variegated training programmes which new member states have been able to draw on as a rich source of inspiration, models and templates (Piana, 2007).

Managerial accountability refers to the need to implement policies of 'judicial administration' (in relation to court backlogs, case flow management, budgets and audits, for instance). In the Regular Reports, the EU does not prescribe any of these practices. However, it is clear that the EU values the efficient performance of courts in judicial systems. Each Regular Report touches on backlogs and timeframes of court proceedings:

> The key areas for further improvement of the judicial system remain the speeding-up of court proceedings, the enforcement of court judgments, training of judges and prosecutors and administrative support for judges and courts. The implementation of the amended Civil Proceedings Code should be underpinned by adequate human and material resources (European Commission, 2001: 19).

Generally speaking, judicial administration is less of a consideration for countries whose judicial systems encountered difficulties in ensuring judicial independence, and vice versa. The latter is true for Poland, Hungary, the Czech Republic, the Slovak Republic and Slovenia. Unlike these countries, for Bulgaria and Romania judicial independence is a crucial and politically controversial issue. For them, the Regular Reports often neglected issues related to judicial administration.

Today, after the accession, all Central and Eastern European countries are involved in extensive processes of standard-setting, addressing the quality and the efficiency of judicial systems. Judicial administration and judicial capacity increasingly draw the attention of experts and members of transnational networks, in particular of the European Commission for the Efficiency of Justice (CEPEJ). The CEPEJ represents the last and most prominent initiative undertaken by the Council of Europe to improve the efficiency of national judiciaries:

> The CEPEJ also has the task of ensuring the effective implementation of the recommendations and resolutions adopted by the Committee of Ministers of the Council of Europe, which set out fairly detailed principles and standards for improving the functioning and efficiency of courts in areas such as mediation, access to justice, legal procedures and the execution of judgments, the use of new information technologies and the role of the various players in the justice system (CEPEJ).

Activities undertaken by CEPEJ working groups are directly related to: (1) monitoring; (2) standard setting; and (3) advising. Unlike standards drawn by judges and members of the Consultative Council of European Judges (CCJE), the CEPEJ has adopted an evidence-based approach to judicial policies. Starting with a first round of reports regarding judicial administration, experts have unpacked the issue of the 'efficiency of the judiciary', working on micro-issues, taking a comparative approach throughout. Pilot courts (CEPEJ, 2002), which have adopted local solutions to problems of judicial administration, are expected to give few hints from which suggestions may be drawn for setting standards. Unlike the top-down approach used so far, the CEPEJ introduced a policy innovation, adopting a bottom-up approach, surveying micro-policy solutions, comparing their results and providing courts with a common grid to assess their efficiency. In that sense, instead of providing standards, the CEPEJ will provide policy solutions, best practices and templates. Pilot courts, which are going to experiment with micro-policies to improve their efficiency, also include courts located in CEE countries. By and large, the organizational models and policy instruments suggested by the external actors aim to promote an incremental introduction of a new public management approach in the judicial system. The basic idea is to promote the implementation of processes and product evaluation (in relation to case backlogs and case flow management, for example).

The type of judge who results from the portrait of the 'good judicial system' depicted by the European standards is a judge with a Janus-like identity. On one hand, he should be respectful of the legality principle and look to the law for the answers to his doubts, problems and questions. On the other hand, he should be respectful of a client-oriented logic of action and find answers to his problems in a different realm – the realm of management. A fair trial is not only one based on procedure: it is also one that is run and managed efficiently and transparently. How to strike a balance between the two is a matter of practical experience. However, the professional identity that comes from the intertwining of these two logics is not easy to foresee, depending, presumably, on the way each single judge, given the material, cognitive and symbolic resources with which he is endowed, interprets his own role. But if this is the case, it would represent a significant deviation from the ideal-typical model of bureaucratic judicial governance.

Leaving Bureaucracy Behind, with Some Reservation

Nietzsche said that human affairs can flow almost without memory, whereas they would never have been able even to exist without oblivion. Harsh as it is, this statement carries with it some truths. In the long term, history matters much more for its exclusion of possible actions than for its determination of specific behaviours. The experiences of the past define the borders for the types of action that are considered to be legitimate and possible. What did not happen in history counts in the way that darkness enables the casting of better and sharper borders around an enlightened space.

The history of post-communist countries dives in between a not fully worked out modernity (Přibáň, Roberts and Young, 2003; Přibáň, 2007) and the experience of a non-democratic rule of law (Sadurski and Morlino, 2010). Post-communist states emerged to see the light of democracy without a solid and cohesive bureaucratic state. Yet, they came to it with a state within which the judicial branch should be placed. The judicial systems of post-communist countries carry in their institutional memories contradictory experiences, which vary depending on the history of the country being considered. The countries that belonged for a period to the Austro-Hungarian empire underwent an important process of modernization following the rationalized and formalized machinery put in motion from Vienna and in the local capitals of the empire. In the Czech-Slovak area and in the area that today corresponds to Hungary, a fairly modernized way of governance was in place before the fall of the empire and the disruptive advance of the world wars. In Bulgaria and in Romania, the experience of the Ottoman empire left a different trace, one factor being that the Ottoman government coped with multiculturalism in the territory it was ruling by means of formidable bureaucratic machinery.

In general, communist rule in all of these Central and South-Eastern countries obscured any possibility of an interpretation of the judiciary as having a public and impersonal role. However, such a possibility emerged clearly from the dust after the fall of communism, when democratic forces assumed a position on the historical stage. The more recent influence of European standards reshuffled the situation and mixed up again the way bureaucracy was conceived during pre-communist and communist eras. Now, standards of institutional accountability promote a model that maximizes guarantees of autonomy and independence of both judge and judicial system. Such a model, as Weber correctly pointed out in his pioneering work at the beginning of the twentieth century, works appropriately in a context in which the judge is actually and really placed in a bureaucratic organizational setting, which isolates any dimension of personal leadership, initiative or subjective interpretation of the role, and which compels judicial actors into the iron cages of their heterogeneously defined roles (Newman, 2005). Moreover, such a model is adequate if the vertical chains of role enforcement perform effectively. External guarantees of independence should go hand-in-hand with an internal cohesive bureaucracy. What happens when this ideal-typical situation is no longer instantiated by a judicial system that had, in the past, instantiated it? What remains in the memory of the institutions and organizational practices to filter and curb eventual new ways of interpreting the judicial role and new practices coming from the external environment? Many scholars who have extensively worked on the concept of institution-building point out the difficulties encountered by institution-builders in artificially building or rebuilding institutions. They seem to embark on an endless task: the more they try to build, the more the elements break down in a myriad of sub-components – practices, routines, implicit know-how and so on – whose collection and embedding in the receiving institution results in a kind of disorder far beyond the control of any human rationality.

The pressure imposed by European institutions, in promoting managerial values in judicial systems that have passed through a number of processes of change (none of which have fully achieved modernity), seems to present a paradox. In promoting the re-bureaucratization of the public sector of the candidate, the EU and the Council of Europe have asked candidates to use the same public sector they had just re-bureaucratized to weaken the bureaucratic cohesiveness of organizations belonging to it. Asking judges to perform as managers or to gain communicational skills and psychological capacities is a more than welcome goal, which should be praised from the point of view of the rule of law. However, it should be viewed with some caution from the historical and perhaps more realistic viewpoint of the organizations and institutions involved. Placing the tender and still porous borders of these renewed judicial systems in a context in which they are supposed to be autonomous (but not too autonomous) is a risky operation, whose consequences have never been fully assessed or foreseen by the European Union.

References

Abbott, A., *The System of Professions* (Chicago, IL: Chicago University Press, 1988).

Ajani, G., *Il modello socialista* (Torino: Giappichelli, 1996).

Albers, P., 'Best practices on the prevention of the unreasonable length of proceedings: Experiences of the CEPEJ'. Communication presented at the UniDem Campus Seminar, organized by the Venice Commission, Trieste (25–28 February 2008).

Albi, A., *The Constitutions of Central and Eastern Europe* (Cambridge: Cambridge University Press, 2005).

Alter, K.J., 'The European Union's legal system and domestic policy: Spillover or backlash?' *International Organization*, 54/3 (2000), 489–518.

Anderson, G., H. Bernstein and J. Gray, *Judicial Systems in Transition Economies: Assessing the Past, Looking to the Future* (Washington, DC: The World Bank, 2005).

Arendt, H., *The Origins of Totalitarianism* (New York: The Free Press, 1951).

Atkins, L., 'The shifting of judicial reform: From independence to capacity' (Budapest: Open Society Institute, EU Accession Monitoring Program, 2002). Available online at <http://www.eumap.org> [accessed 14 April 2010].

Bartole, S. Riforme costituzionali nell'fEuropa centro-orientale: da satellite comunisti a democrazie sovrane (Bologna: Il Mulino, 1993).

Bartolini, S., *Restructuring Europe: Centre Formation, System Building and Political Structuring Between the Nation-State and the European Union* (Oxford: Oxford University, 2005).

Beddard, R., *Human Rights and Europe: A Study of the Machinery of Human Rights Protection of the Council of Europe* (London: Maxwell, 1980).

Benoit-Rohmer, F. and H. Klebcs, *Lc droit du Conseil de l'Europe: vers un espace juridique europeen* (Strasbourg: Le Conseil de l'Europe, 2005).

Berger, P.L. and T. Luckmann, *The Social Construction of Reality* (London: Penguin Books, 1966).

Berkvotz, K., M. Pistor and I. Richard, 'Economic development, legality, and the transplant effect', *European Economic Review*, 47/1 (2001), 165–95.

Bihari, O., *The Constitutional Model of Socialist State Organization* (Budapest: Akademiai Kiado, 1979).

Bobek, M., 'The fortress of judicial independence and the mental transitions of the Central European judiciaries', *European Public Law*, 14/1 (2008), 99–123.

———'Quantity or quality? Reassessing the role of supreme jurisdictions in Central Europe'. EUI Working Paper LAW, 36 (2007), 1–28.

———'A new legal order, or a non-existent one?', *Croatian Yearbook of European Law and Politics*, 2 (2006), 265–98.

Bovens, M., 'Analysing and assessing public accountability: A conceptual framework'. European Governance Paper (EUROGOV) (2006), 1–37.

Caenegem, R.C., *Judges, Legislators and Professors* (Cambridge: Cambridge University Press, 1987).

———*Legal History: A European Perspective* (London: Hambledon, 1991).

Capeta, T., 'Courts, legal culture and enlargement', *Croatian Yearbook of European Law and Policy*, 1 (2005), 23–53.

Castoriadis, C., *La Société bureaucratique* (Paris: Union Générale d'Editions, 1973).

CEPEJ (2002). See online at <http://www.coe.int/t/dghl/cooperation/cepej/default_en.asp> [accessed 14 April 2010].

Contini, F. and G.F. Lanzara, *ICT and Innovation in the Public Sector* (New York: Palgrave, 2009).

Chelabi, H. and J. Linz, *Sultanistic Regimes* (Baltimore: Johns Hopkins University Press, 1998).

Cirtautas, A.M., 'The post-Leninist state: A conceptual and empirical examination', *Communist and Post-Communist Studies*, 28/4 (1995), 379–92.

Coman, R., 'Media, justice and politics, or the independence of the judiciary becomes an issue on the Romanian political agenda', in R. Coman and J.M. de Waele (eds), *Judicial Reforms in Central and Eastern European Countries* (Bruges: Editions Vanden Broele, 2007).

Contini, F. and R. Mohr, 'Reconciling independence and accountability in judicial systems', *Utrecht Law Review*, 3/2 (2007), 26–43. Available online at <http://www.utrechtlawreview.org/> [accessed 14 April 2010].

Cotterrell, R., Law, Culture and Society: Legal Ideas in the Mirror of Social Theory (Aldershot: Ashgate, 2006).

Council of Europe, *Toward a Pan-European Legal Area* (Strasbourg: Official Publications Office, 2005).

———*Recommendation 19* (Strasbourg: Official Publications Office, 2000).

———*Recommendation 12* (Strasbourg: Official Publications Office, 1994).

Court of Auditors, *Report on PHARE* (Luxemburg: Official Publications Office, 2002).

Crozier, M. and E. Friedberg, *L'acteur et le systeme: les contraintes de l'action collective* (Paris: Editions du Seuil, 1977).

Dakolias, M., 'Court performance around the world: A comparative perspective', *Yale Human Rights and Development Law Journal,* 2 (1999), 87–12.

Dallara, C., Uniunea europeana si promovarea statului de drept in Romania, Serbia, si Ucraina (Iasi: Editura Institutul European, 2009).

Damaska, M.R., The Faces of Justice and State Authority: A Comparative Approach to the Legal Process (New Haven, CT: Yale University Press, 1986).

du Gay, P. (ed.), *The Values of Bureaucracy* (Oxford: Oxford University Press, 2005).

European Commission, *Regular Report on Hungary's Process of Accession* (Brussels, 1998a).

———*Report on PHARE PL98/IB-JH-01* (Brussels, 1998b).

———*Regular Report on Poland's process of accession* (Brussels, 1998c).

———*Twinning. An Instrument of Institutional Building* (Brussels, 1998d).

———*Twinning in Action* (Brussels: Office of Official Publication, 2001).

Fabri, M. and F. Contini, Compendium of best practices on time management of judicial proceedings, European Commission for the Efficiency of Justice (CEPEJ) (Strasbourg: Council of Europe, 2006). Available online at <http://www.coe.int/t/dghl/cooperation/cepej/default_en.asp> [accessed 14 April 2010].

Frydman, B., 'L'évolution des critères et des modes de controle de la qualité des décisions de justice'. Working Paper, Centre Perelman de philosophie du droit, 4 (2007). Available online at <http://www.philodroit.be> [accessed 14 April 2010].

Friedrich, C. and Z. Brzezinski, *Totalitarian Dictatorship and Autocracy* (Cambridge: Harvard University Press, 1965).

Garapon, A., *Les Juges dans la mondialization* (Paris: Editions du Seuil, 2005).

Gsovski, V., 'Roman law and Polish jurists', *Seminar Jurists*, 2 (1948), 74–98.

Guarnieri, C. and P. Magalhaes, *Democratic Consolidation, Judicial Reform and the Judicialization of Politics in Southern Europe* (Instituto de Siencias Socialis: Universidade de Lisboa, 2001).

Guarnieri, C. and P. Pederzoli, *The Power of Judges* (Oxford: Oxford University Press, 2002).

Halliday, T., L. Karpik and M. Feeley, Fighting for Political Freedom: Comparative Studies of the Legal Complex and Political Liberalism (Oxford: Hart Publishing, 2007).

Hardin, R., *Liberalism, Constitutionalism and Democracy* (Oxford: Oxford University Press, 1999).

Kallinikos, J., 'The social foundations of the bureaucratic order', *Organization*, 11/1 (2004), 13–36.

———*The Consequences of Information: Institutional Implications of Technological Change* (Cheltenham: Elgar, 2006).

Krygier, M. and A. Czarnota (eds), *The Rule of Law After Communism: Problems and Prospects in East-Central Europe* (Aldershot: Ashgate, 1999).

Kühn, Z., 'Worlds apart: Western and Central European judicial culture at the onset of the European enlargement', *American Journal of Comparative Law*, 3 (2004), 531–67.

———'European law in the empires of mechanical jurisprudence', *Croatian Yearbook of European Law and Policy*, 1 (2005), 55–73.

Lanzara, G.F. and G. Patriotta, 'Technology and the courtroom: An inquiry into knowledge making in organizations', *Journal of Management Studies*, 38/7 (2001), 943–71.

——— 'The institutionalization of knowledge in an automotive factory: Templates, inscriptions, and the problem of durability', *Organization Studies*, 28/1–26 (2007).

Lane, D., *The Rise and the Fall of State Socialism* (Cambridge: Polity, 1996).

Mainwaring, S., 'Democratic accountability in Latin America', in S. Mainwaring (ed.), *Democratic Accountability in Latin America* (Oxford: Oxford University Press, 2003), 3–34.

Merton, R., *Social Theory and Social Structure* (New York: The Free Press, 1949).

Morlino, L. and A. Magen, *International Actors, Democratization and the Rule of Law: Anchoring Democracy* (London: Routledge, 2008).

Newman, J., 'Bending bureaucracy: Leadership and multi-level governance', in P. du Gay (ed.), *The Values of Bureaucracy* (Oxford: Oxford University Press, 2005).

Nicolaides, P., 'Enlargement of the EU and effective implementation of community rules: An integration-based approach'. EIPA Working Paper 99/W/04 (1999).

Oberto, G., *Recrutement et formation des magistrats en Europe: Etude comparative* (Strasbourg: Editions du Conseil de l'Europe, 2003).

Olson, M., *The Logic of Collective Actions* (Cambridge and London: Harvard University Press, 1971).

Papadimitriou, D. and D. Phinnemore, 'The domestic mediation of Europeanization: The twinning exercise and administrative reform in Rumania', *Journal of Common Market Studies*, 42/3 (2004), 619–39.

Peters, G. 'Linking policy instruments and management', *Journal of Public Administration Research and Theory* (2000).

Piana, D., *Judicial Accountabilities in New Europe: From Rule of Law to Quality of Justice* (Aldershot: Ashgate, 2010).

———'When politics comes back from the courts' back-door', *Comparative Political Studies*, 1 (2009), 816–40.

———'Unpacking Policy Transfer, Discover Actor', *French Politics*, 3 (2007), 275–97.

———'Constitutional cultures in new member states: Between tradition and Europeanization', in J. Ziller and W. Sadurski (eds), *After Enlargement* (Dordrecht: Kluwer, 2006).

———'Networking the rule of law'. Paper presented to the UACES conference in Brussels (14 October 2005).

Přibáň, J., *Legal Symbolism: On Law, Time and European Identity* (Aldershot: Ashgate, 2007).

———'Legalism with a human face: Developments in the Czech legal system and theory after 1989', *Ius and Lex in East Central Europe*, 28/1 (2001).

Přibáň, J. and J. Young, *The Rule of Law in Central Europe: The Reconstruction of Legality, Constitutionalism and Civil Society in the Post-Communist Countries* (Dartmouth: Ashgate, 1999).

Přibáň, J., P. Roberts and J. Young, *Systems of Justice in Transition* (Aldershot: Ashgate, 2003).

Raz, J., *The Authority of Law: Essays on Law and Morality* (Oxford: Clarendon Press, 1977).

Rokkan, S. and S. Eisenstadt (eds), *Building States and Nations* (London: Sage, 1973).

Sadurski, W., 'Accession's democracy dividend: The impact of the EU enlargement upon democracy in the new member states of Central and Eastern Europe', *European Law Review*, 10/4 (2004), 371–401.

———'Constitutional courts in the process of articulating constitutional rights in the post-communist states of central and eastern Europe', part IV: Restrictions of constitutional rights. EUI Working Paper LAW, 10 (2003a).

———'Constitutionalization of the EU and the sovereignty concerns of the new accession states: The role of the charter of rights'. EUI Working Paper LAW, 11 (2003b).

——— and L. Morlino, *European Union and Democracy* (London: Routledge, 2010).

Sajó, A., 'The role of lawyers in social change: Hungary', *Case Western Res. Journal International Law*, 25 (1993a), 137–46.

———'The judiciary in contemporary society', *Case Western Res. Journal International Law*, 25 (1993b), 293–301.

Schwartz, H., *The Struggle for Constitutional Justice in Post-communist Europe* (Chicago, IL: University of Chicago Press, 2000).

Selznick, P., *TVA and the Grass Roots: A Study in the Sociology of Formal Organization* (Berkeley, CA: University of California Press, 1949).

Shapiro, M., *Courts. A Comparative and Political Analysis.* (Chicago, IL: University of Chicago Press, 1981).

Solyom, L. and G. Brunner, *Constitutional Judiciary in a New Democracy: The Hungarian Constitutional Court* (Ann Arbor, MI: University of Michigan Press, 2000).

Spendzharova, A., 'Road to Europe I: Legacies, strategies, norms and the development of the rule of law in Hungary and Bulgaria after 1989: The case of human rights', *Southeast European Politics*, 2 (2005), 109–25.

Taylor, J.P., *History of the Balkans* (Cambridge: Cambridge University Press, 1956).

Weber, M., *Economy and Society* (New York: Bedminister Press, [1914] 1968).

Williams, K., A. Szczerbiak and B. Fowler, 'Explaining lustration in Eastern Europe: A post-communist politics approach'. Sussex European Institute Working Paper, 62 (2003).

World Bank, *Initiatives in Legal and Judicial Reform* (Washington, DC: The World Bank, 2004).

———*Diagnostic Surveys on Corruption in Romania* (Washington, DC: The World Bank, 2001).

Wyrzykowski, M., *Constitutional Cultures* (Warsaw: Institute of Public Affairs, 2000).

Chapter 9
Polish Prosecutors, Political Corruption, and Legal Culture

Paulina Polak and David Nelken

> [I]n every case involving a politician, unless a prosecutor is sure his back is well covered, he will not deal with it.
>
> Polish prosecutor (2008)

Introduction

Most of the countries of Central and Eastern Europe are now full members of the European Union, their legal systems are formally, and increasingly substantively, integrated into it, and in constitutional matters they may now often be giving the lead. But, compared with older established members, it still tends to be assumed that they are in need of improvement. They are therefore more often subject to requirements to 'signal conformity' (Nelken, 2006b) to supposed common standards – sometimes even being measured by higher standards.

Our concern here, however, is what most observers admit to be notable weaknesses in the functioning of criminal and civil justice. The present project focuses in particular on the level of independence exercised by Polish prosecutors in sensitive political cases. The earlier communist era was well known for practices of so called 'telephone justice', by which the party tried to influence the outcomes of trials (Markovits, 1995). How much progress has been made since then in Poland? In any society, prosecutorial independence is most likely to be at stake where politicians or other powerful people are under investigation. How does Poland fare in comparison with other places?

Qualitative investigation into the world of different prosecution systems in Europe (and elsewhere) is much needed. Work is currently being sponsored by the EU to harmonize prosecution patterns, as seen especially in the Justis project (Justis, 2009). But this tends to be overly functionalist, assuming both that all prosecutors have to deal with the same problems of increasing caseloads and that expediting matters is what is most needed. It takes no account of the larger political context and shows little awareness of, and no interest in, related differences in the threats or challenges faced by prosecutors in different places. By contrast, this chapter describes empirical research on Polish prosecutors undertaken as part of a wider project on changes in legal culture in Eastern European states. This first section (written by the second-named author) will explain the purpose of the research and offer a brief summary of some of the main conclusions, before going on to consider the relevance of the concept of legal culture. These remarks aim to provide a theoretical context for reading the major part of the chapter, relating to prosecutors under pressure (written by the first-named author), which describes what emerged from the research.

For the purposes of this project a series of semi-structured interviews took place with prosecutors, judges and other legal experts dealing with corruption cases in Poland. Those interviewed were five prosecutors, a former prosecutor, a judge, a law professor, a barrister, a coordinator of a human rights organization, and three police officers from an anti-corruption police force. Interviews lasted an average of one hour and were conducted in Krakow, Warsaw and Katowice. The questions that were asked concerned what prosecutors do in corruption cases, how they do it, whether they feel independent in their work, how their activities are distorted, and how they react to these distortions and pressures – from their superiors, politicians (political patrons?), the public and the media. At one end of the spectrum of independence it was hypothesized that there could be complete independence and autonomy, while at the other end dependence, being put under pressures and political scrutiny.

The interviewees suggested that Polish prosecutors could be located nearer to the latter end of the spectrum, being used as a political tool for dealing with politically chosen and politically important themes. In order to make sense of this a brief history of the condition of Polish prosecution was traced thanks to information given by the interviewees –in terms of both the former communist regime and the past years of democracy. Developments were indicated, charting the changes from a fairly independent prosecution of the 1990s, created in opposition to the fully politicized communist party-serving prosecution, and deterioration of the prosecution over the last years, culminating during the rule of the PiS (Law and Justice) government in the years 2005–2007. In line with overwhelming criticism by the media, legal experts and, obviously, former political opponents, this period was clearly indicated as a marking point for the development of Polish prosecution. However, despite almost unanimous, yet in a number of cases post facto, media condemnation of then Minister of Justice Zbigniew Ziobro's actions, it seems that the potential for a politicized prosecution was underlying, only waiting to be used by one of the coming new authorities.

All those interviewed insisted that Polish prosecutors were not independent, in the sense that it would be very difficult or risky for them to put up resistance if a politician, via the minister of justice, wished to affect the outcome of a case. In addition, the behaviour of politicians in relation to prosecutors strongly resembled that in communist times – it could be summarized as an 'instrumental' approach to law without concern for safeguarding 'the rules of the game'. The same methods were being used – even if the ends – populist nationalism rather than communist subordination – were different. Given the limits of this interview sample, care should be taken in drawing too many conclusions or making generalizations. But, as an initial investigation, combined with whatever can be learned from media reports, it strongly suggests that Polish prosecutors currently lack the power to resist political pressure to prosecute or to refrain from prosecuting corruption. They also, as importantly, *know* that they lack such independence. Prosecutor promotion can depend on prosecutors being willing tools of political machinations. What is more, the explanations provided for this state of affairs also give the impression that, whatever they say in opposition, all political parties are reluctant to grant them greater independence.

These findings raise a number of normative questions about the prosecution of corruption in Poland which have wider relevance. Is it really possible to sustain (let alone justify) a system of 'dual law' and justice – one in which political cases are dealt with differently from the mass of ordinary cases? Hendry (2009: 259) says she has changed her mind over this and now doubts this is possible. Are courts the best way of dealing with corruption? What is the relationship between the advancement of popular democracy and that of the rule of law? (A large proportion of those surveyed in Poland seem to endorse democracy only in so far as it produces better material conditions; and they are used to their views not really being taken into account under past regimes.) Can these values conflict? More specifically, must prosecutor independence be safeguarded in a constitution? What exactly does the rule of law require in the case of prosecutors? Can there be too much independence, too much of a good thing? Many in Italy would say so.

'Undue' interference from politicians within prosecution certainly counts as a serious problem, but what about – as in common law countries – the extent to which public opinion and pressure for punitiveness affects decision-making and is encouraged to do so? A particular issue relates to 'trial by media', as well as 'trials' before parliamentary commissions. The problems of media misrepresentation and the creation of false transparency are felt strongly in Poland – as elsewhere. The media is also said to be another strong influence which weakens the independence of higher prosecutors by shaping their priorities. But if trial by media is such a wide phenomenon, could this be because court sentences arrive too late on the scene? Too often the public would only be informed at a time well after the relevant events about politicians who are suspected of being corrupt. But how can we avoid such accusations being manipulated for political benefit?

The specific research reported here was inspired by a number of the larger questions relevant to this book. How far can the state of affairs amongst Polish prosecutors be seen as a 'carryover' from the legal culture of the previous communist period? Or, given the time that has passed, must it be understood as intrinsic to current constitutional, legal and socio-political arrangements? In a related sense, how different is the Polish situation from other comparable ones – and which countries are appropriate ones for comparison? Not least, how far can the concept of legal culture help us make sense of what goes on? Finding the answers to such questions is not straightforward, and revealing the conduct of the powerful is always more tricky than putting the spotlight on the weak.

Originally the research design of this study was to compare the legal culture of prosecutors in Poland with those in a comparable Eastern European country such as the Czech Republic. The sample of prosecutors was planned to include those at different levels of the official hierarchy and those more or less likely to find themselves dealing with such sensitive cases. There were also to be interviews in both countries with politicians, journalists and other informed parties. The inclusion of these different variables would have provided much needed context for the responses of prosecutors. It would have allowed different groups of actors to give their perceptions of each other, and to learn more about the specificities of these two, in some ways similar, countries. Before the design could be implemented, however, circumstances beyond authorial control meant that any hope of carrying out a properly structured research design had to be abandoned. The first author carried out and wrote up pilot interviews with Polish prosecutors and others reported here. The second author was then invited to add his comments.

Legal Culture and the Study of Prosecution

For comparative purposes, legal culture, in its most general sense, can be defined as:

> [...] one way of describing relatively stable patterns of legally oriented social behaviour and attitudes. The identifying elements of legal culture range from facts about institutions such as the number and role of lawyers or the ways judges are appointed and controlled, to various forms of behaviour such as litigation or prison rates, and, at the other extreme, more nebulous aspects of ideas, values, aspirations and mentalities. Like culture itself, legal culture is about who we are not just what we do (Nelken, 2004: 1).

As this suggests, understanding legal culture properly – the distinctive legally related attitudes and behaviour of prosecutors in Poland – would require study of its internal variation. This would involve comparison within the prosecution service, for example between heads and lower level prosecutors, amongst central, regional and district levels, and between cities and rural areas and so on. The legal culture of prosecutors would also need to be compared with that of others, such as judges and lawyers working in and for legal and political institutions. It would be necessary to consider differences in prosecuting corruption – or, better, different types of corruption – and other crimes. It would also be important to see how work in dealing with corruption relates to that of other agencies and other forms of regulation. In Poland some see the way politicians manipulate the government agency for investigating corruption (the CBA) as itself verging on corruption!

It is plausible to think that the lack of prosecutor independence in Poland is linked to levels of corruption, both because such lack of autonomy blocks investigations and because allowing such institutional weakness is itself a sign of the lack of political will to rein in corrupt practices. But comparative research suggests that the reverse may not always be true. This can be seen by comparing the situation in Italy – the home of the overall project – with that in Poland. Both countries are placed close together in *Transparency International's* classification of expert judgments about which countries are most subject to corruption (TI, 2009). Yet, whatever the situation in Poland may be, Italy has a system that guarantees the highest degree of prosecution autonomy and independence: prosecutors are equated to judges and are constitutionally immovable from their posts, and politicians are excluded from any influence over prosecution policy and priorities (Nelken, 1996; 1997). This has not put an end to political corruption in Italy – though one dreads to think what might happen if Italy's prosecutors were subject to the same level of political interference as in Poland. Looking at Europe more generally, the antibodies to corruption have been found in such different places as the civil service in Germany, parliament in the UK, and the magistracy in Italy (Della Porta and Meny, 1997). But this can change over time, as illustrated by recent corruption scandals in the English parliament.

The issue being considered here, though, is not so much to do with the causes of political corruption as it is to do with understanding the characteristics of a certain kind of prosecution organization that is more or less able to pursue it. Why use the term legal culture? On one hand, it is no more than a classificatory device – whatever Polish prosecutors do illustrates their legal culture. On the other hand, it is more of a challenge to employ the term for explanatory purposes as part of an enquiry seeking to establish how far prosecutors' relative lack of independence is the result of the influence of previous legal culture. There are well-known problems with using legal culture as an explanation (Nelken, 2006a; 2007). It is too easy, for example, for such explanations, like cultural explanations in general, to be tautological (Cotterrell, 1997), determining and unable to explain change (it is change or the lack of change for which explanation is sought here). It adds little to say that Polish prosecutors behave as they do because of their legal culture if, when speaking of legal culture in Poland, it is already in reference to the way prosecutors behave there.

These problems can be side-stepped by turning the question round and asking what could explain the current characteristics of Polish legal culture. Such an enquiry is also more able to avoid 'cultural' determinism (Krygier, 1997) because it suggests looking for historical evidence of how culture itself depends on changing and changeable wider factors. Such factors can and do change – indeed even in Poland, as the following account sets out, the situation changes somewhat from one government to another. What then are the wider social, economic and political conditions that make possible (and necessary) a 'rule of law' type society, in this case one that favours creating a high level of political independence for prosecutors? Comparison with the Italian situation shows that the independence of Italian prosecutors came about because of very special conditions after World War II (Nelken,1996), where neither of the two major political forces – the Christian democrats nor the communists – wanted a prosecution system open to manipulation by the government as it had been under fascism, for fear that it would be turned against them if the other side got into power.

This type of explanation has also been applied to the emergence of effective constitutional courts in some Asian countries (Ginsburg, 2003) and may also apply to constitutional courts in Central and Eastern Europe. Both governing and opposition parties in Italy would now have something to gain from reducing the independence of Italian prosecutors, but they have not overcome their mutual suspicion sufficiently to do this. And any direct attempt to do this would be overturning constitutionally entrenched principles (a variety of indirect methods have been tried and proposed). In Poland, by contrast, prosecutors have no such constitutional guarantees and potential parties of government think rather about the advantages of a prosecution system open to political influence.

It may also be useful to ask how legal culture relates to economic culture (for example, the forms of capitalism that have grown up in the transition from capitalism, as well as the neo-liberal regimes being imposed from the outside), religious culture (including the importance of the Catholic Church in Poland), and – most relevant for present purposes – political culture. Here it is important to recall the useful distinction made by Lawrence Friedman (1975) between what he called 'internal', relating to the culture (or cultures) of those within the legal system, and 'external' legal culture, by which is meant the culture of those outside the system who bring pressure or demands to bear on it. The problems that Polish prosecutors face come partly from the fact that they experience some of the instructions coming from the head of prosecution as 'political' and therefore, in a sense, 'external' to the legal culture they are supposed to be sharing as prosecutors. On the other hand, they can expect little support from 'civil society' if they stand up to such directives – and insofar as they are citizens as well as prosecutors they may also share in such general defeatism. In addition, there is survey evidence in Poland, as in many other Eastern European countries, of low trust in legal institutions and, in particular, widespread suspicion that police and even prosecutors and judges may be susceptible to corruption. Whether this becomes self-fulfilling in the way citizens and politicians avoid law or attempt to influence it is a question that needs investigating.

As always, the key question is whether we are comparing like with like (Nelken, 2010). It is important to be clear what exactly the patterns of 'telephone justice' were in communist times. Interestingly, it has been suggested that it was rarely necessary actually to use the telephone. Appropriate decisions were taken because of the socialization of judges and the fact that they were usually members of the 'party' (Markovits, 1995). It is also necessary to compare and contrast the legal culture of Polish prosecutors with that of prosecutors in other countries for which studies are available, especially early EU members, those from common and civil law countries, those from other Central and Eastern European countries, and those from other countries in the world, including the US and Japan. More information is needed about how prosecution services are organized, controlled and disciplined, what discretion they have in theory and in practice, how much centralization there is, what concern there is about disparity from one area or tribunal to another, their caseloads, the kinds of cases they deal with and so on.

Certainly the way Western legal systems deal with terrorism cases, or even many cases of irregular immigration, suggests little independence from the government. High policing in sensitive cases has always been different from more everyday policing – well before the events of 9/11 (Brodeur, 1983). But different systems also face different external challenges to their integrity. The problem with US prosecutors, for instance, is less to do with direct interference from political superiors than that they are themselves popularly elected. This tends to make them favour harsh responses to crime, which in turn has led to a shameful penal archipelago involving millions of people behind bars. Even under communism there was nothing similar in Poland (Savelsberg, 1999) And it is not always clear in Anglo-American systems how much legitimacy should be given to pressure coming from the community or external legal culture.

Another important point for consideration is how far difficulties in controlling political interference in ex-communist countries are linked to the problems common to all periods of transitional justice. It has been said that the rule of law was declared too quickly in Poland and that this was turned too easily to illiberal purposes under a series of short-lived governments. Study of different countries' practices of lustration shows that in Poland – the first country to break with communism – it 'proved impossible to sustain' institutional discontinuity with the past, for example, most civil servants from the former regime were kept on (Czarnota, 2009). To some extent, those who support the practice of lustration also recognize that it is only possible to avoid the continuation of the past by using similar methods of surveillance as were used in communist times. Not surprisingly, all this provides an easy terrain for mutual suspicions and accusations that those with communist sympathies still exert undue influence.

Although the interviews cited in the present research do not go too deeply into these matters there is one issue where the material presented here is clearly relevant. This has to do with the vexed question of defining both the objective and subjective boundaries of a given 'unit' of legal culture. Are (legal) cultures really separate and separable (Coombe, 1998) given the convergence imposed, for example, by transnational organizations such as the European Union? With what should the Polish system be compared – and what is it actually comparable with? A large part of Poland's heritage from the communist period continues to be low status and pay, which reflects what is and can be expected from prosecutors. But it would be wrong to consider all communist countries as having or having had the same role for prosecutors. Significantly, prosecutors were and are less important figures in Poland than in Russia. As one interviewee concluded:

> In the Communist regime, nobody had any doubts;, one would work in the prosecution because of two reasons. One was that you were from the Party and not good enough to start a judicial legal training, or one could not be involved in the Party but hoped that afterwards, one could switch to being a barrister. And that's what most people did actually. People from small towns, who had worse degrees, or, let's be honest, didn't have connections to be admitted to judicial or

> barrister's legal training. And they all went to prosecution. And it all, of course, caused that there were never the top-class, first-league people there – rather third-league. That's how it worked. I think that if asked which legal profession has the highest esteem in Poland, you would always hear that it's the judges.

In Poland the judges are more authoritative (indeed the *Transparency International* report on 'Judicial Corruption 2007' singles them out for praise). Perhaps this is the reason why politicians were accused of seeking to influence cases before the court hearing stage. But in Russia it was the judges who were less prestigious. Whom do Polish prosecutors compare themselves with – and with whom do they think they should be compared? The evidence from these interviews is unequivocal in finding that prosecutors compare themselves 'ideally' with prosecutors in Western (not Eastern or Central) Europe. Interestingly, they single out the French in particular. Whatever historical reasons there may be for this, it is not unreasonable given that, there too, the Ministry of Justice exercises overall direction over prosecutors in political cases.

Some interviewees found that the countries likely to be the correct comparators are idealized versions of themselves. Comparisons with other places, sometimes even using the term 'legal culture', serve to show how far Poland still needs to go to reach the appropriate 'normal' standards (this approach is especially noticeable in interviews with the human rights activist and the law professor). One prosecutor told us:

> There were several cases where the General Prosecutor would interfere and have files sent to him. He checked the files and gave instructions, directions what to do next. It's unthinkable in a civilized state – it's absolutely against the law! It's disastrous when you consider political culture and legal culture, but it's absolutely lawful, and that's the tragedy of the situation where the General Prosecutor is also the minister of justice.

Some prosecutors (even whilst asking for more independence) also stressed that countries such as France face similar problems of corruption. The author of the previous quotation went on to say:

> When I was doing professional training in France, I was impressed by the news of a female investigating magistrate, who had hidden files of a corruption scandal concerning the use of social security funds of some foundation by one of the parties, which is prohibited in France. And this investigating magistrate simply had all the files missing; they were gone just in the midst of an electoral campaign. And a son of one of the French presidents was also accused of some embezzlement. In Italy we have mafia ties, different networks … so, I think we're in Europe in this respect and we're no different from other countries. But I think one needs to stay reasonable and calm.

The same applied to political control of prosecutors, as she put it:

> It's not independent anywhere in the world. If you look at the French system, the minister of justice can command a prosecutor, even though they have the principle of legalism, which means that a prosecutor decides whether to pursue a case or not, while in Poland we have the principle of opportunism. We have to prosecute everything. We have to instigate proceedings in every case, no matter if public interest demands it or not; we have to start investigating. We can't say: 'It's not a thing for prosecution. If you have anything against each other, hire attorneys and meet in court.'

As this garbled account of different prosecution systems makes clear, however, prosecutors may think they know more about corruption and its prosecution elsewhere than they really do, supposing that it is enough to have attended an EU training course or to have got information from other sources such as the media. This prosecutor also assumed that corruption patterns always take the same form (that which she knew from Poland) whereby governments, whether national or local, only find information about past corruption after a changeover of political parties.

> I think it's similar in other European states, as I've been to a training organized by the EU that dealt with embezzlement of EU funds. And there was a huge scandal in one of the German federal states, where over 20 million Euro of EU subsidies were embezzled, and the case surfaced only after a change in local government. So, based on that modest example, we can assume that this is just what happens because of the power that authorities have.

Rightly or wrongly, it is prosecutors' ideas of what happens elsewhere, rather than what actually goes on, that can condition their behaviour. However, paradoxically, some prosecutors admitted a lack of knowledge of what went on in their own country, in particular concerning how their own police operated in deciding which cases to prosecute. Some prosecutors may even prefer not to know. As one said:

> For years I've been wondering, as the operational section of the police in M. works on 30 thousand cases annually. And I keep wondering how a case that lands on my desk gets there? Why this one? And I can't tell you that. But operational work is done by the police, of course we may commission it from them, but we don't interfere with their work.

A final link with debates over legal culture can be seen by asking whether it is possible to have a culture-free idea of what legal culture means or should mean. In many countries the descriptive/explanatory concept of 'legal culture' is in fact confused with, or assimilated to the more normative idea of 'the culture of legality', which reflects the effort to bring about a society which respects the rule of law. Can description be separated from prescription? Some authors think that even the descriptive/explanatory concept of legal culture is parasitic on normative claims about legal coherence made by legal actors in their institutional roles (see, for example, Webber, 2004).

More generally, is it possible to be sure that there is a culturally neutral place from which to talk about other people's culture? Researchers themselves also are bearers of legal culture. It comes as no surprise that Lawrence Friedman, living in an Anglo-American legal culture, places emphasis on the importance of external legal culture, whereas Erhard Blankenburg, with more experience of Continental state justice systems, sees the 'supply' side of legal institutions as being more important than the 'demand' side (Blankenburg, 1997). American commentators researching into the current situation in communist countries typically argue that no significant change is likely soon, because ordinary people do not see it as their responsibility, as members of civil society, to hold politicians and courts to higher standards (see, for example, Hendry, 2009). For writers like Hendry, ' the rule of law blossoms where the top-down supply of law meets the bottom-up demand for it' (2009). Those influenced by the Continental European tradition, however, are more likely to see the issue – especially in the realm of criminal justice – as one that depends on the state fulfilling its responsibilities rather than needing to rely on input from civil society.

But even if, for argument's sake, it would be possible for a culturally neutral view of legal culture to exist, who would wish to formulate it? Not insiders, those who are actually authorized to speak for legal culture, enact it and change it. The claims about legal culture they make are inherently controversial – telling us as much about the sort of society the author would like to live in as what is actually happening. In the case of the present study, this is certainly true of what the prosecutors tell us about Polish legal culture. Outsiders, on the other hand, while giving more than the 'official' view, often miss the point of local practices and risk imposing their own ethnocentric expectations.

The best accounts therefore are likely to be produced by insider–outsiders (Nelken, 2000). The first author of this paper could be seen as just such a one, both knowing and caring about the culture from the inside and trying through her work both to make an intervention in debates over the future of the justice system and, with the help of social science, to describe it objectively. Whether one is part of or outside a struggle (insofar as this is possible) has implications for how empirical research is conceived and interpreted, especially when dealing with a topic like corruption. Does it make any difference if corrupt gain is sought for oneself, for the party, or for the cause? Hard as it may be to accept being part of the battle, at least it is possible to believe oneself fighting for a different vision. It is often in the name of some noble goal that those in positions of power feel authorized in manipulating prosecution, since they see their own survival as the means of reaching that goal and assume their opponents are willing to resort to the same tricks.

When insider–outsiders claim to speak 'for' the culture they are part of it is important to consider how far they are in fact representative of that culture. By the nature of things, they are often (for better or worse) 'cosmopolitan' rather than 'local' – and commonly share the agenda of other cosmopolitans. In this chapter it is clear that the insider–outsider stance aligns with other 'cosmopolitans', such as many members of the Constitutional Court or human rights activists, rather than with 'locals' who might defend the current system.

The yardstick of what is meant by prosecutor independence is an absolute one – an ideal of the rule of law. Prosecutors, in contrast to judges, are not institutionally independent. They are, by design, hierarchical and subordinate to the prosecutor general. Admittedly, judicial corruption falls foul of even a thin concept of the rule of law. It is assumed that a short period after the end of communism should have been long enough to make more progress, as if patterns of legal culture can change as quickly as a change of regime. A less engaged enquiry might have looked for evidence of improvement since the use of telephone justice under communism (especially in the case of low level political cases). However, given the slowness with which culture changes, it was hardly likely that prosecutors in Poland would be near the independence end of the continuum.

In so far as there are different European ways of law and not just one way of law (Gessner and Nelken, 2007), there are also different meanings of independence and differing thoughts as to how much of it is a good thing. For instance, it might be possible to assume that the prosecutors interviewed here shared concerns about lack of independence, seeing it as a sign that Poland is not a mature democracy. In fact, not all of the prosecutors taking part in this study had the same idea of what independence does and should mean (and a larger sample would probably have brought this out even more). As an example, one prosecutor viewed independence as the ability to 'take decisions consistent with his beliefs and conscience', rather than having to do with being subject to the law and the law alone.

Prosecutors under Pressure

The Polish participants in this project were asked to comment on the changes that there had been in the independence of prosecutors since the collapse of the communist regime. This was in an effort to understand to what extent, and in what ways, politicians continue to use methods like telephone justice ensure that judicial outcomes are as they wish them to be. The first point that emerged was that it would be wrong to consider all communist countries as having or having had the same role for prosecutors. Of course, there were large variations in the role and status of prosecutors in the so-called Soviet bloc, just as there still are in other European countries.

However, soon after the 1989 transition and throughout the early 1990s prosecutors could be treated as fairly independent, at least from national party political influences. If anything, they were more dependent on local networks and connections, than on political powers. Governments changed almost every year in the 1990s. So when prosecutors started to understand what was going on around them, they had to go. The impression this gave is that there was no policy towards prosecution, which would require some systematic actions. If such actions appeared, it was rather in 2001; and, by that time, prosecution had got stronger.

Apparent symbolic change in the rank of the prosecution occurred with the introduction of the new Constitution in 1997. According to an interviewed law professor and long-time legal adviser at the Sejm, the Polish lower parliamentary house:

> And then, in the Constitution – you know how everybody attaches importance to the Constitution – there's no mention of the prosecution. So, everybody thought it wasn't very important, that they were only some better police forces.

Not mentioning the prosecution as one of the institutional pillars of the democratic state or the judicial system evidently deteriorated the rank of the prosecution, making it subordinate as a body to contemporary political arrangements and subject to current judicial policy line.

Changes in Prosecution After 2005

One may say that the situation had degenerated, or even returned full circle, since 1989, which was particularly marked during the period of the PiS governments of Kazimierz Marcinkiewicz (October 2005–July 2006) and Jarosław Kaczyński (July 2006–November 2007). As one of the interviewees, an experienced prosecutor, stated:

> Prosecutors' independence means that nothing depends on a prosecutor. And there was much truth in it, as some extra filters, extra supervision was introduced – a whole system of instruments enabling control of prosecutors' decisions, like periodic reporting, sending files to be checked by superiors, stipulating that some types of decisions must be first consulted with the head of a given prosecution unit, who in turn, in some cases, has this order that proceedings decisions of some high rank in general must be consulted with prosecution of higher rank.

The situation might have begun to improve following the 2007 elections and another change of government, especially with the new radically anti-PiS Minister of Justice Zbigniew Ćwiąkalski. However, no fundamental and necessary reforms granting independence were passed until now. Initial enthusiastic promises of a speedy and radical reform of the prosecution proved empty, especially after Ćwiąkalski was dismissed and replaced by Andrzej Czuma in January 2009. Slightly more emphasis is now placed on providing legal motivations for action, but this cannot ultimately prevent inappropriate action or inaction in sensitive cases.

Other interviewees' criticism of politicization of prosecution that has occurred in the last years was even stronger:

> But what happened then was not even 'manual control'. It was a classic situation of herds of activists doing whatever the top wanted; they were like political commissars. Everybody in Warsaw knew that the District Public Prosecutor's Office in Praga is for special cases. Or, rather, everybody knew who ruled the [District] Prosecution in Ostrołęka and what directions he was given. For instance, there was a case involving the female head of the Tworki hospital (for the mentally ill). An elderly woman, she was accused of accepting a bronze paperweight. They handcuffed her like a criminal and took her off to be examined in a public health centre, putting her in danger of having a stroke. The paperweight was not expensive, maybe 600 zloty (150 Euro), but the prosecution tried to make a big case out of it.

The idea was that a relatively low-value present, though not given as a bribe, could still be the cause of someone's losing their career.

It was not only prosecution which was controlled either. All the detentions and arrests warrants were issued by young people, candidate judges rather than proper judges.[1] Between 2005 and 2007 the prosecution gained the image of being able to do anything needed, follow any given order. It was not so independent and autonomous a body after all, but in fact relatively easy to bend to new state goals.

Such opinions also point to another problem of the professional legal culture of prosecutors – the notion of standards and comparison with other countries. The interviewees here clearly show the tendency of some of the elite members of legal institutions to compare themselves and their institutional setting to others, notably Western states. Their comments also highlight the division between those who seek to obey the post-communist, local rules of politicized and instrumentally treated prosecution, and those with a more cosmopolitan, European-oriented approach, seeking to be similar to others in leading European countries. The latter thus openly criticized the measures and methods rooted in the communist model of prosecution and present in the post-1989 institutional and legal framework concerning prosecution, which were reinstalled at the time of the PiS governments.

Often the interviewees expressed doubts about the true independence of Polish prosecutors. A particular frame of mind was suggested by one of the prosecutors, who stated: 'by law we are independent'. Yet, prosecutors seemed reluctant to discuss their actual independence, as provided by the Act on Prosecution. Article 8 secures prosecutors' independence, at the same time listing exceptions, which encompass

1 Candidate judges are young judges-to-be after they have undergone judge's training and the final judge's examination. Working at least for three years, they can then be nominated for tenure as a judge by the Minister of Justice and appointed by the President. The institution of candidate judges, as a consequence of a negative decision of the Constitutional Tribunal of 24 October 2007 (SK 7/06) was removed in May 2009. See online at http://www.trybunal.gov.pl/OTK/teksty/otkpdf/2007/SK_07_06.pdf [accessed 13 April 2010].

far-reaching subordination to superiors. Therefore, bearing in mind voiced criticism of the period of deep politicization, one should consider whether the prosecution was at all independent before 2005 as well? If it was, could such an obvious shift have happened? One of the interviewees elaborated on the system of prosecution and how it has never fully been freed from political influence:

> It was involved in some structures, networks, and it was going on somehow in the [19]90s, but this recent test showed what it really looks like. Because, if it was really independent, we would have had some defenders, scandals, somebody would've said something, would've complained openly. And here [at the time of the PiS governments], there was nothing like that [among the prosecutors]. Nothing. Up until the end, when everybody knew what was going on, that the [PO] party shall win, so only then did Kaczmarek appear, and some others trying to jump on the bandwagon, complaining.

The interviewee recalled the case of Janusz Kaczmarek, State Prosecutor under Minister of Justice Ziobro (31 October 2005 to 8 February 2007) and Minister of Internal Affairs and Administration (8 February to 8 August 2007), as an example of giving in to politicization and instrumentalization of prosecution. Kaczmarek was dismissed on suspicion of leaking confidential information to hinder a corruption inquiry involving the Minister of Agriculture. On 30 August he was arrested (and detained for 48 hours) on allegations of submitting false testimony and obstructing justice. Only after having been dismissed did Kaczmarek start to openly criticize the government and its judicial policy, mainly the use of prosecution and secret services, among others alleging before a parliamentary commission that Prime Minister Jarosław Kaczyński and other top officials had used the secret services to spy on political opponents and journalists. His criticism, however, came only after being sacked and marginalized in the Polish political scene, on the eve of the parliamentary elections.

The question, then, is to what extent was this potential for instrumentalization of the prosecution underlying? In other words, was it actually only widely used after 2005? As a matter of fact, the 2005 shift in the prosecution policy and activity occurred almost overnight and without introducing any major legal changes. Such a fact clearly implies that the post-communist justice system, and the prosecution in particular, was designed in such a way that it could easily be captured and used for one's immediate political, party, private or other specific goals. It could and, as earlier reports suggest, it was. A 2002 report on corruption in Poland and other EU-candidate countries deals with the problem of prosecutors' independence and their ability to deal with cases of political corruption.

> Prosecutors are organized hierarchically under the Minister of Justice, who simultaneously holds the position of Prosecutor-General. The fact that the Prosecutor General is appointed by the ruling party raises serious doubts about the capacity of the prosecution system to pursue high-level corruption cases. NIK [The Supreme Chamber of Control] officials believe prosecution offices

> are insufficiently specialized to fight against corruption and financial crime, while some other respondents suggested that prosecutors are not sufficiently independent and sometimes operate to protect the politically powerful (Monitoring the EU Accession Process, 2002a: 21).

The same report recommends 'depoliticiz[ing] the prosecution system, [and] consider[ing] separating the positions of Minister of Justice and Prosecutor General' (Monitoring the EU Accession Process, 2002a: 58). It also suggests the need to '[t]ake appropriate measures to protect prosecutors from undue influence' (ibid.: 80).

Reform efforts were undertaken in late 2007 and early 2008 by the new Minister, Zbigniew Ćwiąkalski, who promised to end the Janus-faced coupling of the functions of Minister of Justice and Prosecutor General. The draft of a new Act on Prosecution was prepared in early 2008, yet it was never even discussed by the Parliament. A year later, in January 2009, Ćwiąkalski resigned. His successor Andrzej Czuma also failed to carry out the much-needed and much-discussed prosecutorial reform in the period up until his dismissal in October 2009. The positions of Prosecutor-General and Minister of Justic were separated on 31 March 2010. However, as changes are very recent, no developments regarding them can be discussed now.

What seemed to be the first serious venture to improve the heavily criticized condition of Polish prosecution in over a decade was abandoned. Obviously, one should wonder why, under what pressures and according to what interests this endeavour was never completed, yet such questions would rather involve the problems of political culture and political lobbies, and would surpass the topic of our deliberations on legal culture.

Besides, some institutional and systemic aspects of prosecution's de facto limited independence can be traced. First, it is interesting that prosecutor's independence is not safeguarded in the constitution, held in high esteem and widely regarded in Poland as a fundamental set of guidelines and a matrix for the key institutional framework. As mentioned earlier, exclusion of the prosecution from the constitution has an important symbolic significance, creating the impression of a peripheral service that may be affected by other, seemingly more important, constitutional institutions.

Second, yet even more important, the double role of the Minister of Justice, being at the same time the Public Prosecutor-General (until March 2010) with full authority over the prosecution, plays a major part in the politicization of the prosecution. Depending on his political agenda, the prosecution may be turned into a powerful political instrument. In such a way, lawfully independent and autonomous prosecutors are being 'centrally steered' by their superiors, often with orders being passed down from the highest authorities. According to the Act on Prosecution, Polish prosecutors are independent and autonomous. However, regulations to the given Act empower superiors, including the immediate superiors, Appellate Prosecutors and the Minister of Justice/Prosecutor-General to supervise and change the course of proceedings undertaken by individual prosecutors. In such a way, 'central steering' of cases by superiors, and in special instances by the highest-ranking political patrons, is legitimized.

Such 'manual handling' of individual prosecutors' cases has become a characteristic of the Polish legal system. Provided for by the law, superiors gain full insight into proceedings, an insight often turned into influence.

Several examples of such a tendency were reported by the media. The most noteworthy and symptomatic is that of the Appellate Prosecutors, formerly working on an extensive corruption case in the fuel industry, the so-called 'petrol mafia', who after resigning from the case shed some light on pressures put on them and attempts at influencing the investigation. The media found out about an incident involving the Minister of Justice Ziobro, prosecutor Wojciech Miłoszewski, and Jarosław Kaczyński at the time of the event *éminence grise* behind the PiS government. In late December 2005 and January 2006 Miłoszewski visited Warsaw's Office of the Minister of Justice to report the developments of the investigation on corruption in the petroleum industry. During one of the last visits, he was taken to present files of the case to an unauthorized person, who, according to Minister of Justice Ziobro, could have access to such documents as a member of the National Security Council and a person who 'had at the time the largest influence upon the ruling party's political platform, also in terms of security and [the] struggle against organized crime' (Czuchnowski, 2008).

> Around 5 p.m. Ziobro storms in talking on a cell phone. We didn't talk to each other; he was on the phone all the time, talking even as he was reading testimony of Krzysztof Baszniak, an important witness in the case. All of the sudden he gets up and says: we're going (Hajnosz, Sidorowicz, 2008).

Judging from the context of earlier talks, Miłoszewski expected to go and meet Zyta Gilowska, then Minister of Finance, to discuss the possibility of creating an investigative team of different fiscal officials. 'My first thought was that we were going to the Ministry of Finance. We drove an official car, and I couldn't even ask him anything, as the Minister was talking on the phone for the whole time' (ibid.). Instead, they were driven to the PiS headquarters, where Miłoszewski was told to show files he had brought with him to Jarosław Kaczyński, party chairman and member of parliament not authorized to read prosecution files. Despite initial doubts whether he should present Kaczyński with the records, Miłoszewski did not object – 'I was given an order, and prosecution is like army barracks' (ibid.). In the Appellate Prosecution of Płock, he testified: 'I was surprised with a formula that, as an apolitical prosecutor, I was giving an account of the investigation in the party headquarters to the party's chairman' (Czuchnowski, 2008).

An account of the extent of superiors' supervision over investigations was given by the prosecutor leading the scrutiny of the 'petrol mafia' scandal. In his deposition in the still ongoing case of political pressures on prosecution, Marek Wełna testified about his influence on the corruption case at the time Zbigniew

Ziobro held the position of Minister of Justice. According to his testimony, the prosecutor felt he had no real impact upon the work of the team of prosecutors, and was under constant scrutiny from his highest superiors – Ziobro, Chief of the State Prosecution Janusz Kaczmarek and Bogdan Święczkowski, Head of the Internal Security Agency (ABW) – interested in personal connections and collecting evidence against political opponents. He also recounted his superiors stampeding him into immediate though weak evidence, and charging several prominent left-wing politicians and members of their families. Eventually, the deciding factor behind Wełna's resignation from the case turned out to be a certain command. He was ordered to develop an analysis of 'interesting people, who speak about other interesting people', for obviously political purposes and completely unnecessary for the investigation.

Clearly, interest, insight and ongoing pressures from superiors are imminent in Polish prosecution. Prosecutors are under constant supervision, not only formal, but also stretching to the substance, content and development of investigations. Especially visible in such 'priority cases', they may discourage independent prosecutors from conducting politically important or notorious investigations. However, what is most interesting is how easily prosecutors seem to succumb to such pressures. What must be stressed is that they do not react and stand up to them. Some cases of open criticism and opposition occurred. Yet the only reactions came when prosecutors in question had been fired, as with Janusz Kaczmarek, or interrogated before parliamentary commissions or by the prosecution. In any case, such open words of criticism were uttered only after a change of government and heads of prosecution, as was easily noticeable in 2007.

As mentioned before, the system of Polish prosecution is by its nature highly hierarchical. One of the most evident indicators of this pyramid structure is the way in which heads of prosecutions – State, Appellate, but also Regional and even the lowest District Prosecutions – are appointed. In accordance with the Act on Prosecution (Article 13 (2)), they are designated by the Prosecutor-General/Minister of Justice, who in practice actively uses his prerogatives. Ever since its creation in 1996, the central State Prosecution is being filled by 'trusted' people consisting largely of resigning Ministers of Justice. Already its founder, Leszek Kubicki, assigned seven prosecutors to work in State Prosecution in the last days at his office, and such practice was later repeated by all consecutive Ministers. This institution, mostly supervisory towards other prosecution divisions, which was designed to ensure the independence of prosecutions from the world of politics, has been changed into a political instrument. As Professor Jarosław Gowin, Civic Platform MP, asserted, 'all, and I shall stress all, Ministers of Justice from Leszek Kubicki to Zbigniew Ziobro, instead of taking care of this independence, assign to State Prosecution persons who – let's be honest – have rather stood out with their servilism towards politicians than competence and independence' (Gowin, 2007).

One of the first decisions of every new Prosecutor-General has traditionally involved personal changes of heads of key appellate and regional prosecutions. Such 'purges' were carried out by Zbigniew Ziobro, who appointed his trusted people to several prosecutions, but also earlier, most notably by Lech Kaczyński in 2000. As a consequence, several regional and appellate prosecutions were even called 'Ziobro's prosecutions', owing to very close cooperation and acquiescent prosecutions conducting proceedings and filing charges according to commands from the political top. Appellate prosecutions in Kraków or Katowice were chosen to conduct key political cases of the so-called 'corruption network', mostly involving left-wing party members and the search for incriminating evidence against any prominent opposition politicians or their families, as well as, in some cases, leading investigative journalists. Heads of both were quickly dismissed and replaced by Ziobro's trusted associates or friends. On the other hand, independent prosecutors were deprived of any control or power in corruption and political investigations. Such was the case of Marzena Kowalska, head of Warsaw's Appellate Prosecution, who was ousted from any control over or insight into the investigations of corruption scandal in the Ministry of Agriculture that were conducted by Regional Prosecution in Warsaw, and were formally supervised by none other than Kowalska. Instead, the inquiry was followed and controlled directly by the Ministry (see Newsweek, 2007).

Changes in autumn 2005 were far-reaching. One of the interviewed prosecutors explained how the Minister of Justice and national party political elites may take over individual investigations:

> He first asks for files and then assigns trusted people to highest positions, especially in regional prosecutions, he [Ziobro] change[s] everybody immediately, and then they [take] care that district prosecutions w[ill] also be run by 'appropriate' people in an 'appropriate' way.

However, the situation did not significantly change after the 2007 parliamentary elections and the new government. In December 2007, newly appointed Prosecutor-General Zbigniew Ćwiąkalski dismissed five chiefs of appellate prosecutions and the Head of Regional Prosecution in Warsaw, who supervised a number of political cases. Further personal changes were introduced later, in fact to 'cut off Ziobro's people from key investigations' (PAP, SS, 2007) A vicious circle of personal changes, a characteristic post-electoral 'carousel of positions' once again came about to replace those with unwanted political affiliations.

One must stress that indicators of party politics' influence upon and active use of the prosecution are deeply rooted in the Polish justice system and are an extension of the communist model of politicized prosecution. Leszek Kubicki destroyed his own creation – national State Prosecution, replacing the communist General Public Prosecutor's Office, closed down in 1990 – by appointing political allies instead of professional and independent prosecutors. Lech Kaczyński, Minister of Justice from 2000 to 2001, paved the way for further influence and, as a consequence, Zbigniew Ziobro's political colonization of public prosecution was used as a tool in the struggle against political opponents and the so-called 'corruption network' of post-communist Poland. Symptomatically, soon after his nomination Kaczyński issued guidelines for prosecutors to move for pre-trial detention in all possible cases, leading to abuse of this preventive measure in Poland, which shall be discussed later in the chapter.

The Polish prosecution service has a hierarchical structure. This means that, although the prosecutor is independent in the performance of his duties as set forth in the legislative acts, he is obliged to comply with the orders, guidelines and instructions of the prosecutor to whom he reports. Therefore, as it shall be stressed, prosecutors' potential for being easily influenced mostly lies in the legislation on prosecution, discussed here earlier. The hierarchical nature of the prosecution with strict subordination to the immediate and highest superiors seems to be the key factor opening the path for an almost unlimited influence of the political system upon the prosecution. Possibilities of insight into files, as well as of giving direct orders concerning proceedings, are written into regulations to the Act on Prosecution, allowing de facto full control over the prosecutor's decisions. Some degree of independence may be protected, but it calls for a self-confident and hardly-influenced prosecutor. As one of the interviewees pointed out:

> [P]rosecution in Poland is by nature hierarchical, in the sense that substantially, a higher rank prosecutor may always oblige a lower rank prosecutor to issue a certain decision. If this lower rank prosecutor doesn't agree with it or doesn't like the idea, he may always ask to have the order in writing and may then always defend himself that it was a superior's decision, not his own. But it's difficult. A younger one finds it hard to stand up against his superior, tell him he disagrees with his decision and wants it in writing, as it means declaring war, it's a confrontation. So, that isn't conducive to independence, although formally it is an instrument securing some sort of independence. Prosecutors, in contrast to judges, are not institutionally independent. They are, by design, hierarchical, which means they can't be independent, which even concerns [the] State Prosecutor, who is subordinate to the Prosecutor-General.

The interviewed legal professionals, in line with other legal experts, heavily criticized the structure of Polish prosecution, pointing to politicization as the key problem hindering its actual independence.

Ultimately, it is the superior who can take decisions, which constitutes a major problem for all legal circles. It is seen as wholly inappropriate that the Prosecutor-General is a person who is guided by political matters. It is a tragedy, it is bad and its existence was left over from the communist regime, the essence of which was that political factors could influence the justice system. In a democratic state, such a situation is unacceptable. But each faction that takes over power finds itself unable to end it. It is just too important for them to hold on to their power.

According to a survey measuring the perception of corruption among Polish prosecutors conducted in early 2005, prosecutors do not admit that they are put under pressure. Of the respondents, 12 per cent affirmed they were under pressure from their superiors, 11 per cent were under pressure from other legal professions,

5 per cent from colleagues, while 4 per cent stated the pressures came from local politicians and 4 per cent from representatives of political parties (Kubiak, 2005: 29). Such data do not confirm common opinions about influences put upon the prosecution in Poland. However, one must remember that the survey was conducted before the 2005 elections and the PiS victory. It would therefore be necessary to have more recent data to observe any possible tendencies in declared pressures encountered by prosecutors. On the other hand, it was focused on a very sensitive topic of corruption, clearly repulsing Polish legal professionals. Yet, above all, pressures are often exercised indirectly, in an almost untraceable and very subtle way, often taking the form of allusions and hints, clear to understand by prosecutors, but almost impossible to prove or reconstruct.

The survey respondents in this chapter seemed less reluctant to discuss their experience and opinions on pressures exerted on prosecutors. As stated by the interviewed professionals, pressure upon prosecutors may be exercised in a number of ways, varying from incentives, through subtle suggestions up to almost direct orders.

'Soft' Influence

The pressures to which prosecutors are subject are exercised in a number of ways. The gentlest way may be called 'soft influence', which is very difficult to detect, let alone prosecute and punish. It involves suggestions, incentives, or even being put in a certain position (that is, being forced to move on swiftly with a case, being asked to file charges quickly, or even being told to slow a case down), often brought about by working under certain politically affiliated supervisors.

For example in Regional Prosecution, when a political case appears everybody wants to bluff their way out of it, as they know there is never a good way out. On one hand, if a prosecutor does what he is ordered to do, his compliance renders him a careerist, searching for easy promotion on the back of a particular case. This is something most prosecutors do not want. On the other hand, if he deals with the case substantially, then somebody will cross him out. So, whatever he does, the outcome will be bad. When an obviously political case appears, prosecutors genuinely fear it: from authorial experience, superiors do usually tend to have particular political attitudes. Everybody knows which stance they take and which cases need to be watched out for. Regardless of the truth of the matter, prosecutors remain convinced that politics has a huge influence on what decisions they may or may not take.

Orders

Prosecutors may also be influenced in an official or quasi-official manner by guidelines or direct orders from their immediate or higher superiors. However, such commands may usually not be traced, as they are typically oral, or are simply general and not concerned with a specific inquiry, such as in the case of the Minister of Justice's guidelines.

There are cases direct orders are received, but without anything written in them. Such instructions are never straightforward; there are always hints to be understood, along the lines of 'It would be good if you thought this process decision over once again'.

Prosecutors, told specifically what to do, have practically no way of complaining against the undue influence of their superiors. It is especially so considering that orders are hardly ever written, and that superiors are legally allowed insight into and control over inquires.

Incentives

Incentives are often used to 'soften' an unruly prosecutor in a political corruption case. Quick promotion is the easiest way to entice a prosecutor, exert compliance and eventually gain influence over a given inquiry, at the same time ensuring the prosecutor's future conformity. An interviewed legal professional described a typical mechanism of making quick careers in prosecution:

> It's understood between them. There are whole prosecution careers based on that. One may dislike that, but there are people, who only by taking political orders in preparatory proceedings, were promoted incredibly quickly. So, they were promoted not because of the substance, heart of the matter, but loyalty. And it's because of this hierarchy of the prosecution.

An off-record account was given by another interviewee, who was offered a position in prosecution in Warsaw in return for quitting an inconvenient case. A similar story was recounted by one of the leading prosecutors of Krakow's Appellate Prosecution, holding an extensive inquiry into the corrupt network of the so-called 'petrol mafia'. After having resigned from the case, as discussed earlier in the chapter, Wojciech Miłoszewski shed some light on the incentives offered to prosecutors in return for future conformity or refraining from further investigation of a given case:

> My superior told me that I wouldn't be interrogating Siemiątkowski,[2] as I was excluded from that, yet I would be offered something in three days. And, indeed, I was called to Warsaw and offered a promotion to the State Prosecution. It was

2 Zbigniew Siemiątkowski – Polish left-wing politician; member of parliament from 1991 to 2005; the last head of the Office for State Protection (UOP) in 2001–2002, and later head of the Intelligence Agency; accused of giving false testimony about the arrest of former president of Orlen, the biggest petrol company in Poland; in 2007 found guilty of keeping secret UOP documents at home.

> told by Kaczmarek.[3] […] I answered, that I understood that it's the price for quitting that case and that I would be reassigned to a department not connected to organized crime. 'Well, yes, I think you do understand it,' he replied. […] Needless to say, I declined (Hajnosz, Sidorowicz, 2008).

He did, but many, as stressed in the interviews, chose to cooperate and profit with their flourishing careers.

... and Disincentives

Another famous case which showed mechanisms for influencing prosecutors in their inquiries was revealed in relation to the widely reported arrest and death of Barbara Blida. Blida, former left-wing parliamentary (in the years 1989–2005) and former Minister of Construction and Spatial Economy (1993–1996), committed suicide in still not cleared circumstances in her own bathroom while being arrested, by the Internal Security Agency on 25 April 2007, on charges of corruption.

As the special parliamentary commission investigating the case of Blida found out, all prosecutors holding the inquiry were subject to internal disciplinary proceedings. MP and commission member Danuta Pietraszewska examined the developments of the inquiry: 'I was awestruck when I prepared charts, on which I marked key moments of the Blida investigation and periods when the investigating prosecutors encountered problems themselves. It turned out that these two lines overlapped!' (Manys, 2008). Disciplinary proceedings were initiated against three consecutive prosecutors leading the investigation just after each of them had taken over the case. Trivial and old cases were raked up and used as specific calls to order, subtle threats or hidden blackmail attempts to ensure compliance in such a politically important inquiry, that is, filing charges or soliciting arrest warrants. Interestingly, disciplinary proceedings were terminated at the same time that prosecutors were dismissed from the case, as with Tomasz Balas, who also, shortly after, left public prosecution to go to the Institute of National Remembrance. Balas, who had the court issue the arrest warrant for Blida, took over the case in November 2006. At the beginning of 2007, a disciplinary proceeding was opened in relation to a case that he had held three years earlier, in 2004. Balas signed the arrest warrant in April, and soon after, on 8 June, the disciplinary proceeding was closed (ibid.). Emil Melka, who supervised the Blida case before Balas, was also threatened with disciplinary proceeding. As he testified before the parliamentary commission, pressures in the case almost led to him quitting the Regional Prosecution in Katowice for a lower-ranked position in District Prosecution, a strange and unexpected move in the prosecution hierarchy (see Interia.pl/PAP, 2008).

3 Janusz Kaczmarek, then State Prosecutor from 31 October 2005 to 8 February 2007.

Transfers and relocations of prosecutors – to lower ranks, to other divisions, to lower-ranked prosecution (that is, from Appellate or Regional to District Prosecution), to small centres, such as prosecution offices in small towns – are the best solutions for intractable prosecutors. Such threats or indeed relocations cause fear and encourage the submissiveness that is so often demanded by superiors.

In cases where such scare tactics fail, specifically intimidating legal actions are taken. As mentioned, disciplinary proceedings used to be the easiest way of disciplining unruly prosecutors, though these are now mere empty threats. Probably the best-known case of degradation owing to political reasons happened in June 2006. Former spokesperson for the State Prosecution, Małgorzata Wilkosz-Śliwa, closely associated with the left-wing SLD party, was delegated to work in the lowest-rank District Prosecution in Zabrze for open criticism of then Minister Ziobro. A disciplinary proceeding was also initiated against her (see Siedlecka, 2007; Puchała, 2006).

Similarly, Head of the Regional Prosecution of Opole, Jerzy Niekrawiec, was dismissed after he had started investigation and interrogation of the ruling party PiS local officials from the Opole region in relation to revealing a state secret. Niekrawiec was quickly accused of embezzlement and disciplinarily dismissed. As it turned out, the matter in question amounted to just 300 zł unaccounted for, an equivalent of 66 Euro (see Siedlecka, 2007).

Political Pressures

Apart from the immediate pressure of superiors over prosecutors, direct political influence may also come into question. Problems that occur while political cases are prosecuted were recounted by one of the interviewees:

> And if you add political factors, then not only corruption, but all criminal proceedings, cases that involve a politician, a person holding power or some social influence, these cases are special, as you may presume that in some cases they will try to put pressure. And it requires a huge deal of prosecution's independence, independence of all bodies of justice, of the police, to stand against such services.

One may finally ask how political pressures are applied.

> For example, even through such a gate as the Minister of Justice. He doesn't even have to know that a politician from his party is in the circle of interest, but this politician may refer to him, use his name, suggest that 'you better leave me, you don't know what you're doing, I'm from the same group as your boss'. It's enough even if he doesn't say that, but the policemen and prosecutors are well aware of it, aware that they try to get somebody how is close, from the ruling party.

It seems that the biggest influence of external factors on the prosecution happens before a case goes to court. When the trial begins, as one interviewee suspected, one should not be afraid of any bias:

> I think that we can assume that when there's a court case, court will really be independent. And I think that prosecution will be then as well. If they decide on it, if it goes to court, they have no way out and they will be independent. Nobody will play it soft. But we don't know what happens before it goes to court. There may be very different things happening. And I think everybody will use all the influence they can, which is normal.

With courts widely regarded as truly independent, it is not surprising that prosecution inquiries and police investigations were pointed to as being the stages of the criminal proceedings at which a case may easily be wrenched away. One of the prosecutors with experience in corruption cases elaborated on the ways in which a case may be terminated without merit:

> It may be transferred to another prosecution unit and the case ends its course. At times I've encountered such strange behaviour, which, I reckon, must have had something more to it, its hidden agenda. State or General Prosecutor may order to transfer a case. There must be a reason for that, but you know … you can always find something. And, of course, it's an arbitrary decision, which is grounded in legal provisions. Yet, these provisions can be used in different way, can't they? If one wants … There are sometimes cases which are run in somehow not fully understandable circumstances, but it takes a lot of risk. A prosecutor, an inferior, can write a note, send it officially; which can be very dangerous, it's walking on thin ice.

Interviews showed that prosecutors are well aware of stages at which a case could be wrenched away, or 'killed'. Unsurprisingly, well aware of the consequences of revealing such knowledge, they were not eager to discuss specific examples. When asked if she had heard of any such cases, one prosecutor answered: 'Look, I'm a big girl and I've heard of many things.' However, they did give some general information, including such straightforward statements as this one:

> A case can be killed at every stage. There's no such stage, when one couldn't just kill it, or change its course, if somebody wanted to be dishonest. It's possible. Starting from the operational phase – one may have great information and never reveal it. [Facts] could be somewhere out there in files and nobody might know them. If a case goes to prosecution and a prosecutor, even unwillingly, starts to read the operational files from the very beginning, [he] may find some information irrelevant, if he checks them hastily. I don't even mean killing a case, but if somebody wanted to do it – they could. In preparatory proceedings evidence could be evaluated in a different way than somebody else would treat them, as

> it's an individual decision. So, if they are evaluated dishonestly, one could remit proceedings. And then in court, one could say that evidence doesn't prove the defendant's guilt, dismiss the case or find him innocent. Yes, it could happen, but we shouldn't assume it [...]. The assumption must be that we all work honestly. It's like with doctors in a sense. We diagnose having this specialized knowledge – and my diagnosis may be different than that of a colleague next door. Just like one doctor could tell you that you're healthy, and another one would treat you immediately. Though of course I'd be dishonest if I said that a case can't be killed on purpose – of course it can!

All those interviewed agreed that it was extremely difficult to gain evidence to prosecute everyday corruption by businessmen and politicians. However, they thought that usually the protection of powerful people from prosecution happened at this early stage rather than in open attempts to block proceedings once started. It is possible, but it happens, or rather it used to happen more often for other, commonplace offences, such as driving under the influence or affray. An interviewed barrister and human rights activist shared an interesting thought on the direct influence of national or local politicians upon cases of corruption:

> I know that it is much easier for a politician to influence a non-corruption case. A classic case is a politician detained for drunken driving, or his daughter. Then he calls the Minister of Justice or an acquaintance prosecutor and says – 'look, let's discontinue this case, such a poor girl ...'. And it used to be common, now not so much, but earlier, in the [19]90s it was very common. But when you have a charge of bribery, prosecution is especially sensitive, as killing such a case is also corruption – so, corruption for corruption. Such cases are very difficult to go through with and I personally don't know any from my own experience. I know cases, when people use their influences and refer to their connections – but it was always in cases of ordinary, commonplace offences – driving under [the] influence, a row in a bar, insult[ing] an officer. In these cases, people use their influence to kill them. There is a good chance of success then, when you start talking to a befriended prosecutor, you can approach a prosecutor. It used to be very common, now there are fewer and fewer such cases, fortunately.

These remarks involve political influence and are often not valid when relating to hierarchical, structural influence within the prosecution itself. However, by no means do they exclude inner 'telephone justice', so eagerly executed by immediate and highest superiors, including the Minister of Justice and his associates.

Although not immediately, political influence and pressures upon prosecution were also condemned by the circles of prosecutors. In June 2007, the Association of Polish Prosecutors issued an appeal protesting against the politicization of prosecution and calling for ethical conduct. All troubles were explicitly listed.

> Let us all create professional and objective Prosecution, which does not succumb to influence, free from current political interests, working in an atmosphere of trust, companionship and mutual respect [...]. We are obliged to care and protect prosecutors' independence from actions violating these values (Stowarzyszenie Prokuratorów, 2007).

Soon after the document was published, the Chairman of the Association was called to testify in an explanatory proceeding against him. The investigation was closed after numerous protests of professional associations against limiting freedom of speech, and warning against disciplinary proceedings and charges used as threats and means of silencing prosecutions.

Instruments of Politicization of the Polish Prosecution: From Preventive Detention to 'Extractive Detention'

The Polish prosecution suffers from being institutionally bound with the world of politics. As a consequence, its interface develops some peculiar forms in which prosecution serves the immediate political needs of the ruling parties. The most notable and characteristic of them is a new invention of 'extractive detention' – in a Mertonian sense of the word – innovative, extra-legal use of preventive, pre-trial (also exercised during lengthy trials) detention used in cases regarded as politically crucial.

Widely criticized and regarded as subject to abuse, among others by the Polish Ombudsman (see Rzecznik Praw Obywatelskich, 2007), preventive detention is one of the key instruments used by the Polish prosecution. It was the second most common preventive measure used in preparatory proceedings in 2006, administered in every third case, in total in 34,291 cases (ibid.).

Pre-trial detention is granted by the court on a prosecutor's motion. This measure, in theory limited to three months, may be prolonged by the court to up to a year in preparatory proceedings, and when charged, up to two years, which again might, in special, yet not precisely specified circumstances, be further prolonged by the court if necessary. As a result, a total of 14,268 persons were detained at the beginning of 2007, while at the end of 2006 2,466 persons were held in preventive detention for the period of 12 to 24 months, while 1,054 remained detained for more than two years (ibid.). One must also stress that the number of persons detained constitutes more than 15 per cent of all persons in prison, totalling more than 90 thousand (see Ministerstwo Sprawiedliwości, Centralny Zarząd Służby Więziennej, 2008: 4). It must be stressed that an overwhelming majority of prosecution's motions for pre-trial detention are granted. In 2004, out of all 38,200 filed motions for pre-trial detention, 90 per cent were granted (see Arciszewska-Mielewczyk, 2006).

However, the trend of resorting to preventive detention started to revert after the change of government and the Minister of Justice. The Central Prison Authority stated that as of 31 October 2008, there were 9,464 pre-trial detainees, a distinct drop of approximately 4,500 from March 2007. The drop is partly owing to fewer requests by prosecutors for pre-trial detention and a decline in the number of requests approved by judges (see United States Department of State, 2008, Łukaszewicz, 2008). According to Justice Marek Calej, 'there's no political trend, which would force prosecutors to file for detention almost automatically. More often, they decide to use other preventive measures, by no means less effective' (Łukaszewicz, 2008), especially with less interest and pressure from the Minister of Justice to use pre-trial detention.

What is interesting from the point of view of an analysis of the Polish prosecution is that pre-trial detention was stripped of its actual preventive character and instead changed into a way of 'softening' the accused by lengthy, strenuous detention, thus enabling the acquisition of new burdening evidence (consistent with the prosecutors' line and evidence) from depositions. Resorting to 'extractive detention', a quasi-Stalinist method developed under the rule of Minister Ziobro, meant that otherwise hardly limited preventive detention was extended to critical measures. Former Ombudsman and Chairman of the Polish Constitutional Tribunal, Professor Andrzej Zoll criticized the abuse of preventive detention in Poland: 'We obviously deal with a common use of detention. I'm afraid that its long duration reaches beyond any necessity. I suspect that it serves to extract some specific testimony or to incriminate some specific persons' (Dryszel, 2007).

Extractive detention is not only a media fact. One of the interviewees, a lawyer and human rights activist, recalled:

> There were also objections of the so-called extractive detention, i.e. arresting somebody in order to later extract, force testimony. And here, in my office, we've had at least 4 or 4 people who presented facts and circumstances, which more or less directly pointed to the use of extractive detention. Of course it's such an institution that it's difficult to prove any wrongdoing, as it all happens informally, through intermediaries, through some negotiations, but it indeed happens.

Let us take a look at some examples of such 'extractive detention'. The most notable is that of Marek Dochnal, a businessman and influential informal lobbyist. In September 2004 the Internal Security Agency (ABW) arrested Dochnal for allegedly bribing public officials for information concerning the privatization of a state-owned steel mill and the sale of shares of the country's largest oil company. After 22 months of detention, on 13 July 2007 Dochnal filed a complaint protesting his detention to the European Court of Human Rights (complaint number 31622/07). On 28 January, the ECHR notified the government that the complaint had been accepted. Three days later, the Warsaw Appellate Court refused to further extend his pre-trial detention and freed Dochnal after three and a half years of detention. His trial began on 3 July 2008. However, he was rearrested on 7 August by the Internal Security Agency (ABW) and again put in detention.

Dochnal's complaint to the ECHR was one of a number of cases brought against Poland before the Court. Between 1999 and 2007, the ECHR determined in 113 cases that authorities violated the human rights and fundamental freedom of detained persons owing to lengthy pre-trial detention (see Łukaszewicz, 2008). Such a large number of reproofs plainly shows the magnitude and scale of the problem of the use and abuse of pre-trial detention as a means of 'softening' the accused and extracting incriminating testimony. What must be stressed is that such an instrument is clearly used in politically important cases, where individual prosecutors are under strong pressure from their superiors and political patrons.

New Instruments at the Interface of Politics and Prosecution: 'Hooks' and Leaks

A special term, 'collect hooks', was coined in Poland to describe taking actions to discredit politicians, mainly by collecting and searching for incriminating evidence, often using the police, prosecution, secret services and other investigative means. Several high-profile cases emerged, where the prosecution turned out to be one of the 'centrally-steered' instruments in the political game, providing incriminating evidence against prominent opposition politicians.

A prosecutor gave an account of how his high-profile inquiry was chopped into pieces by the highest superiors and the Ministry of Justice, searching for incriminating evidence against political opponents.

> When a political fraction that is not interested in long-term solution of the problem and finishing of the inquiry, takes over, they are only interested in names, they react to names only – there was this and that name, so they jump on these parts [of the inquiry] and take them out. It's as if somebody wanted to cure [a] rash and would take one pimple after another and investigate them one by one, thinking if this one is pretty, or worse, so we shall start the killing. So were materials taken out of the inquiry, one by one. This is ignorance, lack of experience.
>
> [Interviewer: Why? Somebody wanted it for political reasons?]
>
> Yes, exactly! Names were the target, not solving the case. We have 'hooks', we look for incriminating evidence, for names! […] Many cases are killed like that.

It is at that stage, and often because of such motives, that cases may be wasted, 'killed', that is, terminated, dropped or remitted because of particular interests or, as in the inquiry above, owing to an instrumental hunt for opponents rather than substantial reasons.

Surrounded by Pressures, Opposing Expectations and Conflicting Norms

What emerges is a peculiar form of 'telephone justice' – an unofficial, informal way of forcing justice out of court before it reaches the crucial phase of the procedure in the courthouse. The preparatory, pre-trial part of the proceedings, as one could expect, is ideal for exercising such justice through the use of personal connections.

One may say that a specific 'lex telefonicum' is in force; that one makes a decision based on an official command, or rather on consultation with a superior prosecutor. Obviously, such cases of 'telephone justice' should not be treated as endemic; they were even treated as exceptions by most of the interviewees. However, such backstage justice may prevail and does prevail where political interests (as in the case of Dr G., discussed below) or the interests of the highest-ranking political patrons are at stake.

On one hand, prosecutors are under the constant control, sometimes even the scrutiny, of their superiors and political patrons. On the other hand, they feel that they are left alone when problems arise – for example, criticism, hostility from politicians or the media, public outrage, and also the disapproval or discontent of superiors (including the highest in the Appellate or State Prosecution, and, above all, the Prosecutor-General) – they feel no support and no backing.

Mature democracies may resist such [political] pressures. It is much more difficult, however. One might expect the outrage of a prosecutor who had been put in such a situation to be much stronger, much more unequivocal, and one might anticipate stronger resistance in such cases. Yet prosecutors in Poland are certain that they will lose any confrontation they have with this political power. They believe that, should they stamp their feet and say 'no', there would be nobody standing behind them and nobody supporting them; all the support would be for the politicians. Any daring decision they take must be taken alone.

Prosecutors Facing Media Scrutiny

A further topic for discussion amongst the interviewees was the role the media play in the everyday work of prosecution. On one hand, participants stressed a high level of journalistic scrutiny; though, unsurprisingly, it was perceived as a problem. Yet, on the other hand, the interviewees felt that the quality of journalistic professionalism and knowledge of the justice system was poor.

As stated, prosecutors complained about being under constant watch by the media, which often brought them into the line of fire of public criticism.

> I see the media's role as negative. Media force special interest in a case on our superiors. It's all planned so they can write about what's going on in the case, while it should be enough that only me and my immediate superior is interested, not anyone higher. Yet there is interest – of Regional Prosecution, Appellate and State Prosecution, even from the Ministry of Justice in such media cases.

Confronted with the interest of both the media and their own supervisors, prosecutors often try to evade publicized or political cases, where they would need to operate in the spotlight. Moreover, as several prosecutors complained, superiors' interest is rather limited to public reports on the developments during press conferences and to interviews; it rarely involves backup or support in the case of media attacks or public criticism of prosecution.

Furthermore, as some interviewees suggested, journalists regularly report inaccurately to the public on proceedings they witness, in some cases becoming instruments in political games. Several specific examples of the Polish judiciary's handling of corruption cases were indicated. 'Leaks' play a crucial role in the way that cases are handled by both the media and the prosecution. In recent years, the prosecution's leaking of secret or sensitive information in order to befriend 'investigative' journalists has become the easiest way of publicizing a case without the risk of being accused of revealing secrets of the investigation. Also guilty of such information-leaking have been the Agency of Internal Security, the police, several special parliamentary commissions and the Institute of National Remembrance. Videos, audio tapes, tapped recordings, copies of official records, files and testimonies are all widely used, without much thought about their source or the purpose they will serve once leaked. Such leaks appear immediately in every prominently publicized 'priority case' – one involving corruption and/or high-profile politicians – and, no matter how secret, automatically become of no interest to the prosecution. One of the most obvious examples are the leaked testimonies of key and prominent witnesses in the above-mentioned corruption case of former MP Barbara Blida, which were extensively quoted by leading national newspapers.

Moreover, the media became a new forum for prosecution. Especially under Minister Ziobro, several high-profile cases were handled more by and in the media, than actually by the prosecution, which eagerly leaked crucial information from investigations. The purpose of such leaks was clear: to exert influence on the general public in order to 'try' cases in the media and in the eyes of the public, rather than in the courthouse. Such media trials, obviously, had to play according to the rules of the media sphere – fast, sharp, without hesitation and with ready judgments. Contrary to all principles of the judiciary, violation of individual rights was apparent. The most blatant example of such quick media justice, exercised by the head of the prosecution, was the case of Dr G. (discussed below).

Trial by the Media: Media Trials by the Minister of Justice

In the years 2005–2007, mass media became a powerful instrument used to influence the work of prosecution, especially in cases viewed as politically important.

The best-known instance of media justice was the so-called 'case of Dr G.'. Mirosław Garlicki, an established cardiac surgeon and head of the largest heart transplantation clinic in Poland, was arrested on 12 February 2007, while at work, and led out in handcuffs past stunned co-workers. On the day of his arrest, a press conference was held, which was broadcast live by the major television and radio stations. During the conference, some of the highest-ranking state officials established Dr Garlicki's guilt beyond reasonable doubt, clearly concluding that the prosecution could do without contradictory court proceedings. Standing in the spotlight, Minister of Justice and Prosecutor-General Ziobro stated to the media: 'In this unfortunately sad discovery of the truth, we can say this was an important event in the true sense of that expression, in that no one else ever again will be deprived of life by this man' (Ministerstwo Sprawiedliwości, 2007a). Soon, Garlicki was charged with 20 counts of corruption and one count of murder (which was dropped in May 2008).

The Prosecutor-General's comments on Garlicki's case prompted strong criticism from the former Ombudsman Andrzej Zoll, the National Bar Council, the Polish Helsinki Committee and others. The ECHR will consider the impact of these statements in terms of the right to fair trial and the presumption of innocence.

The prosecutors interviewed for this chapter stressed that incriminating statements such as that made by the Minister of Justice are well-understood among individual prosecutors. They are treated as obvious attempts at influencing their work and showing them the 'official line' of the political superiors of the prosecution.

The case of Dr G. was the most notable example of the political nature and context of the fight against corruption in healthcare. His public arrest proved to be one of many, carried out in an attempt to root out corruption from the Polish healthcare system in particular, and from public life in general. However, for critics, it has become a blatant indicator of the quality of Polishgovernance, as well as of instrumentalization of both the law and the justice system, reducing them to tools for purely political causes and immediate gains.

Still, there have been other examples of the direct influence of the Prosecutor-General on prosecutors, through media appearances, mainly in the form of press conferences. Zbigniew Ziobro, as Minister of Justice, during one such press conference openly defended seven men accused of lynching and murder in the village of Włodowa. He sent an official command to the Regional Prosecution in Olsztyn ordering it to release the detained defendants, an action which he later confirmed publically at another press conference. He also appealed for the charges of murder to be dropped and, in his public statement, repeatedly mentioned the limits of self-defence, as if to influence the indictment. The defendants were immediately released from detention. As the spokesman for the Olsztyn Regional Prosecution briefly commented: 'One doesn't discuss commands of the superior' (Wojciechowska, 2005).

The idea of trying key cases in the media was not abandoned by the next Minister of Justice either. Zbigniew Ćwiąkalski was of the more centrist Civic Platform (PO). Although apparently less eagerly, he also used the media and, to some extent, press conferences as forums for bringing informal influence to bear on individual investigations and proceedings. The most notable example is the case of Aleksandra Jakubowska, Deputy Culture Minister in the left-wing SLD government at the time of the so-called 'Rywin corruption scandal'. On the day that Jakubowska was acquitted of the charges of tempering with the draft of the Media Act in 2002, a key issue in the Rywin scandal, Ćwiąkalski made a number of media appearances. Besides discussing the case outcome, he announced that the prosecution would appeal the verdict. Moreover, the Ministry of Justice issued a statement saying that 'Prosecutor-General Zbigniew Ćwiąkalski ordered the prosecution to lodge an appeal from this verdict' (Ministerstwo Sprawiedliwości, 2007b), not only showing the path for prosecution, but directly and openly commanding future actions.

Interestingly, lawyers stress that such influence violates Article 10 (2) of the Act on Prosecution, which states that directives and orders of the Prosecutor-General may not relate to investigative and court proceedings, thus showing signs of breach of authority by the Prosecutor-General. However, issuing guidelines and direct interventions into inquiries has become standard practice both for consecutive ministers and for individual prosecutors. One might even express fears that young prosecutors or those still gaining experience may contribute to establishing an unwanted practice of accepting all details of proceedings.

The way in which corruption cases are being handled has proved to be a good indicator of the condition of Polish prosecution, showing how political pressure is put on individual prosecutors and how unofficial top-down 'orders' are given. Such pressures become most visible in high-profile cases, especially those involving politicians. However, it is also in such cases that the weakness and actual dependence of the prosecution are most evident.

References

Arciszewska-Mielewczyk, D., 'Oświadczenie złożone przez senator Dorotę Arciszewską-Mielewczyk, skierowane do ministra sprawiedliwości, prokuratora generalnego RP Zbigniewa Ziobry', *Diariusz Senatu Rzeczypospolitej Polskiej Nr 15*, 05.06 (2006). Available online at <http://www.senat.gov.pl/K6/DOK/DIAR/15/1503.htm> [accessed 14 April 2010].

Blankenburg, E., 'Civil litigation rates as indicators for legal cultures', in David Nelken (ed.) *Comparing Legal Cultures* (Aldershot: Dartmouth, 1997), 41–69.

Brodeur, J.-P., 'High policing and low policing: Remarks about the policing of political activities', *Social Problems*, 30 (1983), 507–20.

Coombe, R., 'Contingent articulations: Critical studies of law', in A. Sarat and T. Kearns (eds), *Law in the Domains of Culture* (Ann Arbor, MI: University of Michigan Press, 1998).

Cotterrell, R., 'The concept of legal culture', in D. Nelken (ed.), *Comparing Legal Cultures* (Aldershot: Dartmouth, 1997), 13–32.

Czarnota, A., 'Lustration, decommunisation and the rule of law', *Hague Journal of the Rule of Law*, 1/2 (2009), 307–36.

Della Porta, D. and Y. Meny, *Democracy and Corruption in Europe* (London: Continuum Press, 1997).

Dryszel, A., 'Posiedzisz.. to powiesz', *Przegląd*, no. 24, 12.06 (2007). Available onlineat<http://www.przeglad-tygodnik.pl/index.php?site=kraj&name=2932> [accessed 14 April 2010].

Friedman, L., *The Legal System: A Social Science Perspective* (New York: Russell Sage, 1975).

Gessner, V, and D. Nelken, *European Ways of Law* (Oxford: Hart Publishing, 1997).

Ginsburg, T., *Judicial Review in New Democracies: Constitutional Courts in Asian Cases* (Cambridge: Cambridge University Press, 2003).

Gowin, J., *Wycofanie misji z Iraku w połowie 2008 roku?*, interview in PR1 Sygnały Dnia, 03.11 (2007). Available online at <http://www.polskieradio.pl/jedynka/sygnalydnia/artykul11673.html> [accessed 14 April 2010].

Hendry, K., 'Telephone law and the rule of law: The Russian case', *Hague Journal of the Rule of Law*, 1/2 (2009), 241–306.

Interia.pl/PAP (2008) *Kalisz: Wobec referentów prowadzono postępowania dyscyplinarne*, 10.06, <http://fakty.interia.pl/raport/samobojstwo_minister/news/kalisz-wobec-referentow-prowadzono-postepowania,1125489> [accessed 19 April 2010].

Justis (2009). Available online at <www.eurojustis.eu/> [accessed 14 April 2010]

Krygier, M., 'Is there constitutionalism after communism? Institutional optimism, cultural pessimism, and the rule of law', *International Journal of Sociology*, 26/4 (1997), 17–47.

Kubiak, A., *Opinia publiczna i prokuratorzy o korupcji. Raport z badań 2005* (Fundacja Batorego Program Przeciw Korupcji, Warszawa, 2005). Available online at <http://www.batory.org.pl/doc/opinia_publiczna_i_prokuratorzy_o_korupcji.pdf> [accessed 14 April 2010].

Łukaszewicz, A., 'Przełom w polityce stosowania aresztów', *Rzeczpospolita* 26.09 (2008). Available online at <http://www.rp.pl/artykul/196053.html> [accessed 14 April 2010].

Manys, K., 'Przełom w komisji Blidy?', *Rzeczpospolita*, 11.06 (2008).

Markovits, Inga, *Imperfect Justice: An East-West German Diary* (Oxford: Oxford University Press, 1995).

Ministerstwo Sprawiedliwości, Stenogram konferencji prasowej ministra sprawiedliwości Zbigniewa Ziobro i szefa Centralnego Biura Antykorupcyjnego Mariusza Kamińskiego z dnia 14 lutego 2007 roku (2007a). Available online at <http://www.ms.gov.pl/sprostowania/070226a_stenogram_konf_cba.pdf> [accessed 14 April 2010].

Ministerstwo Sprawiedliwości, *Komunikat prasowy w związku z wyrokiem w sprawie Aleksandry Jakubowskiej*, 20.12 (2007b). Available online at <http://www.ms.gov.pl/aktual/aktualnosci2007.php?m=grudzien> [accessed 14 April 2010].

Ministerstwo Sprawiedliwości, Centralny Zarząd Służby Więziennej (2008) *Informacja o wykonywaniu kary pozbawienia wolności i tymczasowego aresztowania za rok 2007*, Warszawa, <http://www.sw.gov.pl> [accessed 19 April 2010].

Monitoring the EU Accession Process, *Corruption and Anti-corruption Policy in Poland* (Open Society Institute, 2002).

Nelken, D., *Comparative Criminal Justice: Making Sense of Difference* (London: Sage, 2010).

———'Three problems in studying legal culture', in F. Bruinsma and D. Nelken (eds), *Exploring Legal Cultures*, special issue of Recht der Werkelijkheid (2007), 11–28.

——— 'Rethinking legal culture', in M. Freeman (ed.), *Law and Sociology* (Oxford: Oxford University Press, 2006a), 200–24.

———'Signaling conformity: Changing norms in Japan and China', *Michigan Journal of International Law*, 27 (2006b), 933–72.

———'Using the concept of legal culture', *Australian Journal of Legal Philosophy*, 29 (2004), 1–28.

Nelken, D. (ed.), *Contrasting Criminal Justice* (Aldershot, Ashgate, 2000).

——— 'Il significato di Tangentopoli: La risposta giudiziaria alla corruzione e i suoi limiti', in Luciano Violante (ed.) *Storia d'Italia 14: Legge, Diritto e Giustizia* (Turin: Einaudi, 1997), 597–627.

———'Judicial politics and corruption in Italy', in M. Levi and D. Nelken (eds) 'The corruption of politics and the politics of corruption', *Journal of Law and Society*, Special Issue (1996), 95–113.

PAP, SS (2007), Sześciu szefów prokuratury odwołanych', *Wprost24*, 12.12 (2007). Available online at <http://www.wprost.pl/ar/119549/Szesciu-szefow-prokuratury-odwolanych> [accessed 14 April 2010].

Program Monitoringu Akcesji do UE, *Program Monitoringu Akcesji do Unii Europejskiej (UE) Korupcja i polityka antykorupcyjna* (Open Society Institute, 2002). Available online at http://www.batory.org.pl/ftp/program/przeciw-korupcji/publikacje/inne_publikacje/korupcja_i_polityka_antykorupcyjna.pdf [accessed 14 April 2010].

Puchała, E., 'Prokurator na zesłaniu', *POLSKA – Dziennik Zachodni*, 16.06 (2006).

Savelsberg, J., 'Knowledge, domination and punishment revisited: Incorporating state socialism', *Social Problems*, 1 (1999), 45–70.

Siedlecka, E., 'Prokurator o prokuratorach w czasach Ziobry', *Gazeta Wyborcza* (18 August 2007).

Stowarzyszenie Prokuratorów Rzeczpospolitej Polskiej (2007) *Apel o zachowanie etycznych postaw. Uchwała IX Dorocznej Konferencji Stowarzyszenia Prokuratorów Rzeczypospolitej Polskiej* (Poznań, 23 June 2007). Available online at <http://www.sprp.pl/tresc/Apel.pdf> [accessed 19 April 2010].

Szelecki, Łukasz, *Melka boi się przełożonych?*, (30 April 2008). Available online at http://politbiuro.pl/politbiuro/1,85398,5169139.html [accessed 19 April 2010].

Transparency International, *Global Corruption Report 2007: Corruption in Judicial Systems* (Cambridge: Cambridge University Press, 2007).

Transparency International (2009). Available online at <http://www.transparency.org/> [accessed 14 April 2010].

Ulast, PAP (2007) 'Aleksandra Jakubowska uniewinniona w procesie o "lub czasopisma"', *Gazeta Wyborcza*, 20.12 (2007). Available online at <http://wiadomosci.gazeta.pl/Wiadomosci/1,80708,4780458.html> [accessed 14 April 2010].

United States Department of State, *2008 Country Reports on Human Rights Practices – Poland* (2009). Available online at http://www.unhcr.org/refworld/docid/49a8f1615.html [accessed 14 April 2010].

Webber, J., 'Culture, legal culture, and legal reasoning: A comment on Nelken', *Australian Journal of Legal Philosophy* (2004), 25–36.

Wojciechowska, J., 'Ziobro wypuścił podejrzanych o lincz we Włodowie', *Gazeta Wyborcza*, 08.11 (2005).

Chapter 10
Notaries in Central Europe: From State Employment to Professional Independence – A Rocky Path

Gisela Shaw

Introduction

The institution of the notariat is rooted in the transnational tradition of Roman law. Wherever Roman law has retained a strong influence, that is, on the continent of Europe as well as on other continents (by way of export – most particularly Latin America), notaries (also referred to as 'civil law' or 'Latin' notaries) have retained a central role as an independent legal profession. It is an institution charged by respective governments with varying statutory functions within each country's non-contentious jurisdictions. Their main official task is to prevent litigation in the context of property, inheritance, family, commercial and company law. Notarial acts are drawn up after consultation with and agreement of the parties concerned. These acts require detailed information on the legal consequences of the planned action, comply with strict formal rules and are enforceable in court. In their capacity as state officials (the extent of which varies from country to country) civil law notaries have traditionally enjoyed some form of statutory monopoly; their numbers are small, state-controlled and determined according to perceived need;[1] their incomes are generous compared with those of comparable professions; and they have traditionally been mainly male.[2]

While civil law countries subscribe to this more or less interventionist model, with the state creating the institution of notarial acts to provide protection for citizens from unnecessary damage and the need to go to court, common law countries advocate a minimalist role for the state and see no need for what they regard as an obstacle to commerce and individuals' freedom to decide for themselves. Thus, in England and Wales, notarial acts are neither a legal requirement nor are they

1 Austria (2002): 462; France (2003): 7,864; Germany (2002): 1,663 full-time *Nurnotare* and 8,765 *Anwaltsnotare* (that is, practising lawyers (*Rechtsanwälte*) also carrying out notarial functions); the Netherlands (2001): 1,414.

2 Women's share in the profession of notaries: Austria (2002): 3.6%; France (2004): 18.3%; Germany (2003): 18.1% full-time *Nurnotare* (West: 6.1%; East: 46.1%) and 9% *Anwaltsnotare*; the Netherlands (2001): 9.1%.

judicially enforceable. The bulk of the functions that in civil law jurisdictions are given over to notaries, such as conveyancing or the making of wills, are in the hands of solicitors or allied professions. (The large majority of English and Welsh notaries are themselves solicitors.) The profession of notary is only really needed to meet certification requirements of foreign (civil law) jurisdictions.

In line with their political culture of disregarding individuals' rights in favour of central control, authoritarian regimes in the civil law world have tended to go for a particular variant of the civil law notary, the so-called 'state notary'. It was Lenin who, in 1922, introduced this system in the Soviet Union. Although he had initially abolished the institution of the (civil law) notariat altogether in view of its traditionally strong affinities with capitalism, he subsequently discovered its potential usefulness in a centralist political system and reintroduced it, suitably transformed from an independent to a bureaucratic state-controlled profession (Schroeder, 1964). State notaries in the Soviet Union were government officials working in the lower courts, charged with certain functions in non-contentious as well as contentious jurisdictions, mainly in the area of inheritance and property law. After World War II, some variant of the Soviet state notary system was installed in all Central European member states of the Soviet bloc to replace their independent notariats.[3] In contrast to the traditional independent Latin notary, who tends to be male and enjoy high social and economic status, the state notary was most likely a woman and her income the lowest of any professional in the field of law. Once the Soviet bloc collapsed, most of its former member states returned to some version of the independent notarial profession – a step much desired by most of its members but which subsequently proved not to be without its own problems.

What follows is an attempt to trace developments in three former member states in the Soviet Bloc: the German Democratic Republic (which in 1990 became the new federal states of Germany), Poland and Hungary. Developments are traced during two key phases: firstly, during the initial transition from state notariat to the recreation of an independent legal profession; and secondly, during more recent years which have been marked by their common bloc history, gradually giving way to country-specific developments in the face of Europeanization and economic globalization impacting on their respective national contexts.

Socio-legal research on the profession of notaries is thin on the ground generally speaking. This is particularly true of countries where four decades of communism had all but abolished sociological research and where, in any case, notaries had been 'deprofessionalized'. The present study therefore required a good deal of basic fact-finding and fieldwork. Results relating to East Germany are based on longitudinal research starting with that state's demise in 1990. Interviews with a range of actors at all levels and in all regions were carried out in 1990, 1992, 1994, 2002 and 2007, and relied on a network of contacts in both East and West Germany, including regional and national governments, notarial organizations and

3 The one exception was the newly constituted Republic of Yugoslavia where the notariat has not survived in any form (Neschwara, 2000: 91).

individual practitioners. Work on notaries in Poland and Hungary, intended very much as a comparative exercise, began in 2002 with a round of semi-structured interviews conducted with representatives of both countries' regional and national chambers as well as grass-roots members in Warsaw, Krakow and Budapest (Shaw, 2004). A second round of fieldwork, carried out in the spring of 2008, moved beyond the process of transition to democracy, capitalism and the state of law, and included Poland's and Hungary's accession to the European Union and beyond. Also, the main emphasis was on tracking wider developments and on capturing views and perspectives of the professions themselves as well as of institutions and agencies with a say in determining the profession's fate. Interviews therefore targeted representatives of both countries' national chambers, Ministries of Justice and Competition Authorities, as well as socio-legal academics.

Historical Background: Political Turmoil – What's New?

Central Europe has, for centuries, been the site of political upheaval and drama, dominated by power struggles resulting in ever-shifting borders and changing political systems. Civil law notariats, as institutions established by and heavily reliant on governments, have often been directly and drastically affected.

Germany

In keeping with Germany's political history, the history of the German notariat has been shaped by tensions between nationalist and particularist forces. The collapse of the German Empire in 1806 dispelled any hopes of the profession being unified on a national basis. Instead, three broad types of notaries (each divided into further sub-groupings) firmly took root, depending on regional rulers' preferences. These were the *Nurnotariat* (notaries as an independent profession) in regions where French influence had prevailed,[4] the *Anwaltsnotariat* (practising lawyers who also perform notarial duties) in northern Germany under mainly Prussian

4 Rheinpreußen, Rheinhessen, Hamburg, Bavaria. Main features of the French model: an independent legal profession working in the non-contentious judiciary which, in turn, is strictly separate from contentious court work; a professional monopoly regarding, for instance, real estate sales, marriage contracts and wills; a statutory fees scale; probative force of notarial acts; notarial professional organizations wielding considerable autonomy. Cf., for instance, Heinz, 2002. Key distinguishing features of today's German notarial system compared to that of France: a range of prohibitions relating to: nomination of a successor or sale of office, financial involvement in real estate dealings, partnerships with other professions, fees negotiations, involvement of more than one notary in any one transaction, and offering services outside their own district. These prohibitions are balanced by a significant statutory and exclusive role of German notaries in company law matters, which is most lucrative and provides many of them with the bulk of their income (Litzka, 1999).

influence and the *Richternotariat* (notaries as judicial state officers) in Baden and Wurttemberg.[5]

The Soviet-occupied territory, which in 1949 became the German Democratic Republic, had been the stronghold of the Prussian *Anwaltsnotariat*. From 1952 this was phased out and replaced by a Soviet-style state notariat. Notaries' portfolio of duties was much curtailed, their independence was lost and they were expressly charged with 'consolidating the socialist social order, implementing socialist legality, safeguarding socialist property, and protecting the assets of state organs and social organizations'.[6] By contrast to their generally prosperous and male West German colleagues, their social and economic status was low, and almost 70 per cent of them were female.

Poland

Following almost one and a half centuries of division and foreign occupation (1795–1918) the Republic of Poland was set up in 1918. Within the country's newly drawn frontiers there existed at least three notarial systems: the Russian system of 1866 in the eastern provinces, the Prussian *Anwaltsnotariat* in the west and north (Posen, Upper Silesia) and the Austrian system of 1871 in the south (Galicia,[7] Lower Silesia).[8] After intense work on the part of Polish jurists, a range of legislation, including an all-Polish notarial code, was passed in 1933 and came into force on 1 January 1934. This code was largely based on the Austrian model of 1871, which by comparison with other West European countries was rather restrictive in terms of notaries' functions and self-government. But the new Polish system did incorporate a number of components contained in two later and more liberal drafts of the 1871 Austrian model (of 1911 and 1918 respectively) that were never implemented in Austria itself (Neschwara, 2000). The brief life span of this all-Polish notarial code did not even leave sufficient time to eliminate all regional variations, most notably with regard to land registers.

From 1946, the profession's independent status began to be eroded by socialist reforms in the newly established People's Republic of Poland, culminating in

5 In 2009, the long-standing struggle to integrate the Baden-Wurttemberg notariat into the framework of the *Nurnotariat* finally succeeded.

6 'Gesetz über das staatliche Notariat', in *Aufgaben und Arbeitsweize der Staatlichen Notariate*, § 2, Berlin (GDR) 1978. During the last year of the GDR, only eight *Anwaltsnotare* remained in their post (Schippel, 1991), compared with 379 state notaries (Shaw, 2003).

7 Within Galicia, the city of Krakow and its surrounding administrative district had yet a separate (French) tradition which began with French occupation in 1808, continued throughout its existence as a city republic from 1815, survived the annexation of Krakow by Austria in 1846, and was only replaced by the Austrian system in 1858 (Neschwara, 2000: 22–23).

8 In addition, the Hungarian system, which had survived in the former Hungarian comitats of Zips and Arva that were ceded to Poland by Czechoslovakia in 1922, also required integration.

1952 in its abolition and the installation of a socialist state notariat. Professional autonomy gave way to strict government supervision, and notaries were organized in collectives located in the courts. However, by contrast to notariats in other Soviet bloc states, the function of Polish notaries (on average around 900 in number, most of these women) was gradually extended in order to provide relief for the courts. A key year in this context was 1964, when all matters relating to land registers were given over to them, as it turned out that against government expectations a great deal of property in major cities had remained in private hands. Also, smallholders, especially in the south of the country, had resisted nationalization and refused to join a *kolchos*. Over 85 per cent of agricultural land actually remained in private hands and, at the end of the communist regime, the private sector (mainly in agriculture) already employed 30 per cent of the workforce (Kozminski, 1997). Although under communism, Polish notaries' profile lost coherence and identity (Tymecki, 1989; Zmudzinski, 1991), in contrast to their Hungarian colleagues they remained mediators between the state and individual citizens in the context of property transactions.

Hungary

Hungary's history has been no less tumultuous than Poland's, with centuries of extended warfare, foreign domination and political division. Its notariat of modern times was created in 1874, following the restoration in 1867 of the Hungarian Kingdom's special status within the Austro-Hungarian Empire. The Hungarian notarial system was, like Poland's, closely modelled on the Austrian system of 1871, yet managed to acquire a number of more progressive (French) features (Neschwara, 2000). It survived the post-war political upheaval of 1918 and the tumultuous interwar and war period, but following the creation in 1945 of the People's Republic of Hungary, it was demolished step-by-step and replaced by a Soviet-style state notariat. By 1952, Hungarian notaries, too, had become salaried state employees working in teams in the courts, their numbers severely curtailed and their income and social standing much reduced.

However, while Polish notaries remained heavily involved in property transaction and land register work, their Hungarian colleagues had no such opportunities. For one thing, private ownership in Hungary was restricted to one residence and one weekend cottage, and rural areas were practically devoid of real estate business. Hungarian notaries' activities were therefore mostly limited to probate matters and the drawing up of wills, an area where they had sole responsibility. In any case, the need for a public deed had traditionally been very limited in Hungary compared to Poland and applied mainly to the blind and others unable to conduct their own legal affairs. Most citizens could choose between a private deed (drawn up by an advocate) and a public deed (the job of a notary), and usually opted for the former. When, in the late 1980s, private companies began to appear in Hungary, notaries lacked the experience, confidence and numbers to respond to this new challenge. By 1989, there were only 160 notaries left to serve over 10 million people, which put Hungary's per capita rate of notaries lower than that even of Turkey (Gaspardy, 1991).

Yet Another Reversal of Fate

The collapse of communist domination and the introduction of democracy, rule of law and market economies once again brought to the profession a dramatic reversal of fate – but this time it was a return to independence. Amongst the legal professions in Eastern bloc countries, notaries had the most to lose and the most to gain in the transformation process. As state notaries, they had found themselves at the bottom of the pile of legal professionals. Transformation held out the promise of considerable social and economic gains. At the same time, they were better placed than other legal professions to steer developments and to achieve their goal within a very short time. At least three reasons can be identified.

Firstly, the profile of the profession of socialist state notaries as tiny close-knit groups,[9] used to working and communicating in teams as well as being highly committed to reform, greatly facilitated prompt action. Secondly, (former) state notaries in Central European countries enjoyed immediate and wholehearted support (moral, financial and political) from Latin notarial organizations in the West. The latter, acting from sound enlightened self-interest, were keen to expand their own sphere of influence, as well as that of the independent civil law notariat at large, by helping to construct and consolidate a network of allies. Key agents in this context were Germany and Austria. In the case of Germany there was an obvious and immediate interest on the part of West German notaries to integrate their colleagues from the former socialist Germany into their ranks and boost their own numbers and political clout. As for Austria (itself preparing for integration into the European Union), the consideration of notaries' future role in a wider context provided natural motivation to invest in the revival of their historical ties with notariats in countries of the former Austro-Hungarian Empire. What better 'dowry' to bring to the European Union than a clutch of newly restored Latin notariats from Central Europe (Scheich, 1990; Neschwara, 2003)?

What finally clinched the prompt transition from state notariat to independent profession in the three countries considered here was the profession's ability to persuade respective national governments, at an early stage, that a speedy transformation of its role and status and a return to organizational and legal structures that existed prior to the victory of socialism would benefit the state as a whole in three ways. It would highlight countries' national liberal tradition and identity, strengthen bonds with continental European traditions and countries, thereby strengthening integration into the European Union, and facilitate

9 GDR: just under 400 (Shaw, 1997); Poland: around 900 (Neschwara, 2003); Hungary: just under 200 (Neschwara, 2003).

governments' control over economic developments, especially in the context of privatization.

This common denominator notwithstanding, historical and contextual national specificities ensured significant differentiation in the evolution of a restored independent notariat in each of the three countries under discussion.

New Federal States of Germany

In East Germany the notarial transformation agenda was atypical, as it was largely subsumed under and dictated by the agenda of the larger political project of German unification. It had to be fitted into the tight schedule set for the German Democratic Republic's accession to the Federal Republic of Germany within a few months in the spring and summer of 1990, with 3 October 1990 as the final deadline. A 'big bang' approach was the only option. There was never any doubt that some form of independent notariat would be introduced. What was not clear until the summer of that year was which of the two main variants existing in West Germany, the *Nurnotare* and *Anwaltsnotare*, was to be the chosen one.

In the summer of 1990, the organizational framework for the transformation of the East German notariat was created by two statutes rushed through by the GDR parliament just months before its demise. The main aim was to achieve compatibility with conditions in the Federal Republic of Germany, as both notariats would be working within the same legal framework.[10] Precious time had been lost due to internal strife between West German *Nurnotare* and *Anwaltsnotare*, each camp being keen to strengthen its numbers by absorbing the notaries in the newly created five eastern states. The tug-of-war ended with a victory for the full-time notariat (*Nurnotariat*). This was introduced in all regions, with the exception of East Berlin, where an *Anwaltsnotariat* was seen to be more appropriate to match the system already existing in West Berlin (Shaw, 1997).

Promptly from 3 October 1990, in spite of all but insuperable hurdles having to be negotiated by each of them, notaries from the defunct GDR were working to the best of their abilities within an unfamiliar legal, economic and social context (West German law, free market, capitalism, privatization), with personal liability for any mistakes made. Although for a number of years two separate professional codes remained formally in existence, differences between them were of a minor kind. Economic privatization absorbed all their energies as well as offering undreamed of opportunities. The ultimate success of the profession's transformation was owed, to a large extent, to prompt and systematic material and training support by West German notaries, starting even prior to unification. The support system then remained in place for a period of three or four years and was unrivalled by

10 *Verordnung über die Tätigkeit von Notaren in eigener Praxis* of 20 June 1990 (*GBL*, I, no. 37, 475), amended on 22 August 1990 (*GBL*, I, no. 37, 1328).

any other profession in the field of law or elsewhere.[11] It comprised the hurried production of textbooks, the organization of regular training sessions at weekends, and the provision of technical assistance and one-to-one advice. In retrospect, the investment can be seen to have been fully worthwhile for both sides. For East German notaries it meant not only a guarantee of their professional survival,[12] but also a significant upgrading of their economic and social status. Their West German colleagues, in turn, managed to ensure that the full-time Latin notariat they had fought for had proved a success. As privatization dominated the notarial agenda of the early years, the monopoly held by notaries in the context of private and business property transactions ensured their growing prosperity.

A particular gender dimension added an intriguing facet to the transformation process – a fascinating encounter between two contrasting professional cultures. West German *Nurnotare*, traditionally male and recruited from their state's academic legal elite, were coming to the rescue of East German former state notary colleagues, who were mainly female and had little to show for themselves in terms of social status, income or, indeed, relevant professional knowledge or experience. At the time of German unification in early October 1990, the GDR notariat was made up of 257 women and 122 men, a total therefore of 379. The percentage of women notaries across the 14 notarial districts in the GDR ranged from 59 per cent in Gera to 100 per cent in Schwerin, with a national average of 67.8 per cent (Shaw, 1997).

Poland

In Poland, the transformation of the notariat began much earlier than elsewhere as a result of the profession's own initiative. In 1980, a small group of notaries in the city of Poznan felt encouraged by the changing socio-political climate and the creation of the Solidarity movement and began discussions about a possible reprivatization of the Polish notariat. The outcome was a draft bill for a reformed notarial code based on that of 1933. However, this early initiative was overtaken by the imposition of martial law in December 1981 (although suspended in December 1982 and officially lifted in July 1983) (Weclawowicz, 1996: 25). It was only in 1987 that the political climate became more favourable, economic considerations were gaining priority as the Polish market underwent increasing privatization, and work on the reform project could resume. By 1 July 1989 a final draft had been produced and the new professional code for notaries became law with little or no political opposition. The expectation was that an independent notariat would ease

11 While members of the East German judiciary at least benefited from (compulsory) government-funded retraining measures, practising lawyers (*Rechtsanwälte*) were thrown back on their own resources.

12 Had they had to join the profession of practising lawyers (*Rechtsanwalt*), they could not have survived the competition in the free market.

the pressure of the work of the courts, which had been massively increased by privatization.

A three-year transition period was envisaged to allow alternative arrangements to be put into place within the court system. In the definitive Notaries Act of 13 February 1991, the transition period had been reduced to one year and by March 1992 over three-quarters of Polish notaries had moved to fully independent status. On 27 April 1992, the Polish notariat was accepted (along with the Hungarian notariat) as a fully-fledged member of the international union of Latin notariats (UINL).

By international comparison, Polish notaries now enjoy a wide range of reserved tasks, but within an unusually liberal regulatory framework. Their main monopoly concerns the areas of property, family and company law, but they also operate in a competitive legal services market. There is no statutory fixed fees scale, nor are there any explicitly specified criteria for access.[13] Subject to government confirmation, applicants for posts are free to propose the geographical location where they wish to set up office. Notarial chambers, although consulted, find their views are rarely heeded. The result is a trend towards uneven availability of notarial services across the country, driven by significant income differentials between urban and rural areas. As in France and Austria, partnerships among notaries are allowed, and there is no maximum limit governing the number of partners in any one firm. So far, they have concentrated themselves in cities, where there is enough business to make specialization both useful and affordable. By the end of 2006, of a total of 1,302 notarial firms, there were 209 (16 per cent) with two partners, 11 (0.8 per cent) with three partners, and 3 (0.2 per cent) with four partners. The sole notary working on her or his own has, however, remained the norm, possibly (in cities) employing one or two *asesors*, that is, qualified notaries still waiting for their own offices.

The risk of patronage is built into the Polish notarial system. On the one hand, the Ministry of Justice regularly appoints significant numbers of applicants from other legal professions who have at least three years' professional experience but no notarial training or qualifications.[14] On the other hand, office-holders are

13 Published criteria are of a very general kind: minimum age, Polish nationality, good standing and so on.

14 The legal basis for admitting persons without notarial training to the profession was created in 1946 and its continued application is attributed to a disinclination of former Communist elites to relinquish any of their powers (Zmudzinski, 1991). From 1981, mobility between the legal professions became an accepted principle, although in practice movement profiles tend to be rather lop-sided. A sideways route into the notariat also exists in some other countries, but is used less extensively for political appointments than in Poland. In Austria, for instance, it has traditionally been indispensable as a tool to fill vacancies in rural areas for which no notarial candidates can be found (Neschwara, 2000: 48–49). France also has a tradition of admitting sideways entrants to the profession, but anecdotal evidence suggests that numbers involved are small. In Prussia, the award of notarial functions to legal practitioners (*Rechtsanwälte*) without notarial qualifications was

free to propose their own successor, normally their own offspring or trainee, a practice that is well known in France but hard to square with notaries' public role or with a merit-based system. Also, as in France, notaries act as unpaid (but fully accountable) tax collectors for the government. Public confidence in the value and competitiveness of their services is undermined, as clients tend to assume that the often not inconsiderable sums of money handed over to notaries are actually retained by them in full.

In keeping with other former Eastern bloc countries, Poland's notariat has remained highly feminized (65 per cent), while the role of president of the national or of regional chambers has remained mostly in the hands of men.

Hungary

By contrast to Poland, in Hungary it was not the profession itself that took the initiative to push for independence. Rather it was the Austrian National Chamber of Notaries supported by the Austrian government that decided that the time had come to 'reprofessionalize' the Hungarian notariat (Neschwara, 2003). First contacts were made with the Hungarian Ministry of Justice in June 1989. This was followed up only a few months later by a 'Notaries' Colloquium Central Europe' in Keszthely, Hungary, at which the Austrian and the Hungarian Ministers of Justice (both academics) were present. It took little effort and time to persuade them of the mutual benefits of Hungary's return to a professional notariat, as the Hungarian government's declared intention to move towards a democratic system based on the rule of law and a market economy had already created a political framework favourable to the notarial project. Indeed, the Hungarian Minister of Justice Kalman Kulcsar, an outstanding legal sociologist, was also behind the drafting of Hungary's new constitution and the reorganization of the country's legal institutions. By December 1989, he had commissioned a restructuring plan for the notariat, based on the Hungarian notarial act of 1874. Although updated by a number of provisions modelled on current West European systems, the proposed functions of an independent notariat remain modest by comparison with those of their Polish colleagues. In particular, property and corporate law areas were not included, but, in keeping with Hungary's tradition, remained almost exclusively in the hands of advocates. The reform proposal, arrived at by close consultation among government, professional organizations and universities, received government approval by March 1991, was passed unanimously by parliament in September of the same year, and came into force on 1 November 1991, thus also opening the doors to Hungary's membership of the UINL.

---

traditionally used as a means to reward the efforts of the latter and boost their incomes, a tradition which continued in former Prussian territories in the (old) Federal Republic and has only recently stopped. Now access to the *Anwaltsnotariat* in Germany is regulated on the basis of specified qualifications, thus safeguarding quality and excluding the danger of patronage.

Speedy progress and successful completion of the notaries' professional project were owed to a few personalities with the determination and vision to maximize synergies between initiatives at professional, governmental and international levels. On the Hungarian side, this person was Dr Judit Bókai, herself a state notary by training and experience and, at the same time, head of the department in charge of notarial matters in the Ministry of Justice. From 1992 she became the first President of the National Chamber of Hungarian Notaries, a post which she was to hold for 13 years. The 172 (of 182) state notaries who opted for independence could count on considerable support from the Ministry of Justice, including three months' or more free accommodation on state premises to allow them to build up starting-capital and find suitable offices. Their number remained modest in spite of government pressure for an increase to ensure competition.[15] In 2002, the by then 250 notaries catered for a population of just over one-quarter of that of Poland (just over 10 million compared with 38 million), equalling a per capita ratio of one notary per approximately 41,300 people, almost double that of Poland. Access routes to the profession are similar to those in Poland, but selection criteria are more transparent and access via sideways entry from other legal professions has remained the exception (as is the case in Austria) and access not used as a political tool by the government. In contrast to Poland, the regulatory regime is strict. Notaries are appointed to a particular district, where key activities in the law of succession and probate proceedings are confined to that district. Fees are government-regulated, any negotiation of fees is prohibited and the notarial monopoly has remained limited to last will and testament matters of a blind or partially incapacitated person, movables pledge agreements and floating charge contracts. Clients' choice between a notarial public deed and a private deed countersigned by an advocate (the normal procedure) has meant that the general public remains somewhat confused about notaries' roles and the need for their existence. Nevertheless, notarial income levels have a strong appeal and are superior to those of comparable professions, although, as in Poland, there is a wide spectrum ranging from Budapest, where incomes are highest, to regional capitals and, at the bottom of the hierarchy, the provinces (Bókai, 2007). Partnerships between notaries are permitted but have remained the exception, largely due to lack of opportunity for specialization as well as the Hungarian government's express requirement for notaries to deal with any notarial business brought to them and to ensure that their trainees receive comprehensive training in all areas of notarial activity. Women have retained an even stronger grip on the profession in Hungary than in Poland. Not only was the national chamber's founder president a woman (in office until 2005), but quite a few posts on the national chamber's management board are also held by women, and some three-quarters of the total membership is female (2002: 74.4 per cent).

15 2002: 254; 2003: 269; 2004: 283; 2005: 302; 2006: 302; 2007: 309. However, the number of applicants is rising fast: 2002: 42; 2003: 71; 2004: 81; 2005: 91; 2006: 94; 2007: 104.

No Time for Complacency

In tune with the general mood of optimism, not to say euphoria, in the newly established nation states of Central Europe (Sztompka, 1999), national notariats, too, were confident about the profession's ability to hold on to and develop their trusted position in the various social institutional structures. However, from the mid 1990s wider political and economic developments began to threaten the profession's fortunes once again. Underlying the complex network of contributing factors were two key forces at work, both beyond national control: that is, economic globalization on the one hand; and political and economic ambitions on the part of the European Commission on the other. Central European countries that had previously operated within a closed socialist world, immune from capitalist forces, had now become just as exposed to these forces as their neighbours.

For the notarial profession, these developments were of crucial significance. Indicative of the threats posed by economic globalization were the World Bank 'Doing Business' reports, published annually since 2004, which singled out national regulatory restrictions as a main factor in the inhibition of economic growth. 'Where markets are functioning, competition is a substitute for regulation,' the 2004 report claimed, presenting Australia and the Scandinavian countries as examples of best practice in business regulation. '... [H]eavy regulation ... is strongly and consistently associated with lower incomes and with French and socialist legal origins.' And, '[w]here notaries are needed to authorize documents, this is frequently the most expensive part of the company registration'.[16]

The European Commission's attacks on national regulatory barriers governing professions, such as nationality requirements, fixed fees, restrictions on access, advertising, choice of location and organizational structures provided further and more specifically ominous ammunition. A study on regulation of the liberal professions commissioned by the European Commission (Paterson et al., 2003) singled out the profession of (civil law) notary as a prime example of strict regulation, raising serious doubts regarding the appropriateness and proportionality of such regulatory regimes. Subsequent studies in the European context homed in, specifically, on the (allegedly) damaging impact of civil law notariats on the conveyancing market, sparking off heated debates among various interest groups. Not entirely surprisingly, research outcomes and recommendations have tended to reflect the aspirations of commissioning agencies, be they the EU-Commission (Schmid et al., 2007), national governments (Arruñada, 1996, 2005) or professional organizations (Van den Bergh and Montagnie, 2006; Murray, 2007).

Two European directives have proved to be of direct relevance to civil law notariats, namely the Directive on the Recognition of Professional Qualifications of 7 September 2005 (2005/36/EC) and the Directive on Services in the Internal

16 World Bank, 'Doing business in 2004: Understanding regulation' (2004), xvi, 87 and 26, respectively. Available online at <http://www.doingbusiness.org/Documents/DB2004-full-report.pdf> [accessed 2 April 2010].

Market of 12 December 2006 (2006/123/EC). Ultimately, well-targeted and effective lobbying paid off, as notariats were able to escape the immediate impact of these directives by successfully arguing their entitlement to an exemption on account of their exercising official authority (Article 45 EC). However, this was not the end of the matter.

As early as November 2000, the European Commission, urged on by a small but highly effective lobby led by an English solicitor notary, had sent 'letters of formal notice' to seven European states requiring them to open up their notarial markets for international competition by abolishing the nationality requirement.[17] When national governments refused to comply, the matter appeared to have been put to rest. Then, in October 2006, the offending member states received 'reasoned opinions' as a second stage in the infringement process. In June 2007, the case was referred to the European Court of Justice and is as yet undecided.

Why should professional notaries and national Ministries of Justice in Europe be so concerned at this initiative, given that a lack of familiarity with other countries' languages and legal systems can be expected to present a serious obstacle to large numbers of foreign notaries moving in to take away nationals' work? Their real fear, of course, is that a removal of the nationality requirement might represent the start of a slippery slope of wholesale removal of regulatory authority from national governments.

This is an unsettling prospect for both notaries and their governments. Governments are categorically opposed to having their authority curtailed even further, as well as being fully aware of their notariat's social, political and economic benefits to the country. Notaries create legal security at individual and corporate levels thereby lightening the burden on the judiciary and stabilizing the economy. In a number of countries, most prominently France and Poland, other factors come into play, not least the fact that notaries act as unremunerated tax collectors for the government.

Somewhat ironically, though, acknowledging the advantages to a country of a civil law notariat does not prevent national governments from casting a critical eye on the profession, questioning the need for the protective barriers surrounding it and, in some cases, even doubting the very need for its independent existence. This has tended to be in response not only to European and global economic pressures but also to the powerful lobby of advocates who themselves have already been exposed to dramatic deregulation measures and are looking for a level playing field, as well as a stake in the lucrative notarial markets.[18] Added to this is pressure

---

17 The countries concerned were Germany, France, Belgium, the Netherlands, Luxembourg, Austria and Greece. Spain, Italy and Portugal were exempted because they had given a last-minute undertaking to remove the nationality requirement.

18 The most striking example of this is France (the cradle of the modern civil law notariat) where, in April 2009, the advocate Jean Michel Darrois submitted a government-commissioned report proposing the creation of one all-inclusive legal profession, to include the *notaires*.

stemming from national competition authorities (encouraged and supported by relevant EU authorities). In Poland and Hungary these were originally set up in 1990 as monopoly commissions to combat unfair market practices. From 1996 to 1997, their brief was extended to include restrictive market practices. On becoming members of the European Competition Network in 2004, they turned their attention to regulated professions, including notaries.

New Federal States of Germany

Broadly speaking, from 1994 East German notaries had been integrated into the all-German notarial system. Hard work and, in some cases, almost superhuman effort had amply paid off (at least in economic terms), as many a fortune was made in the course of privatization and within the still somewhat sheltered world of heavy subsidies flowing from West to East.

However, from 1997 normalization also meant that privatization was completed, tax subsidies from the West, especially for the construction industry, had been withdrawn and incomes from the corporate and property market sectors were drying up. Falling demand resulted in regional governments not filling notarial vacancies. Attacks from Brussels and the World Bank on strict professional regulatory regimes have been broadly fended off by the profession with the support of the national government. However, long-standing internal tensions threaten to be reignited by European and global developments. *Anwaltsnotare* (the majority of the profession and mainly concentrated in the West) tended to be a good deal more open to deregulatory market-orientated initiatives than their traditionally more conservative colleagues, the *Nurnotare* (now also comprising the five new federal states in the East). Recent efforts to reform overall German federal structures raised another spectre of dread, as the German government got close to trading its (in any case limited) authority over the profession of notaries to the regions, in return for concessions in other areas. This would have been a death-knell to the profession's claim of being a unified group speaking with one voice – a claim of considerable significance for the five new federal states in the East, which needed the support of such economically mighty West German states as Bavaria and Hamburg. By contrast to Poland and Hungary, the German Monopolies Commission has so far failed to turn its critical attention to the profession of notaries. However, its biannual report of 2006 did deal at some length with anti-competitive regulatory regimes of liberal professions in general and of the legal profession in particular,[19] which provided a flavour of possible dangers in store for the notariat as well.

19 <http://www.monopolkommission.de/haupt_16/Summary_HG_XVI.pdf> [accessed 2 April 2010].

Poland

Following a few years of relative regulatory stability, accession to the European Union, the impact of the global economy and unceasing domestic political turbulence soon dispelled the profession's sense of security and optimism (supported by constitutional provisions to strengthen the self-government of professions in Poland).[20] Instead, the prevailing mood over the last decade has become one of concern and anxiety regarding the profession's future.

In 2004, a report on barriers to competition in the liberal professions published by the Polish Competition Authority identified the notaries' strict regulatory regime as one obstacle to the growth of the economy. Criticism centred on barriers on entry (almost exclusively controlled by chambers), fixed fees (freely negotiated but with maximum limits) and the ban on advertising, multidisciplinary partnerships and the operation of more than one office (European Commission, 2004).

The most politically charged of these criticisms was that directed against limitations on access to the profession, as it applied not only to notaries but, even more urgently, to the other legal professions of advocate and legal adviser. The latter division survived the communist era, but has continued to create constant social and political irritation and embarrassment to the government ever since. Advocates (*adwokaci*) are a small and privileged group of approximately 6,000 who, even under communism, had not lost their professional independence. Legal advisers (*radcownie prawni*), on the other hand, are a large and somewhat amorphous group of approximately 20,000 members, created under communism to work as employees in state enterprises and, from 1989, to operate alongside advocates; yet they are excluded from representing clients in criminal and family courts. The massive growth in the number of law graduates looking for legal traineeships has resulted in ever-increasing pressure for reform. The government's response has been dramatic and, in line with unstable governments, erratic. In 2004, the power of professional associations to decide on numbers of trainees as well as on the form and content of entry examinations was ruled unconstitutional. Instead, control over training and examinations was transferred to the Ministry of Justice. This promptly resulted in a radical change of the examination format for legal traineeship applicants. Anyone with a law degree could now register to be

20 Article 17 of the Polish constitution of 1997 reads:

> (1) By means of a statute, self-governments may be created within a profession in which the public repose confidence, and such self-governments shall concern themselves with the proper practice of such professions in accordance with, and for the purpose of protecting, the public interest.
>
> (2) Other forms of self-government shall also be created by means of statute. Such self-governments shall not infringe the freedom to practice a profession nor limit the freedom to undertake economic activity. <http://www.servat.unibe.ch/icl/pl00000_.html> [accessed 2 April 2010].

examined; and the threshold for a pass was lowered significantly, with professional chambers losing any say in the matter.

In 2006, in a measure more specifically directed at notaries, the government increased the share of new notarial appointments from other legal professions to the point where, for the first time, successful candidates without notarial qualifications outnumbered those who had undergone notarial training.[21] At a press conference in August 2006, the Minister of Justice (who himself held no legal qualification) also announced without previous consultation with professional organizations that notaries' maximum fees would be decreased by 50 per cent. Allegedly, this was done to create parity with other legal professions and the judiciary, a claim hotly denied by the notaries who maintained that no statistics on the subject had been made available. Nevertheless, the fee reduction became law on 20 November 2007.

On coming to power in October 2007, the new Civic Platform Government considered another horror scenario: the creation of a single unified legal profession by merging the professions of advocate and legal adviser, which would also be entitled to provide notarial services.[22] However, interest in radical reforms of this kind soon waned, as the realization grew that antagonizing the legal professions was not the best way forward and that consultation with them was needed as a basis for any decision of this kind. For the time being, therefore, any immediate danger to the independent existence of the notariat was staved off. Indeed, even notaries' critics now agree that the profession's traditional dual nature must be preserved and that some regulatory regime, including some form of monopoly, is essential for the benefit of society. Notaries are to remain officers of the state, and their brief within the non-contentious judiciary has even been expanded in order to provide relief for overworked courts. Notaries on their part have welcomed the strengthening of their judicial role, but are equally keen to retain their position in the open legal services market. A degree of calm has returned, at least on the national level. In the face of threats from the European Commission, the government and profession prefer to present a united front and to show international solidarity with other civil law jurisdictions.

Hungary

In post-1989 Hungary, too, legal professions had benefited greatly from the general call for a strengthening of civil and professional organizations at the expense of state powers, and notaries were the first profession to be granted self-government (1991). The Hungarian Competition Authority initially lacked the legal tools

21 Applicants with notarial training: 37; practising advocates: 7; prosecutors: 4; legal advisers: 19; judges: 6; academics: 2.

22 A similar proposition has since shocked and terrified the French notariat after President Sarkozy set up two successive working groups on the legal professions in France, both of which recommended the creation of one *grande profession juridique*.

to challenge what they regarded as professional organizations' and chambers' restrictive practices. From 1997 its power increased, but even then it did not relate directly to notaries, as according to the Notaries Act of 1991 they were part of the judicature, defined as representing the state in all their activities, carrying out state functions and exercising state authority. Nevertheless, the Authority was able to submit recommendations to the Hungarian Parliament for a review of the regulatory regime of notarial services, most particularly their scope for exclusivity, restrictions on territorial competence and entry to the profession, and the fixed fees system. Its main argument was that a distinction was needed between purely administrative (state-authorized) and competitive activities. In May 2007, the Competition Authority reported to the OECD Competition Committee that, unfortunately, nothing had changed. Only the number of notarial posts had been somewhat increased (to 306 by February 2006) (OECD, 2007).

The profession's own response under a new President (from 2005) has been to cut the Gordion knot by taking a dramatic step to secure the profession's future. In consultation with the Ministry of Justice, it was agreed that the role of notaries in Hungary was to be redefined with two aims in mind: firstly, to remove the profession from any possible interference by the European Commission and the Hungarian Competition Authority; and secondly, to draw a clear line of separation between notaries and their major competitors – advocates – so as to exclude any future rivalry and avoid being exposed to attacks by their powerful lobby in parliament. Unsurprisingly, the bar had no objections to notaries leaving the open legal services market to them. Any objections on constitutional grounds had been eliminated by the Hungarian Constitutional Court's decision of 1994, which defined the role of Hungarian (as opposed to Austrian) notaries as part of the judicial system. The timing for the change of strategy has been propitious. As in Poland, courts in Hungary are unable to cope with their ever-growing workload, politicians are urgently looking for solutions and the prospect of notaries taking over some of their non-contentious functions is a welcome one. Also, a recent revision of the Hungarian civil code by parliament offered a golden opportunity to incorporate changes to statutory provisions relating to notaries. Not all members of the profession agree on the advisability of such drastic steps. But they have the support of the overall majority, who are fearful not only of the Competition Authority's attacks, but also of a possible decision by the European Court, stating that notaries, too, are part of the open legal services market and therefore subject to EU rules.

What Future for Notariats in Central Europe?

Generally, civil law notariats have come under threat from previously unknown agents. As economic pressures are taking priority over mainly political ones, they are for the first time in their history having to respond to forces outside their own narrowly national (or even regional) contexts. There is another first: notaries, until recently blissfully unaware of the views of 'consumers', are having to take cognizance of public opinion and the public's trust (or otherwise) in the integrity and usefulness of their profession.

If notaries in Western European countries have reason to be apprehensive, this applies even more to their colleagues in Central and Eastern Europe, where global and European threats are re-enforced by a lack of established traditions and political lobbies within a still unstable national political environment. However, the paths taken by notariats in each of the three countries considered here have increasingly diverged from each other, as bloc history recedes and national characteristics – political, economic, cultural and social – are coming to the fore.

In the former German Democratic Republic the traces left by the socialist system on the country's notaries and their work are fading rapidly. Admittedly, in the over 50 generation, one can still detect a divide between former state notaries and Western imports in terms of the composition of and relations with clientele and their general professional *habitus*, but amongst those trained or newly appointed after 1990 such differences no longer exist. The profession's destiny is, and is seen to be, a joint one. And as long as the Berlin government retains overall authority over the profession, rather than delegating it to regional states, European and global economic challenges can be faced with relative confidence.

In Poland, where a strong notariat had emerged in the wake of transition to the rule of law and a market economy, support from their national government has subsequently been absent. Indeed, notaries have had to cope with serious attacks by their own government and, in the process, have lost some of their professional autonomy and economic advantage, although since 2007 some stability, at least, has returned. Polish notarial organizations are particularly keen to forge and strengthen links with their Western counterparts, especially with France whose (generously designed) notarial system has always been held up by them as an ideal. The strength of their numbers, their comprehensive monopolies portfolio and the fact that they operate in the largest and economically most successful new EU member state fill Polish notaries with hope that their voices are heard both in their own country and in Europe at large.

Hungarian notaries are in a very different situation. They are a tiny and relatively powerless group within a country whose economy is in disarray. For them, the joy of gaining professional independence and subsequently joining the family of European civil law notariats has given way to fear for their continued existence as a separate profession. Consequently, they have chosen what they see as their only chance of survival, that is, a return to total state control and a waiver of all claims to operating in the open legal services market – an occurrence previously unheard of in the history of the civil law notariat.

Looking ahead, the impact on Latin notariats of the recent global banking crisis and economic downturn remains to be seen. On one hand, any economic weakness is bound to have an unwelcome effect on notarial business, most particularly in the context of company activities and property dealings. On the other hand, however, it is not unrealistic to expect that the loss of public confidence in the desirability of a wholly deregulated market will operate in the profession's favour, stifling any immediate threat to the profession's continued existence. Indeed, the need for some (better) regulation, and the rebuilding of trust in the credibility of financial and business transactions as acknowledged, notarial acts – as a guarantee of the legality of such transactions – have a potentially important contribution to make. After all, their sole purpose is to ensure the security of legal transactions and therefore the trust of the parties involved. Already, there is agreement among EU member states that national notarial acts will be recognized across national frontiers, with the French profession and government even pressing for the creation of a European notarial act. Perhaps the banking crisis and its aftermath may even turn out to have been a blessing in disguise, not only for civil law notaries in Central Europe but also, more generally, for the profession at large.

Acknowledgements

The author thanks all those who, over the years, gave up their time to help with research (particularly those from Poland and Hungary, who participated in a language not their mother tongue).

Unless indicated otherwise, all statistical material was kindly provided by notarial chambers.

References

Arruñada, B., 'Managing competition in professional services and the burden of inertia' (2005). Available online at <http://econpapers.repec.org/paper/upfupfgen/827.htm> [accessed 2 April 2010].

———'The economics of notaries', *European Journal of Law and Economics*, 3/1 (1996), 5–37.

Bókai, J., 'The civil law notary in Hungary', in Center of Legal Competence (ed.), *Notaries in Europe – Growing Fields of Competence: Austria, Croatia, Czech Republic, Hungary, Slovenia* (Vienna and Graz: Neuer Wissenschaftlicher Verlag; Antwerp: Intersentia, 2007), 167–208.

European Commission, 'COMP/D3/MK/D: Stocktaking exercise on regulation of professional services: Overview of regulation in the new EU member states (2004). Available online at <http://ec.europa.eu/comm/competition/sectors/professional_services/studies/overview_of_regulation_in_the_eu_professions.pdf> [accessed 2 April 2010].

Gáspárdy, L., Der Weg Ungarns zum Rechtsstaat, *Österreichische Notariatszeitung*, vol. 123, no. 6 (1991) 140–142.

Heinz, V.G., 'Das französische Notariat', *Anwaltsblatt*, 11 (2002), 627–33.

Kozminski, A.K., 'Restitution of private property: Re-privatization in Central and Eastern Europe', *Communist and Post-Communist Studies*, 30/1 (1997), 95–106.

Litzka, P., *Notare in Frankeich und Deutschland: Ein Rechtsvergleich unter besonderer Berücksichtigung der Kautelarpraxis* (Munich: WF, 1999).

Murray, P.L., 'Real estate conveyancing in 5 European Union member states: A comparative study' (2007), commissioned by the Council of the (Latin) Notariats of the European Union (CNUE). Available online at <http://www.cnue-nouvelles.be> [accessed 2 April 2010].

Neschwara, C., 'Restauration als Reform: Das lateinische Notariat im östlichen Europa. Der Beitrag des österreichischen Notariats zu seiner Einführung', in Österreichische Notarkammer (ed.), *Festschrift Georg Weißmann. Freiheit, Sicherheit, Notariat, Gesellschaft* (Vienna: Manz, 2003).

———*Österreichs Notariatsrecht in Mittel- und Osteuropa. Zur Geltung und Ausstrahlung des östereichischen Notariats* (Vienna: Manz, 2000).

OECD, 'DAF/COMP(2007)39: competitive restrictions in legal professions' (2007). Available online at <http://www.oecd.org/dataoecd/12/38/40080343.pdf> [accessed 2 April 2010].

Paterson, I., M. Fink, A. Ogus, J. Merz, F. Fink and H. Berrer, 'Economic impact of regulation in the field of liberal professions in different EU member states' (2003). Available online at <http://ec.europa.eu/competition/sectors/professional_services/studies/prof_services_ihs_part_3.pdf> [accessed 2 April 2010].

Scheich, Manfred, 'Der europäische Integrationsprozeß und die Entwicklung in Ostmitteleuropa', *Österreichische Notariatszeitung*, 122/8 (1990), 185–87.

Schippel, Helmut, 'Das Notariat in den neuen Ländern', *Deutsche Notar-Zeitschrift* (1991), 171–86.

Schmid, C., S. Sebastian, G. Lee, M. Fink and I. Paterson, 'COMP/2006/D3/003: Conveyancing services market' (2007). Available online at <http://ec.europa.eu/comm/competition/sectors/professional_services/studies/studies.html> [accessed 2 April 2010].

Schroeder, F.-C., 'Das Notariatswesen in der Sowjetunion', *Deutsche Notar-Zeitschrift* (1964), 645–71.

Shaw, G., 'Notaries in Central Europe: Transformation as reprofessionalization', *Notarius International*, 9/3-4 (2004), 136–52.

———'Women lawyers in the new federal states of Germany', in U. Schultz and G. Shaw (eds), *Women in the World's Legal Professions* (Oxford: Hart Publishing, 2003), 323–39.

———'Window of opportunity or flash in the pan? Women notaries in the new federal states of Germany', *German Life and Letters*, 50/4 (1997), 557–73.

Sztompka, P., *Trust: A Sociological Theory* (Cambridge: Cambridge University Press, 1999).

Tymecki, B., 'Das Notariat und die notariellen Handlungen in Polen – Bemerkungen zur Verabschiedung der neuen polnischen Notarordnung', *Deutsche Notar-Zeitschrift* (1989), 723–28.

Van den Bergh, R. and Y. Montagnie, 'Theory and evidence on the regulation of the Latin notary profession: A law and economics approach' (2006), commissioned by the notary federations of France, Belgium and the Netherlands. Available online at http://www.ecri.nl/media/publications/theory-and-evidence-regulation-latin-notary-profes.pdf [accessed 18 April 2010].

Weclawowicz, G., *Contemporary Poland: Space and Society* (London: UCL Press, 1996).

World Bank, 'Doing business' (annually since 2004). Available online at <http://www.doingbusiness.org> [accessed 2 April 2010].

Zmudzinski, W., 'Die Notariatsreform in Polen', *Österreichische Notariatszeitung*, 123 (1991), 142–47.

Chapter 11

Multiple Transitions to the EU Constitutional Project: The Case of Eastern European Legal Professions

Vittorio Olgiati

Introduction

As we know, in recent decades the European Union has been officially directed towards gaining quasi-sovereign powers to act at an international level and exclusive internal competences over most relevant national matters. In brief – as the process and policy that, from the early draft of the Maastricht Treaty (1986) onwards, led to the signature of the Treaty on the Functioning of the EU Institutions (2009) demonstrates – the EU tried to become the supreme ruling agent of the entire continental socio-legal dynamic. Therefore no one concerned with the theory and practice of law in action in contemporary Europe can avoid raising two basic questions: how both Western and Eastern European constitutional systems and socio-legal jurisdictions first reacted and then tried to cope with the EU constitutional strategy; and what kind of cultural, political, institutional and socio-technical changes both Western and Eastern European legal professions experienced and/or are now promoting.

Questions of this sort are not new; albeit in a different fashion, they have been raised many times in the recent past. However, they carry a different meaning at present: to the extent that the accession of Eastern European states to the EU (excepting only the Balkans) is a *fait accompli,* they offer the chance to raise – with fewer ideological prejudices and more accurate insights – the problems of both the limits and the potential of the historically-determined socio-legal coupling between the EU's eastward enlargement and EU constitutionalism.

The fact that EU governance, since the Single European Act (1984) and even more so after the enforcement of the Maastricht Treaty (1992), has been implemented in terms of re-proactive 'defensive modernization' *vis-à-vis* the internal and external impact of the two main waves that occurred in the last two decades of the twentieth century in Europe – the rise of the so-called 'American Challenge' or 'Washington Consensus' (later on generically labelled 'globalization') and the collapse, starting with the fall of the Berlin Wall, of the Soviet Union – undeniably played a pivotal role. Yet, beyond the direct and collateral effects of these two waves, EU institutions also had the opportunity to 'accelerate' a third epochal mainstream that has been politically promoted by European unionism since the Rome Treaty (1957), namely the ongoing 'exhaustion' of what was once called 'nation-state building'. In other words, contrary to the amount of studies stressing the rise of an all-encompassing 'global law', the historical sequence of these three waves reveals a significant alteration of the already highly complex '*unitas multiplex*' of European legal experience: an alteration that also included one of its most rewarded socio-legal patterns, that is, the cultural/technical, 'professional mandate' (Sarfatti Larson, 1989) of European legal professions as nation-state builders, as Rudolf von Gneist once put it.

Indeed, legal professions' traditional nation-state-oriented '*Status Activae Civitatis*' – that is, their unique legal position as 'active citizens' within the legal system (Rebuffa, 1990) – can no longer be proclaimed a settled, unequivocal trait of European legal expertise at present (Olgiati, 1996a; 2007a). Besides, to the extent that the epistemic conditions of their traditional *cultural* identity, *technical* speciality and *socio-political* loyalty and commitment have been significantly de-reconverted (Olgiati, 2001; 2003, 2009a), it is likely that their status-role will be further reframed.

This being so, the aim of this study is to draw special attention to the theoretical and practical relevance of such a context. To this end, some major contours of the intertwined impact of the above-mentioned general waves on the European Union's province of law will be discussed. In particular, some exemplary experiences of Eastern European legal professions will be outlined in order to make explicit the link that exists between a given '*Ratio Juris*' and the corresponding socio-legal 'power-knowledge' knot.

The scientific relevance of the case of Eastern European socio-legal systems and legal professions does not deserve to be stressed here. Instead, two additional interrogatives are relevant. Given the contextual overlapping and entanglement of the three above-mentioned waves, what sort of political, cultural and institutional 'organizational brainstorming' – otherwise called 'transition' – have they experienced so far? And in what way, and to what extent, are they technically and culturally 'integrated' into the current EU governance system?

As one can see, these questions raise a theoretical and practical problem whose symbolic and operational implications have not been made explicit so far by current legal and sociological literature. What kind of *new* common professional '*Status Activae Civitatis*'[1] will Eastern *and* Western European legal professions be entitled to claim, in order to be legitimately recognized as veritable 'boundary agents' between EU institutions and European society at large?

1 The '*Status Activae Civitatis*' of legal professions should not to be confused with the notion of 'active citizenship' recently promoted among ordinary (lay) EU citizens to enable them merely to participate in pre-constituted 'deliberative' proceedings and 'subsidiary' activities.

Owing to the complexity of the variables involved in dealing with the matter, the concept of 'positive entropy', borrowed from scientific studies throwing light on the relational co-evolution between energy, substance, space and time, will be implicitly adopted, by analogy, as a leading frame of reference. Indeed, the notion of 'positive entropy' outlines the fact that what we mean when we talk about 'order' is an outcome of processes of internal reorganization accentuated by external disorganizing inputs: processes that occur widely in contemporary society and that, in many respects, seem to concern present-day EU law and society interactions too.

Reframing the Study of European Professionalism

Leafing through scientific literature, one of the most remarkable problems for the study of European professions at present is the assessment of a theoretical approach that may be considered not only analytically plausible (that is, intersubjectively constructed through a rational argument), but also, and above all, socially adequate (that is, grounded on primary claims and fundamental needs) (Luhmann, 1980). Following what has been previously said, it is apparent that the issue at stake lies precisely in what can be called the EU-driven 'positive entropy', that is, the reorganization-through-disorganization of the European professional realm. This was set in motion by the way in which EU governance dealt with each one of the three epochal waves mentioned above, the socio-legal consequences being such that it may be further involved, both in the short and long terms, at regional, national and continental levels.

The multi-layered patterns of this 'de-reconversion' have already been discussed elsewhere with reference to either legal professions (notaries, lawyers, judges) (Olgiati, 1995a; 2000; 2007a) or the overall system of European learned professions (Olgiati, 2001; 2008a). Two major difficulties in this respect came out: (1) how to provide a detailed account of each professional variable while relating the topic to the broader social context and vice versa; and (2) how to provide a reliable 'order of discourse' to such a complex and thorough evolutionary mix of variables.

Given space-time constraints as well as the potentials of EU process and policy, a critical distancing from currently dominating approaches to professions and professionalism is required. In fact, an unprejudiced overview of the scientific literature on contemporary European professions is sufficient to reveal what otherwise should have been self-evident if these approaches had not acted – as Braudel would put it – as veritable *prisons du longue durée*, that is, as mentally stereotyped iron cages of such an extraordinary, historically new, unique character of EU constitutional unionism. This is particularly true of the legal professions, as they experienced, in their turn, a unique unprecedented change, pursued politically 'from above' and propelled technically, at the same time, as both a conscious socio-technical *Strukturbildung* and a veritable 'self-fulfilling prophecy'.

To account for these statements, the following will outline three basic issues that current study and research on the EU, and European professions more generally, has so far practically concealed or underestimated.

The first issue concerns the material and symbolic substance of EU geo-political constructivism. In this respect it can be said, in brief, that since the rise of modern nation-state constituencies, geo-political constructivism has been defined conceptually as the *raison d'état* of a given ruling elite, namely, the coupling of the *ethos* (the foundational ideal and material rule) and the *cratos* (the vital interests of a constituted or constituent political power) (Meineke, 1924). To the extent that this premise is lacking particular or general variables concerned with or related to the status of legal professions as proper 'nomic' agents, that is, as normatively-oriented socio-institutional order builders, it does not make any sense. Even less intelligible, therefore, are the historically determined challenges and cleavages that such powers raise against each other. The problem, in the case of contemporary European legal professions, lies in the fact that (from a socio-legal perspective) the EU *raison d'état* appears at present as a veritable *simulacrum dominations ac libertatis*, as the well-known 'democratic deficit' of EU policy-making demonstrates (Olgiati, 2006; 2007b).

The second issue concerns the core rationale of the EU *raison d'état*; that is, the fact that only those tasks or ideals implying an extraordinary and deep-rooted social achievement, which, in turn, require a systematic socio-technical effort of contextualization and realignment, are significant. Unfortunately, it is impossible to discuss this topic in detail, save to recall attention to the fact that a main pillar of the EU *raison* has been to prevent (as far as possible) undesirable conflicts and constitutional breakdowns (a pillar stemming from 'organizational learning', given the heartbreaking constitutional 'lessons' endured in the course of two world wars). Accordingly, EU 'defensive modernization' policy has been, and still is, enhanced as a top-down (commissarial), reformist (negotiated) 'transposition' strategy about past and present values, as well as prospective interests in mitigating the decline of 'enlightened' European constitutional architecture and lifestyles related to 'classic' political economy standards. Again, it is consequential that no study on any EU issue – legal expertise, in particular – can be taken seriously unless it includes at least a reference to the material and symbolic implications of this socio-legal and political EU imprinting during and after the EU enlargement.

The third issue concerns the role/function of European intellectuals and learned professions in the 'transition' from a country-specific nation-oriented *raison d'état* model to the new, EU-oriented *raison*, in accordance with the above-mentioned EU 'defensive modernization' strategy. Here, what really matters is the rise of a type of EU governmentality, which, at the same time, de-reconstructs the European legal professions' technical 'speciality' and cultural 'identity', and which calls for nothing less than a new, EU-styled constitutional patriotism, otherwise named – according to current managerial culture – 'judicial accountability' (Piana, 2010). In fact, as centuries of political experience teach us, it is not possible to weaken or dismantle settled constituencies or to set up and maintain new legal orders unless a new fundamental rule/ideal is established at a constitutional level and embodied at a social level. In other words, the protection of the available 'cultural capital', as well as the assessment of a new institutional hegemony through organic intellectuals – in particular, the legal professions – are inevitable cultural and political prerequisites (Sarfatti Larson, 2000). This being so, it goes without saying that, in this case too, no studies and research on any EU issue concerning legal professions can be taken seriously if European cultural legacies, learning institutions, educational models and, last but not least, professional knowledge and know-how are not considered as politically relevant sources, agents and targets – subjects and objects – of the same EU governmentality (Olgiati, 2008; 2009a).

Understandably, the three issues outlined above are reciprocally intertwined. Accordingly it is always opportune, if not necessary, to consider – when dealing with European unionism – not only the structural couplings, but also the diverging moves either of general '*fundamental curves*' of European society – as Braudel and Le Goff defined certain basic long-term waves – or of context-specific '*nuances*' of EU process and policy, while focusing on what has happened and is happening to the European professional realm as a part of the overall EU constitutional scenario.

The Many Facets of the So-called 'Transition' in European Countries: A Retrospective Glance

What has been said above is crucial to this chapter. It will now pave the way to a historically determined account of the most relevant variables marking the 'transition' of European legal professions, in general, and Eastern European legal professions, in particular, towards their current, still unsettled '*Status Activae Civitatis*' within both the continental rule of the EU governance system and the national rule of EU member states' constituencies: that is, within the normative domain of a model of legal pluralism that – as will be argued in the course of this chapter – can be roughly compared only to that enforced in Europe after the Treaties of Munster and Osnabruch.

The first variable to deserve specific consideration is the semantic use of the term 'transition'. As we know, after the fall of the Berlin Wall both the EU and the USA engaged in harsh political, economic and cultural competition with regard to the governance (timetable, contents, agents and so on) of what has been called the 'transition' of Eastern European countries towards a new and free socio-institutional system. In actual fact, it is fair to say that such a 'transition' concerned a notable variety of more or less clearly defined 'transitions': 'de-communistization', 'lustration', 'Westernization', 'liberalization', 'modernization', 'democratization', 're-Christianization' and so on. The number of volumes, reports and documents now available on each of these 'transitions' is impressive – needless to say, their insights cannot be summarized here. What is worth stressing about them, however, is that only a minority of these sources account comparatively for the fact that, although these 'transitions' sometimes occurred in parallel, by and large neither their manifest/latent action, nor their impact and final results occurred simultaneously or synchronously. Surely, those sources record, by rule, the strengths and weaknesses of given arrangements, or of specific goals of different agents competing in a given field, offering in turn a general view of different conditions in each country – economic standards, religious attitudes, historical legacies and so on – that enables us to understand achievements and failures, or positive and negative actions or reactions. In most cases, however, a sort of 'social division of disciplinary research work' prevails, to the point that pivotal issues are often neglected, ignored or underestimated. This is particularly apparent in regard to the allegedly converging, but actually competing, US and EU 'transition strategies', specifically in relation to means and procedures, or the final outcome of each 'transition'.

While US agents tried to exert stronger influence and gain larger profits in all fields by imposing their own vision, expertise, technology and so on, EU institutions attempted to assert a veritable 'cybernetic control' – in terms of direction and speed – of the potential structural-functional coupling among all sorts of transitions and ongoing European unionism. This was done by the EU, not so much for its own sake but, rather, to achieve a historical result, that is, to promote socio-legal engineering enabling the same EU to come to terms *peacefully* (as opposed to the attempts of Napoleon and Hitler) with the centuries-old project of European unification under a single continental rule. At the same time, and for the same reason, this 'cybernetic control' set in full motion a political trend otherwise highly questionable, that is, the splitting of national ruling elites, or 'historic blocks', into two factions: the one still nation-oriented, and the other increasingly EU-oriented – thus selectively promoting the rise of new EU-styled geo-political values and interests, while weakening vested local/national issues. Consequently, if it is true that the EU never pursued a purely economist market-driven globalization policy to extremes, it is also true that the EU-driven 'transition' of Eastern countries towards EU governance was never labelled 'annexation' or 'assimilation', but 'Europeanization', 'integration', 'approximation', 'enlargement', 'accession' and so on. Besides, if it is true that the EU transition policy was carried out by means of EU programmes labelled 'EU fundamental rights', 'EU financial aids', 'EU technological support', 'EU parameters', 'EU evaluation' and so on, it is also true that these sub-systemic devices fostered the urge for proper strategy of a *constitutional* nature.

In any case, each kind of 'transition' raised country-specific issues, each one requiring equally specific managerial efforts. Thus, even though all 'transitions' come under the all-encompassing cover of general ideals/values such as 'freedom', 'wealth', 'democracy' and 'rule of law', it is by no means fortuitous that each country-specific transition pattern (in the course of its planning, implementation, degree of variation and so on) was subject to a quite problematic ad hoc operational assessment (Offe, 1997; Přibáň, 2002).

The Semantics of European Legal Professions' 'Transitions'

To the extent that the notion of 'transition' turned into a veritable semantic catch-all for media communications, a rising number of studies, research and official reports began to devote attention to the conceptual framework and empirical treatment of matters under consideration, and to emphasize specific characters of sub-systemic 'transitional' patterns or variables. An emblematic case in point is the literature devoted to cultural/technical 'transitions' towards Euro-Atlantic professional standards in the field of law.

Since 1990 a great deal of scientific literature has attempted to account for the successful 'transplant' of US-styled corporate law firms throughout Europe. Yet ideologically-oriented and one-dimensional viewpoints have often prevailed. For example, if one leafs through socio-legal studies on the role of US lawyers in the 'legal restructuring' of Eastern European countries, one finds that the so-called 'import/export' approach is widely used as an analytical tool (Dezalay, 1995; Dezalay and Garth, 2008) without adopting any clear or proper legal perspective. Needless to say, such a one-sided approach is quite appealing from an economic orientation but highly misleading not only per se (as it does not allow any enlightenment on the complexity of legal professions' 'S*tatus Activae Civitatis*'), but also because it does not allow any full understanding of the extent to which the export/import of a given legal device was a top-down move by US lawyers aiming to compulsorily disseminate certain legal know-how to Europe, or whether European lawyers' legal expertise really needed such a move from US colleagues. Too often the benefit of the exchange ratio for both parties has been taken for granted, while on closer inspection, one might still suppose that, for the most part, the import/export was not at all a matter of direct inter-professional legal relations, but a mere side-effect of the transfer or implantation of organizational/managerial techno-structures embodying normative procedures or binding precautionary provisions. Of course, no one can deny that some sort of 'legal transplants' were necessary and useful, but it is one thing to claim that the kind of legal practice that US law firms were exporting was/is the best way to handle certain local matters technically, and quite another empirically to ascertain their actual effectiveness and/or efficacy in the given country. As official documents show, not only were unsuccessful transplants quite common – as made clear by, for example, the Lawyers Committee for International Human Rights Report as early as 1996 – but the legal practices concerned were, in one way or another, made subject to a number of jurisdictional restrictions by the 'receiving' countries in order to safeguard their own interior public order (Olgiati, 1995; 1999; 2008a). Indeed, looking back, it is also possible to state that the self-claimed 'successful' transplant of US-styled legal devices is at the core of the bankruptcy streams that have characterized the global economic system in the last decade (Flood, 2001), as, for example, the case of the Baltic countries demonstrates.

Another case in point is the emphasis placed on the need for substantial 'de-regulation' and/or 'liberalization' of European professional guilds. Again, if one carefully leafs through accountable sources about the historical progression of many professional reforms on this matter, one cannot but realize that such goals often led, in actual fact, to a veritable de/re-regulation, that is, a mere updating 'adjustment' rather than a full 'de-regulation' or 'liberalization'. The experiences endured by Polish and Hungarian notaries clearly fit into this general trend (Shaw, 2009). But this evidence should not be considered as a failure; it simply reminds us, totally in keeping with the main findings of so-called 'law-and-development' studies, that, as a rule, legal changes, whether labelled 'transitions' or not, are rarely cross-cutting breakdowns but, rather, mere legal discontinuities, whose temporal dimensions raise, in turn, more retrospective and retroactive implications than substantial successful advances. Indeed, one might say that legal 'transitions', being reformist rather than revolutionary processes, are basically socio-legal 'irritants' (as systems theories would call them). It cannot therefore come as a surprise to note that radical legal changes, by means of legal transplants in particular, being instrumental by definition, and often being involuntary, hardly function as such in the long run, for, as Pierre Legrand says, '*extra culturam nihil datur*' (2001).

Despite having said this, however, it does not follow that legal professions in Eastern Europe did not experience a significant foreign-driven 'de-reconversion' at all. On the contrary, a variety of items can be recalled to show that this kind of 'transition' occurred widely, as its main aim was to create institutional, cultural and psycho-attitudinal conditions to *compel* the same legal professions to de-re-construct their own habitual local knowledge and know-how.

Interestingly, looking at the matter from a broader perspective, it is apparent that – albeit on a smaller scale – a quite similar 'transition' occurred at the same time in Western European countries too. Scientific literature devoted to 'transitions' in Eastern European countries in the last decades hardly dealt with this space-time *continental* juncture. Yet, emblematic cases of 'judicial activism', including political 'lustration', or projects for 'transitional justice', such as elite judges' 'legal training', as well as cases of legal practices' import/export 'corporatization', 'liberalization, 'marketization' and so on, also took place within founder members of the EU such as Italy, Germany and France (see, for example, Nelken, 1996). Unfortunately, it is impossible to develop a full comparative analysis here; but it is clear that the 'transitions' experienced in all professional fields in Eastern countries cannot be detached from the mainstream effect on the whole *continental* European professional realm.

This being so, as historical evidence shows, it follows that the analytical horizon of the present discussion needs to be substantially enlarged, not only to decipher the comparative differences, but also to outline the similarities and points of convergence.

As a matter of fact, all kinds of 'transitions' experienced by both Eastern and Western European countries since the Maastricht Treaty are examples of a common legal matrix: namely, the EU governance institutions' 'transition' towards their formal-official constitutionalization.

Undoubtedly, general conditions that compelled, at one point in history or another, all European countries to experience in one way or another the above-mentioned 'transitions', and all EU ruling elites strategically to enhance the process/project of EU constitutionalization, are directly related to distinct, but also overlapping, epochal events that nurtured, in turn, different collateral effects either at international or national levels worldwide.

Even though these events and collateral effects were and are historically intertwined, it is in the interests of clarity to disentangle the matter analytically with respect to the main topic of this study, that is, the changing patterns of the legal professions' '*Status Activae Civitatis*'. The first consideration is the impact of economic globalization. This will be followed by discussion of the impact of EU enlargement. In each case, EU constitutionalization process and policy will be taken on as a context-based general framework.

As will be seen, historical evidence suggests that a sort of 'entropic' movement actually occurred in Europe and that not only entanglements, but also distinctions and contradictions between inter/intra/trans-European endogenous and exogenous variables – as a few political studies on EU 'democratic transition' outlined so far – need to be taken into account.

The Impact of Economic Globalization and the Mismatch between US-driven and EU-oriented Strategies

The impact of US-driven economic globalization on EU law policy-making has been extremely relevant at both political and cultural levels. At the cultural level, in particular, economic theories emphasizing respectively 'market de-regulation' and 'political liberalism' were highly regarded by EU official institutions as inevitable cognitive guidelines for implementing or evaluating any sort of European action system.

Accordingly, it does not come as a surprise to note that, since its early stage of elaboration, EU constitutionalization process and policy was based on a general theory of social action oriented either towards stimulating so-called 'individual flourishing' at any level (Raz, 1986), or eroding the 'normative closure' of both actual and prospective member-state national territorial jurisdictions and political sovereignty, in connection with other issues already well-established (such as free mobility of goods, services, capital and individuals in the socio-legal market). In this respect, the insistence of official EU protocols on the need to anchor such 'individual flourishing' to transnational networks or regional enclaves provided with context-specific knowledge and know-how is not casual at all: it reflected the ideology and practice of the 'global de-regulation agenda' set up by international institutions such as FMI, OECD, Davos-Wef and the World Bank. These institutions lack any formal political legitimation, but are nevertheless able to act as veritable 'constitutional substitutes' of national states (Chalmers, 2000) and are thus also able to re-regulate the broader socio-legal dynamic according to their own market-oriented global normative standards. The problem with this sort of autonomous, exterior and top-down market-driven re-regulation, however, is that it was to a large extent technically and politically contradictory, as demonstrated, for example, by the unsustainable conceptual distinction between 'bureaucratic' and 'political' corruption enforced by the World Bank in an attempt to protect foreign corporations from losing contracts or seeing their property rights undermined (Makowski, 2009). One of the main outcomes of such an instrumentality has been the quest for ever-larger budgets in order to 'increase the political concern' of local authorities about the need to foster additional re-regulatory actions.

In turn, leafing through EU official reports, one notices that the setting up of given political and normative options was coherent with other strategic aims, for example, that of compelling any potential socio-economic and political-institutional resource of prospective member states to 'converge' smoothly not so much towards general ideals or legal principles but, rather, towards the changing patterns of the same EU governance system. Therefore the final outcome of the whole global/local 'liberalization' process and policy in Europe has amounted to an all-encompassing de-re-regulation of the entire European economic and normative realm (Barcellona, 2007) in view of an additional type of transition: the legal-political 'transition' of the same EU towards its own EU constitutionalization.

Unfortunately, it is not possible to focus on the variety of legal issues contained in the number of EU Treaties (Schengen, Laeken, Tampere, Copenhagen, Amsterdam, Nice) that have been signed so far from the Maastricht Treaty up to the completion of the EU enlargement. For the sake of brevity, let us recall one major item only: the officially declared aim of safeguarding and promoting the whole economic, political and institutional patrimony of the European Union by reinforcing the so-called 'EU policy pillars', namely freedom, security and justice. Otherwise, one could not really understand the political meaning of legal reforms enforced up to the Lisbon Treaty (2009), that is, the Treaty that, on the one hand, definitively asserts (as will be seen later) the pivotal importance of the principle of subsidiarity, but, on the other hand, fails to mention explicitly two other principles: (1) 'free competition' (among and within EU countries); and (2) 'EU supremacy' (over member states' constituencies).

Within this general 'playing field', both Eastern and Western European legal professions therefore experienced not only a mere 'transition' to a given socio-legal framework, but also a veritable de-re-regulation. The Eastern legal professions, in particular, also underwent quite a systematic process of socio-technical and cultural-ideological 'legal de-re-education'.

According to the already mentioned import/export theorizing, and the vast majority of studies and research on US 'legal transplant' strategy in Europe of US law firms' expertise, such a 'legal de-re-education' was based largely on a sort of altruistic idea of providing Eastern legal professions with substantial support to fill up the 'modernization gap' and overcome a widespread socio-legal 'backwardness'. Surely humanitarian-styled liberal attitudes cannot be excluded. But these were not always disinterested influences. Indeed, experiencing increasing limits on expansion at home, US law firms – having already established their own branches in Western Europe – flocked to Eastern European countries to promote the post-communist 'free-market transition' in order to further disseminate US economic globalization policy and sustain US corporations in developing their business, while continuing to compete with their Western European counterparts (Dezalay, 1995; Flood, 2001; Madsen, 2008). At any rate Eastern lawyers' professional elites were provided with knowledge about complex transactions, new foreign clients and high-standard techno-structures. In turn, under the cover of promoting the 'rule of law', US law firms offered a variety of legal training courses and exerted strong cultural pressure to reform professional jurisdictions and legal practice according to their own values and interests (Dezalay and Garth, 2008). Demands for mixed partnerships, multi-practice networks, joint ventures and so on were raised and fulfilled. Repeated calls for more suitable 'creative lawyering' and, above all, the dismantling of local professional guild systems were, in turn, ongoing leitmotifs.

A not less relevant but substantially different role was played, in contrast, by the European Union. The main difference *vis-à-vis* US-styled 'legal export/transplant' has been that the EU, while sustaining 'free-market policy' and the European business corporations, also performed – as has already been briefly mentioned – a direct, politically-oriented, quite systematic legal interventionism in terms of plans for legal reforms. As a matter of fact, under the cover of the officially proclaimed principle of the '*Ordoliberalismus*' doctrine, the EU had the opportunity to carry on a veritable 'socio-liberal engineering through law'. Almost all socio-legal fieldwork concerned with professional legal practice was subjected to a flow of top-down legal provisions. Many of them were preceded or followed by the enforcement of more or less detailed EU projects, aimed, as a rule, at imposing ad hoc institutional guidelines and/or administrative and managerial accountability procedures. This has happened in the case of particular jurisdictional settings, such as the Administration of Justice (evaluation of judges' performance, reform of courts' organization, monitoring of length and costs of proceedings and so on), or particular institutional matters of strategic relevance (evaluation and refinement of the timetable agenda of EU Copenhagen parameters as regards fiscal issues; the so-called 'EU Bologna process' about higher education and so on), or particular fields requiring new legal arrangements (surveys and evaluations on welfare, customer satisfaction, citizens' values and so on). General standards about professional legal services were substantially reformed too, either by virtue of ECJ decisions, or through the EU Commission's injunctions to national authorities.

To sum up, if it is true that, by virtue of the ongoing economic globalization wave, US law firms considered Eastern European legal practice to be a veritable 'off-shore market' where it was possible to export cultural and instrumental patterns of the so-called 'American way of law', it is also true that, quite systematically, the EU, by contrast, played a highly normative function in attracting and subsuming US-style legal market professional de-reconversion under the cover of both EU intra-European 'four freedoms' law-making and the emerging EU constitutional project.

Given all of the above, it was not by chance that assenting or dissenting voices and explicit reactions on the part of Eastern European legal professions often became a part of the same 'transitional' scenario. The 'living law' embedded in a number of legal patterns nurtured by local socio-cultural traditions indeed played a significant role. Accordingly, it is possible to argue that even if a process of professional legal re-education occurred under the pressure of foreign US and EU economic and political means, nevertheless a large part of Eastern European legal professions were able to perform a special type of 'transition', that is, a veritable country-specific 'socio-legal adaptation'.

As far as this country-specific legal experience is concerned, studies and research are only now showing up on the scientific agenda. In any case, it is possible to state that those legal professionals who first clamoured for the political overturn of the old regime were somehow ideologically aware of what the political turn could mean, either in legal terms or for their legal practice, while, in turn, those who, during the transition or after the EU accession, were forced to change their traditional professional standards often did so for opportunistic reasons or owing to instrumental and existential constraints (Varga, 2008). In brief, they acted just as ordinary people were currently doing (Stomka, 1996; Kymlika and Opalski, 2001; Bandelj, 2003).

This statement does not reflect a superficial viewpoint: it is supported by similar evidence in the attitudes of other professionals, including politicians, intellectuals, entrepreneurs, civil servants and so on (Galina, 2008). Besides, it is based on what anthropological, cultural and comparative legal studies have often recorded about countries subjected to sudden and contextual forms of cultural, economic, political and legal 'colonization': namely, (1) that modern positive law – as with any law – is always 'local' when actually embodied and applied; (2) that any professional group – as with any social system – is always internally stratified along different, more or less refined, cultural lines; and (3) that any social subject living in a given context is never a *tabula rasa* (Olgiati, 2009). Accordingly, therefore, it is possible to argue that Eastern European legal professions, by embodying and reflecting the legacies of a thousand-year-old legal tradition, have been able to do what their ancestors have done for centuries, that is, as legal scholars as varied as Ehrlich, Gumplowicz and Petrazycki knew well, to become culturally accustomed to dealing with current legal changes and reacting to the given forms of legal pluralism by all means of implicit rejection and distrust or smooth indifference, whatever the circumstances.

Cases in point are countless. For example, the judicial system in democratic Poland has changed substantially since 1989 according to the Italian model. However, its personnel and the social perception of their status and roles have remained largely the same as they were in the socialist days. This is true, in turn, about the legal behaviour of ordinary Polish citizens: as socio-legal scholars such as Fuszara and Kurczewski have ascertained in the course of an empirical survey concerning the treatment of disputes in Poland, political, legal and economic 'transformations' that occurred during the 'transitions' have not been accompanied by an increase in conflicts about property, labour, or commercial matters. Certainly, the socio-legal perception of private rights has been strengthened and there has been an increase in legal actions against public agencies, but legal claims about domestic issues or among neighbours are dealt with outside the courts as in the past. The most significant change that has been noticed is simply the rising number of so-called 'notorious litigants' acting as 'repeat players' (corporate legal actors, as a rule) (Fuszara and Kurczewski, 2009).

Surely, the above empirical findings do not exclude at all that the '*Ratio Juris*' of the legal system and the '*Status Activae Civitatis*' of legal professions did not endure – as we will see in a while – substantial changes. They simply record one of the most apparent consequences of the whole 'legal transition' strategy: namely its own contradictory practical outcomes owing to its own intrinsic conceptual and procedural contradictions. It is true, for example, that, in order to bring the state out of ongoing economic affairs, the militarist tradition of the Socialist Police in Poland was firstly broken (by the Police Act 1990) and subsequently partly restored to reinforce public safety to fight corruption. However, it is also true that the EU Amsterdam Treaty, while asserting that the EU Court of Justice has no jurisdiction to review the validity and proportionality of operations carried out by the police of a member state, at the same time (in Article K.7, paragraphs 5 and 6) stated that the same Court has 'jurisdiction to review the legality of framework decisions' made by a member state 'on grounds of competence [...] of any rule of law relating to [...] misuse of power' (Kadar, 2001).

As one can see, the way in which the economically-driven 'legal transition' occurred in the realm of European legal professions cannot be reduced to legal pressure from economic globalization, but requires us to enlarge the analytical horizon and focus on the most substantial legal impact of EU enlargement.

The Impact of EU Enlargement and the Gap between the Ends and Means of EU Institutional Arrangements

After the collapse of the communist political regime, the accession of Eastern European states to the EU as full members, and consequently the EU enlargement, have been quite troublesome owing either to interior or international variables directly related to the new constitutional nature of the changes implied.

With respect to the evolutionary path of this historical mainstream, it is compelling, first of all, to mention the extraordinary political relevance of the proclamation made by the German Chancellor Helmut Kohl just at the time of the fall of the Berlin Wall: 'A United Germany in a United Europe.' This was a proclamation not only clearly directed at all Germans, but at the whole world also, asserting the guarantee of the political and constitutional equality of all European states within a prospective *peacefully enlarged* Europe.

Unfortunately, owing to geo-strategic reasons and international interests, such a guarantee has not been respected and fulfilled at all. On the one hand, by drafting the Copenhagen Agreements, EU institutions deliberately set up the conditions for the unilateral imposition of 'parameters of convergence' upon all Eastern European states willing to become EU members. On the other hand, by taking on a contradictory policy about the kind of 'transition' that the Balkan region was enduring, EU member states openly infringed nothing less than the core legal and political 'rationale' of the original strategy of European unionism since the Rome Treaty, that is, peaceful inter-European relations.

As far as the Copenhagen Agreements were concerned, the so-called 'EU approximation' parameters were not based solely on top-down and highly selective standards whose merit, methods and temporal junctures were pre-defined around a table, but, neither were they invoked on the occasion of previous accessions (of Western European states). Consequently the EU, by officially undermining the classic liberal-democratic principle of 'self-determination' of each state – EU member states included – created potential conditions for nothing less than a serious constitutional cleavage *vis-à-vis* all EU member states. It was possible for the same EU to take on a normative character similar to that of colonial legal regimes, to the extent that, in spite of its self-styled 'democratic' nature, it evoked the model of a sort of 'double-state' system (Olgiati, 2006). The imposition of the Copenhagen parameters meant that the already established EU *acquis communautaire* was directly enforced as such – that is, without taking into consideration, for example, that part of Eastern European countries' (pre-communist) law that could help to smooth the socio-legal change. Consequently, new problematic outcomes occurred (Poplawska, 2002), owing to the alleged 'confusion' of EU institutions about their own status as promoter of both 'Eastern democratic transition' and 'European unionism'. A case in point is the EU's support for international law-making about minority groups' fundamental rights (never provided for by the EU before 1989): a support that, significantly, raised fierce opposition on the part of Western EU member states (Kymlika, 2005).

If one then considers that, in the same years, not only did the Czechs and Slovaks split up, but some Western EU member states took part in a war on the European continent leading to the decomposition of an Eastern European state such as Yugoslavia, one can easily realize what sort of additional, traumatic 'legal transition' characterized (and still characterizes) EU constitutional process and policy: the failure to complete Eastern Europe's EU integration and a subordinate ranking within the concert of the great world powers.

Having said this, however, what matters here is also that, while all of the above was going on, Eastern European countries really tried to achieve EU standards, taking their own 'transitions' seriously, the accomplishment of 'democratization' of their legal systems included. To this end, in order to distance themselves clearly from communist constitutional rule (that is, to comply explicitly with the principle of the 'rule of law'), they rushed to enforce new constitutional charters in which, in accordance with the European liberal democratic tradition (Suski, 1995), the principle of 'self-determination' was explicitly heralded as a basic democratic value/rule. Paradoxically enough, such a positive disposition turned out to be a 'politically incorrect' interpretation of the EU-styled 'democratic transition'. On the one hand, it clashed with the EU top-down demand for the EU-driven 'approximation' to the Copenhagen parameters; on the other hand, it made apparent the fact that the same 'democratic transition' could also lead legitimately to a deepening of the specific 'identity' of each country and a fostering of the 'diversity' of each national constitutional system, especially regarding constitutionally relevant EU issues such as the assessment of fundamental rights, the definition of 'EU citizenship', the recognition of cultural and ethnic identity and so on.

A large amount of literature on the constitutional relevance of these and other legal variables is now at our disposal. It is possible to see a striking pattern in the extraordinary technical and cultural role played by the judges of national constitutional courts (see, for example, Sadurski, 2001; 2002; 2005).

Comparative studies and research carried out in the last years have shown that (1) EU 'enlargement' policy, (2) EU constitutional policy and (3) the Eastern European states' 'approximation' policy combined to give rise to a veritable and unique model of 'constitutional transition', implying an unusual kind of horizontal and vertical, top-down and bottom-up, socio-legal complexity within and among each Eastern and Western country. For example, while the EU insisted that the UK should provide itself with a constitutional text to better match the EU Nice Charter (a demand the UK legal professions considered a clear threat to their centuries-old common law system), Eastern European courts, in line with the rationale of previous decisions of the Italian, French and German Constitutional Courts, repeatedly reformed their own new and democracy-oriented constitutions to strengthen, rather than co-align or reduce the degree of diversity of their constitutional models according to their internal country-specific balance of powers, in order to affirm their own historically-rooted specificity (Sadurski, 2006b). In short, by reinterpreting in an up-to-date way their own basic cultural values and interests while normatively reassessing the letter and the spirit of the classic liberal principles of the 'rule of law' doctrine, the judges of the constitutional courts in Eastern European countries reaffirmed the primacy of national sovereignty not as a unilateral legal standard, but as a sign of the equal status of their constitutional decision-making *vis-à-vis* each and every Western European constitutional model (Blokker, 2008). Interestingly, by doing so, the same judges did not act as dependent agents of a single ruling political coalition, but as veritable professional agents directly responsible to the people and therefore able to mediate between 'hard liners' and 'soft liners' within the newly created multi-party systems.

As one can see from the scanty hints given above, the EU-driven 'westward legal transition' emphasized – paradoxically – the role and function of the judges of Eastern European constitutional courts in such a way that they became veritable 'coupling pins', regarding the political stability of their countries in terms of being 'wardens of country-specific cultural legacy'. In turn, however, they also played the same role-function as regards ongoing EU legal policy. A clear example is the case of Welfare Directives in Hungary: owing to serious difficulties concerning the enforcement of EU-derived legislation, Hungarian Constitutional judges developed a number of principles around the classic liberal-democratic concept of 'legal certainty' up to the point of declaring in 1995 that: (1) certain welfare legal changes could not enter in force because there was no adequate adjustment period granted; (2) certain restrictions were unconstitutional and therefore void per se; and (3) the court would continue to monitor current and prospective legislation (Sajó and Lauer, 1996).

Given the above, it was by no means fortuitous that, in the meantime, Eastern European judicial institutions were undergoing a comprehensive process of cultural and professional 're-framing'. While the Council of Europe, on behalf of the so-called 'international community', promoted new conceptual standards of quality of justice associated with new managerial action systems designed to achieve the official aims of coordinating context-specific judicial policies, various extra-European non-governmental organizations (such as the American Bar Association or the Open Society Institute) actively took part in the same EU policy, by financially and technically supporting the creation of training centres, consulting agencies, academic seminars and so on, to reshape judicial behaviour and the skills of both judges and prosecutors.

Within this general policy, it is also worth mentioning the attempt to promote educational initiatives at an intra-European level on issues of relevant social impact. The fact that the Ministry of Justice and the Office of Public Prosecutors of the Romanian Supreme Court took part, together with the French Ministry of Justice and the Spanish General Council of Judicial Power, in an EU-sponsored comparative research project promoted by the Italian High Council of Magistracy on the theme of '*participation équilibrée des homes and des femmes dans la prise de decision*', in order to remove obstacles to women judges and ensure equal opportunities and non-discrimination in matters concerning judicial systems (Quaderni del CSM, 2004), is just one of the many examples of the urging by European legal professions to create better conditions for a prospective amalgamation of legal cultures and a more efficient professional practice (Olgiati, 2008a; Piana, 2010).

In brief, to the extent that the broader wave of legal changes – justified by the ideals of the 'democratic transition' – matched programmes of cultural 're-formation' of country-specific patterns of legal knowledge and know-how, the whole province of Eastern European legal expertise underwent a veritable politically-oriented 'professional reconversion' of both their cognitive and institutional '*Status Activae Civitatis*'.

The EU 'Constitutional Transition' Towards an Impossible Isonomic EU Legal Order

What has been said so far about the variety of 'transitions' that Eastern European countries have experienced, owing either to economic globalization or EU enlargement, makes it apparent that, contrary to common stereotyped insights about such 'transitions', the most important 'transition' endured by the entire European society since the collapse of the Berlin Wall has been the whole EU's own formal-official constitutional strategy.

As a matter of fact, the EU 'transition' towards its own constitutionalization process and policy cannot be left aside, hidden or ignored: even at a superficial level, it is apparent that a great deal of its rationale stemmed directly from both the opportunities and the challenges derived from the legal experience of the Eastern European 'de-reconstitutionalizations'. Accordingly, it is possible to state that the structural coupling of both transitions is an unavoidable additional variable in understanding the problematic and unstable socio-legal setting that all European legal professions (Eastern and Western) were and are now enduring while pursuing their everlasting mandate to 'reduce legal complexity' (Luhmann, 1972; Friedman, 1989). Such a mandate, in our case, deals with nothing less that the complexity of the EU dual (continental and national) legal system.

Indeed, such a complex structural coupling raises an unavoidable question. Given the age-old variety of context-specific national traditions and the ongoing multi-layered dynamics of the overall European socio-legal changes, what kinds of 'complexity reduction' were and are the European legal professions substantially called on to perform?

Since the Treaty of Rome, European institutions have pursued a policy specifically oriented towards preventing conflicts, while keeping alive values and interests embedded in the constitutional models rooted in the legal doctrines of the Enlightenment and classic political economy. Needless to say, this sort of policy has required recurrent material and symbolic 'adjustments', including the quite systematic use of legal fictions to support the '*effect utile*' of official narratives (Olgiati, 2005; 2007b; Přibáň, 2002). Slow but relevant semantic 'slippages' regarding the official definition of the EU strategic agenda have also had to be performed, in order to cope with the mismatch between such age-old doctrines and contemporary trends (from unification to harmonization, mutuality, approximation, convergence, diversity and so on). Such 'slippages', in turn, nurtured a growing uncertainty about the driving path towards the EU's real aim (integration, enlargement, or reinforcement?). As these semantic moves were required by the irrepressible functional differentiation and cultural fragmentation of European society as a whole – a reality that could hardly be regulated by legal means – it is remarkable that, as early as the 1980s, in order to prevent foreseeable, disquieting problems at any level, Jacques Delors insisted on breaking with the Enlightenment liberal tradition by claiming that a new principle, that of subsidiarity, had to be officially included in the text of the Maastricht Treaty, that is, the Treaty that officially proclaimed the political nature of European unionism in formal legal terms. In Delors' view, the enactment of the subsidiarity principle was the most reasonable way of politically promoting the institutional intertwining of different, internally fragmented and ever-changing units around common tasks, while driving them towards the general aims of a modern secularized socio-legal order: economic growth (welfare) and social participation (democracy) (1991).

Indeed, the subsidiarity principle implies, by definition, both diversity and asymmetry, for only differentiated but flexible variables can be integrated accordingly. In turn, given such patterns, the expected integration is possible only to the extent that somewhere, at an internal or external level, some common value and/or interest, possibly related to, or stemming from, a minimum common denominator (a common cultural tradition or a common social energetic source) exists. This being so, it is not by chance that in order to achieve – as the Preamble of the rejected EU Constitutional Treaty stated verbatim – 'an ever closer union among European people' (that is, to better rule the variety of local national systems), the subsidiarity principle has been heralded as the basic 'coupling pin' of EU governance, it being envisaged precisely as an asymmetrical and multi-level tool enabling the fostering of integration and cooperation, while at the same time promoting competition and mutual rivalries.

The problem with the subsidiarity principle – enforced in the meantime in the constitutional systems of almost all EU member states – is that it is, undoubtedly, a highly refined legal tool (Castorina, 2007; Bassanini and Tiberi, 2008). Paradoxically, however, it is far from being a 'new' one. As a matter of fact, it is a typical pre-modern device, having qualified for centuries the Gothic law of *Ancien Régime* up to the end of the Holy Roman Empire in 1806. Its current 'added value' within the EU Treaty, therefore, is that it enables many of the democratic formalities of the 'legitimation-through-proceeding' – as Luhmann would put it – to be bypassed, as it allows any political-institutional agency, as well as any social-legal system, to relinquish the nineteenth- and twentieth-century 'government' model and assess what we now call 'governance'. In other words – as eighteenth-century jurist Pufendorf knew perfectly well – it allows asymmetrical socio-political power relations, normatively structured according to a functional logic that, during the Holy Roman Empire, implied binding ties of vassalage, as well as, at present, easily establishing bonds that could be qualified as a type of 'political exchange' (Olgiati, 2007c).

The operations of the so-called 'political exchange' in contemporary society are well known, as specific studies on this topic have been carried out since the 1970s (Rusconi, 1981). In practice they are a never-ending mix of negotiations and competition, collisions and cooperation about any issue, the political legitimacy of *any* (local, regional, national, trans- and supranational) political actor included; in theory (explicitly recalling Schumpeter's school of thought) they form an ideal, never-ending, 'zero-sum' socio-economic-political dynamics, enabling the consolidation of the 'ruler of the game', that is, of EU institutions. Hence, it is theoretically assumed that, by virtue of the (vertical and horizontal) institutionalization of the subsidiarity principle, the necessary persistence of conditions of diversity and asymmetry could be a veritable resource giving rise to 'converging advancements-through-emulative rivalries', or 'competing paths for mutual learning-through-differential achievements', which, in their turn, could advance successful entrepreneurial public/private joint ventures and establish leading territorial enclaves of creativity and excellence. In other words, it is assumed that a systematic enforcement of the same principle excludes a priori the possibility of achieving the opposite outcome, that is, that models of 'multi-level structures', 'differential speeds', 'individual interests' and so on could lead in the end to a 'disintegration-by-differentiation' of the same European Union.

Unfortunately, however, all that glitters is not always gold. In our case, plausibility of the adoption of the subsidiarity principle, either at political or normative level, has already been shown to be seriously problematic and questionable (Amato, 2005). In this respect, it is necessary to consider how far European legal professions could technically and cognitively handle their culture, expertise and commitment *vis-à-vis* a constitutional model that, by implying a differentiated and flexible integration, aims, by definition, to keep steady and alive: (1) a legal functioning; (2) a political legitimation; and (3) a social acceptance of the European Union not as a united and consistent 'legal space' but, on the contrary, as an internally fragmented and fluctuating legal, political and social body/agent (Rolla, 2007).

After all, how can one ignore the fact that the formal-official acknowledgement within the EU *acquis*, of the principles of diversity and flexibility as leading EU guidelines since the Maastricht Treaty (that is, since both globalization and the EU enlargement) shows that the ideal of EU integration, as an expression of potential legal harmonization, social cohesion, economic fairness and so on, has been substantially relinquished at EU governance level? Many examples of such a relinquishment can be mentioned here: the space of EU public order (unequal treatment of freedom, security and justice issues); the EU monetary system (opting out for Denmark and the UK); and the field of fundamental rights (the Nice Charter's degrees of exemption for the UK and Poland). Altogether, these diversified arrangements are now notoriously leading to detrimental consequences for the EU itself, as well as for individual EU member states, as they allow, by and large, various forms of 'social dumping' within and among the same states. In this respect the (deafening) silence of the last version of the constitutional project (the Lisbon Treaty) about the declaration of EU universal values is highly significant. A cluster of EU values were officially proclaimed universal on the occasion of the Laecken Declaration. Yet their 'universality' was soon thrown into doubt, as, soon after the declaration, the EU recognized the 'exit clause' option for any EU member state from the Union in case of its rejection.

In summing up, one might ask another question. If one of the major final outcomes of the EU enlargement so far is to nurture a 'transition' towards a multi-level asymmetric constitutionalism, which, while somehow curtailing traditional constitutional sovereignty of EU member states, opens the way to a highly unsettled legal scenario, what sort of '*nomic*', that is, regulatory, bordering/ordering, function can be ascribed to European legal professions?

This question would not be so extraordinarily relevant if it did not correspond to an additional epochal trend that has not yet been mentioned, but that cannot be ignored: that is, that in the course of economic globalization and EU enlargement, traditional structural and functional patterns of positive state-law models have been, first, flanked, and then openly challenged, by other, radically different systems of legal production and cognition. In turn, radically new legal systems, often based on an asymmetrical, asynchronous co-variance of different sources, emerged. Given the new contours of contemporary legal pluralism, some legal scholars wonder whether, for example, globalization is a legally regulated or a regulating social process or not; while other scholars raise the everlasting problem of the conceptual definition of the 'identity' and 'consistency' of the law as such, or proclaim that it is fruitless to search for legal unity in a general context of legal fragmentation of the same law. The possibility of having to deal with a veritable 'self-deconstruction of Law's hierarchy' (Teubner, 1997) cannot be excluded.

Looking at this academic debate, it turns out that what is under discussion in the final instance is not only the questionable search for a new definition of the whole legal domain, but also, and above all, the practical attempt to somehow reframe the 'state-of-the-art' legal professions, when both their professional jurisdictions and know-how have been fragmented and destabilized.

This being so, it should come as no surprise to note that, in order to counteract powerful international agencies (such as OECD, FMI, Davos Wef and so on) making claims for the full de-regulation of the legal services market, both the Eastern and Western European legal professions are now trying to find out a common entente to counter the dismantling of their guild systems and to restore their social and legal status as veritable wardens and interpreters of the law(s)-in-action (see, for example the 'Declaration of European Intellectual Professions', approved in Madrid in 2005 by all European Bar Associations and Colleges) as a first move towards a new structural and functional identitary model that is now epitomized by the notion of 'post-national intellectuals' (Olgiati, 2009a).

The EU 'Democratic Deficit' and the 'Question of Post-national EU Intellectuals'

The fact that EU institutions strategically promoted a formal-official policy leading to the EU's transition towards its own 'constitutionalization', while enduring the impact of US-driven economic globalization and performing the eastward enlargement, is a historical event that can be defined as an outstanding example of 'structural rupture', fostered by either an 'internal dynamic' or a 'self- transformation' process, and operatively carried out in terms of 'reflexive modernization' in order to bypass the limits of the socio-legal constraints and political-cultural discourses of the 'first Modernity' and gain the opportunities offered by the 'second stage of Modernity' (Beck and Grande, 2006).

If so, one might wonder what sort of normative 'reflexivity' qualified and qualifies such a transition. Paradoxically, an answer to this question can be found only by taking seriously the aggravation of the ongoing problem of the EU 'democratic deficit' during and after the enforcement of the 'transitional' Copenhagen parameters. In fact, it is just such a disquieting issue that helps to explain the political content of that part of the Nice Treaty known as the ‘Charter of Human Rights and Fundamental Freedoms’, now included as a legal text of ‘constitutional’ value in the Lisbon Treaty.

As we know, the Nice Charter document certifies the degree of ‘reflexivity’ – the technical subtlety and ideological refinement – which EU institutions were able to sort out to deal with the management of the variety of ‘transitions’ occurring in the last decades and the prospective outcomes they implied. To explain the point, let us just consider the exemplary case of both Eastern and Western European legal professions.

As has been mentioned already, during and after the ‘transitions’, European legal professions have been confronted not only with the problematic accomplishment of their main professional mandate (that is, their bordering/ordering function), but also with the attempt to dismantle their professional guilds. These general issues are matched with other items such as those raised by the EU Directives on ‘Services, Bids and Goods Supply’, ‘Mutual Recognition of Qualifications’, ‘Services’ Internal Market’ and so on. Interestingly, all these Directives state the necessity: (1) to distinguish the guidelines and models typical of intellectual professions to which there is professional access ruled by state examinations, from the guidelines and models of any other intellectual profession or occupation; (2) to redefine all guidelines and models in relation to each class, sector, type and matter of each professional fieldwork; and all this (3) in accordance with fundamental EU legal values and principles as outlined in the Nice Charter (Alpa, 2005).

In so far as all of the above is based on the distinction between intellectual and non-intellectual professions and must normatively fit with the Nice Charter, it recalls in turn an additional EU institutional strategy specifically devoted to speeding up the entanglement of Eastern and Western European professionalism: the so-called EU ‘Bologna process’. Significantly, within this process, the Single European Higher Education Space was officially set up to promote scientific research and professional knowledge and know-how, but also as a way of facing fierce international competition and reducing, at the same time, either the pre-existing EU ‘democratic deficit’ or the ‘democratic deficit’ of Eastern European countries.

As soon as this Space began to run, the EU enforced a highly specific, institutional coupling between European science production and EU governance policy, in order to establish a visible and solid EU-organic power-knowledge nexus (CEC, 2000). More precisely, in 2001 (the year in which the Nice Treaty was signed), the Commission of the European Community officially outlined in its White Book on European Governance a new concept of science and a new concept of governance: the concept of European science as a ‘policy-related science’ and the concept of EU governance as the institutional outcome (or, better, a political synthesis) of a sort of ‘social contract’ between European science and European society (CEC, 2001). Accordingly, European higher knowledge since then has stopped being conceived in the traditional sense, that is, according to the scientific, ‘cultural’ meaning of the term, being defined as a veritable ‘science devoted to public issues', for its premises, results, means and so on, as well as its agents or 'carriers'. In other words, learned professions are called to be committed to and accountable for the kinds of performances, plans, activities and so on that European society (individuals and organizations) is entitled to carry on within the constitutional framework of EU governance.

Interestingly, such a 'knowledge-based transition' – otherwise conceptualized as 'epistemic drift' – is strictly related to the innovative legal principles that were firstly assessed by the creative activism of the European Court of Justice and then codified in the Nice Charter. Therefore reference to the letter and spirit of this Charter is now absolutely necessary to fully understand the new 'legal rationale' not only of European higher studies and research, but also of the knowledge and know-how that all European learned professions are meant to accomplish in Europe today.

By signing the Nice Charter, EU institutions proclaimed the *ontological* equalization of all rights and freedoms that the ECJ recognized as a constitutive part of the so-called 'common European legal tradition'. In turn, such a conceptual move has been made possible by virtue of the proclamation of the new legal principle of the *axiological* indivisibility of all the values contained in the same tradition. Besides, the Charter states that (1) techno-scientific achievements; (2) economic activity; and (3) social dynamics are veritable socio-legal sources of the EU legal order as a whole, and therefore also official sources of cognition and interpretation for any sort of EU decision-making (Olgiati, 2005b; 2008a).

As a result of such an extraordinary legal conceptualization, the Charter now includes a number of rights and freedoms that were previously assessed in different European legal systems, according to different, country-specific space-time conditions by different local socio-political forces, according to different values and interests. Nevertheless, they are all now recognized as having the same value, being indivisibly equal as fundamentals of the EU legal order. This means, for example, that freedoms such as economic competition and rights such as human solidarity are not detachable, but have the same fundamental importance for EU governance. Given the above technicalities, it follows that any actor, field, performance or structure (professions included) cannot but be directly concerned. For example, within any professional realm, programmes for economic competition only, based or not based solely on market freedom, can no longer be pursued, for they clash with the EU values of human solidarity, social security and so on.

The above example is not an abstract teaching case for law students. In March 2003, during a conference on European professional services, the EU Commissioner for Competition stressed, as he was used to doing, the need for a de-regulation policy in legal services to promote market competition. To that end, he relied on data provided by OCSE research. Two months later, in May 2003, the CCBE, the Consulting Committee of European Bars, formally contested the method and merit of the OCSE research as well as the Commissioner's argument in so far as neither considered all professional mandates and services to be covered by the human and social rights of the Nice Charter (Alpa, 2005). In short, under the rule of the Nice Charter, no professional issue can be conceived in formal or official legal terms from a single one-dimensional perspective (that is, market imperatives) anymore, but must be evaluated from the point of view of the irrepressible relational entanglement involving knowledge production, economic growth, institutional framework and social dynamics.

An outstanding example of this is the case that occurred in February 2006, concerning the so-called 'Bolkestein EU Directive' aimed at assessing the fundamental freedom of both semi-professional and professional services throughout Europe. The content of the so-called 'Polish plumber Directive' has been somewhat revised not only because of strong socio-political pressures from Western European countries, but also owing to the existence of an *overall* set of fundamental rights and freedoms in the Nice Treaty.[2] This being so, it follows that neither the status nor missions of learned professions and professionalism in the enlarged Europe (legal professions included) are as they were before. In particular, it is now already apparent that, by virtue of the *de jure* ontological equalization and axiological indivisibility of *de facto* radically diverging and incoherent rights and freedoms, the European Court of Justice gained the power to 'balance' the enforcement according to its autocratic and discretional legal decision-making: a fact that could certainly give rise, in turn, to cultural and political disputes, within and outside EU institutions, about the specific nature of the professional values and interests involved.

In any case, professions in general, but learned professions in particular, will have to face the challenge of assessing their technical specificity, cultural identity and socio-institutional loyalty in a totally new culturally plausible and politically adequate manner. In fact, owing to the above-mentioned 'conceptual drift' (as a constitutive part of the wider EU 'reflexive modernization'), traditional, self-referential professional values and interests are no longer socially and legally self-evident.

This means that a new professional discourse based on newly-created assertions is required. Clearly, the issue is not a matter of mere semantic make-up. What is needed, from now on, is the ability to state nothing less than a new Foucaultian 'authority of speech' compatible with the new complexity of the whole EU socio-legal dynamics: that is to say, to be able to enforce a new systematic professional *doxa*. The 'transition' towards a veritable 'post-national question of *organic* intellectuals' is now on the scientific agenda of EU governance (Olgiati, 2008).

2 It is interesting here to note that the metaphor of the 'plumber' as a mere service provider has been used by William Twining in his paper on English lawyers' education, 'Pericles and the plumber: Prolegomena to a working theory for lawyers' education', *The Law Quarterly Review*, 83 (1967).

Concluding Remarks: The Problematic Professional Bordering/Ordering Function and the Search for a Neo-Gothic EU Legal Order

As we have seen, the process and policy of EU eastward enlargement, set in motion by epochal global-local mainstreams, changed the original EU 'integration' strategy to such an extent as to foster the rise of an extraordinary socio-legal 'positive entropy' (a sort of dis-reintegration), which, in turn, called for a new, broader EU strategic design: that of an EU epitomized by its 'transition' towards a 'reflexive modernization' of constitutional nature.

In general terms, one can say that the 'cybernetic' potential of EU constitutional process and policy led far more to a growing socio-legal complexity than to a 'sustainable' normative order. At the same time, one can also add that, owing to the increasing country-specific socio-legal differentiation, EU institutions are now trying to empower a variety of top-down 'flexsecurity' arrangements, rather than making use of an isonomic constitutional model. Certainly, the EU has abandoned a great deal of that idealistic, formalistic and positivist legal culture that it had wished to enforce at the time of the Rome Treaty: the 'operational transition' to the subsidiarity principle is now supported by the 'conceptual transition' of the Nice Charter.

If the above is true – as empirical evidence shows – it follows that, owing to the official recognition of the subsidiarity principle within the EU *aquis communautaire,* additional forms of legal pluralism could spread from now on. It is foreseeable, therefore, that the search for a new political and normative equilibrium of continental dimensions will *not* be abandoned. However, its features call to mind – *mutatis mutandis,* of course – those features typical of a veritable neo-Gothic legal equilibrium, such as that envisaged, in particular, after the Westphalia Treaty up to the time of the French Revolution.

This statement should not come as a shock. Paradoxically enough, in spite of what official narratives suggest, the subsidiarity principle structurally and functionally implies, by definition, a multi-level socio-legal pluralism (Olgiati, 2007a; 2009b). Both elements can work together easily and fruitfully (Delmas-Marty, 2009), just as occurred for centuries at a European continental level during *Ancien Régime*. On the other hand, if EU institutions reject and abandon the principle, they will lose any credibility, as well as the possibility of ruling both social differentiation and legal complexity.

Having said this, it is worth drawing attention, in conclusion, to a highly significant symbolic historical legal experience: the theory and practice of the pre-modern European constitutional tradition of the Holy Roman Empire.

Leafing through the work of Samuel Pufendorf, *De Statu Imperii Germanici* (published under the pseudonym Severinus de Mozambano in 1668), it is surprising to note how topical are the problems that were on the agenda at that time: what sort of sovereignty and character should be chosen for either a unitary or a federal state, or a federation of states; what sort of power should be limited and which kind of rights should prevail (those of the people or of the ruler) in the case of incorporations or partitions; which kinds of interests and values should be guaranteed; what sort of historical conditions could be relevant as far as the validity or the efficacy of the legal order is concerned and so on. In short, what sorts of historically determined 'bodily irregularities' should be taken into consideration when raising a solid strategic vision that will enable one to assess a real European '*Ratio Status*' (Severinus de Mozambano, 1668)?

As one can see, these few accounts suffice to explain how and why the centuries-old legal experience of the Holy Roman Empire after the Munster and Osnabruck Treaties, particularly that of the so-called *Reichspublizistik*, should be reconsidered – according to contemporary standards, of course – not only to face past and present problematic issues, but also to elaborate a more refined reference model that could guarantee the protection of a future necessary European equilibrium.

References

Alpa, G., 'Disciplina della concorrenza e regolamentazione delle professioni liberali. La prospettiva economica', in Ce.R.D.E.F. (a cura di), *Rivista della Scuola Superiore dell'Economia e delle Finanze* (2005), n. 5, 49–59.

Amato, G., *Conclusioni del Congresso dell'Associazione Italiana dei Costituzionalisti* (2005). Available online at www.associazionedeicostituzionalisti.it [accessed 15 April 2010].

Bandelj, N., 'Particularizing the global: Reception of foreign direct investments in Slovenia', *Current Sociology*, 51/3–4 (2003), 375–92.

Barcellona, M., 'L'interventismo europeo e la sovranità del mercato', in P. Barcellona (a cura di), *La società europea. Identità, simboli, politiche* (Torino: Giappichelli Ed., 2009), 45–67.

Bartole, S., *Riforme costituzionali nell'Europa centro-orientale. Da satelliti comunisti a democrazie sovrane* (Bologna: Il Mulino, 1993).

Bassanini, F. and G. Tiberi, (a cura di), *Le nuove istituzioni europee. Commento al Trattato di Lisbona* (Bologna: Il Mulino, 2008).

Beck, U. and E. Grande, *L'Europa Cosmopolita. Società e politica nella seconda modernità* (Rome: Carocci, 2006).

Blokker, P., Multiple democracies: Political cultures and democratic variety in post-enlargment Europe, *Contemporary Politics*, 14/2 (2008), 161–78.

Castorina, E., *Profili attuali e prospettive di diritto costituzionale europeo* (Torino: Giappichelli, 2007).

CEC, Commission of the European Communities (2001), *European Governance: A White Paper*. Available online at http://europa.eu.int/comm. [accessed 15 April 2010].

CEC, Commission of the European Communities (2000), *Governance and Expertise*. Available online at <http://governance.jrc.it> [accessed 13 April 2010].

Chalmers, D., 'Post-nationalism and the quest for constitutional substitutes', *Journal of Law and Society*, 27/1 (2000), 178–217.

Coman, R. and J.M. de Waele (eds), *Judicial Reforms in Central and Eastern European Countries* (Bruges: Editions Vanden Broele, 2007).

Council of Bars and Law Societies of the EC, *Compendium of Legal Practice for Lawyers in Central and Eastern Europe* (Strasburg: Council of Europe, 1998).

Council of Europe Legal Co-Operation with Central and Eastern Europe Countries, *The role and Responsibilities of the Lawyer in a Society in Transition Proceedings* (Strasbourg: Council of Europe, 1999).

Czarnota, A., M. Krygier and W. Sadurski (eds), *Rethinking the Rule of Law after Communism* (Budapest and New York: Central European University Press, 2005).

Delmas-Marty, M., *Ordering Pluralism: A Conceptual Framework for Understanding the Transnational Legal World* (Oxford: Hart Publishing, 2009).

Delors, J., *Subsidiaritè: defi du changement* (Maastricht: Institute Europèen d'Administration Publique (EIPA), 1991).

Dezalay, Y., 'Technological warfare: The battle to control the mergers and acquisitions market in Europe', in Y. Dezalay and D. Sugarman (eds), *Professional Competition and Professional Power: Lawyers, Accountants and the Social Construction of Markets* (London: Routledge, 1995), 77–103.

Dezalay, Y. and B. Garth, 'Re-structuring states by exporting law: American law firms and the genesis of a European legal market', in H. Petersen, A.L. Kjaer, H. Krunke and M.R. Madsen (eds) *Paradoxes of European Legal Integration* (Aldershot: Ashgate, 2008), 75–88.

Dupré, C., *Importing the Law in Post-Communist Transitions: The Hungarian Constitutional Court and the Right to Human Dignity* (Oxford: Hart Publishing, 2003).

EU Accession Monitoring Program (ed.), *Monitoring EU Accession Process: Judicial Capacity* (Budapest and New York: Open Society Institute, 2002).

Flood, J., 'The vultures fly east: The creation and globalization of the distressed debt market', in D. Nelken and J. Feest (eds), *Adapting Legal Cultures* (Oxford: Hart Publishing, 2001), 257–78.

Friedman, L.M., 'Lawyers in cross-cultural perspective', in R. Abel and P.S.C. Lewis (eds), *Lawyers in Society*, 3 (1989), 1–26.

Fuszara, M. and J. Kurcewski, 'Disputes and courts in Poland 25 years later', in *Societas/Communitas, Journal of Institute of Applied Sciences, University of Warsaw*, 1/7 (2009), 101–33.

Galina, N., *Political Elites in East central Europe: Paving the Way for 'Negative Europeanization'?* (Opladen: Budrich UniPress, 2008).

Galligan, D.J. and M. Kurkchiyan (eds), *Law and Informal Practices: The Post-Communist Experience* (Oxford: Oxford University Press, 2003).

Kadar, A. (ed.), *Police in Transition: Essays on the Police Forces in Transition Countries* (Budapest and New York: Central European University Press, 2001).

Kotkin, S. and A. Sajó (eds), *Political Corruption in Transition: A Skeptic's Handbook* (Budapest and New York: Central European University Press, 2002).

Kymlika, W., 'The moral foundations and geopolitical functions of international minority rights: A European case study', in M. Escamilla and M. Saavedra (eds), *Anales de la Catedra Francisco Suarez, IVR 2005, Law and Society in a Global Society* (Granada: University of Granada, 2005), 199–230.

Kymlika, W. and M. Opalski (eds), *Can Liberal Pluralism Be Exported? Western Political Theory and Ethic Relations in Eastern Europe* (Oxford: Oxford University Press, 2001).

Krygier, M. and A. Czarnota (eds), *The Rule of Law After Communism: Problems and Prospects in East-Central Europe* (Aldershot: Dartmouth, 1999)

Legrand, P., 'What "Legal Transplant"?', in D. Nelken and J. Feest (eds), *Adapting Legal Cultures* (Oxford: Hart Publishing, 2001), 55–70.

Luhman, N., *Gesellschaftsstruktur und Semantik* (Frankfurt am Main: Suhrkamp Verlag, 1980).

———*Rechtssoziologie* (Hamburg: Suhrkamp Verlag, 1972).

Madsen, M.R., 'Introduction: An ever closer union – An ever larger market: Lawyers and the transnational construction of European institutions and markets', in H. Petersen, A.L. Kjaeder, H. Krunke and M.R. Madsen (eds), *Paradoxes of European Legal Integration* (Bodmin: Ashgate, MPG Books, 2008), 67–73.

Matyk, S. et al. (eds), (2007), *Notaries in Europe: Growing Fields of Competence. Austria, Croatia, Czech Republic, Hungary, Slovenia*, Neuer Wissenschaftlicher Verlag, Wien-Graz.

Meineke, F., *Die idée der Staatrason in der Neure Geschichte* (Munchen-Berlin: Oldenbourg, 1924).

Offe, C., *Varieties of East European and East German Experience* (Cambridge, MA: MIT Press, 1997).

Olgiati, V., 'Potentials and obstacles in the promotion of higher knowledge in the European area: The post-national question of European intellectuals', in J. Langer, J. Pavicic and N. Alfirevic (eds), *Knowledge Region: The Alps-Adriatic Challenges*, vol. I, *General Perspective* (Frankfurt-am-Main: P. Lang GmbH, 2009a), 35–57.

———'The notion of legal pluralism: A theoretical assessment', *Societas/ Communitas*. Journal of the Institute of Applied Social Sciences, University of Warsaw, 1/7 (2009b), 173–97.

———'The European learned professions and the EU higher education projects', *European Societies*, 10/4 (2008a), 545–64.

———'On women lawyers' voice in Europe: Scenarios for a legal education agenda', European Women Lawyers Association 8th Congress, 'Being Heard in the Future Europe', 4–5 July 2008 (London: (in print), 2008b).

———'Le trasformazioni costituzionali del professionalismo giuridico europeo', in R. Roselli (a cura di), *Osservatorio sulla formazione giuridica* (Napoli: ESI, 2007a), 53–80.

———'The preamble of the treaty that institutes a constitution for Europe: A question of virtual reality', in P. Cserne, I.H. Szilagy, M. Konkzol, M. Pasksy,

P. Takacs and S. Tattay (eds), *Theatrum Legale Mundi: Symbola Cs Varga Oblate* (Biblioteca Juridica, Liber Amicorum 24) (Budapest: Societas Sancti Stephani, Domus Editoria S.Sedis Apostolicae, 2007b), 321–37.

———'Le condizioni epistemiche del ritorno al principio di sussidiarietà', in C. Magnani (a cura di), *Beni pubblici e servizi sociali in tempi di susssidiarietà* (Torino: Giappichelli, 2007c), 150–72.

———'The eastern EU enlargement and the Janus-headed nature of the constitutional treaty', in W. Sadurski, A. Czarnota and M. Krygier (eds), *Spreading Democracy and the Rule of Law? Implications of EU Enlargement for the Rule of Law, Democracy and Constitutionalism in Post-Communist Legal Orders* (Dordrecht: Springer, 2006), 51–71.

———'The EU charter of fundamental rights. Text and context to the rise of "public interest" EU-oriented European lawyers', *International Journal of the Legal Profession*, 9/3 (2005), 235–50.

———'Geo-political constructionism: The challenge of Europe to comparative sociology of professions', in L. Svensson and J. Evetts (eds), *Comparative Studies of Continental and Anglo-American Professions*, Department of Sociology Research Report n. 129 (Goteborg: Goteborg University, 2003), 55–77.

———'Vers une refonte des communautés èpistemiques en Europe', in L. Parini (dir.), *Etats et Mondialization: strategies et roles* (Paris: L'Harmattan, 2001), 191–223.

———'Identidad y papel de la abogacia en Europa', *Revista de Ciencia Politica: Estudios politicos*, n. 25 (Mexico City: UNAM, 2000), 183–97.

———'The policy of legal higher education in Europe', in F. Cownie (ed.), *The Law School: Global Issues, Local Problems* (Aldershot: Ashgate, 1999), 163–94.

———'Risk, professions and the claim for human rights', in V. Olgiati, L.H. Horzak and M. Saks (eds), *Professions: Identity and Order in Comparative Perspective*, Onati Papers (IISL-Onati 1998), 379–98.

———*Le professioni giuridiche in Europa. Politiche del diritto e dinamiche sociali* (Urbino: E. Quatroventi, 1996).

———'Process and policy of legal professionalization in Europe: The de-construction of a normative order', in Y. Dezalay and D. Sugarman (eds), *Professional Competition and Professional Power: Lawyers, Accountants and the Social Construction of Markets* (London and New York: Routledge, 1995), 170–204.

Pernice, I., 'Multilevel constitutionalism', *European Law Review*, 5 (2002), 51–529.

Petersen, H., A.L. Kjaer, H. Krunke and M.R. Madsen (eds), *Paradoxes of European Legal Integration* (Aldershot: Ashgate, 2008).

Piana, D., *Judicial Accountabilities in New Europe: From Rule of Law to Quality of Justice* (Aldershot: Ashgate, 2010).

Poplawska, E., 'The new constitutional principle of subsidiarity and "the diminishing state" in Poland', *Journal of Constitutional Law in Eastern and Central Europe*, 9/1 (2002), 51–95.

Přibáň, J. *Dissidents of Law: On the Velvet Revolutions, Legitimations, Fictions of Legality and Contemporary Version of the Social Contract* (Aldershot: Dartmouth, 2002).

Přibáň, J. and J. Young (eds), *The Rule of Law in Central Europe. The Reconstruction of Legality, Constitutionalism and Civil Society in the Post-Communist Countries* (Aldershot: Ashgate, 1999).

Přibáň, J., P. Roberts and J. Young (eds), *Systems of Justice in Transition: Central European Experiences Since 1989* (Aldershot: Ashgate, 2003).

Raz, J., *The Morality of Freedom*, (Oxford: Clarendon Press, 1989).

Rebuffa, G., *Costituzioni e Costituzionalismi* (Torino: Giappichelli, 1990).

Rechberger, W.H. and E.O. Albert (eds), *Notarbild in Mitteleuropa* (Wien: Neuer Wissenschaftlicher Verlag, 2003).

Rolla, G., 'Lo sviluppo del regionalismo asimmetrico e il principio di autonomia nei nuovi sistemi costituzionali: un approccio di diritto comparato', *Quaderni Regionali*, 1–2 (2007), 387–99.

Rusconi, G., 'Scambio politico', *Laboratorio Politico*, n.2 (Torino: Einaudi, 1981), 65–87.

Sadurski, W., *Postcommunist Constitutional Courts in Search of Political Legitimacy* (Fiesole: EUI, 2001).

——— 'Solange, Chapter 3rd: Constitutional Court in Central Europe – Democracy – European Union', EUI Working Papers LAW, n. 2006/40 (2006).

———*Rights Before Courts: A Study of Constitutional Courts in Postcommunist States of Central and Eastern Europe* (Dordrecht: Springer, 2005).

Sadurski, W. (ed.), *Constitutional Justice, East and West: Democratic Legitimacy and Constitutional Courts in Post-Communist Europe in a Comparative Perspective* (The Hague and New York: Kluwer Law International, 2002).

Sadurski, W., A. Czarnota and M. Krygier (eds), *Spreading Democracy and the Rule of Law? The Impact of EU Enlargement on the Rule of Law, Democracy and Constitutionalism in Post-Communist Legal Orders* (Dordrecht: Springer, 2006).

Sajó, A. and K. Lauer, *Western Rights? Post-Communist Applications* (The Hague and London: Kluwer Law International, 1996).

———'The role of lawyers in social change: Hungary', *Case Western Res. Journal International Law*, 25 (1993), 137–46.

Sarfatti Larson, M., 'The professions:Nomic functions and the end of modernity', in A. Febbrajo, D. Nelken and V. Olgiati (eds), *Social Processes and Patterns of Legal Control*, European Yearbook in the Sociology of Law (Milan: Giuffrè, 2000), 145–72.

———'The changing functions of lawyers in the liberal state: Reflections for comparative analysis', in R. Abel and P.S.C. Lewis (eds), *Lawyers in Society:*

Comparative Theories (Berkeley, CA: University of California Press, 1989), 427–77.

Severinus de Mozambano (alias S. Pufendorf), 'De statu imperii Germanici', *Klassiker der Politik*, vol. III (1870 [original 1668]).

Smilov, D. and J. Toplak (eds), *Political Finance and Corruption in Eastern Europe: The Transition Period* (Aldershot: Ashgate, 2007).

Suski, M., *Making a Constitution: The Outline of an Argument* (Abo: Abo Akademy Trikeri, 1995).

Sztompka, P., 'Trust and emerging democracy: Lessons from Poland', *International Sociology*, 11/1 (1996), 37–62.

Varga, C., *Transition? To Rule of Law? Constitutionalism and Transitional Justice Challenged in Central & Eastern Europe* (Pomaz: Krater, 2008).

Voigt, S. and H.-J. Wagner (eds), *Constitutions, Markets and Law: Recent Experiences in Transition Economies* (Cheltenham and Northampton, MA: Edward Elgar, 2002).

Selected International Bibliography 1989–2009

Edited by Stefania Porfiri
Librarian at the University of Macerata, Italy

Summary

Preliminary Note

This is a select bibliography of the material published about the subjects of the transition to democracy and the entry of the CEE countries into the European Union. The first criterion of selection was the language of the publications. The books chosen were principally those written in the four main European languages: English, German, French and Spanish.

The bibliographic records are organized in conformity with the scheme of *Dewey Decimal Classification* (*DDC*), 22nd edition. The opening summary shows the numerical classes with their description and the page where it is possible to find the related titles of the books.

Some subjects, like human rights, are represented by more than one class (according to the DDC indications).

Within each class, the records are organized in chronological reverse order and, within each year of publication, in alphabetic order of the author's name.

Catalogue

I. 302.2309437 – Media (Means of communication)

[2009], Imre, Anikó, *Identity Games. Globalization and the Transformation of Media Cultures in the New Europe*. Cambridge, MA: MIT Press.

[2008], Jakubowicz, Karol, and Miklós Sükösd (eds), *Finding the Right Place on the Map. Central and Eastern European Media Change in a Global Perspective*. Bristol: Intellect.

[2007], Bayer, József, and Jody Jensen (eds), *From Transition to Globalization. New Challenges for Politics, the Media and Society*. Budapest: MTA Politikai Tudományok Intézete.

[2007], Jakubowicz, Karol, *Rude Awakening. Social and Media Change in Central and Eastern Europe*. Cresskill, NJ: Hampton Press.

[2006], Coman, Mihai, and Peter Gross, *Media and Journalism in Romania*. Berlin: Vistas.

[2006], Huber, Silvia, *Media Markets in Central and Eastern Europe. An Analysis on Media Ownership in Bulgaria, Czech Republic, Estonia, Hungary, Latvia, Lithuania, Poland, Romania, Slovakia and Slovenia*. Wien: Lit; London: distrib. in the UK by Global; Piscataway, NJ: distrib. in North America by Transaction Publ.

[2006], Ramet, Sabrina P., and Danica Fink-Hafner (eds), *Democratic Transition in Slovenia. Value Transformation, Education and Media*. College Station, TX: Texas A&M University Press.

[2005], Szilágyi, Zsófia, *Media Reform in Post-Communist Europe. Case Studies of Hungary, Ukraine and Kosovo*. San Domenico di Fiesole, FI: European University Institute.

[2004], Berry, David, *The Romanian Mass Media and Cultural Development*. Aldershot, Hampshire and Burlington, VT: Ashgate.

[2004], Londo, Ilda et al., *Media Ownership and its Impact on Media Independence and Pluralism. [Albania, Bosnia and Herzegovina, Bulgaria, Croatia, Czech Republic, Estonia, Hungary, Kosovo, Latvia, Lithuania, Macedonia, Moldova, Montenegro, Poland, Romania, Serbia, Slovakia, Slovenia]*. Ljubljana: Peace Institute, Institute for Contemporary Social and Political Studies.

[2003], Huber, Silvia (ed.), *Medien in den neuen EU-Staaten Mittel- und Osteuropas. Inklusive Beitrittskandidat Türkei*. Krems: Donau-Univ. Krems.

[2003], Paletz, David L., and Karol Jakubowicz, *Business as Usual. Continuity and Change in Central and Eastern European Media*. Cresskill, NJ: Hampton Press.

[2003], Sükösd, Mikloś, and Péter Bajomi-Lázár (eds), *Reinventing Media. Media Policy Reform in East-Central Europe*. Budapest and New York: Central European University Press.

[2003], Spassov, Orlin, and Christo Todorov (eds), *New Media in Southeast Europe*. Sofia: Southeast European Media Centre.

[2002], Boskovska, Nada (ed.), *Wege der Kommunikation in der Geschichte Osteuropas*. Köln: Böhlau.

[2002], Gross, Peter, *Entangled Evolutions. The Media and Democratization in Eastern Europe*. Baltimore, MD: The Johns Hopkins University Press.

[2002], Tzankoff, Michaela, *Der Transformationsprozess in Bulgarien und die Entwicklung der postsozialistischen Medienlandschaft*. Münster and Hamburg: Lit.

[2001], Bajomi-Lázár, Péter, and István Hegedüs (eds), *Media and Politics. Conference Papers on the Interplay of Media and Politics*. Budapest: Új Mandátum.

[2001], Giles, Robert, Robert W. Snyder, and Lisa DeLisle (eds), *Reporting the Post-Communist Revolution*. New Brunswick, NJ and London: Transaction.

[2001], Gritti, Roberto, *Postcomunismo e media*. Roma: Meltemi.

[2001], Thomass, Barbara, and Michaela Tzankoff (eds), *Medien und Transformation in Osteuropa*. Wiesbaden: Westdeutscher Verl.

[2000], Milton, Andrew K., *The Rational Politician. Exploiting the Media in New Democracies*. Aldershot and Brookfield, VT: Ashgate.

[1999], Kaid, Linda Lee (ed.), *Television and Politics in Evolving European Democracies*. Commack, NY: Nova Science.

[1998], Graber, Doris, Denis McQuail, and Pippa Norris (eds), *The Politics of News. The News of Politics*. Washington, DC: CQ Press.

[1997], O'Neil, Patrick (ed.), *Post-Communism and the Media in Eastern Europe*. London and Portland, OR: Frank Cass.

[1996], Downing, John Derek Hall, *Internationalizing Media Theory. Transition, Power, Culture. Reflections on Mass Media in Russia, Poland and Hungary, 1980-95*. London: Sage.

[1996], Gross, Peter, *Mass Media in Revolution and National Development. The Romanian Laboratory*. Ames, IA: Iowa State University Press.

[1995], Casmir, Fred L. (ed.), *Communication in Eastern Europe. The Role of History, Culture and Media in Contemporary Conflicts*. Mahwah, NJ: L. Erlbaum.

[1995], Paletz, David L., Karol Jakubowicz, and Pavao Novosel (eds), *Glasnost and After. Media and Change in Central and Eastern Europe*. Cresskill, NJ: Hampton Press.

[1994], Goban-Klas, Tomasz, *The Orchestration of the Media. The Politics of Mass Communications in Communist Poland and the Aftermath*. Boulder, CO: Westview Press.

[1994], Splichal, Slavko, *Media beyond Socialism. Theory and Practice in East-Central Europe*. Boulder, CO: Westview Press.

[1992], Ecoistituto del Friuli-Venezia Giulia, Tra Stato e mercato. Seminario sull'informazione nell'Europa dell'Est. Atti del Convegno organizzato dall'Ecoistituto del Friuli-Venezia Giulia, Trieste, 30 novembre–1 dicembre 1990. Trieste: Ecoistituto del Friuli-Venezia Giulia.

[1989], Curry, Jane Leftwich, *Poland's Journalists. Professionalism and Politics*. Cambridge: Cambridge University Press.

II. 303.37209437 – Social processes. Belief systems and customs

[2008], Wöll, Alexander, and Harald Wydra (eds), *Democracy and Myth in Russia and Eastern Europe*. London and New York: Routledge.

[2005], Svašek, Maruska, *Postsocialism. Politics and Emotions in Central and Eastern Europe*. New York: Berghahn Books.

[2002], Czobor-Lupp, Mihaela, and J. Stefan Lupp (eds), *Moral, Legal and Political Values in Romanian Culture*. Washington, DC: Council for Research in Values and Philosophy.

[2002], Delsol, Chantal, Michel Maslowski, and Joanna Nowicki (eds); Pierre Chaunu (pref.), *Mythes et symbols politiques en Europe centrale*. Paris: Presses universitaires de France.

[1999], Golubović, Zagorka, and George F. McLean (eds), *Models of Identities in Postcommunist Societies*. Washington, DC: Council for Research in Values and Philosophy.

[1999], Makariev, Plamen, Andrew M. Blasko, and Asen Davidov (eds), *Creating Democratic Societies. Values and Norms*. Washington, DC: Council for Research in Values and Philosophy.

[1998], Tismaneanu, Vladimir, *Fantasies of Salvation. Democracy, Nationalism and Myth in Post-Communist Europe*. Princeton, NJ: Princeton University Press.

III. 303.483309437 – Social change. Communications

[2000], Banse, Gerhard, Christian J. Langenbach, and Peter Machleidt (eds), *Towards the Information Society. The Case of Central and Eastern European Countries*. Berlin and New York: Springer.

[2000], Lengel, Laura (ed.), *Culture and Technology in the New Europe. Civic Discourse in Transformation in Post-Communist Nations*. Stanford, CT: Ablex.

IV. 305.5209437 – Social classes. Upper class

[2008], Gallina, Nicole, *Political Elites in East Central Europe. Paving the Way for 'Negative Europeanisation'?* Opladen and Farmington Hills, MI: Budrich UniPress.

[2007], Digol, Diana, *Emerging Diplomatic Elites in Post-Communist Europe*, San Domenico di Fiesole, FI: European University Institute.

[2003], Eyal, Gil, *The Origins of Postcommunist Elites. From Prague Spring to the Breakup of Czechoslovakia*. Minneapolis, MN: University of Minnesota Press.

[2000], Higley, John, and Lengyel György (eds), *Elites after State Socialism. Theories and Analysis*. Lanham, MD: Rowman & Littlefield.

[1998], Higley, John, Jan Pakulski, and Włodzimierz Wesołowski (eds), *Postcommunist Elites and Democracy in Eastern Europe*. Basingstoke: Macmillan.

[1994], Institute of Economics (ed.), *Elites in Eastern Europe: Old and New*, Budapest: Hungarian Academy of Sciences.

[1993], Derlien, Hans-Ulrich, and George J. Szablowski (eds), *Regime Transitions, Elites, and Bureaucracies in Eastern Europe*. Cambridge, MA: Blackwell.

V. 305.55209437 – Social classes. Intelligentsia

[2006], Wachtel, Andrew, *Remaining Relevant after Communism. The Role of the Writer in Eastern Europe*. Chicago, IL: University of Chicago Press.

[2003], Falk, Barbara J., *The Dilemmas of Dissidence in East-Central Europe. Citizen Intellectuals and Philosopher Kings*. Budapest and New York: Central European University Press.

[2001], Congdon, Lee, *Seeing Red. Hungarian Intellectuals in Exile and the Challenge of Communism*. DeKalb, IL: Northern Illinois University Press.

[1999], Bozóki, András (ed.), *Intellectuals and Politics in Central Europe*. New York: Central European University Press.

[1999], Suny, Ronald Grigor, Michael D. Kennedy (eds), *Intellectuals and the Articulation of the Nation*. Ann Arbor, MI: University of Michigan Press.

[1993], Lüdke, Martin (ed.), *Die innere Grenze. Die Intellektuellen und die sozialen Veränderungen in Mittel- und Osteuropa*. Reinbek bei Hamburg: Rowohlt.

VI. 305.8009437 – Ethnic and national groups

[2008], Friberg, Erik et al., *Institutions for the Management of Ethnopolitical Conflict in Central and Eastern Europe*. Strasbourg: Council of Europe Publ.

[2008], Genov, Nikolai (ed.), *Interethnic Integration in Five European Societies*. Hamburg: Krämer.

[2008], Haslinger, Peter, K. Erik Franzen, Martin Schulze Wessel (eds), *Diskurse über Zwangsmigrationen in Zentraleuropa. Geschichtspolitik, Fachdebatten, literarisches und lokales Erinnern seit 1989*. München: Oldenbourg.

[2007], Jenne, Erin K., *Ethnic Bargaining. The Paradox of Minority Empowerment*. Ithaca, NY: Cornell University Press.

[2006], Kelley, Judith Green, *Ethnic Politics in Europe. The Power of Norms and Incentives*. Princeton, NJ: Princeton University Press.

[2006], Ladányi, János, *Patterns of Exclusion. Constructing Gypsy Ethnicity and the Making of an Underclass in Transitional Societies of Europe*. Boulder, CO: East European Monographs; New York: distrib. by Columbia University Press.

[2006], Rizman, Rudolf Martin, *Dall'autoritarismo alla democrazia attraverso l'indipendenza. Il caso sloveno*. Ravenna: Longo.

[2006], Vermeersch, Peter, *The Romani Movement. Minority Politics and Ethnic Mobilization in Contemporary Central Europe*. New York: Berghahn Books.

[2005], Barany, Zoltan, and Robert G. Moser (eds), *Ethnic Politics after Communism*. Ithaca, NY: Cornell University Press.

[2005], Kemény, István (ed.), Andrew Gane (transl.), *Roma of Hungary*. Boulder, CO: Social Science Monographs; Highland Lakes, NJ: Atlantic Research and Publications; New York: distrib. by Columbia University Press.

[2005], Roe, Paul, *Ethnic Violence and the Societal Security Dilemma*. London and New York: Routledge.

[2005], Tóth, Ágnes (ed.), Nora Arato (transl.), *National and Ethnic Minorities in Hungary, 1920–2001*. Boulder, CO: Social Science Monographs; Highland Lakes, NJ: Atlantic Research and Publications; New York: distrib. by Columbia University Press.

[2004], Neumann, Victor, *Conceptually Mystified. East-Central Europe Torn between Ethnicism and Recognition of Multiple Identities*. Bucharest: Encyclopedica Publishing House.

[2004], Szarka, László (ed.), *Hungary and the Hungarian Minorities. Trends in the Past and in our Times*. Boulder, CO: East European Monographs; New York: distrib. by Columbia University Press.

[2003], Eberhardt, Piotr; Jan Owsinski (transl.), *Ethnic Groups and Population Changes in Twentieth-Century Central-Eastern Europe. History, Data, and Analysis*. New York and London: M.E. Sharpe.

[2003], Jarab, Jan (ed.), *The Search for Effective Strategies against Racism. When to Educate, when to Legislate?* Background Paper. Geneva: Office of the UN High Commissioner for Human Rights.

[2003], Robotin, Monica, Levente Salat (eds), *A New Balance. Democracy and Minorities in Post-Communist Europe*. Budapest: Local Government and Public Service Reform Initiative, Open Society Institute.

[2002], Barany, Zoltan D., *The East European Gypsies. Regime Change, Marginality, and Ethnopolitics*. Cambridge and New York: Cambridge University Press.

[2002], Fowkes, Ben, *Ethnicity and Ethnic Conflict in the Post-Communist World*. Basingstoke and New York: Palgrave Macmillan.

[2002], Meinhof, Ulrike Hanna (ed.), *Living (with) Borders. Identity Discourses on East-West Borders in Europe*. Aldershot and Burlington, VT: Ashgate.

[2002], Pajnik, Mojka (ed.), *Xenophobia and Post-Socialism*. Ljubljana: Mirovni Institut.

[2002], Petersen, Roger Dale, *Understanding Ethnic Violence. Fear, Hatred, and Resentment in Twentieth-Century Eastern Europe*. Cambridge: Cambridge University Press.

[2001], Bíró, Anna-Mária, and Petra Kovács (eds), *Diversity in Action. Local Public Management of Multi-Ethnic Communities in Central and Eastern Europe*. Budapest: Local Government and Public Service Reform Initiative, Open Society Institute.

[2001], Guy, Will (ed.), *Between Past and Future. The Roma of Central and Eastern Europe*. Hatfield: University of Hertfordshire Press.

[2001], Inder Singh, Anita, *Democracy, Ethnic Diversity and Security in Post-Communist Europe*. Westport, CT and London: Praeger.

[2001], Kaufman, Stuart J., *Modern Hatreds. The Symbolic Politics of Ethnic War*. New York: Cornell University Press.

[2001], Kymlica, Will, and Magdalena Opalski (eds), *Can Liberal Pluralism Be Exported? Western Political Theory and Ethnic Relations in Eastern Europe*. New York: Oxford University Press.

[2001], Lord, Christopher, and Olga Strietska-Ilina (eds), *Parallel Cultures. Majority/Minority Relations in the Countries of the Former Eastern Bloc*. Aldershot and Burlington, VT: Ashgate.

[2001], Manssen, Gerrit, and Bogusław Banaszak (eds), *Minderheitenschutz in Mittel- und Osteuropa*. Frankfurt am Main and New York: P. Lang.

[2000], Mandelbaum, Michael (ed.), *The New European Diasporas. National Minorities and Conflict in Eastern Europe*. New York: Council on Foreign Relations Press.

[2000], Morison, John (ed.), *Ethnic and National Issues in Russian and East European History*. Fifth World Congress for Central and East European Studies, Warsaw, Poland, 1995. New York: St. Martin's Press.

[2000], Open Society Institute (ed.), *Racism in Central and Eastern Europe and Beyond. Origins, Responses, Strategies. Report*. Budapest: Open Society Institute.

[2000], Wolff, Stefan (ed.), *German Minorities in Europe. Etnic Diversity and Cultural Belonging*. New York: Berghahn Books.

[1999], Aklaev, Airat, *Democratization and Ethnic Peace. Patterns of Ethnopolitical Crisis Management in Post-Soviet Settings*. Aldershot and Burlington, VT: Ashgate.

[1999], Krasteva, Anna (ed.), *Communities and Identities in Bulgaria*. Ravenna: Longo.

[1999], Poppe, Edwin, *National and Ethnic Stereotypes in Central and Eastern Europe. A Study among Adolescents in Six Countries*. Amsterdam: Thela Thesis.

[1999], Wallace, Claire, *Xenophobia in Post-Communist Europe*. Glasgow: University of Strathclyde, Centre for the Study of Public Policy.

[1998], Hroch, Jaroslav, David Hollan, and George F. McLean (eds), *National, Cultural and Ethnic Identities. Harmony beyond Conflict*. Washington, DC: Council for Research in Values and Philosophy.

[1998], Taras, Ray (ed.), *National Identities and Ethnic Minorities in Eastern Europe*. Selected Papers from the Fifth World Congress of Central and East European Studies, Warsaw, 1995. Houndmills, Basingstoke: Macmillan.

[1997], Klinke, Andreas, Ortwin Renn, and Jean-Paul Lehners (eds), *Ethnic Conflicts and Civil Society. Proposal for a New Era in Eastern Europe*. Aldershot and Brookfield, VT: Ashgate.

[1997], Kürti, László, and Juliet Langman (eds), *Beyond Borders. Remaking Cultural Identities in the New East and Central Europe*. Boulder, CO: Westview Press.

[1996], Altermatt, Urs (ed.), *Nation, Ethnizität und Staat in Mitteleuropa*. Wien: Böhlau.

[1996], Brunner, Georg; Gabriele Schroers (transl.), *Nationality Problems and Minority Conflicts in Eastern Europe. Strategies for Europe*. Gütersloh: Bertelsmann Foundation.

[1996], Ekiert, Grzegorz, *The State against Society. Political Crises and their Aftermath in East Central Europe*. Princeton, NJ: Princeton University Press.

[1996], Held, Joseph (ed.), *Populism in Eastern Europe. Racism, Nationalism and Society*. Boulder, CO: East European Monographs.

[1996], Caplan, Richard, and John Feffer (eds), *Europe's New Nationalism. States and Minorities in Conflict*. New York: Oxford University Press.

[1993], Brunner, Georg, and Hans Lemberg (eds), *Volksgruppen in Ostmittel- und Südosteuropa*. Baden-Baden: Nomos.

[1993], Cuthbertson, Ian M., and Jane Leibowitz (eds); Joseph S. Nye, Jr. (foreword), *Minorities. The new Europe's Old Issue*. Prague and New York: Institute for EastWest Studies; Boulder, CO: distrib. by Westview Press.

[1993], Hermacora, Felix (ed.), *Volksgruppen im Spammungsfeld von Recht und Souveränität in Mittel- und Osteuropa*. Internationale Symposion am Institut für Staats- und Verwaltungsrecht der Universität Wien vom 13. bis 15 November 1991. Wien: Braumüller.

[1992], Bowers, Stephen R. (ed.), *Ethnic Politics in Eastern Europe*. London: Research Institute for the Study of Conflict and Terrorism.

[1992], Rupesinghe, Kumar, Peter G. King, and Olga Vorkunova (eds), *Ethnicity and Conflict in a Post-Communist World. The Soviet Union, Eastern Europe, and China*. Basingstoke: Macmillan.

VII. 306.209437 – Political institutions

[2008], Buzalka, Juraj, *Nation and Religion. The Politics of Commemorations in South-East Poland*. Münster: Lit; London: Global (distrib.).

[2008], Norton, Philip, David M. Olson (eds), *Post-Communist and Post-Soviet Parliaments. The Initial Decade*. London and New York: Routledge.

[2007], Bozóki, András, *Ars Politica*. Budapest: Jószöveg.

[2007], Gaber, Rusanna, *Politische Gemeinschaft in Deutschland und Polen. Zum Einfluss der Geschichte auf die politische Kultur*. Wiesbaden: VS Verlag für Sozialwissenchaften.

[2007], Gherghina, Sergiu, *Institutional Design and Party Development in Post-Communist States. The Key-Role of National Parliaments*. Iaşi: Lumen.

[2006], Dimitrov, Vesselin, Klaus H. Goetz, and Hellmut Wollman; with contributions by Radoslaw Zubek, and Martin Brusis, *Governing after Communism. Institutions and Policymaking*. Lanham, MD: Rowman & Littlefield.

[2006], Gherghina, Sergiu, *The Relationship between the Strength of Parliament and Party Development in Post-Communist Countries*. Budapest: CEU, Budapest College.

[2006], Kiiver, Philipp (ed.), *National and Regional Parliaments in the European Constitutional Order*. Gröningen: Europa Law Publ.

[2006], Meyer, Gerd (ed.), *Formal Institutions and Informal Politics in Central and Eastern Europe: Hungary, Poland, Russia and Ukraine*. Opladen and Farmington Hills, MI: Budrich.

[2006], Rindzevičiūtė, Eglė (ed.), *Re-Approaching East Central Europe. Old Region, New Institutions?*. Huddinge: Center for Baltic & East European Studies, Södertörns högskola.

[2006], Seleny, Anna, *The Political Economy of State-Society Relations in Hungary and Poland. From Communism to the European Union*. Cambridge and New York: Cambridge University Press.

[2005], Ágh, Attila, *Institutional Design and Regional Capacity-Building in the Post-Communist Period*. Budapest: Hungarian Centre for Democracy Studies.

[2005], Whitefield, Stephen (ed.), *Political Culture and Post-Communism*. New York: Palgrave Macmillan; Oxford: in association with St. Anthony's College.

[2004], Kornai, János, and Susan Rose-Ackerman (eds), *Building a Trustworthy State in Post-Socialist Transition*. New York: Palgrave Macmillan.

[2004], Roger, Antoine (ed.), *Le 'champ politique' dans les sociétés post-communistes. Une notion en debat*. Bruxelles: Institut de Sociologie, Université libre de Bruxelles.

[2003], Campos, Nauro F., and Jan Fidrmuc (eds), *Political Economy of Transition and Development. Institutions, Politics and Policies*. Boston, MA, Dordrecht and London: Kluwer Academic.

[2003], Stan, Lavinia, *Leaders and Laggards. Governance, Civicness and Ethnicity in Post-Communist Romania*. Boulder, CO: East European Monographs; New York: distrib. by Columbia University Press.

[2002], Batt, Judy, and Kataryna Wolczuk (eds), *Region, State, and Identity in Central and Eastern Europe*. London and Portland, OR: Frank Cass.

[2002], Meier Dallach, Hans-Peter, and Jakob Juchler (eds), *Postsocialist Transformations and Civil Society in a Globalizing World*. Huntington, NY: Nova Science.

[2002], Pollack, Detlef et al., *Political Culture in Post-Communist Europe. Attitudes in New Democracies*. Aldershot and Burlington, VT: Ashgate.

[2000], Hinrichs, Karl, Herbert Kitsschelt, and Helmut Wiesenthal (eds), *Kontingenz und Krise. Institutionenpolitik in kapitalistischen und postsozialistischen Gesellschaften. Claus Offe zu seinem 60. Geburtstag*. Frankfurt am Main and New York: Campus.

[1999], Matthes, Claudia-Yvette, *Polen und Ungarn- Parlamente im Systemwechsel. Zur Bedeutung einer politischen Institution für die Konsolidierung neuer Demokratien*. Opladen: Leske + Budrich.

[1999], Millard, Frances, *Polish Politics and Society*. London: Routledge.

[1999], Nunberg, Barbara, *The State after Communism. Administrative Transitions in Central and Eastern Europe*. Washington, DC: The World Bank.

[1999], Widmayer, Ulrich, Andrea Gawrich, and Ute Becker, *Regierungssystem Zentral- und Osteuropas*. Opladen: Leske + Budrich.

[1998], Elster, Jon, Claus Offe, and Ulrich K. Preuss; with Frank Boenker, Ulrike Goeting, and Friedbert W. Rueb, *Institutional Design in Post-Communist Societies. Rebuilding the Ship at Sea*. Cambridge and New York: Cambridge University Press.

[1996], Norton, Philip, and David M. Olson (eds), *The New Parliaments of Central and Eastern Europe*. London: Frank Cass.

[1996], Plasser, Fritz, and Andreas Pribersky (eds), *Political Culture in East Central Europe*. Aldershot and Brookfield, VT: Avebury.

[1994], Offe, Claus, *Designing Institutions in East European Transitions*. Wien: Institut für höhere Studien.

[1993], Meyer, Gerd (ed.), *Die politischen Kulturen Ostmitteleuropas im Umbruch – The Political Cultures of Eastern Central Europe in Transition*. Tübingen, etc.: Francke.

[1993], Whitefield, Stephen (ed.), *The New Institutions Architecture of Eastern Europe*. Basingstoke: Macmillan.

[1992], Kéri, László, *Between Two Systems. Seven Studies on the Hungarian Political Changes*. Budapest: MTA Politikai Tudományok Intézete.

[1989], Meyer, Gerd, and Franciszek Ryszka (eds), *Die Politische Kultur Polens*. Tübingen: Francke.

VIII. 306.409437 – Specific aspects of culture

[2007], Böllmann, Felix (ed.), *Intellectual and Cultural Change in Central and Eastern Europe*. Frankfurt am Main, etc.: P. Lang.

[2006], Ostermann, Patrick, Karl-Siegbert Rehberg, and Karen Voigt, *Transformationsprozesse im Kulturbereich. Eine vergleichende Studie zum 'Dritten System' in Mittel- und Osteuropa*. Leipzig: Leipziger Univ. Verl.

[2005], Adam, Frane et al., *The Challenges of Sustained Development. The Role of Socio-Cultural Factors in East-Central Europe*. Budapest and New York: Central European University Press.

[2005], Bialecki, Ireneusz et al., *The Bridge Generation. Complexity, Issues and Perspectives of Youth in Poland*. Milano: B. Mondadori.

[2004], Forrester, Sibelan, Magdalena J. Zaborowska, and Elena Gapova (eds), *Over the Wall, after the Fall. Post-Communist Cultures through an East-West Gaze*. Bloomington, IN, etc.: Indiana University Press.

[2004], Marga, Andrei, *Die kulturelle Wende. Philosophische Konsequenzen der Tranformation = Cotitura culturală. Consecinte filosofice ale tranzitiei*. Cluj-Napoca: Cluj University Press.

[2003], Gorzka, Gabriele (ed.), *Transformation der Wissenschaften in Mittel- und Osteuropa: Polen, Rumänien, Russland, Slowakei, Tschekien, Ungarn*. Kassel: Kassel Univ. Press.

[2001], Höhmann, Hans-Hermann (ed.), *Kultur als Bestimmungsfaktor der Transformation im Osten Europas: konzeptionelle Entwicklungen, empirische Befunde*. Bremen: Temme.

[2000], Engel, Christine, and Renate Reck (eds), *Frauen in der Kultur. Tendenzen in Mittel- und Osteuropa nach der Wende*. Konferenz, Innsbruck, 1997. Innsbruck: Institut für Sprachwiss.

[2000], Grzinic, Marina, *Fiction Reconstructed. Eastern Europe, Post-Socialism & the Retro-Avant-Garde*. Wien: Selene.

[1998], Mayntz, Renate, Uwe Schimank, and Peter Weingart (eds), *East European Academies in Transition*. Dordrecht, etc.: Kluwer Academic.

[1995], Mayntz, Renate (ed.), *Transformation mittel- und osteuropäischer Wissenschaftssysteme. Länderberichte*. Opladen: Leske + Budrich.

[1994], Fuchs, Dieter, and Edeltraud Roller, *Cultural Conditions of the Transition to Liberal Democracy in Central and Eastern Europe*. Berlin: Wissenschaftszentrum Berlin, Abt. Institutionen und Sozialer Wandel.

IX. 320.5409437 – Political ideologies. Nationalism

[2009], Krueger, Rita, *Czech, German, and Noble. Status and National Identity in Habsburg Bohemia*. New York: Oxford University Press.

[2008–2009], Egbert, Jahn (ed.), *Nationalism in Late and Post-Communist Europe*. 3 vols. Baden-Baden: Nomos.

[2008], Kanet, Roger E. (ed.), *Identities, Nations and Politics after Communism*. London: Routledge.

[2008], Mitu, Sorin, *The Bibliography of Romanian Nationalism and Ethnicity in Western Language*. Cluj-Napoca: International Book Access.

[2008], Saideman, Stephen M., and R. William Ayres, *For Kin or Country. Xenophobia, Nationalism and War*. New York: Columbia University Press.

[2007], Valota, Bianca (ed.), *National Stereotypes. Correct Images and Distorted Images*. Alessandria: Edizioni dell'Orso.

[2006], Delanty, Gerard, and Krishan Kumar (eds), *The Sage Handbook of Nations and Nationalism*. London and Thousand Oaks, CA: Sage.

[2006], Kelly, T. Mills, *Without Remorse. Czech National Socialism in Late-Habsburg Austria*. Boulder, CO: East European Monographs; New York: Columbia University Press.

[2006], Melegh, Attila, *On the East-West Slope. Globalization, Nationalism, Racism and Discourses on Eastern Europe*. New York: Central European University Press.

[2006], Weaver, Eric Beckett, *National Narcissism. The Intersection of the Nationalist Cult and Gender in Hungary*. Bern: P. Lang.

[2006], Zubrzycki, Geneviève, *The Crosses of Auschwitz. Nationalism and Religion in Post-Communist Poland*. Chicago, IL: The University of Chicago Press.

[2005], Kolstø, Pål (ed.), *Myths and Boundaries in South-Eastern Europe*. London: Hurst & Co.

[2004], Auer, Stefan, *Liberal Nationalism in Central Europe*. London and New York: RoutledgeCurzon.

[2004], Mungiu-Pippidi, Alina, and Ivan Krastev (eds), *Nationalism after Communism. Lessons Learned*. Budapest and New York: Central European University Press.

[2003], Fawn, Rick (ed.), *Ideology and National Identity in Post-Communist Foreign Policies*. London and Portland, OR: Frank Cass.

[2002], Dević, Ana, *Nationalism, Regional Multiculturalism and Democracy*. Bonn: ZEI (Zentrum für Europäische Integrationsforschung).

[2002], Donskis, Leonidas, *Identity and Freedom. Mapping Nationalism and Social Criticism in Twentieth-Century Lithuania*. London and New York: Routledge.

[2002], Tismaneanu, Vladimir (ed.), *Discomforts of Victory. Democracy, Liberal Values and Nationalism in Post-Communist Europe*. San Domenico di Fiesole, FI: European University Institute, Robert Schuman Centre.

[2001], Jubulis, Mark A., *Nationalism and Democratic Transition. The Politics of Citizenship and Language in Post-Soviet Latvia*. Lanham, MD: University Press of America.

[2001], Keating, Michael, and John McGarry (eds), *Minority Nationalism and the Changing International Order*, Oxford and New York: Oxford University Press.

[2001], Kłoskowska, Antonina, *National Cultures at the Grass-Root Level*. Budapest and New York: Central European University Press.

[2000], Csepeli, György, Antal Örkény, and Mária Székelyi; Éva Szalay (transl.), *Grappling with National Identity. How Nations See Each Other in Central Europe*. Budapest: Akadémiai Kiadó.

[2000], Laitin, David D., and Robert Schuman, *Culture and National Identity. 'The East' and European Integration*. San Domenico di Fiesole, FI: European University Institute, Robert Schuman Centre.

[2000], Matteucci, Silvia (ed.), I*l nazionalismo. Culture politiche, mediazione e conflitto*. Ravenna: Longo.

[1999], Cohen, Shari J., *Politics without a Past. The Absence of History in Postcommunist Nationalism*. Durham, NC: Duke University Press.

[1999], Kemp, Walter A., *Nationalism and Communism in Eastern Europe and the Soviet Union. A Basic Contradiction?* New York: St. Martin's Press.

[1999], Sugar, Peter F., *East European Nationalism, Politics and Religion*. Aldershot and Burlington, VT: Ashgate.

[1998], Duțu, Alexandru, Andrei Pippidi et al., *Culture and the Politics of Identity in Modern Romania*. Bucharest: Fundatia Cultura Europeana.

[1998], Koszel, Bogdan (ed.), *Länder Mittel- und Südosteuropas auf der Suche nach neuer Identität. Identität im eneuerten Nationalstaat*. Potsdam: Brandeburgische Landeszentrale für Politische Bildung.

[1998], Pryzel, Ilya, *National Identity and Foreign Policy. Nationalism and Leadership in Poland, Russia, and Ukraine*. Cambridge and New York: Cambridge University Press.

[1998], Smith, Graham et al., *Nation-Building in the Post-Soviet Borderlands. The Politics of National Identities*. Cambridge and New York: Cambridge University Press.

[1997], Bollerup, Søren Rinder, and Christian Dons Christensen, *Nationalism in Eastern Europe. Causes and Consequences of the National Revivals and Conflicts in Late-Twentieth-Century Eastern Europe*. New York: St. Martin's Press.

[1996], Augustinos, Gerasimos (ed.), *The National Idea in Eastern Europe. The Politics of Ethnic and Civic Community*. Lexington, MA: D.C. Heath.

[1996], Brubaker, Rogers, *Nationalism Reframed. Nationhood and the National Question in the New Europe*. Cambridge and New York: Cambridge University Press.

[1995], Latawski, Paul (ed.), *Contemporary Nationalism in East Central Europe*. Basingstoke and New York: Palgrave Macmillan.

[1995], Sugar, Peter F. (ed.), *Eastern European Nationalism in the Twentieth Century*. Washington, DC: American UP.

[1994], Bugajski, Janusz, *Ethnic Politics in Eastern Europe. A Guide to Nationality Policies, Organizations, and Parties*. New York: M,E. Shape.

[1994], Privitera, Francesco (ed.); essays of Francesco Benvenuti, et al., *L'Europa orientale e la rinascita dei nazionalismi*. Milano: Guerrini.

[1993], Faulenbach, Bernd, and Heinz Timmermann (eds), *Nationalismus und Demokratie. Gesellschaftliche Modernisierung und nationale Idee in Mittel- und Osteuropa*. Essen: Klartext.

[1993], Pasquali, Luigi, *Nazionalismo e steccati interetnici. La nuova minaccia in Europa orientale. Origini storiche delle tensioni nazionaliste*. Roma: Poetica.

[1993], Suny, Ronald Grigor, *The Revenge of the Past. Nationalism, Revolution, and the Collapse of the Soviet Union*. Stanford, CA: Stanford University Press.

[1992], Motyl, Alexander J. (ed.), *Post-Soviet Nations. Perspectives on the Demise of the USSR*. New York: Columbia University Press.

[1992], Waldenberg, Marek, *Kwestie narodowe w Europie Środkowo-Wschodniej. Dzieje, idee*. Warszawa: PWN (Ital. ed., transl. by Maria Olszańska e Salvatore Esposito, Le questioni nazionali nell'Europa centro-orientale. Storia e attualità. Milano: Il Saggiatore, 1994).

[1990], Karnoouh, Claude, *L'invention du peuple. Chroniques de Roumanie*. Essai. Paris: Arcantere.

X. 320.809437 – Local government

[2007], Lankina, Tomila, Anneke Hudalla, and Hellmut Wollmann, *Local Governance in Central and Eastern Europe. Comparing Performance in the Czech Republic, Hungary, Poland and Russia*. Basingstoke and New York: Palgrave Macmillan.

[2006], Paraskevopoulos, Christos J., Panagiōtēs Getimēs, and Nicholas Rees (eds), *Adapting to EU Multi-Level Governance. Regional and Environmental Policies in Cohesion and CEE Countries*. Aldershot and Burlington, VT: Ashgate.

[2006], Campbell, Adrian, and Andrew Coulson (eds), *Local Government in Central and Eastern Europe. The Rebirth of Local Democracy*. London and New York: Routledge.

[2004], Tatur, Melanie (ed.), *The Making of Regions in Post-Socialist Europe. The Impact of Culture, Economic Structure and Institutions. Case Studies from Poland, Hungary, Romania and Ukraine*. Wiesbaden: VS Verl. für Sozialwissenschaften.

[2003], Baldersheim, Harald et al., *Local Democracy in Post-Communist Europe*. Opladen: Leske + Budrich.

[2003], Pamfil, Claudia, *Evolving Intergovernmental Relations for Effective Development in the Context of Regionalization*. Budapest: Local Government and Public Service Initiative, Open Society Institute.

[2002], Davey, Kenneth (ed.), *Balancing National and Local Responsibilities. Education Management and Finance in Four Central European Countries*. Budapest: Local Government and Public Service Initiative, Open Society Institute.

[2002], Marcou, Gérard (ed.), *Regionalization for Development and Accession to the European Union. A Comparative Perspective*. Budapest: Local Government and Public Service Initiative, Open Society Institute.

[2002], Soós, Gábor, Gábor Tóka, and Glen Wright (eds), *The State of Local Democracy in Central Europe*. Budapest: Local Government and Public Service Initiative, Open Society Institute.

[2002], Swianiewicz, Pawel (ed.), *Consolidation or Fragmentation? The Size of Local Governments in Central and Eastern Europe*. Budapest: Local Government and Public Service Initiative, Open Society Institute.

[2002] Tishkov, Valery, and Elena Filippova (eds), *Local Governance and Minority Empowerment in the CIS*. Budapest: Local Government and Public Service Initiative, Open Society Institute.

[1998], Strezhneva, Marina V., *Social Culture and Regional Governance. Comparison of the European Union and Post-Soviet Experiences*. Commack, NY: Nova Science.

[1996], Mesa 10. Center for Economic & Social Analysis; Ivan Miklos et al., *A New System of Funding Local Government Institutions. Proposal for a Radical Change*. Bratislava: Mesa 10.

[1995], Coulson, Andrew (ed.), *Local Government in Eastern Europe. Establishing Democracy at the Grassroots*. Aldershot and Brookfield, VT: Edward Elgar.

[1995], Friedrich Ebert Stiftung; Ludmila Malíková, et al., *Localities and Politics in the Transformation Process. The Slovak and Czech Experiences*. Conference Proceedings, 8–9 June 1995, Bratislava, Slovak Republik. Bratislava: Slovak Political Science Association.

[1992], Dostál, Petr et al., *Changing Territorial Administration in Czechoslovakia. International Viewpoints*. Amsterdam: University of Amsterdam, Faculty of Environmental Sciences, Department of Human Geography.

XI. 320.9437 – Political situation and conditions

[2009], Buffet, Cyril, *Le jour où le mur est tombé*. Paris: Larousse.

[2009], Deckert, Renatus (ed.), *Die Nacht, in der die Mauer fiel. Schriftsteller erzählen vom 9. November 1989*. Frankfurt am Main: Suhrkamp.

[2009], Demke, Elena, *Die friedliche Revolution, 1989–1990. Quellen, Fragen, Kontexte*. Berlin: Landesbeauftragter für die Unterlagen des Staatssicherheitsdienstes der Ehemaligen DDR.

[2009], Hertle, Hans-Hermann, *Chronik des Mauerfalls. Die dramatischen Ereignisse um den 9. November 1989*. 11th edn. Berlin: Links.

[2009], Kotkin, Stephen; with a contribution by Jan Tomasz Gross, *Uncivil Society. 1989 and the Implosion of the Communist Establishment*. New York: Modern Library.

[2009], Nieder, Johannes, *Fall der Mauer: Berlin 9.11.1989*. Hamburg: Fantictures Foto- und Medienverl.

[2009], Pleshakov, Konstantin, *There is no Freedom without Bread! 1989 and the Civil War that Brought down Communism*. New York: Farrar Straus Giroux.

[2009], Schabowski, Günter; Frank Sieren (conversation), *Wir haben fast alles falsch gemacht. Die letzen Tage der DDR*. 2nd edn. Berlin: Econ.

[2009], Schuller, Wolfgang, *Die Deutsche Revolution 1989*. Berlin: Rowohlt.

[2009], Stude, Sebastian, *Die friedliche Revolution 1989/90 in Halle/Saale. Ereignisse, Akteure und Hintergründe*. Frankfurt am Main, etc.: Lang.

[2008], Blasko, Andrew M., and Diana Januauskiene (eds), *Political Transformation and Changing Identities in Central and Eastern Europe*. Washington, DC: Council for Research in Values and Philosophy.

[2008], Elsuwege, Peter van, *From Soviet Republics to EU Member States. A Legal and Political Assessment of the Baltic States' Accession to the EU*. Leiden and Boston, MA: M. Nijhoff.

[2008], Epstein, Rachel A., *In Pursuit of Liberalism. International Institutions in Postcommunist Europe*. Baltimore, MD: Johns Hopkins University Press.

[2008], Heintz, Monica (ed.), *Weak State, Uncertain Citizenship: Moldova*. Frankfurt am Main: P. Lang.

[2008], Koczanowicz, Leszek, *Politics of Time. Dynamics of Identity in Post-Communist Poland*. New York: Berghahn Books.

[2008], Pusca, Anca, *Revolution, Democratic Transition and Disillusionment. The Case of Romania*. Manchester and New York: Manchester University Press; New York: distrib. in the United States exclusively by Palgrave Macmillan.

[2008], Wolchik, Sharon L., and Jane Leftwich Curry (eds), *Central and East European Politics. From Communism to Democracy*. Lanham, MD: Rowman & Littlefield.

[2007], Bideleux, Robert, and Ian Jeffries, *A History of Eastern Europe. Crisis and Change*. Milton Park, Abingdon and New York: Routledge.

[2007], Böhmer, Jule (ed.), *Osteuropa Heute: Entwicklungen, Gemeinsamkeiten, Unterschiede*. Münster: Lit.

[2007], Buzogány, Aron (ed.), *Osteuropa. Politik, Wirtschaft und Gesellschaft*. Baden-Baden: Nomos.

[2007], Forbrig, Joerg, and Pavol Demeš (eds), *Reclaiming Democracy. Civil Society and Electoral Change in Central and Eastern Europe*. Washington, DC: German Marshall Fund of the United States.

[2007], Ganev, Venelin I., *Preying on the State. The Transformation of Bulgaria after 1989*. Ithaca, NY and London: Cornell University Press.

[2007], Marin, Noemi, *After the Fall. Rhetoric in the Aftermath of Dissent in Post-Communist Times*. New York: P. Lang.

[2007], Riscassi, Andrea; Pietro Marcenaro (pref.), *Bandiera arancione la trionferà. Le rivoluzioni liberali nell'Est europeo*. Milano: Melampo.

[2007], White, Stephen, Judy Batt, and Paul G. Lewis (eds), *Developments in Central and East European Politics*. Houndmills, Basingstoke and New York: Palgrave Macmillan.

[2007], Wydra, Harald, *Communism and the Emergence of Democracy*. Cambridge and New York: Cambridge University Press.

[2006], Avioutskii, Viatcheslav, *Les revolutions de velours*. Paris: A. Colin.

[2006], Bafoil, François, *Europe centrale et orientale. Mondialisation, européanisation et changement social*. Paris: Presses de Sciences politiques.

[2006], Diewald, Martin, Anne Goedicke, and Karl Ulrich Mayer (eds), *After the Fall of the Wall. Life Courses in the Transformation of East Germany*, Stanford, CA: Stanford University Press.

[2006], Fisher, Sharon, *Political Change in Post-Communist Slovakia and Croatia. From Nationalist to Europeanist*. New York: Palgrave Macmillan.

[2006], Iliescu, Ion, Vladimir Tismaneanu (interviewed), Dinu C. Giurescu (intr.), *Communism, Post-Communism and Democracy. The Great Shock at the End of a Short Century*. Boulder, CO: East European Monographs; New York: distrib. by Columbia University Press.

[2006], Kenney, Padraic, *The Burdens of Freedom. Eastern Europe since 1989*. Black Point, Nova Scotia: Fernwood; London and New York: Zed Books (Ital. ed., *Il peso della libertà. L'Europa dell'Est dal 1989*. Torino: Edt, 2008).

[2006], Klingemann, Hans-Dieter, Dieter Fuchs, and Jan Zielonka (eds), *Democracy and Political Culture in Eastern Europe*. London and New York: Routledge.

[2006], Kott, Sandrine, Martine Mespoulet, and Antoine Roger, *Le postcommunisme dans l'histoire*. Bruxelles: Éditions de l'Université de Bruxelles.

[2006], Kutter, Amelie, and Vera Trappmann (eds), *Das Erbe des Beitritts. Europäisierung in Mittel- und Osteuropa*. Baden-Baden: Nomos.

[2006], Pickel, Gert (ed.), *Osteuropas Bevölkerung auf dem Weg in die Demokratie. Repräsentative Untersuchungen in Ostdeutschland und zehn osteuropäischen Transformationsstaaten*. Wiesbaden: VS Verlag für Sozialwissenschaften.

[2006], Rizman, Rudolf Martin; Sabrina P. Ramet (foreword), *Uncertain Path. Democratic Transition and Consolidation in Slovenia*. College Station, TX: Texas A&M University Press.

[2006], Schmemann, Serge, *When the Wall Came Down. The Berlin Wall and the Fall of Soviet Communism*. London: Kingfisher.

[2005], Arias King, Fredo, *Transiciones. La experiencia de Europa del Este*. Buenos Aires: Cadal; Bratislava: Pontis Fundation; Hialeah, FL: Ceon.

[2005], Devaux, Sandrine, *Engagements associatifs et postcommunisme. Le cas de la République Tchèque*. Paris: Belin.

[2005], Donskis, Leonidas; Zygmunt Bauman (pref.), *Loyalty, Dissent, and Betrayal. Modern Lithuania and East-Central European Moral Immagination*. Amsterdam: Rodopi.

[2005], Frison-Roche, François; Michel Lesage (pref.); Slobodan Milacic (foreword), *Le 'modèle semi-présidentiel' comme instrument de la transition en Europe post-communiste: Bulgarie, Lituanie, Macédoine, Pologne, Roumanie et Slovénie*. Bruxelles: Bruylant.

[2005], Hauswald, Harald, and Lutz Rathenow, *Ost-Berlin. Leben vor dem Mauerfall*. Berlin: Jaron.

[2005], Judson, Pieter M., and Marsha L. Rozenblit (eds), *Constructing Nationalities in East Central Europe*. Oxford and New York: Berghahn Books.

[2005], Mires, Fernando, *El orden del caos. Historia del fin del comunismo*. Buenos Aires: Libros de la Araucaria.

[2005], Ost, David, *The Defeat of Solidarity. Anger and Politics in Postcommunist Europe*. Ithaca, NY: Cornell University Press.

[2004], Fulga, Gheorghe, *Europa dell'Est. Dal comunismo alla democrazia*. Trento: Curcu & Genovese.

[2004], Gyárfášová, Olga, and Grigorji Mesežnikov (eds.), *Party Government in Slovakia. Experience and Perspectives*. Bratislava: Institute for Public Affairs.

[2004], Jeffries, Ian, *The Countries of the Former Soviet Union at the Turn of the Twenty-First Century: the Baltic and European States in Transition*. London and New York: Routledge.

[2004], McFaul, Michael, and Kathryn Stoner-Weiss (eds), *After the Collapse of Communism. Comparative Lessons of Post-Communist Transitions*. Cambridge and New York: Cambridge University Press.

[2004], Richard, Yann, and André-Louis Sanguin (eds), *L'Europe de l'Est quinze ans après la chute du mur. Des Pays baltes à l'ex-Yougoslavie.* Actes du Colloque de la Sorbonne, 25–27 September 2001. Paris: L'Harmattan.

[2004], Shanor, Donald R., and Constance Shanor, *After the Russians. Eastern Europe Joins the West*. Philadelphia, PA: Xlibris.

[2004], Thompson, Mark R., *Democratic Revolutions. Asia and Eastern Europe*. London and New York: Routledge.

[2003], De Nevers, Renée, *Comrades no more. The Seeds of Political Change in Eastern Europe*. Cambridge, MA: MIT Press.

[2003], Guida, Francesco (ed.), *L'altra metà del continente. L'Europa centro-orientale dalla formazione degli Stati nazionali all'integrazione europea*. Padova: Cedam.

[2003], Howard, Marc Morjé, *The Weakness of Civil Society in Post-Communist Europe*. Cambridge and New York: Cambridge University Press.

[2003], Kopecký, Petr, and Cas Mudde (eds), *Uncivil Society? Contentious Politics in Post-Communist Europe*. London and New York: Routledge.

[2003], Mögelin, Chris, *Die Transformation von Unrechtsstaaten in demokratische Rechtsstaaten. Rechtlicher und politischer Wandel in Mittel- und Osteuropa am Beispiel Russlands*. Berlin: Duncker & Humblot.

[2003], Observatoire des Etats post-soviétiques; Radvanyi, Jean (ed.), *Les états postsoviétiques. Identités en construction, transformations politiques, trajectoires économiques*. Paris: A. Colin.

[2003], Sharman, Jason Campbell, *Repression and Resistance in Communist Europe*. New York: RoutledgeCurzon.

[2003], Smith, Simon (ed.), *Local Communities and Post-Communist Transformation: Czechoslovakia, the Czech Republic and Slovakia*. London and New York: RoutledgeCurzon.

[2003], Špiewak, Paweł (ed.), *Anti-Totalitarismus. Eine Polnische Debatte*. Frankfurt am Main: Suhrkamp.

[2003], Stiftung Ettersberg; Hans-Joachim Veen (ed.), *Nach der Diktatur. Demokratische Umbrüche in Europa, zwölf Jahre später*. First Internationale Symposium, 2002. Köln: Böhlau.

[2003], Stöber, Georg (ed.), *Der Transformationsprozess in (Ost-)Deutschland und in Polen*. Hannover: Hahn.

[2003], Szachi, Jerzy; Friedrich Griese (transl.), *Der Liberalismus nach dem Ende des Kommunismus*. Frankfurt am Main: Suhrkamp.

[2003], Williams, Kieran, Brigid Fowler, and Aleks Szczerbiak, *Explaining Lustration in Eastern Europe. A Post-Communist Approach*. Brighton: University of Sussex.

[2002], Bianchini, Stefano, George Schöpflin and Paul Shoup (eds), *Post-Communist Transition as a European Problem*. Ravenna: Longo.

[2002], Colas, Dominique (ed.); in collaboration with Anne Gazier, et al., *L'Europe post-communiste*. Paris: Presses universitaires de France.

[2002], Gill, Graeme J., *Democracy and Post-Communism. Political Change in the Post-Communist World*. London and New York: Routledge.

[2002], Harris, Erika, *Nationalism and Democratisation. Politics of Slovakia and Slovenia*. Aldershot: Ashgate.

[2002], Kennedy, Michael D., *Cultural Formations of Postcommunism. Emancipation, Transition, Nation and War*. Minneapolis, MN and London: University of Minnesota Press.

[2002], Lovell, David W. (ed.), *The Transition. Evaluating the Postcommunist Experience*. Aldershot and Burlington, VT: Ashagte.

[2002], Rothacher, Albrecht, *Im wilden Osten. Hinter den Kulissen des Umbruchs in Osteuropa*. Hamburg: Krämer.

[2001], Anderson, Richard et al., *Postcommunism and the Theory of Democracy*. Princeton, NJ: Princeton University Press.

[2001], Habermas, Jürgen; Max Pensky (transl., ed., and intr.), *The Postnational Constellation. Political Essays*. Cambridge, MA: MIT Press.

[2001], Kumar, Krishan, *1989: Revolutionary Ideas and Ideals*. Minneapolis, MN: University of Minnesota Press.

[2001], Light, Duncan, and David Phinnemore (eds), *Post-Communist Romania. Coming to Terms with Transition*. Basingstoke: Palgrave.

[2001], Schultz, Helga (ed.), *Grenzen im Ostblock und ihre Überwindung*. Berlin: Berlin-Verl. Spitz.

[2001], White, Stephen, and Daniel N. Nelson (eds), *The Politics of the Postcommunist World*. Aldershot and Burlington, VT: Ashgate.

[2000], Boer-Ashworth, Elizabeth de, *The Global Political Economy and post-1989 Change. The Place of the Central European Transition*. New York: St. Martin's Press.

[2000], Gitelman, Zvi (ed.), *Cultures and Nations of Central and Eastern Europe. Essays in Honor of Roman Szporluk*. Cambridge, MA: Ukrainian Research Institute, Harvard University Press.

[2000], Goehrke, Carsten (ed.), *Transformation und historisches Erbe in den Staaten des europäischen Ostens*. Bern, etc.: P. Lang.

[2000], Janos, Andrew C., *East Central Europe in the Modern World. The Politics of the Borderlands From Pre- to Postcommunism*. Stanford, CA: Stanford University Press.

[2000], Sorin, Antohi, and Vladimir Tismaneanu (eds), *Between Past and Future. The Revolutions of 1989 and Their Aftermath*. New York: Central European University Press.

[2000], Wydra, Harald, *Continuities in Poland's Permanent Transition*. Basingstoke: Macmillan; New York: St. Martin's Press.

[1999], Braun, Aurel, and Zoltan Barany (eds), *Dilemmas of Transition. The Hungarian Experience*. Lanham, MD: Rowman & Littlefield.

[1999], Burawoy, Michael, and Katherine Verdery (eds), *Uncertain Transition. Ethnographies of Change in the Postsocialist World*. Lanham, MD: Rowman & Littlefield.

[1999], Mink, Georges, and Jean-Charles Szurek, *La grande conversion. Le destin des communistes en l'Europe de l'Est*. Paris: Editions du Seuil.

[1999], Smith, Julie, and Elizabeth Teague (eds), *Democracy in the New Europe. The politics of Post-Communism*. London: Greycoat Press.

[1999], Unverhau, Dagmar (ed.); Roland Lucht (coll.), *Lustration, Aktenöffnung, demokratischer Umbruch in Polen, Tschechien, der Slowakei und Ungarn*. Referate der Tagung des BStU und der Akademie für Politische Bildung Tutzing vom 26-28.10.1998. Münster: Lit.

[1998], Berglund, Sten, Tomas Hellén, and Frank H. Aarebrot (eds), *The Handbook of Political Change in Eastern Europe*. Cheltenham and Northampton, MA: Edward Elgar.

[1998], Brabant, Jozef M. van, *The Political Economy of Transition. Coming to Grips with History and Methodology*. London and New York: Routledge.

[1998], Ferry, William E., and Roger E. Kanet (eds), *Post-Communist States in the World Community*. Selected Papers from the Fifth World Congress of Central and East European Studies, Warsaw, 1995. New York: St. Martin's Press.

[1998], Klein, Patricia Vawter, Arthur Wesley Helweg, and Barbara P. McCrea (eds), *Struggling with the Communist Legacy. Studies of Yugoslavia, Romania, Poland and Czechoslovakia*. Boulder, CO: Eastern European Monographs; New York: distrib. by Columbia University Press.

[1998], Koenig, Helmut, Michael Kohlstruck, and Andreas Woell (eds), *Vergangenheitsbewältigung am Ende des zwanzigsten Jahrhunderts*. Opladen: Westdeutscher Verl.

[1998], Mandel, David (ed.), *Looking Left Eastwards*. Montréal and New York: Black Rose Books.

[1998], Michnik, Adam, and Irena Grudzińska Gross (eds), Ken Jowitt (foreword), Jane Cave (transl. from the Polish), *Letters from Freedom. Post-Cold War Realities and Perspectives*. Berkeley, CA: University of California Press.

[1998], Plasser, Fritz, Peter A. Ulram and Harald Waldrauch, *Democratic Consolidation in East-Central Europe*. New York: St. Martin's Press.

[1998], Potel, Jean Yves, *Les 100 portes de l'Europe centrale et orientale*. Paris: Editions de l'Atelier-Editions Ouvrières.

[1997], Holmes, Leslie, *Post-Communism. An Introduction*. Cambridge: Polity Press.

[1997], Offe, Claus, *Varieties of Transition. The East European and East German Experience*. Cambridge, MA: MIT Press.

[1997], Plasser, Fritz, Peter A. Ulram, and Harald Waldrauch, *Politischer Kulturwandel in Ost-Mitteleuropa. Theorie und Empirie demokratischer Konsolidierung*. Opladen: Leske + Budrich.

[1997], Ramet, Sabrina P., *Whose Democracy? Nationalism, Religion, and the Doctrine of Collective Rights in Post-1989 Eastern Europe*. Lanham, MD: Rowman & Littlefield.

[1997], Sørensen, Lene Bøgh, and Leslie C. Eliason (eds), *Forward to the Past? Continuity and Change in Political Development in Hungary, Austria, and the Czech and Slovak Republics*. Aarhus: Aarhus Universitet.

[1997], Stokes, Gale, *Three Eras of Political Change in Eastern Europe*. New York: Oxford University Press.

[1997], Zacek, Jane Shapiro, and Ilpyong J. Kim (eds), *The Legacy of the Soviet Bloc*. Gainesville, FL: University Press of Florida.

[1996], Elster, Jon (ed.), *The Roundtable Talks and the Breakdown of Communism*. Chicago, IL: University of Chicago Press.

[1996], Hodenius, Birgit (ed.), *Transformationsprozesse in Mittelost-Europa. Zwischenbefund*. München: Oldenbourg.

[1996], Rosenberg, Tina, *The Haunted Land. Facing Europe's Ghosts after Communism*. New York: Vintage Books.

[1996], Ziolkowski, Andrzej, *Konversion: Polen, Ukraine. Geschichte, Ökonomie, Politik*. Frankfurt am Main, etc.: P. Lang.

[1995], Barany, Zoltan, and Ivan Volgyes (eds), *The Legacies of Communism in Eastern Europe*. Baltimore, MD and London: John Hopkins University Press.

[1995], Wollmann, Hellmut (ed.); Attila Ágh (with contributions of), *Transformation sozialistischer Gesellschaften. Am Ende des Anfangs*. Opladen: Westdt. Verl.

[1994], Altmann, Franz-Lothar (ed.); Anneli Ute Gabanyi (coll.), *Reformen und Reformer in Osteuropa*. Regensburg: Pustet.

[1994], Brown, James F., *Hopes and Shadows. Eastern Europe after Communism*. Harlow: Longman.

[1994], Gombár, Csaba, et al., *Balance. The Hungarian Government, 1990–1994*. Budapest: Korridor Politikai Kutatások Központja.

[1994], Jannazzo, Antonio, *Trasformazioni economiche, classi sociali e politica in Ungheria, 1945–1990*. Palermo: La Zisa.

[1994], Kennedy, Michael D. (ed.), *Envisioning Eastern Europe. Postcommunist Cultural Studies*. Ann Arbor, MI: University of Michigan Press.

[1994], Michta, Andrew A., *The Government and Politics of Postcommunist Europe*. Westport, CN: Praeger.

[1994], Serafin, Joan (ed.), *East-Central Europe in the 1990s*. Boulder, CO etc.: Westview Press.

[1994], Szomolányi, Soňa, and Grigorij Mesežnikov (eds), *The Slovak Path of Transition: to Democracy?*. Bratislava: Slovak Political Science Association.

[1993], Kraljic, Matthew A. (ed.), *The Breakup of Communism. The Soviet Union and Eastern Europe*. New York: H.W. Wilson.

[1993], Lampe, John R., Daniel N. Nelson (eds); Roland Schönfeld (coll.), *East European Security Reconsidered*. Washington, DC: Woodrow Wilson Center Press. Südosteuropa-Gesellschaft; Baltimore, MD: distrib. by the Johns Hopkins University Press.

[1993], Schöpflin, George, *Politics in Eastern Europe, 1945–1992*. Oxford and Cambridge, MA: Blackwell.

[1993], University of Warsaw. Institute of Sociology; Jerzy J. Wiatr (ed.), *The Politics of Democratic Transformation. Poland after 1989*. Warsaw: Scholar Agency.

[1992], Ackerman, Bruce A., *The Future of Liberal Revolution*, New Haven, CT: Yale University Press.

[1992], Feffer, John, *Shock Waves. Eastern Europe after the Revolutions*. Boston, MA: South End Press.

[1992], Lewis, Paul G. (ed.), *Democracy and Civil Society in Eastern Europe*. Selected Papers from the Fourth World Congress for Soviet and East European Studies, Harrogate, 1990. New York: St. Martin's Press.

[1992], Nation, Robert Craig, *Political Differentiation in Eastern Europe since 1989*. Bologna: Johns Hopkins University. Bologna Center. Research Institute.

[1992], Rozman, Gilbert, Seizaburō Satō, and Gerald Segal (eds), *Dismantling Communism. Common Causes and Regional Variations*. Washington, DC:

Woodrow Wilson Center Press; Baltimore, MD: Johns Hopkins University Press.

[1991], Belohradsky, Vaclav, Pierre Kende, and Jacques Rupnick (eds), *Democrazie da inventare. Culture politiche e Stato in Ungheria e Cecoslovacchia.* Torino: Edizioni della Fondazione Giovanni Agnelli.

[1991], Delli Zotti, Giovanni (ed.), *Attori del mutamento nell'Est europeo.* Milano: F. Angeli.

[1991], Skilling, H. Gordon, and Paul Wilson (eds), *Civic Freedom in Central Europe. Voices from Czechoslovakia.* London: Macmillan.

[1990], Bradley, John, *Eastern Europe. The Road to Democracy.* New York: Gloucester Press.

[1990], Brinton, William M., and Alan Rinzler (eds), *Without Force or Lies. Voices from the Revolution of Central Europe in 1989–90. Essays, Speeches, and Eyewitness Accounts.* San Francisco, CA: Mercury House.

[1990], Dahrendorf, Ralf, *Reflections on the Revolution in Europe. In a Letter Intended to Have Been Sent to a Gentleman in Warsaw.* London: Chatto and Windus.

[1990], Gremion, Pierre, and Pierre Hassner (eds); with László Bruszt et al., *Vents d'Est. Vers l'Europe des Etats de droit?* Paris: Presses universitaires de France.

[1990], Habermas, Jurgen, *Kleine politische Schriften*, vol. 7: *Die nachholende Revolution.* Frankfurt am Main: Suhrkamp.

[1990], White, Stephen (ed.); Patrick Artesian et al., *Political and Economic Encyclopaedia of the Soviet Union and Eastern Europe.* Chicago, IL: St. James Press.

[1989], Mazowiecki, Tadeusz; Eric Morin-Aguilar (transl.); Jean-Marie Domenach (pref.), *Un autre visage de l'Europe.* Montricher: Noir sur blanc.

XII. 321.809437– Democratic government

[2008], Goehring, Jeannette (ed.), *Nations in Transit 2008. Democratization from Central Europe to Eurasia.* New York, Washington, DC and Budapest: Freedom House.

[2007], Blondel, Jean et al., *Governing New European Democracies.* Basingstoke and New York: Palgrave Macmillan.

[2007], Forum Centra za politološka istraživanja; Dvořáková, Vladimíra, and Anđelko Milardović (eds), *Lustration and Consolidation of Democracy and the Rule of Law in Central and Eastern Europe.* Zagreb: Cpi.

[2007], Ramet, Sabrina P., *The Liberal Project and the Transformation of Democracy. The Case of East Central Europe.* College Station, TX: Texas A&M University Press.

[2006], Hasselmann, Chris, *Policy Reform and the Development of Democracy in Eastern Europe.* Aldershot and Burlington, VT: Ashgate.

[2006] Hutcheson, Derek S., and Elena A. Korosteleva (eds), *The Quality of Democracy in Post-Communist Europe*. London and New York: Routledge.

[2006], Krasteva, Anna, and Francesco Privitera (eds), *Democratization in Post-Communist Transition Processes in the 1990s. Lights and Shadows*. Ravenna: Longo.

[2006], Sticht, Monika, *Der Beitrag des Europarats zur demokratischen Transformation in Mittel- und Osteuropa seit 1989 am Beispiel von Ungarn, Rumänien und Aserbaidschan*. Berlin: WVB (Wissenschaftlicher Verlag Berlin).

[2006], Tatar, Marius I., *Importing Democracy from Abroad. International Assistance for Civil Society in Romania*. Oradea: Editura Universitatii din Oradea.

[2006], Wiarda, Howard J.; Dale R. Herspring, and Esther M. Skelley (coll.), *Development on the Periphery. Democratic Transitions in Southern and Eastern Europe*. Lanham, MD: Rowman & Littlefield.

[2005], Emerson, Michael, and Senem Aydin Dügzit (eds), *Democratisation in the European Neighbourhood*. Brussels: Centre for European Policy.

[2005], Flockhart, Trine (ed.), *Socializing Democratic Norms. The Role of International Organizations for the Construction of Europe*. Basingstoke and New York: Palgrave Macmillan.

[2005], Pridham, Geoffrey, *Designing Democracy. EU Enlargement and Regime Change in Post-Communist Europe*. Basingstoke and New York: Palgrave Macmillan.

[2004], Jacobs, Jörg, *Tücken der Demokratie. Antisystemeinstellungen und ihre Determinanten in sieben post-kommunistischen Transformationsländern*. Wiesbaden: Verl. Für Sozialwissenschaften.

[2003], Åberg, Martin, and Mikael Sandberg, *Social Capital and Democratisation. Roots of Trust in Post-Communist Poland and Ukraine*. Aldershot and Burlington, VT: Ashagte.

[2003], Andreev, Svetlozar A., *Consolidating Democracies. The Theory and Practice of Democratization in Post-Communist Eastern Europe (1989–2000)*. San Domenico di Fiesole, FI: European University Institute.

[2003], Badescu, Gabriel, and Eric M. Uslaner (eds), *Social Capital and the Transition to Democracy*. London and New York: Routledge.

[2003], Ekiert, Grzegorz, and Stephen E. Hanson (eds), *Capitalism and Democracy in Central and Eastern Europe. Assessing the Legacy of Communist Rule*. Cambridge and New York: Cambridge University Press.

[2003], Karatnycky, Adrian, Alexander J. Motyl, and Amanda Schnetzer (eds), *Nations in Transit 2003. Democratization in East Central Europe and Eurasia*. Lanham, MD and Oxford: Rowman & Littlefield; New York: Freedom House.

[2003], Kelley, Donald R. (ed.), *After Communism. Perspectives on Democracy*. Fayetteville, AR: University of Arkansas Press.

[2003], Milacic, Slobodan (ed.), *La reinvention de l'Etat. Démocratie politique et ordre juridique en Europe centrale et orientale*. Colloque international, Paris, Senat-Palais du Luxembourg, 5–6 April 2002. Bruxelles: Bruylant.

[2002], Clark, Terry D., *Beyond Post-Communist Studies. Political Science and the New Democracies of Europe*. New York: M.E. Sharpe.

[2002], Diamond, Larry, and Marc F. Plattner (eds), *Democracy After Communism*. Baltimore, MD and London: Johns Hopkins University Press.

[2002], Dryzek, John S., and Leslie Holmes (eds), *Postcommunist Democratization. Political Discourses across Thirteen Countries*. New York: Cambridge University Press.

[2002], Haerpfer, Christian W., *Democracy and Enlargement in Post-Communist Europe. The Democratisation of the General Public in Fifteen Central and Eastern European Countries, 1991–1998*. London and New York: Routledge.

[2002], Mendelson, Sarah Elizabeth, and John K. Glenn (eds), *The Power and Limits of NGOs. A Critical Look at Building Democracy in Eastern Europe and Eurasia*. New York: Columbia University Press.

[2002], Pisciotta, Barbara, *Istituzioni europee e consolidamento democratico. Le politiche di privatizzazione e tutela della concorrenza in Polonia, Ungheria e Repubblica Ceca*. Napoli: Edizioni scientifiche italiane.

[2002], Wejnert, Barbara (ed.), *Transition to Democracy in Eastern Europe and Russia. Impact on Politics, Economy and Culture*. Westport, CT: Praeger.

[2001], Auer, Andreas, and Michael Bützer (eds), *Direct Democracy. The Eastern and Central European Experience*. Aldershot and Burlington, VT: Ashgate.

[2001], Berg-Schlosser, Dirk, and Raivo Vetik (eds), *Perspectives on Democratic Consolidation in Central and Eastern Europe*. New York: distrib. by Columbia University Press.

[2001], Breglund, Sten et al., *Challenges to Democracy. Eastern Europe Ten Years After the Collapse of Communism*. Cheltenham and Northampton, MA: Edward Elgar.

[2001], Pickel, Gert, and Jörg Jacobs, *Einstellungen zur Demokratie und zur Gewährleistung von Rechten und Freiheiten in den jungen Demokratien Mittel- und Osteuropas*. Frankfurt an der Oder: Fit.

[2001], Zielonka, Jan, and Alex Pravda (eds), *Democratic Consolidation in Eastern Europe*. 2 vols. Oxford and New York: Oxford University Press.

[2000], Colomer, Josep Maria, *Strategic Transitions. Game Theory and Democratization*. Baltimore, MD: Johns Hopkins University Press.

[2000], Klingemann, Hans-Dieter, and Friedhelm Neidhardt (eds), *Zur Zukunft der Demokratie. Herausforderungen im Zeitalter der Globalisierung*. Berlin: Sigma.

[2000], Larsen, Stein Ugelvik (ed.), *The Challenges of Theories on Democracy. Elaborations over New Trends in Transitology*. Boulder, CO: Social Science Monographs; New York: distrib. by Columbia University Press.

[2000], Mangott, Gerhard, Harald Waldrauch, and Stephen Day (eds), *Democratic Consolidation. The International Dimension: Hungary, Poland and Spain*. Baden-Baden: Nomos.

[2000], Mezzetti, Luca, *Le democrazie incerte. Transizioni costituzionali e consolidamento della democrazia in Europa orientale, Africa, America Latina, Asia*. Torino: Giappichelli.

[1999], Hauser, Ewa, and Jacek Wasilewski (eds), *Lessons in Democracy*. Kraków: Jagiellonian University Press; Rochester, NY: University of Rochester Press.

[1999], Kaldor, Mary, and Ivan Vejvoda (eds), *Democratization in Central and Eastern Europe*. London and New York: Pinter.

[1999], Merkel, Wolfgang (ed.), *Demokratie in Ost und West. Für Klaus von Beyme*. Frankfurt am Main: Suhrkamp.

[1999], Nagle, John D., and Alison Mahr, *Democracy and Democratization. Post-Communist Europe in Comparative Perspective*. London and Thousands Oaks, CA: Sage.

[1999], Sakwa, Richard (ed.), *The Experience of Democratization in Eastern Europe*. Selected Papers From the Fifth World Congress of Central and East European Studies, Warsaw, 1995. Basingstoke, etc.: Macmillan.

[1998], Bartole, Sergio, and Pietro Grilli di Cortona (ed.), Transizione e consolidamento democratico nell'Europa centro*-orientale. Élites, istituzioni e partiti*. Torino: Giappichelli.

[1998], Milacic, Slobodan (ed.), *La Democratie constitutionnelle en Europe centrale et orientale. Bilans et perspectives*. Colloque international, Bordeaux, 28–30 November 1996. Bruxelles: Bruylant.

[1998], Rose, Richard, William Mishler, and Christian Haerpfer, *Democracy and its Alternatives. Understanding Post-Communist Societies*. Cambridge: Polity Press.

[1998], Stankovsky, Jan, Fritz Plasser, and Peter A. Ulram, *On the Eve of EU Enlargement. Economic Developments and Democratic Attitudes in East Central Europe*. Wien: Signum.

[1998], Ziccardi Capaldo, Giuliana (ed.); Sergio Moccia et al., *Democratizzazione all'Est e diritto internazionale*. Atti del Convegno di studi, Università di Salerno, 8 May 1997. Napoli: Edizioni scientifiche italiane.

[1997], Dawisha, Karen, and Bruce Parrott (eds), *The Consolidation of Democracy in East-Central Europe*. Cambridge and New York: Cambridge University Press.

[1997], Pridham, Geoffrey, Eric Herring, and George Sanford (eds), *Building Democracy? The International Dimension of Democratisation in Eastern Europe*. Rev. edn. (1st edn 1994). London and Washington, DC: Leicester University Press.

[1996], Beyme, Klaus von, *Transition to Democracy in Eastern Europe*. Basingstoke: Macmillan, in association with International Political Science Association.

[1996], Einhorn, Barbara, Mary Kaldor, and Zdenek Kavan (eds), *Citizenship and Democratic Control in Contemporary Europe*. Cheltenham and Brookfield, VT: Edward Elgar.

[1996], Linz, Juan J., and Alfred C. Stepan, *Problems of Democratic Transition and Consolidation: Southern Europe, South America and Post-Communist Europe*. Baltimore, MD: Johns Hopkins University Press.

[1996], Matynia, Elżbieta (ed.), *Grappling with Democracy. Deliberations on Post-Communist Societies (1990–1995)*. Prague: Sociologické nakl.

[1996], Open Media Research Institute (ed.); James F. Brown (intr.), *Building Democracy*. New York: M.E. Sharpe.

[1995], Mommsen, Margareta (ed.), *Demokratie-Experimente im Postkommunismus. Politischer und institutioneller Wandel in Osteuropa*. Münster: Lit.

[1995], Varga, Csaba, *Transition to Rule of Law. On the Democratic Transformation in Hungary*. Budapest: Project on Comparative Legal Cultures of the Faculty of Law of Loránd Eötvös University and of the Hungarian Academy of Sciences, Institute for Legal Studies.

[1994], Berglund, Sten, and Jan Åke Dellenbrandt (eds), *The New Democracies in Eastern Europe. Party Systems and Political Cleavages*. 2nd edn. Aldershot and Brookfield, VT: Edward Elgar.

[1994], Pridham, Geoffrey, and Tatu Vanhanen (eds), *Democratization in Eastern Europe. Domestic and International Perspectives*. London and New York: Routledge.

[1994], Stiftung Mitarbeit (ed.); Renate Schmidt et al., *Wieviel Demokratie verträgt Europa? Wieviel Europa verträgt die Demokratie?* Opladen: Leske + Budrich.

[1993], Frenztel-Zargoska, Janina (ed.), *From a One-Party State to Democracy. Transition in Eastern Europe*. Amsterdam, etc.: Rodopi BV.

[1993], McFaul, Michael; Stephen Sestanovich (foreword), *Post-Communist Politics. Democratic Prospects in Russia and Eastern Europe*. Washington, DC: Center for Strategic and International Studies.

[1992], Bermeo, Nancy Gina (ed.), *Liberalization and Democratization. Change in the Soviet Union and Eastern Europe*. Baltimore, MD: Johns Hopkins University Press.

[1991], Meyer, Gerd, and Franciszek Ryszka (eds), *Political Participation and Democracy in Poland and West Germany*. Warsaw: Osrodek Badan Spolecznych.

[1990], Volten, Peter (ed.), *Uncertain Futures. Eastern Europe and Democracy*. New York: Institute for East-West Security Studies.

XIII. 323.09437 – Civil and political rights

[2006], Azzariti, Gaetano, *Studi sui diritti in Europa*. Roma: Aracne.

[2006], Einhorn, Barbara, *Citizenship in an Enlarging Europe. From Dream to Awakening*. Basingstoke and New York: Palgrave Macmillan.

[2006], Sadurski, Wojciech (ed.), *Political Rights under Stress in 21st Century Europe*. Oxford, etc.: Oxford University Press.

[2005], Cassese, Antonio, *I diritti umani oggi*. Roma-Bari: GLF Laterza.

[2005], De Búrca, Gráinne, and Bruno de Witte (eds); Larissa Ogertschnig (coll.), *Social Rights in Europe*. Oxford: Oxford University Press.

[2005], May, Rachel, and Andrew Milton (eds), *(Un)civil Societies. Human Rights and Democratic Transitions in Eastern Europe and Latin America*. Lanham, MD: Lexington Books.

[2005], Uildriks, Niels A. (ed.), *Police Reform and Human Rights. Opportunities and Impediments in Post-Communist Societies*. Antwerpen: Intersentia; Holmes Beach, FL: distrib. for North America by Gaunt Inc.

[2002], Feldbrugge, Ferdinand J. M., and William B. Simons (eds), *Human Rights in Russia and Eastern Europe. Essays in Honor of Ger van den Berg*. The Hague and New York: M. Nijhoff; Norwell, MA: sold and distrib. in North, Central, and South Carolina by Kluwer Law International.

[2000], Pagon, Milan (ed.), *Policing in Central and Eastern Europe. Ethics, Integrity and Human Rights*. Ljubljana: College of Police and Security Studies.

[2000], Voiculescu, Aurora, *Human Rights and Political Justice in Post-Communist Eastern Europe. Prosecuting History*. Lewiston, NY: E. Mellen Press.

[1999], Alston, Philip, Mara Bustelo, and James Heenan (eds), *The EU and Human Rights*. New York: Oxford University Press.

[1996], Sajó, András; Katherine Lauer (ed. supp.); Joseph Raz (intr.), *Western Rights? Post-Communist Application*. The Hague and London: Kluwer Law International.

[1989], US. Congress. Commission on Security and Cooperation in Europe (ed.), *Reform and Human Rights in Eastern Europe*. Report Submitted to the Congress of the United States. Washington, DC: US GPO, Congressional Sales Office.

XIV. 323.1437 – Civil and political rights of nondominant groups

[2009], Rechel, Bernd (ed.), *Minority Rights in Central and Eastern Europe*. London and New York: Routledge.

[2004], Gozzi, Gustavo, and Fabio Martelli (eds), *Guerre e minoranze. Diritti delle minoranze, conflitti interetnici e giustizia internazionale nella transizione alla democrazia dell'Europa centro-orientale*. Bologna: Il Mulino.

[2004], Meijknecht, Anna, *Minority Protection Standards and Reality. Implementation of Council of Europe Standards in Slovakia, Romania and Bulgaria*. The Hague: T.M.C. Asser Press; Cambridge: Cambridge University Press.

[2003], Diaconu, Ion (ed.), *The Challenge Ahead. Regional Trends and Recommendations for the Elimination of the Discrimination of Persons Belonging to National, Ethnic, Religious and Linguistic Minorities. Background Paper*. Geneva: Office of the UN High Commissioner for Human Rights.

[2003], UN. Office of the High Commissioner for Human Rights; Kehris, Ilze Brands (ed.), *The Role of Non-Governmental Organizations in the Protection and Promotion of the Rights of Persons Belonging to National, Ethnic, Religious and Linguistic Minorities*. Background Paper. Geneva: Office of the UN High Commissioner for Human Rights.

[2003], UN. Office of the High Commissioner for Human Rights; Petrova, Dimitrina (ed.), *Legal Avenues for Advancing the Rights of Persons Belonging to National, Ethnic, Religious and Linguistic Minorities*. Geneva: Office of the UN High Commissioner for Human Rights.

[2003], UN. Office of the High Commissioner for Human Rights; Raykova, Alexandra (ed.), *Roma Youth. A Voice to Be Reckoned with.* Background Paper. Geneva: Office of the UN High Commissioner for Human Rights.

[2002], Cahn, Claude, *Roma Rights. Race, Justice and Strategies for Equality*. New York: International Debate Education Association.

[2002], EU Accession Monitoring Program, *Monitoring the EU Accession Process. Minority Protection*. Budapest and New York: Open Society Institute.

[2001], Crisen, Sabina A. M. (ed.), *Minorities and Tolerance. Central and Eastern Europe & the NIS.* Proceedings of the Conference, Washington, DC, 24 April 2001. Washington, DC: Woodrow Wilson International Center for Scholars.

[2000], Böszörményi, Jenö, and Márta Józsa (eds), *Caught in the Trap of Integration. Roma Problems and Prospects in Hungary.* International Conference, Budapest, 22–23 June 1999. Budapest: Bureau for European Comparative Minority Research.

[1996], Bîrzea, Cézar (ed.), *Human Rights and Minorities in the New European Democracies. Educational and Cultural Aspects.* Report on the Workshop Held at Lohusalu (Estonia), 20–23 October 1994. Strasbourg: Council of Europe.

XV. 323.44209437 – Freedom of conscience and religion

[2009], Murzaku, Ines Angjeli (ed.), *Quo vadis Eastern Europe? Religion, State and Society after Communism*. Ravennna: Longo.

[2006], Manssen, Gerrit (ed.), *Religionsfreiheit in Mittel- und Osteuropa zwischen Tradition und Europäisierung*. Symposium 29 September to 3 October 2004 in Lemberg, Ukraine. Frankfurt am Main, etc.: Lang.

[2005], Merdjanova, Ina, Rota Vavilova, and Myroslav Marynovych, *Religion in Post-Communist Europe*. Antwerpen: Universitari Centrum Sint-Ignatius Antwerpen.

[2004], Durham, W. Cole Jr., and Silvio Ferrari (eds), *Laws on Religion and the State in Post-Communist Europe*. Leuven: Peeters (Ital. ed., Diritto e religione nell'Europa post-comunista. Bologna: Il Mulino.

[2002], Danchin, Peter G., and Elizabeth A. Cole (eds), *Protecting the Human Rights of Religious Minorities in Eastern Europe*. New York and Chichester: Columbia University Press.

[2002], Merdjanova, Ina, *Religion, Nationalism and Civil Society in Eastern Europe. The Postcommunist Palimpsest*. Lewiston, NY: Edwin Mellen Press.

[1992], Ramet, Sabrina P. (ed.), *Protestantism and Politics in Eastern Europe and Russia.The Communist and Postcommunist Eras*. Durham, NC etc.: Duke University Press.

[1990], Ramet, Sabrina P., and Pedro Ramet (eds), *Catholicism and Politics in Communist Societies*. Durham, NC etc.: Duke University Press.

XVI. 324.209437 – Political parties

[2008], Hanley, Seán, T*he New Right in the New Europe. Czech Transformation and Right-Wing Politics, 1989–2006*. London and New York: Routledge.

[2008], Roper, Steven D., and Jānis Ikstens (eds), *Public Finance and Post-Communist Party Development*. Aldershot and Burlington, VT: Ashgate.

[2008], Veen, Hans-Joachim (ed.), *Parteien in jungen Demokratien. Zwischen Fragilität und Stabilisierung in Ostmitteleuropa*. Köln-Weimar-Wien: Böhlau.

[2007], Grzymała-Busse, Anna Maria, *Rebuilding Leviathan. Party Competition and State Exploitation in Post-Communist Democracies*. Cambridge and New York: Cambridge University Press.

[2007], International Institute for Democracy and Electoral Assistance; Stojarová, Věra et al., *Political Parties in Central and Eastern Europe. In Search of Consolidation. Central and Eastern Europe Regional Report, Based on Research and Dialogue with Political Parties*, Stockholm: International Idea.

[2007], Meleshevic, Andrey A., *Party Systems in Post-Soviet Countries. A Comparative Study of Political Institutionalization in the Baltic States, Russia, and Ukraine*. New York: Palgrave.

[2007], Webb, Paul, and Stephen White (eds), *Party Politics in New Democracies*. Oxford and New York: Oxford University Press.

[2006], Hough, Dan, William E. Paterson, and James Sloam (eds), *Learning from the West? Policy Transfer and Programmatic Change in the Communist Successor Parties of Eastern and Central Europe*. London and New York: Routledge.

[2006], Jungerstam-Mulders, Susanne (ed.), *Post-Communist EU Member States. Parties and Party Systems*. Aldershot and Burlington, VT: Ashgate.

[2006], Kopecký, Petr (ed.), *Political Parties and the State in Post-Communist Europe*. Abingdon: Routledge.

[2006], Lewis, Paul G., and Zdenka Mansfeldová (eds), *The European Union and Party Politics in Central and Eastern Europe*. Basingstoke and New York: Palgrave Macmillan.

[2006], Rohrschneider, Robert, and Stephen Whitefield (eds), *Public Opinion, Party Competition and the European Union in Post-Communist Europe*. Basingstoke and New York: Palgrave Macmillan.

[2005], Migalski, Marek (ed.), *Parties and Party Systems in Central and Eastern Europe*. Sosnowiec: Wyższa Szkoła Zarządzania i Marketingu. (1st edn 1997).

[2005], Schmitt, Hermann, and Jacques J. A. Thomassen, *The EU Party System after Eastern Enlargement*. Wien: IHS (Institut für höhere Studien).

[2004], Bender, Katrin, *Entstehung und Entwicklung der politischen Parteien in Mittel- und Osteuropa: Polen, Ungarn, die Tschechische Republik und die Slowakei im Vergleich*, Osnabrück: Univ., Masterarbeit im Master-Studiengang Europäische Studien.

[2004], Millard, Frances, *Elections, Parties and Representation in Post-Communist Europe*. Basingstoke and New York: Palgrave Macmillan.

[2004], Waele, Jean-Michel de (ed.), *Les clivages politiques en Europe centrale et orientale*. Bruxelles: Editions de l'Université de Bruxelles.

[2003], Roger, Antoine (ed.), *Des partis pour quoi faire? La représentation politique en Europe centrale et orientale*. Bruxelles: Bruylant.

[2003], Rose, Richard, and Neil Munro, *Elections and Parties in New European Democracies*. Washington, DC: CQ Press.

[2003], Tworzecki, Hubert, *Learning to Choose. Electoral Politics in East-Central Europe*. Stanford, CA: Stanford University Press.

[2002], Bugajski, Janusz, *Political Parties of Eastern Europe. A Guide to Politics in the Post-Communist Era*. New York and London: M.E. Sharpe.

[2002], Kostelecký, Tomáš, *Political Parties after Communism. Developments in East-Central Europe*. Washington, DC: Woodrow Wilson Center Press; Baltimore, MD and London: The Johns Hopkins University Press.

[2002], Luther, Kurt Richard, Ferdinand Müller-Rommel (eds), *Political Parties in the New Europe. Political and Analytical Challenges*. Oxford: Oxford University Press.

[2002], Waele, Jean-Michel de (ed.), *Partis politiques et démocratie en Europe centrale et orientale*. Bruxelles: Editions de l'Université de Bruxelles.

[2001], Lewis, Paul G. (ed.), *Party Development and Democratic Change in Post-Communist Europe. The First Decade*. London and Portland, OR: Frank Cass.

[2001], Lewis, Paul G., *Political Parties in Post-Communist Eastern Europe*. London and New York: Routledge.

[2000], Klingemann, Hans-Dieter (ed.), *Elections in Central and Eastern Europe. The First Wave*. Third Berlin Conference on Comparative Political Research in Central and Eastern Europe. Held in December 1997. Berlin: Sigma.

[1999], Cook, Linda J., Mitchell A. Orenstein, and Marilyn Rueschemeyer (eds), *Left Parties and Social Policy in Postcommunist Europe*. Boulder, CO: Westview Press.

[1999], Kitschelt, Herbert et al., *Post-Communist Party Systems. Competition, Representation and Inter-Party Cooperation*. Cambridge and New York: Cambridge University Press.

[1999], Lawson, Kay, Andrea Römmele, and Georgi Karasimeonov (eds), *Cleavages, Parties and Voters. Studies from Bulgaria, the Czech Republic, Hungary, Poland and Romania*. Westport, CT: Praeger.

[1999], Norris, James Arthur, *Completing Democracy. Party Systems and Democratic Consolidation among Mass Publics in East-Central Europe*. Ann Arbor, MI: UMI Dissertation Services.

[1999], Ramet, Sabrina P. (ed.), *The Radical Right in Central and Eastern Europe since 1989*. University Park, PA: Pennsylvania State University Press.

[1997], Grilli di Cortona, Pietro, *Da uno a molti. Democratizzazione e rinascita dei partiti in Europa orientale*. Bologna: Il Mulino.

[1997], Segert, Dieter, Richard Stöss, and Oskar Niedermayer (eds), *Parteiensysteme in postkommunistischen Gesellschaften Osteuropas*. Opladen: Westdeutscher Verl.

[1996], Segert, Dieter (ed.), *Spätsozialismus und Parteienbildung in Osteuropa nach 1989*. Berliner Debatte. Berlin: Bugrim.

[1995], Segert, Dieter, and Csilla Machos; Lubomír Brokl (coll.), *Parteien in Osteuropa. Kontext und Akteure*. Opladen: Westdeutscher Verl.

[1994], Segert, Dieter (ed.), *Konfliktregulierung durch Parteien und politische Stabilität in Ostmitteleuropa*. Frankfurt am Main, etc.: P. Lang.

XVII. 327.17094 – International cooperation. Europe

[2009], Loth, Wilfried (ed.), *Experiencing Europe. 50 Years of European Construction, 1957–2007*. Baden-Baden: Nomos.

[2009], Teló, Mario (ed.), *The European Union and Global Governance*. London and New York: Routledge.

[2008], DeBardeleben, Joan (ed.), *The Boundaries of EU Enlargement. Finding a Place for Neighbours*. Basingstoke and New York: Palgrave Macmillan.

[2008], Diez, Thomas, Mathias Albert, and Stephan Stetter (eds), *The European Union and Border Conflicts. The Power of Integration and Association*. Cambridge and New York: Cambridge University Press.

[2008], Kogan, Irena, Michael Gebel, and Clemens Noelke (eds), *Europe Enlarged. A Handbook of Education, Labour and Welfare Regimes in Central and Eastern Europe*. Bristol: Policy Press.

[2008], Sajdik, Martin, and Michael Schwarzinger, *European Union Enlargement. Background, Developments, Facts*. New Brunswick, NJ: Transaction.

[2007], Akule, Dace, T*he Future of EU Enlargement. On Track or Derailed, Debates in New Member States, Candidates and Neighbours*. Riga: Centre for Public Policy, Providus.

[2007], Dezséri, Kálmán, *New Modes of Governance and the EU Structural and Cohesion Policy in the New Member States*. Budapest: Akadémiai Kiadó.

[2007], Gatnar, Lumír, and David Lane (eds), *Popular Opposition and Support for Different Types of the EU Integration*. 3rd International Conference, Prague, 17–18 February 2006. Brno: Tribun EU.

[2007], Hofbauer, Hannes, *EU-Osterweiterung: historische Basis, ökonomische Triebkräfte, soziale Folgen*. Wien: Promedia.

[2007], Kuus, Merje, *Geopolitics Reframed. Security and Identity in Europe's Eastern Enlargement*. New York: Palgrave Macmillan.

[2007], Segre, Umberto, Vera Segre, and Paolo Mugnano (eds), *L'Europa senza ideologia tra capitalismo e socialismo*. Roma: Edizioni Associate.

[2007], Sissenich, Beate, *Building States without Society. European Union Enlargement and the Transfer of EU Social Policy to Poland and Hungary*. Lanham, MD: Lexington Books.

[2007], Stivachtis, Yannis A. (ed.), *The State of European Integration*. Aldershot and Burlington, VT: Ashgate.

[2007], Tiersky, Ronald, and Erik Jones (eds), *Europe Today. A Twenty-First Century Introduction*. Lanham, MD: Rowman & Littlefield.

[2006], Di Sarcina, Federica, Laura Grazi, Laura Scichilone (eds); Ariane Landuyt (pref.), *Europa in progress. Idee, istituzioni e politiche nel processo di integrazione europea*. Milano: Angeli.

[2006], Dyson, Kenneth H. F. (ed.), *Enlarging the Euro Area. External Empowerment and Domestic Transformation in East Central Europe*. Oxford and New York: Oxford University Press.

[2006], Heinrichs, Anja, *Die europäische Integration aus Sicht Mittel und Osteuropas: Polen, Tschechische Republik und Ungarn in der EU-Verfassungsdebatte*. München: Utz.

[2006], Infante, Davide (ed.), *Crescita e prospettive dell'Unione europea allargata*. Bologna: Il Mulino.

[2006], Kaźmierkiewicz, Piotr (ed.), *The Future of EU Enlargement. Debates in New Member States, Candidates and Neighbours*. Warsaw: Instytut Spraw Publicznych [Institute of Public Affairs].

[2006], Neumayer, Laure, *L'enjeu européen dans les transformations postcommunistes: Hongrie, Pologne, République Tchèque, 1989–2004*. Paris: Belin.

[2006], O'Brennan, John, *The Eastern Enlargement of the European Union*. London and New York: Routledge.

[2006], Pasquinucci, Daniele (ed.), *Dalla piccola alla grande Europa. Gli allargamenti della CEE/UE*. Bologna: Clueb.

[2006], Sadurski, Wojciech, Jacques Ziller, and Carolina Zurek (eds), *Après enlargement. Legal and Political Responses in Central and Eastern Europe*. San Domenico di Fiesole, FI: European University Institute, Robert Schuman Centre.

[2006], Sander, Gerald G., and Monica Vlad (eds), *Quo vadis, Europa? Europas Verfassung und künftige Erweiterungen*. Hamburg: Kovač.

[2006], Stephanou, Constantine A. (ed.), *Adjusting to EU Enlargement. Recurring Issues in a New Setting*. Cheltenham and Northampton, MA: Edward Elgar.

[2006], Vacca, Giuseppe, and José Luis Rhi-Sausi (eds), *I dilemmi dell'integrazione. Il futuro del modello sociale europeo. Rapporto 2006 sull'integrazione europea*. Bologna: Il Mulino.

[2005], Adviesraad Internationale Vraagstukken (ed.), *The European Union's New Eastern Neighbours*. The Hague: Advisory Council on International Affairs.

[2005], Beria di Argentine, Camilla (ed.), *L'allargamento da 15 a 25 paesi rafforzerà l'Unione Europea?* Congresso internazionale, Grand Hôtel des Îles Borromées, Stresa, 21–22 May 2004. Milano: Giuffrè.

[2005], DeBardeleben, Joan (ed.), *Soft or Hard Borders? Managing the Divide in an Enlarged Europe*. Aldershot and Burlington, VT: Ashgate.

[2005], Dupont, Bernard (ed.), *La Pologne dans l'Europe. Une intégration achevée?* Paris and Budapest-Torino: L'Harmattan.

[2005], Kannwischer, Christian, *Die Stabilisierungs- und Konsolidierungspolitik der EU gegenüber Mittel- und Osteuropa. Anbindung im Spannungsfeld zwischen konsistenter Politikausrichtung und strategischer Interaktion*. Remscheid: Gardez!-Verlag.

[2005], Lippert, Barbara, and Gaby Umbach, *The Pressure of Europeanisation. From Post-Communist State Administrations to Normal Players in the EU System*. Baden-Baden: Nomos.

[2005], Mammarella, Giuseppe, and Paolo Cacace, *Storia e politica dell'Unione europea, 1926–2005*. New ed. adj. Roma-Bari: GLF Laterza.

[2005] Mansfeldová, Zdenka, Vera Sparschuch, and Agnieszka Wenninger (eds), *Patterns of Europeanisation in Central and Eastern Europe*. Hamburg: Krämer.

[2005], Olivi, Bino, and Roberto Santaniello, *Storia dell'integrazione europea. Dalla guerra fredda alla Costituzione dell'Unione*. Bologna: Il Mulino.

[2005], Raspadori, Fabio, and Marcello Signorelli (eds), *L'Unione Europea tra allargamento e trattato costituzionale*. Torino: Giappichelli.

[2005], Reichart, Susanne, *Zum Konvergenzprozess der mittel- und osteuropäischen EU-Beitrittsländer*. Frankfurt am Main, etc.: Lang.

[2005], Scartezzini, Riccardo, and Jimmy O. Milanese (eds), *L'allargamento dell'UE nello scenario geopolitico europeo*. Milano: Angeli.

[2005], Schimmelfennig, Frank, and Ulrich Sedelmeyer (eds), *The Europeanization of Central and Eastern Europe*. Ithaca, NY: Cornell University Press.

[2005], Schimmelfennig, Frank, and Ulrich Sedelmeyer (eds), *The Politics of European Union Enlargement. Theoretical Approaches*. London and New York: Routledge.

[2005], Sedelmeyer, Ulrich, *Constructing the Path to Eastern Enlargement. The Uneven Policy Impact of EU Identity*. Manchester and New York: Manchester University Press; New York: distrib. exclusively in the USA by Palgrave.

[2005], Skuhra, Anselm, *The Eastern Enlargement of the European Union. Efforts and Obstacles on the Way to Membership*. Innsbruck: StudienVerlag; New Brunswick, NJ: distrib. in North and South America by Transaction.

[2005], Vachudová, Milada Anna, *Europe Undivided. Democracy, Leverage and Integration after Communism*. Oxford and New York: Oxford University Press.

[2004], Baleanu, Adelina (coord.), *Romania and the EU Enlargement. Public Debates Organized by the European Institute of Romania, Year 2003*. Bucharest: Institutul European din România.

[2004], Berger, Helge, and Thomas Moutos (eds), *Managing European Union Enlargement*. Cambridge, MA: MIT Press.

[2004], Dimitrova, Antoaneta L. (ed.), *Driven to Change. The European Union's Enlargement Viewed from the East*. Manchester and New York: Manchester University Press.

[2004], Favaretto, Tito (ed.), *Allargamento a Est e integrazione europea*. Milano: F. Angeli.

[2004], Hillion, Christophe (ed.), *EU Enlargement. A Legal Approach*. Oxford: Hart Publishing.

[2004], Hughes, James, Gwendolyn Sasse, and Claire Gordon, *Europeanization and Regionalization in the EU's Enlargement to Central and Eastern Europe. The Myth of Conditionality*. Basingstoke and New York: Palgrave Macmillan.

[2004], Kaźmierkiewicz, Piotr (ed.), *Neighbourhood across a Divide? Borderland Communities and EU Enlargement*. Warszawa: Institute of Public Affairs.

[2004], Kłoczowski, Jerzy (ed.), *East-Central Europe's Position within Europe. Between East and West [L'Europe du Centre-Est dans l'espace européen. Entre l'Est et l'Ouest]*. Lublin: Instytut Europy Środkowo-Wschodniej.

[2004], Kohler, Wilhelm, *Eastern Enlargement of the EU. A Comprehensive Welfare Assessment*. Hamburg: HWWA (Hamburgisches Weltwirtschaftsarchiv).

[2004], Mattina, Liborio (ed.), *La sfida dell'allargamento. L'Unione europea e la democratizzazione dell'Europa centro-orientale*. Bologna: Il Mulino.

[2004], Messina, Patrizia (ed.), *EU Enlargement. Borders, Boundaries and Constraints*. Padova: Cleup.

[2004], Podkaminer, Leon (ed.), *Transition Countries on the Eve of EU Enlargement*. Wien: WIIW (Wiener Institut für internationale Wirtschaftsvergleiche).

[2004], Rizzo, Alfredo, *L'allargamento ad Est dell'Unione europea. Problematiche del Trattato di adesione*. Napoli: Editoriale scientifica.

[2004], Wood, Stephen, *Germany and East-Central Europe. Political, Economic and Socio-Cultural Relations in the Era of EU Enlargement*. Aldershot and Burlington, VT: Ashgate.

[2004], Zucconi, Mario (ed.), *Post-Communist Transition in Europe and its Broader International Implications*. Ravenna: Longo.

[2003], Barbé, Esther, and Elizabeth Johansson (eds), *Beyond Enlargement. The New Members and New Frontiers of the Enlarged European Union*. Barcelona: Institut Universitari d'Estudis Europeus.

[2003], Batt, Judy et al., *Partners and Neighbours. A CFSP for a Wider Europe*. Paris: European Union Institute for Security Studies.

[2003], Cremona, Marise (ed.), *The Enlargement of the European Union*. Oxford and New York: Oxford University Press.
[2003], Fry, John, *The Helsinki Process. Negotiating Security and Cooperation in Europe*. Honolulu, Hawaii: University Press of the Pacific.
[2003], Henderson, Karen (ed.), *Back to Europe. Central and Eastern Europe and the European Union*. London and New York: Routledge.
[2003], Hörburger, Hortense (ed.), *EU Enlargement. Our Neighbours' View*. Marburg: Schüren.
[2003], Kempe, Iris, and Wim P. van Meurs (eds), *Prospects and Risks beyond EU Enlargement*. 2 vols. Opladen: Leske + Budrich.
[2003], Letta, Enrico, *L'allargamento dell'Unione europea*. Bologna: Il Mulino.
[2003], Poole, Peter A., *Europe Unites. The EU's Eastern Enlargement*. Westport, CT, etc.: Praeger.
[2003], Raik, Kristi, *Democratic Politics or the Implementation of Inevitabilities? Estonia's Democracy and Integration into the European Union*. Tartu: Tartu University Press.
[2003], Rösch, Olga (ed.), *Osterweiterung der Europäischen Union und kulturelle Grenzen. Zur Ausgangslage*. Berlin: News & Media.
[2003], Srubar, Ilja (ed.), *Problems and Chances of the East Enlargement of the EU*. Hamburg: Krämer.
[2003], Tupy, Marian L. (ed.), *EU Enlargement. Costs, Benefits and Strategies for Central and Eastern European Countries*. Washington, DC: Cato Institute.
[2003], UN. Economic Commission for Europe, *The Impact of EU Enlargement on Non-Candidate Countries in Eastern Europe and the CIS*. Geneva: UN, ECE.
[2003], Vaughan-Whitehead, Daniel, *EU Enlargement versus Social Europe? The Uncertain Future of the European Social Model*. Cheltenham and Northampton, MA: Edward Elgar.
[2002], Bingran, Dai, and Jian Junbo (eds), *The Enlarged European Union. Diversity and Adaptation*. London and Portland, OR: Frank Cass.
[2002], Felderer, Bernhard, Helmut Frisch, and Bernhard Boehm (eds), *Hungary and EU Eastern Enlargement*. Wien: IHS (Institut für Höhere Studien).
[2002], Franzen, Wolfgang, Hans Peter Haarland, and Hans-Joachim Niessen, *Osteuropa auf dem Weg in die Europäische Union*. Frankfurt am Main, etc.: Campus- Verl.
[2002], Heijdra, Ben J., Christian Keuschnigg, and Wilhelm Kohler (eds), *Eastern Enlargement of the EU. Jobs, Investment and Welfare in Present Member Countries*. München: Center for Economic Studies & Ifo-Institut für Wirtschaftsforschung.
[2002], Ingham, Hilary C., and Mike Ingham (eds), *EU Expansion to the East. Prospects and Problems*. Cheltenham and Northampton, MA: Edward Elgar.
[2002], Inotai, András (ed.), *Some Reflections on Possible Scenarios for EU Enlargement. Some Key Issues in Understanding the Negotiations on Accession*

to the European Union. Budapest: Hungarian Academy of Sciences. Institute for World Economics.

[2002], Mair, Peter, and Jan Zielonka (eds), *The Enlarged European Union. Diversity and Adaptation*. London and Portland, OR: Frank Cass.

[2001], Dehaene, Jean-Luc, and Ania Krok-Paszkowska (eds), *The Political Dimension of EU Enlargement. Looking towards Post-Accession. Report of the Reflection Group*. San Domenico di Fiesole, FI: European University Institute.

[2001], Drulák, Petr (ed.), *National and European Identities in EU Enlargement. Views from Central and Eastern Europe*. Prague: Institute of International Relations.

[2001], Kostrzewa-Zorbas, Wiesława (ed.), *Strengthening Good-Neighbourly Relations in Central and Eastern Europe in Preparation for EU Enlargement*. Seminar Organised Jointly by the Council of Europe and the European Commission Hosted by the Republic of Poland, Lublin, 11–12 December 2000. Warsaw: Warsaw University Centre, Information Centre on the Council of Europe.

[2001], Olivi, Bino, *L'Europa difficile. Storia politica dell'integrazione europea, 1948–2000*. New ed. Bologna: Il Mulino.

[2001], Polska. Ministerstwo Spraw Zagranicznych, *The Eastern Policy of the European Union in the Run-up to the EU's Enlargement to Include the Countries of Central and Eastern Europe. Poland's Viewpoint*. Warsaw: Ministry of Foreign Affairs.

[2000], Cowles, Maria Green, and Michael Smith, *The State of the European Union*, vol. 5: *Risks, Reform, Resistance and Revival*. Oxford and New York: Oxford University Press.

[2000], Danta, Darrick R., and Derek Hall (eds), *Europe Goes East. EU Enlargement, Diversity and Uncertainty*. London: Stationery Office.

[2000], Dorodnova, Jekaterina, *EU Concerns in Estonia and Latvia. Implications of Enlargement for Russia's Behaviour towards the Russian-Speaking Minorities*. San Domenico di Fiesole, FI: European University Institute, Robert Schuman Centre.

[2000], EU. Committee of the Regions, *A Europe of Regions and Cities. Strategies and Prospects for EU Enlargement*. Luxembourg: Office for Official Publications of the European Communities.

[2000], Gligorov, Vladimir, *Delaying Integration. The Impact of EU Eastern Enlargement on Individual CEECs non Acceding or Acceding only Later*. Wien: Wiener Institut für Internationale Wirtschaftsvergleiche.

[2000], Konitzer, Werner, and Kristian Bosselmann-Cyran (eds), *Ein erweitertes Europa verstehen. Die Rolle der Geistes-, Sozial- und Wirtschaftswissenschaften*. Frankfurt am Main, etc.: P. Lang.

[2000], Nunberg, Barbara, *Ready for Europe. Public Administration Reform and European Accession in Central and Eastern Europe*. Washington, DC: World Bank.

[2000], Richter, Sándor et al., *EU Eastern Enlargement. The Case of the Former 'Second Wave' Applicant Countries*. Wien: WIIW (Wiener Institut für Internationale Wirtschaftsvergleiche).

[2000], Smith, Alan, *The Return to Europe. The Reintegration of Eastern Europe into the European Economy*. London: Macmillan.

[2000], Tang, Helena (ed.), *Winners and Losers of EU Integration. Policy Issues for Central and Eastern Europe*. Washington, DC: World Bank.

[2000], Thom, Rodney (ed.), *EU Enlargement. The Effect on Third Countries*. Dublin: University College Dublin, Dept. of Economics.

[1999], Häußer, Ilse, and Berud-Michael Kruse, *Die Ost- Erweiterung der Europäischen Union. Rohstoffwirtschaftliche Bestandsaufnahme zu ausgewälten Ländern Mittel- und Osteuropas (Bulgarien, Estland, Lettland, Litauen, Polen, Rumänien, Slowakei, Slowenien, Tschechische Republik, Ungarn)*. Hannover, etc.: BGR (Bundesanst. für Geowissenschaften und Rohstoffe).

[1999], Mallossek, Jörg, *Die Erweiterung der Europäischen Union um Mittel- und Osteuropäische Länder. Wirtschaftspolitischer Reformbedorf bei gegebenen Budgetsrestriktionen*. Köln: Inst. für Wirtschaftspolitik.

[1999], Price, Victoria Curzon, Alice Landau, and Richard G. Whitman (eds), *The Enlargement of the European Union. Issues and Strategies*. London and New York: Routledge.

[1998], Mayhew, Alan, *Recreating Europe. The European Union's Policy Towards Central and Eastern Europe*. Cambridge and New York: Cambridge University Press.

[1997], Commission of the European Communities, *Commission Opinion on Estonia's Application for Membership of the European Union*. Luxembourg: OOPEC (Office for Official Publications of the European Communities).

[1995], Pasinato, Antonio (ed.), *Deutschland und Europa. Materialien zum Maastrichter Vertrag über die Europaische Union*. Padova: Libreria Rinoceronte.

[1995], Schulze, Hagen; Angelo Bolaffi (intr.); Camilla Miglio (transl.), *Il ritorno di Europa. La nuova Germania e il vecchio continente*. Roma: Donzelli.

[1995], Tabboni, Simonetta, *Identità europea, identità nazionale, identità etnica*. Milano: Fondazione Cariplo-I.S.MU.

[1994], Amato, Amedeo, and Franco Praussello (eds), *L'Unione europea di fronte alle sfide dell'allargamento*. Bari: Cacucci.

[1994], Letta, Enrico, *Passaggio a Nord-Est. L'Unione europea tra geometrie variabili, cerchi concentrici e velocità differenziate*. Bologna: Il Mulino.

[1993], Castellano, Danilo (ed.), *Nuove integrazioni dell'Europa*. Napoli: Edizioni scientifiche italiane.

[1992], Decaux, Emmanuel (ed.), *Securité et cooperation en Europe. Les texts officials du processus de Helsinki (1973–1992)*. Paris: La documentation française.

XVIII. 328.24 – The legislative process. Initiative and referendum. Europe

[2005], Szczerbiak, Aleks, *EU Enlargement and Referendums*. London and New York: Routledge.

[2005], Waele, Jean-Michel de, *European Union Accession Referendums*. Brussels: Editions de l'Université de Bruxelles.

[2002], Hug, Simon, *Voices of Europe. Citizens, Referendums, and European Integration*. Lanham, MD: Rowman & Littlefield.

XIX. 340.023437 – Law as a profession, occupation, hobby

[2007], Center of Legal Competence; Stephan Matyk et al., *Notaries in Europe. Growing Fields of Competence: Austria, Croatia, Czech Republic, Hungary, Slovenia*. Wien-Graz: Neuer Wissenschaftlicher Verl.

[2003], Rechberger, Walter H. (ed.); Erika Orsolya Albert (coll.), *Notarbild in Mitteleuropa*. Wien: NWV (Neuer Wiss. Verl.).

[2003], Schultz, Ulrike, and Gisela Shaw (eds), *Women in the World's Legal Profession*. Oxford: Hart Publishing.

[1999], Council of Europe. Legal Co-Operation with Central and Eastern Europe Countries, *The role and Responsibilities of the Lawyer in a Society in Transition*. Proceedings. Strasbourg: Council of Europe.

[1998], Council of Bars and Law Societies of the European Community, *Recueil sur les règles de la profession d'avocat en Europe centrale et orientale [Compendium of Legal Practice for Lawyers in Central and Eastern Europe]*. Strasbourg: Council of Europe Publ.

XX. 340.11509437 – Law and society

[2005], Czarnota, Adam, Martin Krygier, and Wojciech Sadurski (eds), *Rethinking the Rule of Law after Communism*. Budapest and New York: Central European University Press.

[2003], Galligan, Denis J., and Marina Kurkchiyan (eds), *Law and Informal Practices. The Post-Communist Experience*. Oxford and New York: Oxford University Press.

[2002], Hoff, Karla Ruth (ed.), *After the Big Bang? Obstacles to the Emergence of the Rule of Law in Post-Communist Societies*, Washington, DC: World Bank, Development Research Group, Investment Climate Team.

[2002], Přibáň, Jiří, *Dissidents of Law. On the Velvet Revolutions, Legitimations, Fictions of Legality and Contemporary Version of the Social Contract*. Aldershot: Ashgate.

[1999], Krygier, Martin, and Adam Czarnota (eds), *The Rule of Law after Communism. Problems and Prospects in East-Central Europe*. Aldershot: Ashgate.

[1996], Council of Europe (ed.), *The Role of the Judiciary in a State Governed by the Rule of Law. Proceedings*. Round Table of the Ministers of Justice from Countries of Central and Eastern Europe, Warszawa, 1995. Strasbourg: Council of Europe Publ.

XXI. 341.48 – Human rights

[2009], Christoffersen, Jonas, *Fair Balance. Proportionality, Subsidiarity and Primarity in the European Convention on Human Rights*. Leiden and Boston, MA: M. Nijhoff.

[2007], Arold, Nina-Louisa, *The Legal Culture of the European Court of Human Rights*. Leiden and Boston, MA: M. Nijhoff.

[2007], Goldhaber, Michael D., *A People's History of the European Court of Human Rights*. New Brunswick, NJ: Rutgers University Press.

[2006], Dembour, Marie-Bénédicte, *Who Believes in Human Rights? Reflections on the European Convention*. Cambridge and New York: Cambridge University Press.

[2005], Carletti, Cristiana, *I diritti fondamentali e l'Unione europea tra Carta di Nizza e Trattato-Costituzione*. Milano: Giuffrè.

[2005], Castellano, Danilo, and Federico Costantini (eds), *Costituzione europea, diritti umani, libertà religiosa*. Napoli: Edizioni scientifiche italiane.

[2005], Gardino Carli, Adriana, *Stati e Corte europea di Strasburgo nel sistema di protezione dei diritti dell'uomo. Profili processuali*. Milano: Giuffrè.

[2002], Comba, Mario E. (ed.); Joseph Weiler (intr.), *Diritti e confini. Dalle costituzioni nazionali alla Carta di Nizza*. Torino: Edizioni di Comunità.

[2002], United States Congress. Commission on Security and Cooperation in Europe (ed.), *Democracy and Human Rights Trends in Eurasia and East Europe. A Decade of Membership in the Organization for Security and Cooperation in Europe*. A Report. Washington, DC: CSCE.

[2001], Blackburn, Robert, and Jörg Polakiewicz (eds), *Fundamental Rights in Europe. The European Convention on Human Rights and Its Member States, 1950–2000*. Oxford and New York: Oxford University Press.

[2001], Thomas, Daniel C., *The Helsinki Effect. International Norms, Human Rights and the Demise of Communism*. Princeton, NJ and Oxford: Princeton University Press.

[1995], Council of Europe, *A Guide to the Role and Functioning of Non-Governmental Human Rights Organisations*. Proceedings. Report from an International Conference for Non-Governmental Human Rights Organisations from Central and Eastern European Countries, Ljubljana, 11–13 November 1994. Strasbourg: Council of Europe; Croton-on-Hudson, NY: Manhattan Publ. Co.

[1994], Mullerson, Rein A., *International Law, Rights and Politics. Developments in Eastern Europe and the CIS*. London and New York: Routledge.

XXII. 342.437 – Constitutional and administrative law

[2009], Manssen, Gerrit (ed.), *Die verfassungsrechtlich garantierte Stellung der Abgeordneten in den Ländern Mittel- und Osteuropas*. Frankfurt am Main, etc.: Lang.

[2008], Ajani, Gianmaria; Alex Gilardini, and Ugo Sebastiani (colls.), *Il modello post-socialista*. 3rd edn. adj. Torino: Giappichelli.

[2008], Kortmann, Constantijn, Joseph Fleuren, and Wim Voermans (eds), *Constitutional Law of 2 EU Member States: Bulgaria and Romania. The 2007 Enlargement*. Deventer: Kluwer BV.

[2008], Massias, Jean-Pierre et al., *Droit constitutionnel des États d'Europe de l'Est*. 2nd edn. entièrement revue. Paris: Presses universitaires de France.

[2008], Petersen, Hanne (ed.) et al., *Paradoxes of European Legal Integration*. Aldershot and Burlington, VT: Ashgate.

[2008], Varga, Csaba, *Transition? To Rule of Law? Constitutionalism and Transitional Justice challenged in Central & Eastern Europe*. Pomáz: Kráter.

[2006], Sadurski, Wojciech, Adam W. Czarnota, and Martin Krygier (eds), *Spreading Democracy and the Rule of Law? The Impact of EU Enlargement on the Rule of Law, Democracy and Constitutionalism in Post-Communist Legal Orders*. Dordrecht: Springer.

[2005], European Commission for Democracy through Law (ed.), *Evaluation of Fifteen Years of Constitutional Practice in Central and Eastern Europe*. UniDem Seminar, 19–20 November 2004, Warsaw, Poland. Strasbourg: Council of Europe.

[2005], Uitz, Renata, *Constitutions, Courts and History. Historical Narratives in Constitutional Adjudication*. Budapest and New York: Central European University Press.

[2004], Bermann, George A., and Katharina Pistor (eds), *Law and Governance in an Enlarged European Union*. Oxford and Portland, OR: Hart Publishing.

[2004], Calhoun, Noel, *Dilemmas of Justice in Eastern Europe's Democratic Transitions*. Basingstoke and New York: Palgrave Macmillan.

[2003], Gambino, Silvio (ed.), *Costituzionalismo europeo e transizioni democratiche*. Milano: Giuffrè.

[2003], Sadurski, Wojciech, *'Decommunisation', 'Lustration', and Constitutional Continuity. Dilemmas of Transitional Justice in Central Europe*. San Domenico di Fiesole, FI: European University Institute.

[2003], Şerban Rosen, Mihaela (ed.), *Constitutionalism in Transition, Africa and Eastern Europe*. International Conference on Comparative Constitutionalism, Warsaw, Poland, 17–20 May 2001. Warsaw: Helsinki Foundation for Human Rights.

[2002], Prochazka, Radoslaw, *Mission Accomplished on Founding Constitutional Adjudication in Central Europe*. Budapest and New York: Central European University Press.

[2002], Voigt, Stefan, Hans-Jürgen Wagener (eds), *Constitutions, Markets and Law. Recent Experiences in Transition Econonomies*. Cheltenham and Northampton, MA: Edward Elgar.
[2001], Czarnota, Adam W. (ed.), *Ius and Lex in East Central Europe. Socio-Legal Conditions of the Rule of Law amid Post-Communist Transformation*. Budapest: Collegium Budapest.
[2001], Dzialocha, Kazimierz, Ryszard Mojak, and Krzysztof Wojtowicz (eds), *Ten Years of Democratic Constitutionalism in Central and Eastern Europe*. Lublin: Morpol.
[1999], Přibáň, Jiří, and James Young (eds), *The Rule of Law in Central Europe. The Reconstruction of Legality, Constitutionalism and Civil Society in the Post-Communist Countries*. Aldershot and Brookfield, VT: Ashgate.
[1999], Sarnecki, Pawel, Andrzej Szmyt, and Zbigniew Witkowski (eds); Albert Pol (transl.), *The Principles of Basic Institutions of the System of Government in Poland*. Warsaw: Sejm Publ. Office.
[1998], Brzezinski, Mark, *The Struggle for Constitutionalism in Poland*. New York: St. Martin's Press.
[1998], Wyrzykowski, Mirosław (ed.), *Constitution-Making Process*. Warsaw: Institute of Public Affairs, Center for Constitutionalism and Legal Culture.
[1997], Mögelin, Chris, *Die Rezeption des Rechtsstaats in Mittel- und Osteuropa*. Frankfurt an der Oder: Frankfürter Institut für Transformationsstudien.
[1996], Hofmann, Rainer (ed.); Maria Lúcia Amaral (coll.), *Rechtsstaatlichkeit in Europa*. Heidelberg: C. F. Müller.
[1995], Dąbrowska, Ewa et al., *Konstytucja w służbie demokracji [Constitution in Service of Democracy]*. 10–12 March 1995, Kraków. Kraków: Wydawn Ad Laborem.
[1994], Grudzińska-Gross, Irena (ed.); Paula Sawicka (coll.), *Constitutionalism in East Central Europe. Discussions in Warsaw, Budapest, Prague, Bratislava*. Bratislava: Czecho-Slovak Committee of the European Cultural Foundation.
[1994], Katz, Stanley N., *Constitutionalism in East Central Europe. Some Negative Lessons from American Experience*. Providence, etc.: Berghahn Books.
[1991], Biscaretti di Ruffia, Paolo, *1988–1990: un triennio di profonde trasformazioni costituzionali: in Occidente, nell'URSS e negli Stati socialisti dell'Est europeo. Aggiornamento all'Introduzione al diritto costituzionale comparato*. Milano: Giuffrè.
[1990], Ajani, Gianmaria, *Diritto dei paesi socialisti*. Torino: Utet Libreria.

XXIII. 342.43702 – Basic instruments of government

[2007], Loughlin, Martin, and Neil Walker (eds), *The Paradox of Constitutionalism. Constituent Power and Constitutional Form*, Oxford and New York: Oxford University Press.
[2005], Albi, Anneli, *EU Enlargement and the Constitutions of Central and Eastern Europe*. Cambridge and New York: Cambridge University Press.

[2004], Constantinescu, Mihai et al., *Constituția României revizuită. Comentarii și explicații*, Bucharest: All Beck.

[2002], Gönenç, Levent (ed.), *Prospects for Constitutionalism in Post-Communist Countries*. The Hague and New York: M. Nijhoff.

[1999], Roggemann, Herwig (ed.), *Die Verfassungen Mittel- und Osteuropas. Einführung und Verfassungstexte mit Übersichten und Schaubildern*. Berlin: Berlin- Verl. Spitz.

[1999], Sarnecki, Pavel, Andrzej Szmyt, and Zbigniew Witkowski (eds); Albert Pol (transl.), *The Principles of Basic Institutions of the System of Government in Poland*. Warsaw: Sejm Publ. Office.

[1996], The International Institute for Democracy (ed.), *The Rebirth of Democracy. 12 Constitutions of Central and Eastern Europe*. 2nd edn. rev. Strasbourg: Council of Europe.

[1996], Ludwikowski, Rett R., *Constitution making in the Region of Former Soviet Dominance*. Durham, NC: Duke University Press.

[1995], Lesage, Michel (ed.), *Constitutions d'Europe centrale, orientale et balte*. Paris: Documentation française.

[1995], Raina, Peter K. (ed.), *The Constitutions of New Democracies in Europe*. Braunton, Devon: Merlin.

[1993], Howard, A.E. Dick (ed.), *Constitution Making in Eastern Europe*. Washington, DC: Woodrow Wilson Center Press; Baltimore, MD: distrib. by the Johns Hopkins University Press.

[1992], Wawrzyniak, Jan, *La Polonia e le sue costituzioni dal 1791 ad oggi. Le radici istituzionali della svolta polacca*. Rimini: Maggioli.

XXIV. 342.437020269 – Basic instruments of government. Courts and procedure

[2001], Fede, Fabio, *La giurisdizione costituzionale nelle repubbliche europee della ex Unione Sovietica*. Padova: Cedam.

[1999], Mazza, Mauro, *La giustizia costituzionale in Europa orientale*. Padova: Cedam.

[1997], Verdussen, Marc, and Mariana T. Karagiozova-Finkova (eds), *La justice constitutionnelle en Europe centrale*. Bruxelles: Bruylant.

XXV. 342.43703 – Revision and amendment of basic instruments of government

[2007], Coman, Ramona, and Jean-Michel de Waele (eds), *Judicial Reforms in Central and Eastern European Countries*. Brugge: Vanden Broele; Baden-Baden: Nomos.

[2003], Fogelklou, Anders, and Fredrik Sterzel (eds), *Consolidating Legal Reform in Central and Eastern Europe. An Anthology*. Stockholm: Rättsfonden.

[1998], Müllerson, Rein, Malgosia Fitzmaurice, and Mads Tønnesson Andenæs (eds), *Constitutional Reform and International Law in Central and Eastern Europe*. The Hague, London and Boston, MA: Kluwer Law International.

[1996], Hungary. Legfőbb Ügyészség (ed.), *The Transformation of the Prokuratura into a Body Compatible with the Democratic Principles of Law.* Proceedings. Strasbourg: Council of Europe Publ.; Croton-on-Hudson, NY: Manhattan Publ. Co. (distrib.).

[1994], Beatty, David M. (ed.), *Human Rights and Judicial Review. A Comparative Perspective*. The Hague: Kluwer.

[1993], Bartole, Sergio, *Riforme costituzionali nell'Europa centro-orientale. Da satelliti comunisti a democrazie sovrane*. Bologna: Il Mulino.

XXVI. 342.437085 – Rights and personal activities

[1995], Pogany, Istvan (ed.), *Human Rights in Eastern Europe. Law in its Social Setting*. London: Edward Elgar.

[1993], Dailey, Erika, Jeri Laber, and Lois Whitman (eds), *Human Rights in Moldova. The Turbulent Dniester*. New York: Human Rights Watch.

[1991], Helsinki Watch; Human Rights Watch; Cartner, Holly (ed.), *Since the Revolution. Human Rights in Romania*. New York: Human Rights Watch.

XXVII. 345.43705 – Criminal law. Criminal procedure

[2009], Nalepa, Monika, *Skeletons in the Closet. Transitional Justice in Post-Communist Europe*. New York: Cambridge University.

[2009], Stan, Lavinia (ed.), *Transitional Justice in Eastern Europe and the Former Soviet Union. Reckoning with the Communist Past*. London and New York: Routledge.

[2003], Přibáň, Jiří, Pauline Roberts, and James Young (eds), *Systems of Justice on Transition. Central European Experiences since 1989*. Aldershot and Burlington, VT: Ashgate.

[2000], De Vergottini, Giuseppe (ed.), *Giustizia costituzionale e sviluppo democratico nei Paesi dell'Europa centro-orientale. Atti del convegno tenuto a Bologna nel 1999*. Torino: Giappichelli.

[2000], Schwartz, Herman, *The Struggle for Constitutional Justice in Post-Communist Europe*. Chicago, IL: University of Chicago Press.

[1998], Massias, Jean-Pierre, *Justice constitutionnelle et transition démocratique en Europe de l'Est*. Clermont-Ferrand: Presses universitaires de la Faculté de droit de Clermond-Ferrand; Paris: L.G.D.J.

[1997], Borneman, John, *Retribution and Judgment. Violence, Democratic Accountability, and the Invocation of the Rule of Law*. Ithaca, NY: Cornell University Press.

[1997], Borneman, John, *Settling Accounts. Violence, Justice and Accountability in Postsocialist Europe*. Princeton, NJ: Princeton University.

[1997], *Judicial Systems in a Period of Transition*. Multilateral Meeting Organised by the Council of Europe and the Hungarian Supreme Court, Budapest, 25–27 October 1995. Strasbourg: Council of Europe.

[1997], McAdams, A. James (ed.), *Transitional Justice and the Rule of Law in New Democracies*. Notre Dame, IA and London: University of Notre Dame.

[1996], *The Role of the Judiciary in a State Governed by the Rule of Law*. Proceedings. Round Table of the Ministers of Justice from Countries of Central and Eastern Europe, Organised by the Council of Europe with the Co-Operation of the the Minister of Justice of the Republic of Poland, Warsaw (Poland), 4 April 1995. Strasbourg: Council of Europe.

XXVIII. 347.437014 – Civil procedure and courts. Judges

[2002], EU Accession Monitoring Program (ed.), *Monitoring the EU Accession Process. Judicial Capacity*. Budapest and New York: Open Society Institute.

[2001], Oberhammer, Paul, and Aleš Galič (eds), *Richterbild und Rechtsreform in Mitteleuropa*. Wien: Manz.

XXIX. 347.437035 – Courts of last resort (Supreme courts)

[2007], Luchterhandt, Otto, Christian Starck, and Albrecht Weber (eds), *Verfassungsgerichtsbarkeit in Mittel- und Osteuropa*. Baden-Baden: Nomos.

[2006], Gargarella, Roberto, Pilar Domingo, Theunis Roux (eds), *Courts and Social Transformation in New Democracies. An Institutional Voice for the Poor?*. Aldershot and Burlington, VT: Ashgate.

[2005], Sadurski, Wojciech, *Rights Before Courts. A Study of Constitutional Courts in Postcommunist States of Central and Eastern Europe*. Dordrecht-Norwell, MA: Springer.

[2004], Hagedorn, Amelie, *Gleiche Maßstäbe für Ost und West? Die Staaten Ost- und Mitteleuropas vor dem EGMR unter besonderer Berücksichtigung des Art. 5 EMRK*. Frankfurt am Main, etc.: Lang.

[2003], Dupré, Catherine, *Importing the Law in Post-Communist Transitions. The Hungarian Constitutional Court and the Right to Human Dignity*. Oxford and Portland, OR: Hart Publishing.

[2003], *L'influence de la jurisprudence de la Cour Européenne des Droits de l'Homme sur l'activité des cours constitutionnelles d'Europe centrale et orientale*. Actes du colloque international de Clermont-Ferrand organisé les 15 et 16 novembre 2002 par le Groupe de Recherche sur le Droit et la Transition de la Faculté de Droit, Laboratoire des Politiques Publiques, Université d'Auvergne. Clermont-Ferrand: Presses Univ. De la Faculté de Droit, Univ. D'Auvergne.

[2003], Sadurski, Wojciech, *Constitutional Courts in the Process of Articulating Constitutional Rights in the Post-Communist States of Central and Eastern Europe*, Pt. II, *Personal, Civil and Political Rights and Liberties*. San Domenico di Fiesole, FI: European University Institute.

[2003], Sadurski, Wojciech, *Constitutional Courts in the Process of Articulating Constitutional Rights in the Post-Communist States of Central and Eastern*

Europe, Pt. III, *Equality and Minority Rights*. San Domenico di Fiesole, FI: European University Institute.

[2003], Sadurski, Wojciech, *Constitutional Courts in the Process of Articulating Constitutional Rights in the Post-Communist States of Central and Eastern Europe*, Pt. IV, *Restrictions and Constitutional Rights*. San Domenico di Fiesole, FI: European University Institute.

[2002], Sadurski, Wojciech, *Constitutional Courts in the Process of Articulating Constitutional Rights in the Post-Communist States of Central and Eastern Europe*, Pt. I, *Social and Economic Rights*. San Domenico di Fiesole, FI: European University Institute.

[2002], Sadurski, Wojciech (ed.), *Constitutional Justice, East and West. Democratic Legitimacy and Constitutional Courts in Post-Communist Europe in a Comparative Perspective*. The Hague and New York: Kluwer Law International.

[2001], Sadurski, Wojciech, *Postcommunist Constitutional Courts in Search of Political Legitimacy*. San Domenico di Fiesole, FI: European University Institute.

[2000], Sólyom, László, and Georg Brunner; Stefen G. Breyer (foreword), *Constitutional Judiciary in a New Democracy. The Hungarian Constitutional Court*, Ann Arbor, MI: University of Michigan Press.

[2000], Stone Sweet, Alec, *Governing with Judges. Constitutional Politics in Europe*, Oxford and New York: Oxford University Press.

[1999], Council of Europe, *The Competences of Supreme Courts*. Strasbourg: Council of Europe Publ.

[1998], Frowein, Jochen Abr., and Thilo Marauhn (eds), *Grundfragen der Verfassungsgerichtsbarkeit in Mittel- und Osteuropa*. Berlin, etc.: Springer.

XXX. 361.6109437 – Social policy

[2009], Klenner, Christina (ed.), *Wohlfahrtsstaaten und Geschlechterungleichheit in Mittel- und Osteuropa. Kontinuität und postsozialistische Transformation un den EU-Mitgliedsstaaten*. Wiesbaden: VS Verl. Für Sozialwiss.

[2008], Baum-Ceisig, Alexandra (ed.), *Wohlfahrtsstaaten in Mittel- und Osteuropa. Entwicklungen, Reformen un Perspektiven im Kontext der europäischen Integration*. Baden-Baden: Nomos.

[2008], Inglot, Tomasz, *Welfare States in East Central Europe, 1919–2004*. Cambridge and New York: Cambridge University Press.

[2007], Cook, Linda J., *Postcommunist Welfare States. Reform Politics in Russia and Eastern Europe*. Ithaca, NY: Cornell University Press.

[2005], De Búrca, Gráinne (ed.), *EU Law and the Welfare State. In Search of Solidarity*. Oxford: Oxford University Press.

[2004], Tomka, Béla, *Welfare in East and West. Hungarian Social Security in an International Comparison, 1918–1990*. Berlin: Akademie Verlag.

[2003], Dragoš, Srečo, and Vesna Leskošek, *Social Inequality and Social Capital*. Ljubljana: Peace Institute.

[2003], Kovács, János Mátyas (ed.); Helmut K. Anheier (coll.), *Small Transformations. The Politics of Welfare Reform, East and West*. Münster, etc.: Lang.

[2002], Funck, Bernard, and Lodovico Pizzati (eds), *Labor, Employment and Social Policies in the EU Enlargement Process. Changing Perspectives and Policy Options*. Washington, DC: World Bank.

[2002], Kapstein, Ethan B., Branko Milanovic (eds), *When Markets Fail. Social Policy and Economic Reform*. New York: Russell Sage Foundation.

[2002], Stropnik, Nada, Zsuzsa Ferge et al., *Combating Poverty and Social Exclusion*. 2 vols. Budapest: Ilo.

[2001], Kornai, János, and Karen Eggleston, *Welfare, Choice and Solidarity in Transition. Reforming the Health Section in Eastern Europe*. Cambridge and New York: Cambridge University Press.

[2001], Kornai, János, Stephan Haggard, and Robert R. Kaufman (eds), *Reforming the State. Fiscal and Welfare Reform in Post-Socialist Countries*. Cambridge: Cambridge University Press.

[2000], Boeri, Tito, *Structural Change, Welfare Systems and Labour Reallocation. Lessons from the Transition of Formerly Planned Economies*. New York: Oxford University Press.

[2000], Braithwaite, Jeanine, Christiaan Grootaert, and Branko Milanovic, *Poverty and Social Assistance in Transition Countries*. Basingstoke: Macmillan.

[2000], Iatridis, Demetrius S. (ed.), *Social Justice and the Welfare State in Central and Eastern Europe. The Impact of Privatization*. Westport, CT: Praeger.

[2000], Kovács, János Mátyás, *Approaching the EU and Reaching the US? Transforming Wlfare Regimes in East-Central Europe*. San Domenico di Fiesole, FI: European University Institute.

[2000], Micklewright, John, and Kitty Stewart (eds), *Child Well-Being in the EU and Enlargement to the East*. Firenze: Unicef-Innocenti Research Centre.

[2000], World Bank. Europe and Central Asia Region. Human Development Sector Unit. Social Protection Team, *Balancing Protection and Opportunity. A Strategy for Social Protection in Transition Economies*. Washington, DC: World Bank.

[1998], Götting, Ulrike, *Transformation der Wohlfahrtsstaaten in Mittel- und Osteuropa. Eine Zwischenbilanz*. Opladen: Leske + Budrich.

[1996], Götting, Ulrike, *A New Social Contract? In Defense of Welfare. Social Protection and Social Reform in Eastern Europe*. Firenze: Unicef.

[1994], Cornia, Giovanni Andrea, *Income Distribution, Poverty and Welfare in Transitional Economies. A Comparison Between Eastern Europe and China*. Firenze: Unicef.

[1994], Ringen, Stein, and Claire Wallace (eds), *Social Reform in the Czech Republic*. Prague: Prague Digital Arts.

[1993], Barr, Nicholas A. (ed.), *Poland. Income Support and the Social Safety Net During the Transition*. Washington, DC: World Bank.

[1992], Benson, Charlotte, *Eastern Europe and the Former Soviet Union. Economic Change, Social Welfare and Aid*. London: Overseas Development Institute.

[1992], Deacon, Bob (ed.), *Social Policy, Social Justice and Citizenship in Eastern Europe*. Aldershot: Avebury.

[1992], Deacon, Bob et al., *The New Eastern Europe. Social Policy, Past, Present and Future*. London: Sage.

[1992], Dixon, John, and David Macarov (eds), *Social Welfare in Socialist Countries*. London and New York: Routledge.

[1992], Svetlik, Ivan (ed.), *Social Policy in Slovenia. Between Tradition and Innovation*. Aldershot: Avebury.

[1992], World Bank (ed.), *Hungary: Reform of Social Policy and Expenditures*. Washington, DC: World Bank.

[1991], Cornia, Giovanni Andrea, and Sándor Sipos (eds), *Children and the Transition to the Market Economy. Safety Nets and Social Policies in Central and Eastern Europe*. Aldershot and Brookfield, VT: Avebury.

[1990], Deacon, Bob, and Júlia Szalai (eds), *Social Policy in the New Eastern Europe. What Future for Socialist Welfare?* Aldershot and Brookfield, VT: Avebury.

XXXI. 363.209437 – *Police services*

[2003], Uildriks, Niels A., and Piet van Reenen, *Policing Post-Communist Societies. Police-Public Violence, Democratic Policing and Human Rights*. Antwerp, Oxford and New York: Intersentia-Open Society Institute; Ardsley, NY: distrib. for North America by Transnational Publishers.

[2001], Kádár, András (ed.), *Police in Transition. Essays on the Police Forces in Transition Countries*. New York: Central European University Press.

XXXII. 364.132309437 – *Criminology. Corruption*

[2009], Küpper, Herbert, *Korruptionsbekämpfung in Osteuropa. Berichte zu Ungarn, Kroatien, Bulgarien, der Slowakischen und der Tschechischen Republik, Polen und Rumänien*. München: Forost.

[2007], Center for the Study of Democracy, *Anti-Corruption Reforms in Bulgaria. Key Results and Risks*. Sofia: Center for the Study of Democracy.

[2007], Smilov, Daniel, and Jurij Toplak (eds), *Political Finance and Corruption in Eastern Europe. The Transition Period*. Aldershot and Burlington, VT: Ashgate.

[2006], Holmes, Leslie, *Rotten States? Corruption, Post-Communism and Neoliberalism*. Durham, NC: Duke University Press.

[2002], Kotkin, Stephen, and András Sajó (eds), *Political Corruption in Transition. A Skeptic's Handbook*. Budapest and New York: Central European University Press.

[2002], Open Society Institute; EU Accession Monitoring Program; Sajó, András (foreword), *Monitoring the EU Accession Process. Corruption and Anti-Corruption Policy*. Budapest and New York: Open Society Institute.

[2001], Miller, William Lockley, Åse B. Grødeland, Tatyana Y. Koschechkina, *A Culture of Corruption? Coping with Government in Post-Communist Europe*. Budapest and New York: Central European University Press.

[2000], World Bank; Sanjay Pradhan (ed.), *Anticorruption in Transition. A Contribution to the Policy Debate*. Washington, DC: World Bank.

XXXIII. 364.1509437 – Offenses against persons

[2007], Locher, Birgit, *Trafficking in Women in the European Union. Norms, Advocacy-Networks and Policy-Change*. Wiesbaden: VS Verlag für Sozialwissenschaften.

[2005], Unicef; UN. Office of the High Commissioner for Human Rights; Organization for Security and Cooperation in Europe. Office for Democratic Institutions and Human Rights, *Trafficking in Human Beings in South Eastern Europe, 2004. Focus on Prevention in: Albania, Bosnia and Herzegovina, Bulgaria, Croatia, the Former Yugoslav Republic of Macedonia, Moldova, Romania, Serbia and Montenegro, the UN Administered Province of Kosovo*. Available online at <http://www.iom.md/materials/1_traff_human_beings_se.pdf> [accessed 13 April 2010].

[2004], El-Cherkeh, Tanja (ed.), *EU-Enlargement, Migration and Trafficking in Women. The Case of South Eastern Europe*. Hamburg: Hamburgisches Weltwirtschaftsarchiv.

XXXIV. 364.94 – Historical, geographic, persons' treatment of crime and its alleviation. Europe

[2008], Melossi, Dario, *Controlling Crime, Controlling Society. Thinking about Crime in Europe and America*. Cambridge: Polity Press.

[2008], Zauberman, Renée (ed.), *Victimation et insécurité en Europe. Un bilan des enquêtes et de leurs usages*. Paris: L'Harmattan.

[2007], Hyde-Price, Adrian G.V., *European Security in the Twenty-First Century. The Challenge of Multipolarity*. London and New York: Routledge.

[2005], Henderson, Karen (ed.), *The Area of Freedom, Security and Justice in the Enlarged Europe*. Basingstoke and New York: Palgrave Macmillan.

[2004], Bia, Maria Teresa, *Internal Security and the Making of a Federal Europe*. San Domenico di Fiesole, FI: European University Institute.

[2004], Fijnaut, Cyrille, and Letizia Paoli (eds), *Organised Crime in Europe. Concepts, Patterns and Control Policies in the European Union and Beyond*. Dordrecht, etc.: Springer.

[2002], Entfort, Horst, and Hannes Spengler, *Crime in Europe. Causes and Consequences*. Berlin-Hong Kong: Springer.

[2001], Duyne, Petrus C. van et al., *Cross-Border Crime in a Changing Europe*. Huntington, NY: Nova Science.

[1999], Outrive, Lode van, and Philippe Robert (eds), *Crime et justice en Europe depuis 1990. Etat des recherches, évaluation et recommandations*. Paris: L'Harmattan.

[1994], Zimmermann, Hans-Martin, and Dietrich Sauer (eds), *Die Zusammenarbeit mit Ost- und Mitteleuropa in der Kriminalitätskontrolle*. Sclußbericht über das internationale Seminar, 4–6 July 1994. Münster: Polizei-Führungsakademie.

[1991], Heidensohn, Frances, and Martin Farrell (eds), *Crime in Europe*. London and New York: Routledge.

Index

Page numbers in italic refer to Tables and Figures, and numbers like 25n6 refer to notes (page 25 note 6).